Romans 13 and Covid 19

Knowledge, Warnings and Encouragement for the Church and World

BY

J.L. FULLER

Copy Editor:
S. Camacho

Line Editor:
Heather G.

Interior Formatter:
Farhan Iqbal

Interior and Cover Designer:
Etheal Publishing

ISBN: Print 978-1-9196224-0-8

First published in 2021.

For more information and resources and to contact the Author, please go to: www.Romans13Revival.com.

Romans 13
and Covid 19

ETHEAL PUBLISHING

FREE COMPANION RESOURCES

You can download a free PDF of all the references and resources given in this book, so you can easily access them as clickable links.

Please go to: www.Romans13Revival.com/references.html

Acknowledgements

This book is dedicated to Jesus, my Lord, Saviour, our Bridegroom and Head of the Church, to You be all the glory and honour. We eagerly await Your return.

I would like to thank my good friends, advisors, prayer supporters, editors and encouragers, especially Stephen, Roy, Angela, Tony, Hilary, Val, Howard, Jonathan, Heather, Shalle, Ruth, Scott, Sophie and Sam. I also thank the people who have expressed loving disagreement and concern, it has helped sharpen me and refine the book.

"Take heed that no man deceive you." – Matthew 24:4

"Who rises up for me against the wicked? Who stands up for me against evildoers?" – Psalm 94:16

"For the grace of God has appeared that offers salvation to all people. It teaches us to say "No" to ungodliness and worldly passions, and to live self-controlled, upright and godly lives in this present age, while we wait for the blessed hope—the appearing of the glory of our great God and Saviour, Jesus Christ, who gave himself for us to redeem us from all wickedness and to purify for himself a people that are his very own, eager to do what is good. These, then, are the things you should teach. Encourage and rebuke with all authority. Do not let anyone despise you." – Titus 2:11-15

"The night is far spent, the day is at hand: let us therefore cast off the works of darkness, and let us put on the armour of light." – Romans 13:12

Endorsements

In more than 25 years of Christian leadership, I have not read a book which sets out the truths behind the headlines in such a fearless and relevant way for the times we now live in. This is a must-read for every Christian. The facts will shake you to the core; they did me, but they are vital for us to know, so that we can effectively pray God's kingdom into a world where hope is fast disappearing.

– Roy Beaumont, Pray Plymouth

****

The title of J.L. Fuller's book, 'Romans 13 and Covid 19 – Knowledge, Warnings and Encouragement for the Church and World' is self-explanatory, and it does exactly what it says on the tin. This is essential reading for every Church leader – from those who are at a loss to understand what is happening in the world and the Church and have no idea how to explain it to their flocks, to those who are well aware of what is going on, but need help and encouragement to share what they know and stand for Truth. No matter how much you already know, this book will tell you something more. It has been extensively and very well researched, and I particularly like the fact that the sources and resources are listed for you to check out for yourself, if you feel so inclined. It is an excellent resource in itself for anyone called to teach and lead a Church through the challenging times we find ourselves living in.

– Ian Dodgson, Pastor, Vale Christian Fellowship, UK

****

We now live in a world where freedom and liberty has turned to forced masking and lock-down, when medical professionals and pharmaceutical industry insiders are being silenced and censored from exposing the bald-faced lies of the international elite's well-orchestrated global media machine, and when the governments of the world are taking their orders from that same global elite's UN and (so-called) 'World Health Organization'. At the same time, many, if not most of the supposed 'men of God' who occupy the pulpits of Christian Churches have shirked their responsibility to guard their flocks from the wolves and have instead allowed the wolves to dictate their terms of service and close their doors. Speaking directly and authoritatively in response to these issues, <u>Romans 13 and Covid-19</u> courageously and meticulously presents much-needed light to a very darkened world. I heartily recommend this book as a thoroughly documented 'must-read' for all Christians, both pastors and Church members, especially those who have believed the controlled media's lies about the hyped-up 'pandemic' and the vaccines being pushed – to begin to understand not only the agenda and devices behind the entire UN/WHO Covid-19 deception, but also their own responsibility under Christ to resist government tyranny at any cost in order to restore the Lord Jesus to His rightful place as the sole head of their local churches – "that in all things he might have the pre-eminence" (Colossians 1:18).

– Sam Adams, Pastor, Independence Baptist Church, Ocala, Florida, USA www.IndependenceBaptist.com

****

Reading this is akin to reserving for yourself and your loved ones the best seats in the lifeboat just before the Titanic hits the iceberg. This book will appeal to two groups of readers. First, those who instinctively sense something has not been right in the last year in government and media. Why were so many leading scientists, medical researchers and frontline workers bullied into silence? Why was a traditionally robust and fearless UK media muzzled? Seekers wanting hard facts to go with their intuition will find the research here. Moreover, the author points not just to the root of the problem but to a crystal-clear solution. One you can apply yourself, in good conscience, without seeking permission of the government and their advisors. Second, it is for Christian leaders who sincerely want to see a genuine revival of passionate, raw, mountain-moving Biblical faith in our nation. The faith which built everything that is good and wonderful about this land. It is not for those who want a lukewarm Church of Laodicea. It is for those seeking a Church of Philadelphia, which delights the real Jesus Christ of the Bible. They will rejoice and be emboldened by the contents. It will give you ammunition to persuade others of the serious times we are living in. Jesus Christ, Creator of the universe, who shed His Blood to pay off the sin mortgage owed by every human, guarantees He will spit out lukewarm Christians. He guarantees to curse anyone who removes one line from the Bible. He gives clear signs of His soon return to the Mount of Olives in Jerusalem to rule the nations, bringing in His Kingdom for eternity. This book brings clarity, focus and urgency. Jesus warned that in the end times there will be seducing evil spirits and doctrines of demons in the Church itself. That there will be those creating counterfeit Jesus Christs within the Church. That there will be at the very end a true Church and a False Christian Church. One will go up the ladder and receive divine protection and blessing. The other will slide down the snake, completely unprotected, into the period Jesus describes as the worst years in the whole of history. For Christians in the West, business as usual is no longer an option.

– Jonathan Stuart-Brown LLB, Author and Journalist. Sheffield University. Chester Law College. The Alliance Française de Rouen-Normandie, France. The Raindance Film Festival. Hollywood Film Institute.

****

In an age of spin, fake news, lies, propaganda and manipulation by media and governments alike, it is refreshing to find an author who clearly questions the current given narrative of Covid, along with the concomitant reaction of the Church in general. This is a must-read for all Berean Christians, who would claim to be men and women of Issachar, able to read the signs of the times. The author is not only very well-qualified to deal with many of the questions that pastors and truth-loving, Bible-believing Christians are asking, but has thoroughly researched every angle of this 'Plandemic', all backed up by wide research. Having myself spent hours online watching many teaching videos, reading reports, listening to Frontline Doctors, epidemiologists, prophetic teachers and pastors explain the God-revealed truth about what is happening in line with Biblical prophecy, only to have their evidence removed from the internet as 'fake news', this book was really a God-send as it has compiled, under one cover, the information I have gleaned over the past year. I cannot recommend it more highly for truth seekers!

– Ruth Campbell, Retired International Schools Teacher

****

In this book J.L. Fuller has done a timely and excellent job in investigating and deconstructing the hidden agendas, nefarious intent and identities of the shadowy parties behind the non-existent pandemic and what is one of the greatest crimes ever committed on humanity. The magnitude of the crime is breath-taking in its audacity and scope and this book serves as a timely must-read wake-up call.

– James Newman, Chartered Surveyor, Brampton, Canada

****

'Romans 13 and Covid 19' will both enlighten and shock you in equal measure. It is probably one of the most timely and relevant books published in the advent of Covid, speaking directly into the situation we all find ourselves in – the coronavirus minefield and the world of 'the Global Elite' agenda. Not only a 'now book' but also gives vital information as to what has led us to this point in time and where it's going. Plus, it has something to say to everyone, whether you are a lay person, like me, or the head of the Church. It may even open the eyes of the 'man on the

street' who is discerning the times in which he lives. It has practical suggestions on 'what to do next' and even has a section on how we can prepare our hearts for what is on the horizon. I've never read a book that covers such a diverse range of relevant and intertwined subjects, such as what is going on in the world in terms of genetics but also give down to earth advice on what to eat! Make no mistake, this book will open your eyes but also equip you to be the Church of tomorrow in an ever-changing world that may never go back to 'normal' again. The only question I ask is 'are you ready for it?'

– Val Thorpe, BA Hons

****

If, as Christians believe, the Bible is the living and active Word of God, then we should use it daily to guide how we relate to God and live our lives. We should also use the it as a benchmark to assess the current actions of other individuals, influencers, governments and countries in the world. The Bible contains history and prophesy and we need to be aware of Bible prophesies yet to be fulfilled; how might the activities of key influencers in the world be working towards events lining up to allow as yet unfulfilled prophesies to come to fruition? We should assess history, watch events unfold and listen carefully to what we are being told (and perhaps more importantly what we are not told, but can uncover with some research and applying critical thought) in the news and other media, reading our Bibles alongside and interpreting these things accordingly.

In this Biblically grounded thesis, which has been written with God-given conviction, J.L. Fuller identifies some key events that have occurred before and during the 'Covid 19 crisis' and demonstrates how governments have gone beyond their 'Romans 13 remit' in the policies they have effected. J.L. goes on to highlight the ramifications and dangers of these policies and shows how these may be accelerating progress towards what the Bible tells us will be features of the 'end times' in terms of world his-

tory. Much of it is uncomfortable reading and J.L. calls Christians espe-cially to exercise careful discernment at these times. The points made are thoroughly researched and evidenced to credible third-party links and primary sources. All readers will benefit from knowing about the impact of current world events, but I would particularly urge all professing Christians to read this book alongside their Bibles to help discern what is truth and seek God for guidance in the light of it.

– Tony Jopson, FCA and member and Treasurer of Hope Baptist Church, Devon, UK

****

The Church today finds itself amidst very troublesome times, and this study seeks to raise and resolve many of the questions in respect to this. Whatever your views on prophecy or power, the sections contained in this book on Paul's instructions regarding Christian obedience and freedom and the historical observations and lessons in respect to prior times of difficulty are essential to the very fabric and nature of our faith, and need to be taken to heart in these current circumstances.

Whilst difficult to deal with, it is imperative that we examine the issues the author has ably addressed in this work if we are to face the key chal-lenges of today. This publication, whilst tackling several thorny issues, is a good way to begin and advance that conversation.

– Howard Nowlan, Author, 'Preparing for Heaven on Earth: An In-troduction to Creational Christianity'

****

'Romans 13 and Covid 19' is unique book, written for such a time as this, when things are moving and shaking rapidly in our society. J.L. Fuller has spent much time in research and soul searching to present a book that flies against the culture of fear, confusion, ease and political correctness, often uninformed as to what is really going on behind the scenes world-wide and dictated to by the media. There is a bigger picture we must see;

it has been planned for centuries by the Global Elite and this book condenses it into a wonderful resource. When Government censoring causes the daily disappearance of 'voices of truth' from the internet and social media, we know there's a problem and this book puts the information into our hands.

Martin Luther King said, "The ultimate measure of a man is not where he stands in moments of comfort and convenience, but where he stands at times of challenge and controversy." J.L.'s deep heart of passion, not only for the Church, but for all people, to know and understand the truth being presented here, is commendable and making a stand comes with a price, not all of us would wish to pay. A 'must read' for everyone who is 'open to hear', Revelation 2:7. An invaluable resource, one I will certainly recommend to family and friends.

– Anon, Israel

****

J.L. Fuller is a Christian with unflinching honesty and searing intelligence. This isn't a book for the faint-hearted, but it is manna for those who have deep and serious questions about 'what on earth is going on in the world today?'. It's amazing to find such a complex and wide range of subjects brought together in one volume, and ultimately what is so exciting is that it is SO readable!

– Cynthia Wilson, UK

CONTENTS

PART 1: The Current Problem and Context (Romans 13:1-7)

PART 2: Authority, Tyranny and the Wider Problems

PART 3: The Solution

Foreword

The book you have before you is not a casual, easy read. It's not the kind of book you read to help you sleep at night. Actually, I suspect it may have just the opposite effect. It's a challenging read and its conclusions are painful.

That's not exactly a ringing endorsement. You may be wondering, *"why should I bother?"* My hope is that you will read it for the same reason you pick up and read a book like 'A Problem from Hell' or 'Gulag Archipelago' or 'Night' or even 'A Theatre in Dachau'. Simply put, it's honest. J.L. Fuller's arguments are important and the message urgent. We have all read heart wrenching accounts of the deeds of previous generations. This is like that, except it is present day; which means there is still something you can do about it. In that sense it is urgent. But it is also important in that it touches on freedoms which once lost are not easily regained.

We are often told that we are living in unprecedented times. I am not inclined to argue. I think they are unprecedented. But I believe the times are unprecedented for a whole different set of reasons than what you may have been led to believe. What is *unprecedented* is the mass closure of Churches worldwide. What is *unprecedented* is the almost universal agreement among nations and governments both in terms of messaging and regulation. What is *unprecedented* is the way that the media in nations around the world have managed to sell the same message – all repeating the same words as if quoting from the same playbook. What is *unprecedented* and frightening is the willingness of freemen everywhere to so cheaply give up their freedom.

This book won't be popular with many because it takes issue with the prevailing opinion. I suspect it won't be liked for another reason. It isn't comfortable. But for both reasons it is urgently needed.

You may not agree with all its conclusions, but you would be reckless to dismiss it without first prayerfully considering its arguments.

I believe we need this voice of reason very badly. I have been personally staggered by the silent complicity of our Church leaders. Make no mistake, their silence makes them party to the problem. History will not look favourably on them.

I sincerely wish there were many more with courage to speak. But I am profoundly thankful for those like J.L. Fuller whom God has surely raised up for such a time as this ... to sound the alarm.

Reader, with all my heart I believe that alarm needs sounding. I certainly hope that you will read, pray, act and then pray again. My prayer is that you will put this book down, determined that you will not so easily surrender the freedoms which cost your forefathers so much to buy. But I have prayed that the Lord would use this book for something much more than that. Civil liberties are precious, but they have value only insofar as they serve the glory of God. It is my prayer that the Lord may use this book to remind His people that He is King, and that *He is worthy*!

– Steve Richardson, Pastor, Faith Presbyterian Church, Ontario, Canada.

Author Biography

When the LORD put it on my heart to embark on this writing project, my first and subsequent thoughts were *"LORD, I'm not qualified nor experienced to write this thing!"* Whilst I was aware that God delights in taking the unqualified but willing and uses them to display His handiwork, it took me longer to realise, mainly highlighted by others, that I do have some experience to bring to the table in the areas that are relevant to Covid and its entourage of new directives. Namely, a portfolio career in the spheres of Medical Research Law and Health Policy, as well as business experience that has given me first-hand knowledge of the strategies of powerful elites. I also had a long spell in the New Age world, both professionally and as my adopted religion.

These fields of my professional interest are very relevant to all-things Covid 19 and beyond (which we'll look at in detail in the body of the book) and there was a common denominator that I eventually recognised in them all: high-level, subtle and systematic deception, especially when it comes to determining who controls the purse strings and for what purposes. It's sad to say that I see the same in much of what has taken place in the advent of our so-called 'pandemic', on a rather more monumental scale. Let me expand a little on my background …

After graduating with a Law degree, I spent years managing Medical Research and the ethical and legal aspects of clinical trials. I wrote the Government reports which intimately highlighted to me the huge influence of Big Pharma funding on what actually makes it to full trial and the bias in results and outcome for patients, as well skewed information given to sincere medical professionals. Separately, I also worked on writing the legal policies for a large institution where I saw the systematic legalisation of evil practices, squeeze on free speech and the creeping of government authoritarianism. For two decades, I have worked in natural health and have been delighted to see that so many 'incurable diseases' (including viruses) are quite rapidly curable, with the right diet and lifestyle. All of this has enabled me to detect very early on the huge problems, on many levels, with the rushed experimental vaccination rollout that began in 2020.

In my decade of business and marketing consultancy, I worked amongst very powerful businessmen who knew how to manipulate large groups of people to sell them products and ideas, using sophisticated and deceptive techniques, such as mass-hypnotism and Neuro-Linguistic Programming (NLP). I witnessed the professionalised and highly effective use of fear, scarcity and appealing to people's greed, pride and desire for comfort to control actions and attitudes, without the target audience's knowledge or awareness.

As a New Ager, I ascribed to various aspects of humanism, 'mother earth' worship, positive Psychology and channelling. I also delved deep into re-search on the Luciferian New World Order agenda. So, you could say I have a working knowledge of how the devil and his demons can masquer-ade very convincingly as 'angels of light', bringing much spiritual and physical devastation.

Thankfully for me and all glory and praise to my Father in Heaven, the LORD Jesus Christ saved me from all that a good while ago and I have been an avid Bible student and disciple of Christ ever since. But I will never forget those experiences and I recognise the same deception in the ministries of false preachers and apostate Churches, but also sneaking into the true Church, which we need to be more vigilant about swiftly removing.

I have a burning and single-minded devotion to God and echo Fanny Crosby's sentiments to 'take the world, but give me Jesus' and I have suffered and lost a lot as a consequence. I have no personal ambition at this point in my life, I love Him far above all else and I long to see our God glorified in and by His Church, albeit in my weakness, sin and frailty. I love the local Church, God's people on earth, and I long to see a return to holiness. I long for repentance within the Body of Christ and to walk in truth, radical faith and good conscience, all of which have been dangerously and often subtly eroded in many ways.

The Satanic Babylonian system is all around us and advancing rapidly in the advent of the Covid 19 medical crisis, traversing across both pragmatic scientism and religion and seeking to conflate the two. We need to be a Church who can successfully separate herself and launch a holy counter-attack in the spiritual realms for Christ's Kingdom, binding up the broken hearted, proclaiming the Gospel to those who are in captivity to sin and setting people free, even as the world seeks to imprison us. To do this, we need to be 'men of Issachar' and I believe that I am one of them, owing to my peculiar professional and spiritual background and God's gracious salvation, communion and revelation. So, here's my book on these times.

"And of the children of Issachar, which were men that had understanding of the times, to know what Israel ought to do" – 1 Chronicles 12:32.

Preface

Geonge Orwell once claimed that he has 'an ability to face unpleasant facts'. I have this ability too. I've seen many 'unpleasant facts' in my own life, heart and relationships, like all sinners in need of a Saviour, but also in various work settings and false religion, as I've just outlined. Throughout my portfolio career I've explored things that people often turn a blind eye to, for various reasons of convenience and sometimes self-preservation.

As an avid researcher, I've dedicated by far the most of my time, energy and passion to understanding worldviews and the nature of reality; consequently, experiencing many rabbit holes and causing changes of thought and direction along the way that have helped me to grow in truth and knowledge. This has cost a lot – loss of finances, relationships, status, comfort and more. Having the boldness to ask those probing, socially inappropriate or politically incorrect questions that others often don't wish to address, doesn't always win friends and influence people!

My desire to be a truth seeker, no matter what I may find, or what consequences may arise, has led me to seeing the devastating level of deception in all aspects of life, especially the motivating factors behind world events and politics. Oftentimes, the deep, dark subject matter that I've found myself delving into began as genuine enquiry into what I thought was a happy, positive subject, but instead I discovered very alarming realities. 'Health care' is one of these areas, for example. By God's grace, I've been able to maintain calm resolve and critical thought which has allowed me to keep pressing in to face the facts full-on, with a heart to see my insights inform wise actions – to forewarn others, lament the situation and take it to the LORD in prayer. In tandem with this, I've sought to live as a law-abiding (latterly Christian) citizen, in peace with my neighbour and enjoying a 'normal life' as far as possible.

As I pen this work, we are knee-high in a world crisis 'pandemic', with governmental measures in place that even the most sceptical would say is nonsensical and confusing at best and utterly tyrannical at worst. I've seen this coming and perceive it to be the unfolding of a very carefully planned set of events towards a specific agenda. You won't see it outlined on television or mainstream media and where information about it is disseminated on social media, it is swiftly stamped as 'fake news', censored and removed. Isn't it correct that once you see behind a magician's trick, you have a revelation that you can't undo? Once you see the 'smoke and mirrors' for what it is, your subjective reality shifts. The fog gives way to clarity of view and true insight. So, I'll say this: If truth and the present world crisis, the matter at hand, is something you prefer not to address, then this book could be a challenge for you. Ignorance is indeed often bliss in many ways. But this book is written for the believer in Christ who wishes to live in truth and courage (with love and respect), being wise to the enemy's tactics (but innocent of partaking in the evil itself) and contending for the faith accordingly. Our LORD warns us many times not to be deceived and to worship Him in spirit and truth and to turn away from evil. So, if you are committed to your obedience to Him, at any cost, and wish to be a light in the world and grow in your discernment ... I urge you to read on, read in full and prayerfully consider what's written here and let it be a factor in your actions.

[**SIDE NOTE:** If you're not yet a follower of the Jesus Christ, then before you make a start on this book, please first go to Chapter 14 on 'Your One and Only True Solution to Overcome this Mess'. Friend, your biggest problem is not this current world crisis and craziness, it's that you're not in a right relationship with the Living God and that if you die in your sins, you will face eternal wrath. Jesus is Creator of the heavens and the earth and everything in them. He is God and He also came to earth as a man to pay for your sins (the bad deeds that we all do and the good things we've failed to do) on the cross but you need to accept that gift to receive forgiveness. I urge you, today, to get right with Him. Believe that Jesus laid down His life to take the penalty for your sins. Confess them to Him and repent (turn away from them). Turn to King Jesus as Lord of your life.

Read His Word, the Bible and seek out a local fellowship group of believers. This is vitally important!]

Winston Churchill once said this: *"In wartime, truth is so precious that she should always be attended by a bodyguard of lies."* He was a Freemason[1] and Druid[2] – a member of organisations shrouded in secrecy and deception, even to its members, until they achieve the higher degrees. So, he would know a lot about truth and lies, especially on a geopolitical level. There is one great truth that Christians hold onto – that Jesus is LORD, creator, sustainer and redeemer of the heavens and the earth and all therein. We know that the devil sets up an untold multitude of lies to try and keep people from recognising this reality.

According to Scripture, we are in wartime now. I believe that there is so much deception going on and lies being told that we need to fervently pray for our eyes to be opened and for the LORD to deliver us. We must ask Him what we, personally, in our own particular setting, gifting and area of responsibility should do for the best, in order to stick closest to our Shepherd and to shepherd others, glorify Him and lead others to a personal relationship with Jesus. The wisdom we're all looking for needs to come directly from that relationship and the fountain of living water instead of worldly 'broken cisterns' (Jeremiah 2:13). John 10:27 states that *"my sheep hear my voice"*. If you are in a leadership position especially, then I would offer the suggestion that just maybe, the LORD has brought you here for a reason. Maybe the information and wisdom you're looking for on what to do in this crisis won't be found from world leaders and governmental bodies but discerned from within the Body of Christ … I'll let you decide.

---

[1] 'Winston Churchill'. *United Grand Lodge of England*. https://www.ugle.org.uk/about-freemasonry/famous-masons/17-winston-Churchill. Accessed 1 May 2021.

[2] 'The History of Modern Druids'. *Order of Bards, Ovates & Druids*. https://druidry.org/druidway/what-druidry/recent-history. Accessed 1 May 2021.

Why I Wrote This Book

My motivations for writing this book are certainly not to rant about conspiratorial matters and 'fight the powers that be' merely for the sake of human rights (much as I used to like listening to Public Enemy in the 80s). Rather, my motivations are twofold: First, a concern for right and proper worship of the Living God, in all the ways He instructs us to, in spirit, truth and freedom as His gathered, called out Church – 'ekklesia'. Second, a concern for effective evangelisation of the lost world and seeking to bring souls to a saving faith in the LORD Jesus Christ.

I found that trying to have one-to-one conversations with many people on these matters was a job left half done at best. So, I took it to God and felt a clear prompt in the Spirit to write about it, confirmed by others. It made sense as I have the prior experience of authoring several major-published books. As I have undertaken this research and writing project, it has not been at the expense of other more 'regular' Christian duties and account-abilities, nor speaking to people in person about these things.

Here's some of the actions I've taken:

- In February 2020, I petitioned several Church leaders to keep our Churches open. I explained that the crisis involved much govern-ment deception and that we should resist the things that directly imposed on our gathered worship of the Living God. This ap-peared to be largely unheard.
- I have laboured in prayer and fasting consistently to repent and ask the LORD to have mercy on us and give us the courage and faith to re-open Churches (with wisdom) – to worship and go about Church business unrestricted by governments and fear.
- I have continued to meet, in person, for Church fellowship in some form or other throughout the lockdowns.

25

- My 1-1 evangelism increased. I have shared the Gospel with many atheists, Muslims, New Agers, family members, friends in person and online, clients, social activists, people I've met whilst out walking and more.

- Joining a group to do open air preaching and evangelism which has continued in city centres locally.

- I have continued to serve in Church – visit and take food to elderly people, look after my vulnerable relatives, participate on various Church rotas and attend prayer and Bible study meetings.

- In the research and writing of this book, I have interviewed many leaders of Churches from differing denominations, locations and underground fellowship groups, Christian organisations and other ministries. I have solicited feedback, critique and suggestions from those who are favourable to my plight, conclusions and suggestions and also from those who are not wholly in agreement and some who are outright hostile. I have taken these things to God in prayer and fasting and amended my writing accordingly. I have also sought out the insights and experiences of people who have been very negatively affected by all things Covid.

I know that many Church leaders are reluctant to listen to 'conspiracy theories', looking to focus on making Jesus known and the task at hand rather than digging into deception or 'wacky nonsense', as many perceive it! Their call is to preach the Word and shepherd the sheep (pastoral), while mine is to bring truth and exposure to deception (watchman or prophetic). However, the body of Christ works best when we all function in our varying gifts, for the edification of all and we are all eventually heading towards the final goal, the return of our Messiah Jesus.

I have written this book with a humble desire for it to be a thorough and clear means to bring the knowledge and rally-call to Christians and leaders that is so desperately needed at this time. I have taken the considered decision to let it be longer than it essentially needs to be, with many full quotations and primary source excerpts. The main reason for this is that both truth and open discussion about all things Covid are being heavily censored and quite possibly eliminated altogether in the near future. I wanted people to have a comprehensive physical resource that they could keep and refer to into the future. I would advise getting several copies in paperback form; not so that I sell more books, but as a matter of wisdom and the sharing of truth with your loved ones. You may not agree with everything in this book and there are certainly aspects that I have posed as musings and considerations, or as my current opinion, rather than un-equivocal fact (namely around future events). However, there is more than enough in here to make it an invaluable, in-depth resource for truth on Covid and the Church and wider society's response. I hope and pray it is a helpful blessing to you and your brothers and sisters in Christ. I hope too that the people who read it and are not yet followers of Christ, will become ones.

"Wherever you hear the sound of the trumpet, rally to us there. Our God will fight for us." – Nehemiah 4:20 (NKJV)

Romans 13 – The Relevance of All Fourteen Verses

This book ties together three weighty issues that might at first blush seem rather unrelated:

1. The first seven verses of Romans 13, addressing the Christian's subjection and attitude to governing authorities over us.
2. Covid 19 mandates, with the most pressing being the rushed, enforced 'vaccination' programme.
3. The Babylonian landscape around us, as most clearly depicted in Revelation chapters 13, 17 and 18. This encompasses the worldly political, commercial and religious structures in place that are set up against Jesus and His Biblical commands.

We will explore each of these in detail and the connection between the three, in an effort to discern the times, heed Jesus' warnings to us to not be led astray by deceptive people and teachings, and to prepare ourselves for what's ahead. The first seven verses of Romans 13 provide the most obviously relevant and naturally discussed verses in connection to the Church's situation under Covid. However, the latter seven verses are also highly relevant and I tie these in with material throughout the book, to a lesser or greater extent. Namely those things are:

- Fulfilling our obligations to one another by loving our neighbour and not wronging them (Romans 13:8-10).
- Waking up from deception and apathy (Romans 13:11).
- Casting off the works of darkness; turning from evil and putting on the armour of the light of Christ (Romans 13:12).
- Making no provision for the flesh – to neither gratify its desires nor seek to impress others by making a good showing in the flesh in order to avoid persecution. (Romans 13:14, also Galatians 6:12)

Finally, I am a sinner saved by grace and claim to be no more than that. I am not a Church leader or preacher, nor do I hold a theology degree. But I have had the time needed that many Church leaders just didn't seem to have, with all that's happened since Covid. The LORD has set me aside to write this, with the headspace, degree of objectivity, energy, quiet space and prayerfulness to do it. I have a burning heart for evange-lism and hope for a prepared Bride and army of the Lord that can discern the deceptive times we're in and avoid deceitful spirits. *"Now the Spirit expressly says that in latter times some will depart from the faith, giving heed to deceiving spirits and doctrines of demons"* – 1 Timothy 4:1 (NKJV).

Let's open with an intriguing and rather sobering allegory…

The Modern Metal Image – An Allegory

"Cursed be the man that maketh any graven or molten image, an abomination unto the Lord, the work of the hands of the craftsman, and putteth it in a secret place. And all the people shall answer and say, Amen." – Deuteronomy 27:15

The nineteenth century heralded the triumphal entry of the prototype metal image and the people hailed *"Blessed is he who comes in the name of the Lord!"*. The god of this world sent out his creeds across his territory – the airwaves – and into every home across the land. The message of the Nazarene was swapped for the Nazi regime in the 1930s and the enemy of the Living God rejoiced at what destruction he was able to accomplish with this modest molten thing.

By the middle of the twentieth century, the metal image was given a face, as well as speech, and was set up in the corner of every living room. The gods of the metal image were consulted several times a day by family members and the image, known as the 'television set', was keenly polished and cared for.

This new and upgraded metal image was at first small and fairly unassuming, complementing daily life rather than intruding upon it. But by the 1960s it had gained traction with a generation: having great influence over the actions and ethics of the youth, who saw less need for outdated Christian doctrines and more desire for pleasure. The metal image declared the glory of the god of this world and day after day it poured forth speech of all kinds of debauchery, drunkenness, gluttony, witchcraft, sorcery, orgies, fornication, promiscuity … Sodom and Gomorrah would have loved it.

The nations continued to conspire and the peoples plotted in vain. The kings of the earth set themselves, and the rulers took counsel together, against the LORD and against his Anointed – and the metal image was their prime vehicle. The LORD God looked down from Heaven on the children of man and was perplexed and dismayed at what He saw. He held them in derision.

As the decades went on, the metal image became a bigger and much more prominent feature in everyday life. It was happy to offer relief from the strains of life, information, entertainment and delight. Like a kind of philanthropic big brother to both families and singles, in exchange for just a pinch of incense. It was a fair swap and it reassured Christians that it could happily coexist with their God without interference.

Satan continued his roam across the world and largely passed over all who had faithfully erected their metal image black box altars in their homes and were seen bowing down to them several times a day at least. There were a few who sought to get rid of the metal image, suspecting that it had a grip on them that was not altogether healthy and in their best interests, but they were maligned, even by Christians, as being 'out of touch with reality'.

By the end of the twentieth century, the metal image had gained two metal allies – the personal computer and the smartphone. These allowed people to really deepen their faith in the god of the metal image and their daily spiritual practices. The fuzzy airwaves from the prince of the power of the air caused much static to hinder the voice of the Holy Spirit in the Christian's life and served to resist the prayers of the saints, much like a prince of Persia.

Strangely, the Christians did not seem to grasp that the god of this world had instituted all this and that they were willingly inviting him into their homes each day. The occultists in high places delighted in the image's powers of deception and control of the masses by its veritable and captivating fare. Satan's end-times masterstroke, if he did say so himself.

Hedonism, humanism, scientism, pragmatism and collectivism took precedent over truth, faith, depth of enquiry and individual critical thought. Everyone was becoming united under a banner of groupthink and falsehood, led by metal image. By 2019, all but a few people had come to depend on their metal images for comfort, social life and communication. Practically all of their thinking on worldview issues (in fact, nearly all other issues too) was able to be done for them. No longer did people have to spend time weighing up how to best live their lives and what action they wished to take, it was conveniently outsourced to the image, for everyone's good. The stage was set ...

In the year 2020, the metal image announced a worldwide plague.

The people became afraid and confused and wondered what to do. There was apparently a virus that was sweeping the nations. You couldn't see it – there was no one dying in the streets, people looked normal, life looked normal, after all illnesses had been a part of human life since the beginning of creation, but they were warned not to be under any illusions; this was deadly and a grave threat to all of humanity. What to do? Thankfully the benevolent metal image issued decrees and mandates that would let the people know what to believe, how to act and prescribe the reasonable and rational solution.

The threefold pronouncement was made – the metal image's antidote to the heinous plague: fear, compliance and absurdity. The people should fear death, fear governments (they knew best, don't dare question) and most of all, fear other people. Each person was now deemed to be a plague bearer and each other person was to fear them as such and stay as far away as possible, for the good of everyone.

The people should comply – with any and all mandates given by the authorities. Stay at home. Close businesses. Open businesses for a month then close them again. Close Churches. Close schools. No travelling. Quarantine both the sick and healthy. The message was clear – whatever the governments say, the people should obey. Some would muse that it seemed a little heavy-handed and one-sided but you have to understand, it was all in the name of keeping everyone safe. And the Christians would open their Bibles to Paul's letter to the Romans, find verse one of chapter 13 and be reassured that this was all good and right.

The people should embrace absurdity – they were to cover their faces with an old ragged cloth or two, or three – one of the more prominent sacrificial shackles, denoting allegiance. Avoid all family members for months. Don't hug grandchildren. Let the government know every time they entered a new place. Stick a virus test swab up their nose, regularly – that even the inventor said was ineffective, but no matter, a positive result is a positive result: no questions, they were to quarantine themselves, despite how well they felt. They were to remember that it was illegal and dangerous to sit and have a coffee with a friend in a park but totally fine and safe to do an indoor group gym class. They began to realise that it was necessary to give up living in order to protect life. They kept in mind that no one was doing these things for themselves – that would be selfish and damnable – instead, it was all for the good of others. They let the governments inject them with a rushed and experimental wonder drug containing all sorts of known toxins and new technologies but unknown long-term effects. The fact that the main philanthropist behind much of this was actively championing population control seemed to be a minor and inconsequential point. Absurdity was the new normal. They could almost be encouraged to champion the wise words of an old prophet: War is Peace, Freedom is Slavery and Ignorance is Strength. This was beginning to make real sense in 2020.

The bottom line was clear: So long as one was not overly concerned with truth, one's existence could assume an unreflective contentment. And if it wasn't for the metal image, people would not have known all these things and they wondered just what kind of devastation the plague would have caused to health, families, jobs, the economy, life, liberty and Church, had it not been around.

The metal image continued to preach and repeat its sermons with great fervour and with the help of its multitude of priests and elders all across the world and in every language. It tantalised the people's senses in multimedia technicolour. Graphs and tickers and news anchors repeated the creeds of the message that everyone needed to hear and heed. Billions were captivated.

Now, all this said, there were more than a few who questioned the novel commandments but unless their ideas made it onto the altar of the metal image, they were dismissed as strange fire; unacceptable worship and heresy. The people did not want to arouse the anger of the capricious gods of the metal image, so they continued to reverently obey.

Those Christians who refused to bow to the metal image were thought of as disruptive. After all, the gracious metal image gods had let them keep their Churches (albeit modified and prescribed, but that wasn't seen as a big deal) and had also given them their own metal image online services by which to serve their God. They could have the best of both worlds and both gods (where the metal image could keep an eye on them and later prescribe and censor the content), so what an earth was their problem? Pah! They clearly needed a re-read of Romans 13. These ungrateful, ungracious, uncompromising radicals. They needed to be dealt with, and the metal image god had made provisions for that.

There were health service evangelists (namely doctors and nurses) stationed in prominent positions in Churches, who ensured ongoing and unified ecclesiastical allegiance. Any Christian who dared to debate the metal image's decrees were sharply asked if they actually cared about people's lives at all? These cold and heartless folk clearly didn't get it, or so it was said.

It was a sad reality that even those who had been set free from the bondage of evil, sin and death and had a relationship with the loving and Living God, bowed down before the metal image, along with the pagans. There was not much distinguishable difference between the two groups.

Satan had not taken away Bibles yet: There was no need since there was no real threat, as Christians preferred to consult and make offerings to the metal image gods many times a day instead. Yes, the Christians still had their Bibles – lots of them – but they did not much care for them like they really ought to have. They decided in their hearts that there must be an error or at least an exception to what the scriptures said around gathering for worship, singing in the congregation and living in freedom and without fear; since the metal image, which had been such a familiar family friend for so many years, told them differently. After all, the gods of safety, pragmatism, scientism and collectivism and their zealous evangelists, were all in agreement and the people seemed to think it was all quite judicious.

A full year after the metal image pronounced the plague, Christians had still forfeited their weapons of warfare in a one-sided armistice: Corporate prayer gatherings were gone, or remote and lacklustre. Hymns of praise in the congregation were shut up or quietly apologetic. Anointing to break yokes and laying on of hands was nowhere to be seen. The Lord's Supper to remember the body and blood of Jesus availed for each believer was suspended or reduced to a 50% version – now the wine that represents the blood that brings life, could bring death. Public evangelism disappeared.

A little light in the darkness … the need of the hour and the technology available enabled astute believers from around the world to convene and repent in prayer together. The metal image gods were not happy about this illegitimate use of their altar, but it was waived for a time as minor collateral damage. The Living God heard and thought differently.

Meanwhile, the god of this world advanced his army with great force and urgency: Government edicts, unjust laws, snappy 3-pronged newspeak soundbites, emotive psy-ops and magical sleight of hand reports of death tolls. It was all quite a spectacle and the whole world continued to follow and marvel.

By 2021, the metal image had firmly persuaded the people that they should embrace Satan's new pharmakeia. Like all good drug dealers worth their salt, the image showed people how life would be so much better when they rolled up their sleeve and received an intravenous hit of a magical but unknown substance that would allow them to escape from the hard truths of reality ... and that one hit was never going to be enough. Where did it come from? What's in it? Why are we being offered it and so quickly? There was no need to worry – this was the new saviour of the world to deliver them from the humdrum, burdens, frustrations and anxieties of everyday plague and lockdown life since 2020.

Any reports of adverse reactions, overdose, and pure and simple death from poisoning did not make it onto the news report altar, naturally, although there were many. And as the programme rolled out, in accordance with the affable technocrat eugenicists (key high priests of the metal image god), this new witches' brew began to include chips and bots that wowed the crowd, mostly by way of capturing the last of their mind and freewill that the metal image had not yet accrued. Just like Huxley's soma, it had raised a quite impenetrable wall between the actual universe and their minds.

And so it came to be that, like the five wanting virgins, there was almost a full complement of slumbering bodies in (online) Churches. The unregenerate were content as there was nothing required of them to claim membership to the community club of Jesus. And even many of those with oil in their lamp were in a spiritual stupor, cosily preferring their Egyptian cotton bedsheets to the harsh winds of discipleship. In fact, their God seemed quite distant to them and pretty silent on all of this stuff that the metal image was so vocal about ... So, what else was there to do but settle down, build houses, plant vineyards and sleep it all off?

They supposed that their God must not have really meant what He said when He told them that they should expect to suffer, even die for their faith: Those hot-tempered men of old with ruffled feathers must have made much ado about nothing over the things of Christ and His holiness. And so, their stories of martyrdom and patient endurance under persecution were looked upon fondly and compassionately as the stuff of cute myth.

The resolution of the matter was this: It was much better to be on the right side of the metal image god, since it seemed so much more relevant to daily life and curried so much favour with the pagans. Besides, what witness would it be if Christians recklessly disregarded the hymns of fear and incense of safety in favour of joy, hope and freedom? No, they saw that they must be just like the world in order to win the world ... but that they'd leave the winning to when the metal image allowed them to go out again.

Now, I won't spoil the rest of the story for you, you'll have to see for yourself how it all pans out in the last days before Christ returns ... I wouldn't want to turn this unsettling fable into an outright horror story. Let's just say that the technocratic trinity – the metal image god and its two allies – went on to develop a supremely sophisticated fantasyland of stealth terror and death, that the world had already obtained its ticket to, from racking up decades of entertainment loyalty points. Multifaith Churches were standard, holographs, aliens, more outbreaks, a Jesus here, a Jesus there! Quite wondrous ... And I won't even mention that son of perdition. True and committed followers of Jesus had to resolve to 'live not by lies' (as Solzhenitsyn once said) and against all odds and norms. It was near impossible because of the all-pervading magnitude of the metal image deception – but it could be done, by the grace of the Living God. It was there that the beauty of sweet communion with Christ was found.

One has to reflect though on how things might have been quite different, had the Christians smashed their metal images, or not brought them into their homes at all. What if they had asked the Living God in all earnestness to deliver them from the shackles of lies and comfort and cowardice? What if, when the metal image first announced the plague and orders to shut Churches, they unwaveringly followed Christ and His commands instead, saying *"We must obey God rather than men"*? What if the Christians resolved to shine more brightly with their open Churches in the dark and closed world? How would things have looked if they'd spent more time thinking and praying about lost souls on their way to hell and doing evangelism, rather than hand sanitisers and safety risk assessment reports? If they had discussed and delved into what Romans 13 actually meant and laboured in prayer for even a third of the time that they spent consuming newspeak and metal image box sets? Remember, Elijah was a man just like us.

Anyway, as I write this, from the largest correction centre that the world has ever known and with great risk to my life, since pens and notebooks are now deemed the most dangerous of weapons, my deepest wish is this: To be able to wind the clock back to early 2020 and plead with the Christians to resist the lies of the god of the metal image, to make a stand for Christ and His worship and be willing to be counted worthy to suffer for Him – and to know the great joy and intimacy with our Saviour as a result of costly and wholehearted obedience ... before it's too late.

"What profiteth the graven image that the maker thereof hath graven it; the molten image, and a teacher of lies, that the maker of his work trusteth therein, to make dumb idols?" – Habakkuk 2:18

"Blessed are they which are persecuted for righteousness' sake: for theirs is the kingdom of heaven. Blessed are ye, when men shall revile you, and persecute you, and shall say all manner of evil against you falsely, for my sake. Rejoice, and be exceeding glad: for great is your reward in heaven: for so persecuted they the prophets which were before you." – Matthew 5:10-12

Part 1: The Current Problem & Context (Romans 13:1-7)

CHAPTER ONE

Cold, Hard Covid Facts and Uncovering Initial Insights

L et's open this chapter with 20 pithy facts around all things Covid. They are things that are undisputable, but mostly hidden or censored by mainstream and social media.

#1 PCR Tests do not work – they do not accurately detect any virus. *(See full details and evidence in Chapter 3.)*

PCR tests are expressly not approved for diagnostic purposes – as is correctly noted on official literature coming with these tests[3], and as the inventor of the PCR test, Kary Mullis, has repeatedly emphasised. Instead, they're simply incapable of diagnosing any disease.

"...if a person gets a 'positive' PCR test result at a cycle threshold (Ct) of 35 or higher (as applied in most US labs and many European labs), the chance that the person is infectious is less than 3%. The chance that

---

[3] 'PCR Test Revelations From Official Literature; They Expose Their Own Lies'. *LewRockwell.com*, https://www.lewrockwell.com/2021/02/jon-rappoport/pcr-test-revelations-from-official-literature-they-expose-their-own-lies/. Accessed 1 May 2021.

the person received a 'false positive' result is 97% or higher." – Swiss Policy Research[4]

#2 Masks do not work – they don't stop virus particles but are dangerous to health. *(See full details and evidence in Chapter 3.)*

An under-reported CDC study, which surveyed symptomatic Covid 19 patients, found that 70.6% of Covid patients reported 'always' wearing a mask and 14.4% say they 'often' wear a mask[5]. That means a whopping 85% of infected Covid patients are habitual mask wearers. Only 3.9% of those infected said they 'never' wear a face covering.

"Masks have been shown to inhibit breathing and increase the chance of infection. Reports coming from my colleagues all over the world are suggesting that the bacterial pneumonias are on the rise, as a result of moisture collecting in face masks." – Dr James Meehan[6]

"By all means people can wear masks – or not wear masks. Policy can make the decision, but what they can't do is say that it's an evidence-based decision." – Dr Carl Henegan[7], Professor of Evidence-Based Medicine, University of Oxford.

#3 Lockdowns do not work – they do not inhibit virus transmission, but do cause major devastation to relationships, work, health and the economy. *(See full details and evidence in Chapter 3.)*

Amongst many others, Pandemics Data and Analytics (PANDA) have proved that not only do lockdowns not work but they contradict a century

---

[4] 'The Trouble With PCR Tests'. *Swiss Policy Research*, 4 Oct. 2020, https://swprs.org/the-trouble-with-pcr-tests/.

[5] Fisher, Kiva A. 'Community and Close Contact Exposures Associated with COVID-19 Among Symptomatic Adults ≥18 Years in 11 Outpatient Health Care Facilities — United States, July 2020'. *MMWR. Morbidity and Mortality Weekly Report*, vol. 69, 2020. *www.cdc.gov*, doi:10.15585/mmwr.mm6936a5.

[6] 'Medical Doctor Warns That "Bacterial Pneumonias Are on the Rise" from Mask Wearing' – *MuchAdoAboutCorona.Ca*, https://muchadoaboutcorona.ca/bacterial-pneumonias/. Accessed 1 May 2021.

[7] Bruce, Damian. 'In Vaccines We Trust'. *Damian Bruce,* https://damianbruce.substack.com/p/in-vaccines-we-trust. Accessed 1 May 2021.

of pre-Covid science[8] and are much deadlier than the Covid 19 virus in their negative impact on all areas of life and society.

#4 Suicide, divorce rates and mental health decline have spiked. *(See full details and evidence in Chapter 3.)*

By April 2020, the interest in divorce had already increased by 34% in USA[9] and divorce rates have continued to show a marked increase. Studies show that Covid is associated elevated with social isolation, distress, anxiety, fear of contagion, depression and insomnia[10] in the general population and among healthcare professionals. This can lead to the development or exacerbation of depressive, anxiety, substance use and other psychiatric disorders in vulnerable populations. Stress-related psychiatric conditions, including mood and substance use disorders, are associated with suicidal behaviour. It has been estimated that the Covid crisis is increasing suicide rates significantly[11].

#5 Abortions by post were instituted by health services under Covid. *(See full details and evidence in Chapter 5.)*

The UK, USA and other locations have made abortions at home by pill sent in the mail[12] available, billed as *"a safe and legal way to end a pregnancy at an early gestation without needing to attend a clinic for treatment."* Abortion clinics remained open as 'essential services' all through

---

[8] 'Lockdowns Contradict a Century of Pre-Covid Science'. *PANDA*, 14 Feb. 2021, https://www.pandata.org/lockdowns-contradict-a-century-of-pre-covid-science/.

[9] 'Lockdowns Contradict a Century of Pre-Covid Science'. *PANDA*, 14 Feb. 2021, https://www.pandata.org/lockdowns-contradict-a-century-of-pre-covid-science/.

[10] Sher, Leo. 'The Impact of the COVID-19 Pandemic on Suicide Rates'. *QJM: Monthly Journal of the Association of Physicians*, vol. 113, no. 10, Oct. 2020, pp. 707–12. *PubMed*, doi:10.1093/qjmed/hcaa202.

[11] 'The Impact Of Covid-19 On Suicide Rates'. *Psycom.Net - Mental Health Treatment Resource Since 1996*, https://www.psycom.net/covid-19-suicide-rates. Accessed 1 May 2021.

[12] 'Abortion Pill Treatment at Home'. *British Pregnancy Advisory Science*. https://www.bpas.org/abortion-care/abortion-treatments/the-abortion-pill/remote-treatment/. Accessed 1 May 2021.

lockdowns, while Churches shut in order to 'save the national health services and hospitals'.

#6 Children are being institutionally traumatised. *(See full details and evidence in Chapters 3 and 4.)*

Return to school is with many traumatic restrictions[13] – children are given invasive and ineffective Covid tests weekly, forced to wear masks and with a big push for vaccination.

#7 Huge legal cases of Covid crimes against humanity are being brought right now across the world. *(See full details and evidence in Chapter 3.)*

A team of over 1,000 lawyers and over 10,000 medical experts are mounting legal proceedings against the CDC, WHO & the Davos Group for crimes against humanity. German defence lawyer, Dr Reiner Fuellmich, is leading the German Corona Investigative Committee, which is bringing crimes against humanity charges against the world's lockdown and other Covid mandates promoters[14] – using the Nuremberg Code. Many other legal cases are being brought too, and have won, as in Austria, where the courts rules that PCR tests are not suitable for Covid 19 diagnosis and that lockdowns have no legal basis[15].

#8 Many Churches have closed for long periods under lockdown, shut down completely, or are compromised in their worship. *(See full details and evidence in Chapters 3 and 4.)*

Across the world, established denominational Churches have closed their buildings and conducted their services online. Where they are open, most

---

[13] 'COVID 19 / Safe Steps to Safe Schools - Daily Pass'. *Los Angeles Unified School District*, https://achieve.lausd.net/dailypass. Accessed 1 May 2021.

[14] 'Dr Reiner Fuellmich Is Currently Preparing the Largest Class Action Lawsuit in History'. *BitChute*, https://www.bitchute.com/video/CmqSEvg8psGV/. Accessed 1 May 2021.

[15] 'Austrian Court Rules PCR Test Not Suitable For COVID-19 Diagnosis And That Lockdowns Has No Legal Basis'. *GreatGameIndia*, 8 Apr. 2021, https://greatgameindia.com/austria-court-pcr-test/.

have continued to refrain from congregational singing, observing the Lord's Supper, baptisms, fellowship meals, in-person prayer meetings, Bible studies, Gospel outreach and continue to enforce social distancing and masks. Many have taken the stance of governments, that opening back up 'largely depends on vaccine rollout'.

#9 Pastors have been jailed for opening their Churches and given astronomical fines. *(See full details and evidence in Chapter 3 and 5.)*

Pastors such as James Coates from Alberta, Canada have been jailed[16] for continuing to open their Churches when ineffective and heavy-handed lockdowns have been instituted. Many others have been issued with very heavy fines and threats of imprisonment, such as Pastor Jacob Reaume at Trinity Bible Chapel in Ontario, Canada. TBC has been issued with $40 million of fines[17] (yes, *forty million), including $83,000 given for a single service, which cannot be waived, removed, or appealed.

#10 The Covid 'vaccine' is an experimental, untested 'gene tampering injection'. *(See full details and evidence in Chapter 4.)*

Millions of people have taken a rushed, new injectable technology which has only been approved for emergency use and is funded by known eugenicists and medical companies who have been granted complete freedom from any liability. Many expert medical professionals have expressed grave concern over these 'gene therapy shots' and there are worrying reports of many serious side effects and deaths – all of which are being heavily censored.

---

[16] 'Canadian Pastor James Coates Reveals Powerful Moment When He Was Released from Jail'. *CBN News*, 4 Apr. 2021, https://www1.cbn.com/cbnnews/cwn/2021/april/canadian-pastor-james-coates-reveals-powerful-moment-when-he-was-released-from-jail.

[17] 'After $40,000,000 in Fines, Police To Lock Doors and Take Over Canadian Church'. *Protestia*, 1 May 2021, https://protestia.com/2021/05/01/after-40000000-in-fines-police-to-lock-doors-and-take-over-canadian-Church/.

#11 Vaccine 'passports' are enforcing a two-tier society of medical segregation and complete loss of liberty. *(See full details and evidence in Chapter 4.)*

Starting in Israel in February 2021 and sweeping across the world, vaccine passports were introduced to verify and distinguish between those who have received the experimental Covid injections from those who have not. The vaccinated class is granted permission to re-enter society and enjoy 'privileges' such as air travel, access to sporting events, theatres, restaurants. Even the ability to work in employment, shop for food and attend Church have been restricted to those with a vaccine pass in many places. This is complete medical segregation, marginalising the 'unvaccinated' from all aspects of society. If governments have their way, this will seal the deal for a complete totalitarian regime across the world. IBM, who created the Nazi Germany concentration camp punch cards, is a leader in this initiative, with its 'Digital Health Pass'[18], tethering vaccine records to a blockchain digital wallet for employers and businesses.

Author of 'The End of America', Naomi Wolf, along with many others, has repeatedly warned, *"I cannot say this forcefully enough: This is literally the end of human liberty in the West if this plan unfolds as planned."*[19]

#12 Clergy Response Teams (CRTs) have been used to spread Covid and vaccine propaganda within Churches and to quell any questioning or dissent. *(See full details and evidence in Chapters 4 and 10.)*

---

[18] 'IBM Digital Health Pass – Overview'. *IBM*, https://www.ibm.com/products/digital-health-pass. Accessed 1 May 2021.

[19] Hains, Tim. 'Naomi Wolf: Mandatory Vaccine Passport Could Lead To The End Of Human Liberty In The West'. *RealClear Politics*, 29 Mar. 2021, https://www.realclearpolitics.com/video/2021/03/29/naomi_wolf_mandatory_vaccine_passport_could_lead_to_end_of_human_liberty_in_the_west.html#!. Accessed 1 May 2021.

Governments have been fervently recruiting 'Clergy Response Teams' and 'Places of Worship Task Forces'[20] to massage the views of Christians and Churchgoers, to persuade them that not only is the experimental Covid pseudo-vaccine 'safe and effective' but that taking it is the most loving, Christlike thing to do. It is not.

#13 Draconian legislation has been passed to remove liability of vaccine manufacturers and grant governments authoritarian powers. *(See full details and evidence in Chapters 4 and 5.)*

The USA Public Readiness and Emergency Preparedness (PREP) Act[21] of 2005 was updated in 2020 to provide complete immunity from liability to vaccine manufacturers and administrators. This is just one example of complete indemnity given across the world to medical companies and professionals – so there is zero recourse for any harm done by the experimental Covid vaccine.

In March 2020, Denmark's parliament unanimously passed an emergency coronavirus law[22] and the UK passed its Coronavirus Act[23], both of which gives health authorities powers to force testing, treatment and quarantine with the backing of the police. Emmanuel Macron's 'Global Security Bill'[24] was passed in 2020, granting dictatorial provisions to governments akin to the 1933 Nazi Enabling Act, which 'enabled' Hitler's government

[20] 'New Taskforce Developing Plan to Reopen Places of Worship'. *GOV.UK*, https://www.gov.uk/government/news/new-taskforce-developing-plan-to-reopen-places-of-worship. Accessed 1 May 2021.

[21] 'Public Readiness and Emergency Preparedness Act'. *U.S. Department of Health & Human Services – Public Health Emergency*, https://www.phe.gov/Preparedness/legal/prepact/Pages/default.aspx. Accessed 1 May 2021.

[22] 'Denmark Rushes Through Emergency Coronavirus Law'. *The Local DK*, 13 Mar. 2020, https://www.thelocal.dk/20200313/denmark-passes-far-reaching-emergency-coronavirus-law/. Accessed 1 May 2021.

[23] 'Coronavirus Act 2020'. *The National Archives - Legislation.gov.uk,* https://www.legislation.gov.uk/ukpga/2020/7/contents. Accessed 1 May 2021.

[24] Torres, Anthony. 'Macron Prepares "Global Security" Law Banning the Filming of French Police'. *World Socialist Web Site*, 18 Nov. 2020, https://www.wsws.org/en/articles/2020/11/19/macrn19.html. Accessed 1 May 2021.

to issue decrees independently of the Reichstag and the presidency and gave him a clear path in his genocide of the Jews.

#14 The 'Great Reset' technocracy is being forced upon us by the World Economic Forum (WEF). *(See full details and evidence in Chapter 10.)*

Led by Klaus Schwab, the unelected WEF Great Reset[25] movement is rolling out a detailed grand plan for a cashless, one world currency and one world order. It's socialism repackaged and boosted. In a 2020 short video, the WEF gave eight bold and coercive predictions for 2030, which includes the surrender of the United States to the United Nations, as well as a major economic crash.

#15 Governments want to implant biosensors in everyone, hook up humanity to the Internet of Things and roll out a global social credit system. *(See full details and evidence in Chapter 4.)*

The political left has united with Big Tech to implement a social credit model like the one rolled out in China in 2020, openly operational in Canada in April 2021[26]. This is being facilitated with the big push for vaccine passports, implantable biosensor nanochips, blockchain and 5G. With complete surveillance of all of society, income and releasing payments to civilians is dependent on complying with the authoritarian governments' mandates. In April 2021, the Pentagon's military research lab, DARPA revealed its implantable biosensor[27] to 'detect Covid 19'.

---

[25] 'The Great Reset'. *World Economic Forum*, https://www.weforum.org/great-reset/. Accessed 1 May 2021.

[26] 'China's Social Credit Program Creeps into Canada'. *The Sunday Guardian Live*, 17 Apr. 2021, https://www.sundayguardianlive.com/news/chinas-social-credit-program-creeps-canada.

27 'The DARPA Difference: Pivoting to Address COVIS'. *DARPA - Defense Advanced Research Projects Agency*, 19 Mar. 2021, https://www.darpa.mil/work-with-us/covid-19. Accessed 1 May 2021.

#16 The USA Equality Act, passed during Covid, erases God-given gender distinctions from law. *(See full details and evidence in Chapter 5.)*

The Equality Act, passed in February 2021[28], enforces transgender rights and removes religious freedoms with serious Gospel implications. This legislation has been called the most invasive threat to religious liberty ever passed in America because of its mandating universal liberal 'understandings' of sexual orientation and gender identity for all aspects of society. Anyone who maintains a traditional understanding of human sexuality, gender identity, and marriage will be treated as one guilty of discrimination.

#17 Anti-Christian 'conversion therapy' bills are being passed to try to outlaw prayer and Gospel witness to certain groups. *(See full details and evidence in Chapter 5.)*

Legislation to ban 'conversion therapy' is being pushed in Canada[29] and the UK, with activists targeting Bible-believing Churches[30]. Conversion therapy means *"a practice, treatment or service designed to change a person's sexual orientation to heterosexual or gender identity to cisgender, or to repress or reduce non-heterosexual attraction or sexual behaviour."* This would effectively outlaw Gospel freedom to pray and witness to gay and trans people, cutting across the ordinary work of Churches and could even affect Christian parenting.

#18 The Pope is ushering in 'Chrislam' and a 'one world religion'. *(See full details and evidence in Chapter 10.)*

---

28 Cicilline, David N. 'H.R.5 – Equality Act: 116th Congress (2019-2020)'. *Congress.gov*, 20 May 2019, https://www.congress.gov/bill/116th-congress/house-bill/5/text.

29 'Bill C-6: An Act to amend the Criminal Code (conversion therapy)'. *Government of Canada – Department of Justice*, 27 Oct. 2020, https://www.justice.gc.ca/eng/csj-sjc/pl/charter-charte/c6b.html.

30 'An Open Letter to the Rt Hon Liz Truss'. *Ban Conversion Therapy*, 9 July 2020. https://www.ban-conversiontherapy.com/the-letter. Accessed 1 May 2021.

Pope Francis has been signing ecumenical deals with Islamic leaders[31] and advocating the establishment of 'Abrahamic worship centres' – to conflate Christianity, Islam and Judaism.

#19 Church leaders are using Romans 13 verses 1-7 as a means of justifying their compliance with all the above lies and evil. *(See full details and evidence in Chapter 2 and 5.)*

The Church at large has justified its blanket submission to the Covid mandates with the Romans 13 passages[32] concerning how Christians should be subject to rulers and governments. This is an immature or wilfully ignorant perspective, not fully worked through and is a misinterpretation of the scriptures.

#20 Jesus says *"Take heed that no man deceive you."* **– Matthew 24:4.**

The Unfolding Deception

The events that have unfolded around the world since the start of 2020 have been mind boggling, fear inducing and have impacted every corner of life so massively that life 'pre-coronavirus' seems almost like a lifetime ago. To think we actually met freely and got close to each other, unafraid and unashamed; it feels like an age of innocence that's lost forever. Of course, as Christians, we know that there is nothing innocent about us human beings. We are bound up in sin and we know that the whole of creation groans as we wait for the glorious appearing of our dear Saviour, the Lord Jesus Christ, who will put all things right and will usher us into glory with Him forevermore. When He comes to claim His Bride,

---

[31] Randolph, Jason. 'Announcement of the Chrislam "Abraham Accord" Between Israel and UAE was Missing Link Needed to Launch Vatican Abrahamic Faiths Initiative'. *Gospel News Network*, 17 Aug. 2020, https://gospelnewsnetwork.org/2020/08/17/announcement-of-the-chrislam-abraham-accord-between-israel-and-uae-was-missing-link-needed-to-launch-vatican-abrahamic-faiths-initiative/.

[32] Jarrett, Ed. 'How Should Christians Be Responding to COVID-19'. *Christianity.Com*, 1 Apr. 2020, https://www.christianity.com/wiki/christian-life/how-should-christians-be-responding-to-covid-19.html. Accessed 1 May 2021.

there will be no more sin, no fear, no death, no deception and no bondage. That'll all be displaced by perfect holiness and we'll experience blissful life with our God for eternity. Hallelujah!

"And there shall be no more curse: but the throne of God and of the Lamb shall be in it; and his servants shall serve him." – Revelation 22:3

Yes, we wait for His appearing on that great Day. But in the meantime, we are here, now. We've been dealing with a virus and all the craziness and political power moves that have resulted from it (or so we're told). Whichever way you look at it or what you think of it all, there is one thing that is for certain – our lives have changed forever. As an MIT Technology Review article[33] brazenly stated right back in March 2020 – 'we're not going back to normal'.

The magnitude of what has happened and the rate at which it's all developed could be predicted by few. But it could be predicted by those who have eyes to see and ears to hear and have been watching the higher political arena, closely, for a good while before 2020. I've had many discussions with people over the past two decades on exactly what we are seeing before our eyes now in the name of a pandemic. How? We'll get into that. But, most significantly, having access to the throne room of Heaven to ask my Father for wisdom and discernment on these matters and in reading the signs of the times we are living in (as do you, of course, if you're a follower of Jesus). The evidence is there for all to see, if only we would look. If we ask our Father for eyes to see and the humility to accept the truth and then the boldness to act upon what He reveals, I believe our discernment and insight will grow hugely. But if we're not focused on truth or are not prepared to act upon it, then the news media will resonate much more with us and we'll desire the comfort of the world and the mainstream crowd.

---

[33] Lichfield, Gideon. 'We're Not Going Back to Normal'. *MIT Technology Review*, 17 Mar. 2020, https://www.technologyreview.com/2020/03/17/905264/coronavirus-pandemic-social-distancing-18-months/. Accessed 1 May 2021.

This book is not full of end times speculation and conjecture or over-hyped fear mongering, though there is discussion of where this is heading. I have rooted it in the facts of both the past and what's happening right now and have used primary source materials and evidence where possible – getting information 'straight from the horse's mouth' so to speak, where it's available. My aim is to show the truth that can be seen, the ramifications of what's going on in our world and the implications for the body of Christ. There are suggestions for what we can do moving forward, to navigate through these troubling times in a Biblical and righteous way.

My number one concern is that we worship our LORD Jesus in spirit and truth and that He receives the glory due to Him, by His Bride, the true Church, undeceived and unobstructed by secular opinion and the anti-worship, anti-Gospel, anti-Christ rules imposed upon our Church family fellowship by the state.

In His sermon on the mount, Jesus says: *"Blessed are they which are persecuted for righteousness' sake: for theirs is the kingdom of heaven."* (Matthew 5:10) Interestingly, He does not say 'persecuted for sharing the Gospel' or 'persecuted by coronavirus regulations'. No, we are persecuted for righteousness: doing good. Doing the God-ordained right and worshipful things in the face of evil and opposition. Persecution therefore comes when we make a concerted stand in the face of wrong. Judgement and persecution are two very different things. The LORD could well be judging His Church by sending us into a kind of exile during lockdowns and forced isolation, or He could be testing us to see whether we'll stand and faithfully obey Him instead and keep on gathering for worship, with the possibility of incurring persecution as a result, as some pastors and Churches are facing right now. Whichever way we look at it, we're on a spiritual battlefield and there are obstacles and landmines that we need to navigate around. However, if we're not prepared to repent, turn from and intercede for secular humanism, lukewarmness, abortion and other types of bloodshed and idolatry, then we should expect God's judgement. The Body of Christ is the gatekeeper of truth and only we can intercede for the ungodliness and sin of the world around us.

We also need to be prepared for persecution and to see things clearly and as they really are and to gird our loins to stand up for our faith in Christ. The true Christ-follower is sold out for Him and all He's done for us and we're committed to evangelising the lost world, to see souls saved, and living in holiness. Let's keep that the main focus and walk daily with our LORD, humbly and boldly, ready to face what's ahead. I pray the LORD strengthens and blesses you in doing this.

How Could Covid 19 Be Deception?

I have found that there are two main objections people give to the notion that any or all of the mandates rolled out under Covid 19 and beyond are deceptive or tyrannical.

The first objection is that any speak of this is merely 'conspiracy theories', to which I would say that the term 'conspiracy theory' has been weaponised and is clearly being used towards anyone who seeks to use discernment and apply a level of critical thinking to what's going on. This is evidenced by the heavy suppression, censorship and immediate removal of information, as well as a lack of any meaningful official discussion or argument against masks, vaccines and the like. Actually, **a 'conspiracy theorist' is simply someone who questions the statements and motives of *known liars*.** More importantly, the Bible is absolutely full of real conspiracies, so we should 100% expect them to be in action in our world right now. Jesus' crucifixion – divinely ordained and the most glorious event in history – was also a human conspiracy. We have to ask, is the beast system spoken of in Revelation that rises with a False Prophet and Antichrist at the helm, and beguiles the whole world, a conspiracy? If not and Scripture prophecy is true, then how can it be implemented by our benevolent world leaders?

I have also heard people say that conspiracy theories appeal to one's pride – *"I know something that others don't know"* – to try and trump or silence any talk of this nature. To which I would say that it only takes time, effort, focus and courage in doing some discerning research to know and prove the truth, guided by the Spirit and in prayer. It's not easy or pleasant but it's there for all to see … at least for the moment while we still have some degree of freedom of information over the internet. However, even this is being rapidly eroded. It is not pride to genuinely want to help people see that something isn't right with the world and warn them of dangers ahead; it's a godly concern.

The second objection people have to the notion that the Covid rules are deceptive and tyrannical is that **there is no way that the powers that be could have orchestrated all of this in a matter of weeks or months**, since the end of 2019 and into early 2020, when lockdowns were first ordered. This is absolutely correct – there is no way it could have been masterminded so quickly. Rather, it has taken decades, centuries, even *millennia* of collusion and planning. What we are seeing now is moving towards the full culmination of the stealth atrocities and complete control that Satan is instituting via 'Mystery Babylon', spoken about in the Book of Revelation and has been at work since his first attempt through Nimrod building the Tower of Babel in Genesis.

Let me state an obvious truth: Deception is, well, deceptive. Deception is something insidiously malignant working upon our highest, even purest desires to enslave us to corruption – to bend all that is good to tyranny. Lies are sometimes subtle and sometimes so big and bold that they couldn't possibly be lies, could they? Our spiritual adversary uses both. He's a master at it and we are told that the whole world lies in the power of the evil one. So, we should not be surprised at deception, but also not fearful; Our great LORD Jesus has overcome the powers of darkness, sin and death through His life, death, resurrection and ascension, and we know how this story ends, don't we? Hallelujah!

Theologian, Howard Nolan[34], writes: *"Evil does not parade its true nature and ramifications in a fashion that will leave us appalled and angered. It will work softly, methodically, appealing to our sense that it is best to tolerate and co-exist with what is not deemed or perceived as an immediate threat to us. It draws alongside, and then, requesting what is clearly good or sensible for us, gradually encroaches upon what it should not have until it erodes away our actual freedom by luring us with something it defines as better than what we had, until we are entirely ensnared by its pervasive systems and choked by the poison of its ideals, defined as being 'for the best'."*

George Orwell's final warning before he died, referring to his infamous book which prophesies a totalitarian state, '1984', was *"Don't let it happen; it depends upon you"*. It does, indeed, depend upon us – as believers with the wisdom and mind of Christ. We need to recognise what's going on under the guise of a pandemic and be shrewd but also gentle with the truth of what we see, as our LORD commands us. If you haven't read or watched the film '1984', spend 7:34 minutes watching a helpful and interesting summary now.[35]

"Now as He sat on the Mount of Olives opposite the temple, Peter, James, John, and Andrew asked Him privately, "Tell us, when will these things be? And what will be the sign when all these things will be fulfilled?" And Jesus, answering them, began to say: **"Take heed that no one deceives you. For many will come in My name, saying, 'I am He,' and will deceive many.** *But when you hear of wars and rumors of wars, do not be troubled; for such things must happen, but the end is not yet. For nation will rise against nation, and kingdom against kingdom. And there will be earthquakes in various places, and there will be famines and troubles. These are the beginnings of sorrows. "But watch out*

---

[34] Howard. 'Rebel by Nature, Righteous by Force'. *Justified Sinner* (blog), 31 May 2021, https://wwwjustifiedsinner.blogspot.com.

[35] 'Video SparkNotes: Orwell's 1984 Summary'. *Youtube*, https://www.youtube.com/watch?v=h9JlKngJnCU. Accessed 4 May 2021.

for yourselves, for they will deliver you up to councils, and you will be beaten in the synagogues. You will be brought before rulers and kings for My sake, for a testimony to them. And the gospel must first be preached to all the nations." – Mark 13:3-10 (NKJV)

CHAPTER TWO

Thesis Statement and Exploring Submission in Romans 13

I had originally planned for this book to be a much shorter thesis. But after doing my research and prayerfully considering it all, and given the gravity of the situation, I felt it really needed to be a book with a thesis section and this next section is it. That is, I am stating a position that I am arguing for and will present my Biblical, prayerful reasoning and support for that position. Unlike an academic paper, it's written conversationally and plainly with a slight edge to it in places, which I believe is warranted under the circumstances and to act as an alarm call on this matter.

This book is predominantly for 'the Church', so let me define what I mean by that, so we're on the same page. I simply mean the Body of Christ, the Ekklesia, the gathered communion of saints, a fellowship of believers in Christ, the faithful remnant – who are holding to Biblical truths and want to see Jesus' name lifted high. So, the term 'Church' encompasses gatherings of believers in all formats – from the established, structural, denominational Churches, to small, underground house Churches. Churches can look very different from each other, depending on location, how sympathetic the ruling government is towards Christianity in that location, as well as one's own persuasion on what local 'Church' looks like. I am writing to all, from Messianic Jews in Israel, to Baptists in USA to the underground Church of Iran. However, I believe that the Church in the Western world is experiencing the biggest shake-up right now, so I suspect that this information is most needed there.

Here's my thesis statement:

The Church must resist rules being imposed on her by the State in the name of 'peace and safety' under Covid 19+ (lockdown restrictions, masks, virus testing, vaccinations) since adherence is aiding and abetting deceptive lies, is a dangerous misapplication of Romans 13 and granting authority that belongs to the Living God only; thereby partaking in State idolatry.

Romans 13 (verses 1-7) is about subjection by the Christian to authorities or 'higher powers', which can include Civil government – the 'State'. Here's the full text (KJV):

*"[1] Let every soul be subject unto the higher powers. For there is no power but of God: the powers that be are ordained of God. [2] Whosoever therefore resisteth the power, resisteth the ordinance of God: and they that resist shall receive to themselves damnation. [3] For rulers are not a terror to **good** works, but to the evil. Wilt thou then not be afraid of the power? do that which is **good**, and thou shalt have praise of the same: [4] For he is the minister of God to thee for **good**. But if thou do that which is evil, be afraid; for he beareth not the sword in vain: for **he is the minister of God**, a revenger to execute wrath upon him that doeth evil. [5] Wherefore ye must needs be subject, not only for wrath, but also for conscience sake. [6] For for this cause pay ye tribute also: for they are God's ministers, attending continually upon this very thing. [7] Render therefore to all their dues: tribute to whom tribute is due; custom to whom custom; fear to whom fear; honour to whom honour."*

And Romans 13:1-7 in the NKJV:

"Let every soul be subject to the governing authorities. For there is no authority except from God, and the authorities that exist are appointed by God. [2] Therefore whoever resists the authority resists the ordinance of God, and those who resist will bring judgment on themselves. [3] For rulers are not a terror to good works, but to evil. Do you want to be unafraid of the authority? Do what is good, and you will have praise from the same. [4] For he is God's minister to you for good. But if you do evil, be afraid; for he does not bear the sword in vain; for he is God's minister, an avenger to execute wrath on him who practices evil. [5] Therefore you must be subject, not only because of wrath but also for conscience' sake. [6] For because of this you also pay taxes, for they are God's ministers attending continually to this very thing. [7] Render therefore to all their due: taxes to whom taxes are due, customs to whom customs, fear to whom fear, honor to whom honor."

Here's my paraphrase and emphases:

1. Every Christian's default position should be to submit to the higher powers which are set in place over us by God.
2. To take a different position, to rebel against the authorities that the LORD has appointed, will be judged and not go well for us.
3. If we act **righteously**, we have nothing worry about – people placed in authority by God are there to aid us and for the **good** of everyone and we will be blessed by Him in **doing good**.
4. Rulers are there to uphold **good works** (as defined by God; His laws) and as such, are no problem to us or need not be feared when we too engage in good conduct. Further, **the rulers will honour, praise, approve of and commend us when we engage in good conduct.**
5. If we act in bad conduct however (again, defined by God; evil), we should fear the consequences. That is, if we want to be unafraid of the authorities, **we must do the good that God defines.**

6. A person in authority (now singular) is **put in place by God to serve for good (to uphold His laws)**. But if we do **evil**, we should fear because that person, who is a **servant of God for good**, will administer God's justice against the person who does **evil**.

7. With this in mind, we must submit under the authority of the person placed and serving for good, to both avoid God's anger and to keep a **clear conscience**. (Our conscience should align with the 'good works' defined by God in His Word and therefore also be aligned with the good works that the rulers are to uphold. We submit on this basis.)

8. In line with this, you also pay taxes, since the authorities are put in place to be **ministers of God** and are to be paid as such.

9. Give to everyone what you owe them: pay taxes to whom you owe them, revenue to whom you owe, respect to whom you owe, honour to whom you owe. (We give this to be repaid in all the blessings and advantages of good public government.)

There is a lot in here about doing good and doing wrong and a lot of pre-suppositions are made by Paul; namely, that authority figures are there to do GOOD, by upholding God's laws. In line with that, we submit under them. Peter echoes this in his statements on submitting to authorities:

*"Therefore submit yourselves to every ordinance of man for the Lord's sake, whether to the king as supreme, or to governors, as to those who are sent by him **for the punishment of evildoers and for the praise of those who do good**. For this is the will of God, that by **doing good** you may put to silence the ignorance of foolish men – as free, yet not using liberty as a cloak for vice, but as bondservants of God. Honor all people. Love the brotherhood. Fear God. Honor the king."* – 1 Peter 2:13-17

But what if our authorities and governments are not acting as ministers of God for our good, but are acting for evil instead? Are we always to obey them? It is interesting that Paul uses the Greek word '*hypotassō*'[36], meaning 'to subject' or 'be subject to', in Romans 13:1. There's another word, '*hupakouo*'[37], which literally means 'to obey a command' or 'to conform'. Peter and Paul could have used this stronger, more black-and-white word, 'obey', but they both chose not to. Hupokouo is used 21 times in the New Testament and always denotes a hierarchical context, as in the relationship between children or slaves and their parents or masters (Ephesians 6:1 and 6:5).

Other examples of hypotassō (limited subjection):

- *"**Submitting** yourselves one to another in the fear of God."* – Ephesians 5:21
- *"Wives, **submit** to your own husbands, as is fitting in the Lord."* – Colossians 3:18 (NKJV)
- *"Likewise you younger people, **submit** yourselves to your elders. Yes, all of you be submissive to one another, and be clothed with humility, for "God resists the proud, But gives grace to the humble."* – 1 Peter 5:5 (NKJV)

Examples of hupakouo (unconditional obedience to a command):

- *"And they feared exceedingly, and said one to another, What manner of man is this, that even the wind and the sea **obey** him?"* – Mark 4:41 (NKJV)
- *"And if anyone does not **obey** our word in this epistle, note that person and do not keep company with him, that he may be ashamed."* – 2 Thessalonians 3:14 (NKJV)

---

[36] 'G5293 - Hypotassō - Strong's Greek Lexicon (KJV)'. *Blue Letter Bible*, https://www.blueletterbible.org/kjv/gen/1/1/s_1001.

[37] 'G5219 - Hypakouō - Strong's Greek Lexicon (KJV)'. *Blue Letter Bible*, https://www.blueletterbible.org/kjv/gen/1/1/s_1001.

- *"By faith Abraham **obeyed** when he was called to go out to a place that he was to receive as an inheritance. And he went out, not knowing where he was going."* – Hebrews 11:8 (NKJV)

We can see then, from the New Testament Greek, that to submit does not always mean to obey. They are two separate actions or postures. **Thus, Romans 13 does not prescribe *unlimited* obedience to the authorities. In fact, it's a great and clear statement on the <u>limits</u> set on civil government, which is not at liberty to make up its own power structures, void of God.**

A common objection to this that is often heard is that Paul was speaking these verses about obedience at the time of the Emperor Nero, who was anything but a godly leader. Therefore, if submission applied then, it surely must for us! Samuel Rutherford corrects this kind of thinking in 'Lex, Rex'[38]: *"If Paul had intended that they should have given obedience to Nero, as the only essential judge, he would have designed him by the noun in the singular number."* In other words, Rutherford is explaining that Paul is not writing about Nero any more than he is writing about any current president, prime minister or king. Rather, he is describing what *ought to be* in the designated offices of authority. These words are *prescriptive* rather than descriptive. Paul was simply admitting that there are some things that belong to Caesar and that we must render those things to him. He wasn't for a moment suggesting that the king could demand along with taxes what belonged to God. Paul wrote at a time when 'civil disobedience' was an ordinary part of Christian life. In Acts, we read repeated instructions and warnings to the apostles and early believers plainly telling them what they must not do, irrespective of what the authorities may or may not think and prescribe. Let's explore, then, the extent and limits of submission in the context of Romans 13 and its surrounding chapters.

---

[38] Rutherford, Samuel. *Lex, Rex: The Law and the Prince*. Sprinkle Publications, 1955. (Original work published 1644).

Exploring Submission to the Authorities in Romans 13

In Romans 13:1-7, we can clearly see that people in authority and governmental positions have two key responsibilities. These people are:

1. In place to **do good as servants of Jesus.**
2. To **administer justice against evil behaviour.**

We, as members of Jesus' Church, have three key responsibilities, which are:

1. To have a general **attitude of submission and respect** to people placed in authority.
2. To **do good, not wrong** – which should result in harmony with the authorities (and to avoid God's wrath).
3. To **check our conscience** – that we are indeed doing good and that we are submitting to leaders who are acting for good.

We see that there is a common thread that unites both the people in authority and people in submission: **doing good.**

In chapter 12 of Romans, Paul says to:

"I beseech you therefore, brethren, by the mercies of God, that you present your bodies a living sacrifice, holy, acceptable to God, which is your reasonable service. And do not be conformed to this world, but be transformed by the renewing of your mind, that you may prove what is that good and acceptable and perfect will of God." – Romans 12:1-2 (NKJV)

Further: *"Let love be without dissimulation[39]. Abhor that which is evil; cleave to that which is good."* – Romans 12:9

So, he directly commands us to:

1. Dedicate our body (and all its faculties, including our minds) as a living and holy sacrifice to God.
2. NOT be conformed to the world; in our thinking or living.
3. Renew our minds (with Scripture) and test things around us.
4. Thereby discern the will of God – what is good, in our conscience.

Remember that 'good' is the opposite of evil and is defined by the Godhead. Father, Son and Holy Spirit are our ultimate authority on everything and we delight in that as Christians. We were bought at a price and are not our own, but slaves to righteousness and heirs who have been translated out of this world and into Jesus' Kingdom. Therefore, doing good is that which is in accordance with God's Word and will for us. We are to check our conscience on this, to make sure that the requirements of authority over us are in alignment with God's Word – 'from the love of virtue', as Matthew Henry remarks in his commentary. If both the requirements of the authorities and God's Word are in alignment – harmony and peaceful submission should occur and that sits well with our consciences.

A good conscience has the capability to tell right from wrong and is free from guilt. A person with a good conscience maintains their integrity. A seared conscience has been desensitised and has dulled the sense of right and wrong.

Good conscience is maintained irrespective of whether anyone else recognises it or approves it. It is the antithesis of the new darling of

---

[39] Without pretence, dishonesty, duplicity.

modern ethics, Pharisaic 'virtue signalling'[40]. Because of this, maintaining good conscience will ALWAYS require us, at some point or other, to be brave and stand up for what we know to be right. Our Christian confessions are great examples of the fruit of good conscience and have been borne out of much bravery and integrity, at great personal cost.

In relation to our conscience, Article 20.2 of the Westminster Confession addresses this directly:

"God alone is Lord of the conscience, and hath left it free from the doctrines and commandments of men, which are, in anything, contrary to his Word; or beside it, if matters of faith, or worship. So that, to believe such doctrines, or to obey such commands, out of conscience, is to betray true liberty of conscience: and the requiring of an implicit faith, and an absolute and blind obedience, is to destroy liberty of conscience, and reason also."

Chapter 14 of Romans is clear on matters of the conscience – *"Who are you to judge another's servant? To his own master he stands or falls. Indeed, he will be made to stand, for God is able to make him stand."* – Romans 14:4 (NKJV)

And: *"So then every one of us shall give account of himself to God."* – Romans 14:12

The section on subjection to authorities in Romans 13 is sandwiched between chapter 12, which deals with discerning what is good and having sober and sound judgement and shunning evil, and chapter 14, which deals with conscience and not causing each other to stumble in the area

---

[40] Oxford Dictionary defines virtue signalling as "the action or practice of publicly expressing opinion or sentiments intended to demonstrate one's good character or the moral correctness of one's position on a particular issue."

of individual conscience and judgements. He finishes that chapter by saying *"for whatsoever is not of faith is sin."* – Romans 14:23

We can conclude from all of this that we are to discern and do good and act in line with our good conscience; to do otherwise on either count is sin. Harmony arises when authorities do good and we do good and submit (with good conscience).

So how can problems occur in the model of authority and subjection? In simple terms, and omitting short-term misunderstandings or mistakes from either side, there are three main scenarios:

1. If the authorities do good and we don't do good or don't submit (we go against our conscience or our conscience is seared).
2. If the authorities don't do good and we submit (with good and gracious conscience but with concern, or from the seared conscience of fear, cowardice or apathy).
3. If the authorities don't do good and we don't submit (from a good or possibly seared conscience).

The issues we are exploring in this thesis are scenarios 2 and 3 – what to do when the authorities don't do good and how we, as the Church, respond.[41]

Let's look at scenario 2: If the authorities don't do good and we submit (with good and gracious conscience but with concern, or from the seared conscience of fear, cowardice or apathy).

There are many ways in which authorities in charge, placed there by God to do good, may not actually always do good. The thrust of what Paul

---

[41] Scenario 1 of a wayward Church or individual in the context of good authority is not the issue or scope of this thesis. The simple answer to that is that we should repent and joyfully submit to honour Christ and live peaceably with our neighbours.

says in Romans 13, however, is that governments are nonetheless placed there by God – better a bad government than none at all.

Examples of scenario 2 could be: heavy or unfair taxes or bungling or overreactive laws in response to crises. In such cases, we should always err on the side of gracious obedience. Our consciences may or may not be completely sure on the 'goodness' of the authority's requirements but if our submission is a response of proactive graciousness and charity, our conscience can be settled in this act of submission, done for the sake of Christ. If, however, in scenario 2 our consciences are seared by fear, cowardice or apathy and that is the reason for our submission, that is a matter of great concern. If we recognise that something is not good and are fearful or lacking courage in challenging it, we are in sin.

Let's relate all this to our current situation ...

Back in March of 2020, when lockdown orders were announced across the world, many Churches shut down. We are aware that we should 'not forsake the assembling of ourselves together' (Hebrews 10:25), but in the name of safety and trusting government guidelines on the severity of the so-called pandemic, we succumbed to the lockdown and closed our doors. I believe this was done, against our good conscience in most cases – we are the Church of Jesus Christ, a city on a hill in this dark world – but nonetheless, we trusted that there was a genuine reason for this short-term rule, laid out by our governments.

But what about now? We are long into this situation and many Churches are still closed on Sundays and running services online instead of gathering in person. Government advice has been patchy, unclear, restrictive and the goal posts seem to keep moving. So, what do we do? Many Churches will submit to everything the government says. Is this right? Some Churches opened back up quickly and disregarded restrictive rules on masks and distancing and no singing – most notably led by John MacArthur at Grace Church in California. Is this right?

We can see Scenarios 2 and 3 arising for us right now and issues of good and bad conscience – and we're getting into deeper waters. So let's put our diving gear on and jump in to explore the many and complex Covid issues in the next two chapters. Then we'll revisit Romans 13 and look at the four main types of authorities set in place over us, the Church-State relationship and the limits to our submission to authorities.

CHAPTER THREE

The Problems with What We've Submitted to Under Covid 19

B y all accounts, we can now see that this crisis situation that descended upon us in March 2020 has been a shambles.

We were told that we're facing a world-wide pandemic that's highly contagious and is killing indiscriminately and prolifically; so dangerous that life as we knew it had to come to a grinding halt. A universal lockdown needed to be enforced, resulting in an economic crash that's going to be near impossible to recover from, families and loved ones kept apart for months and Churches, schools and businesses all shut. This has been a devastating time for many, to say the least, and the real ramifications of all these reactive measures of lockdown, 'self-isolating', quarantining, social distancing, masks, screen schooling, vaccines and the rest of the hoopla, have yet to be fully seen.

As a health practitioner of almost two decades (working in both allopathic and natural health settings) and working one-to-one with over a thousand people in that time, I am all-too-familiar with the nuanced ramifications of social isolation, the psychology of fear, trauma and stress, over-hyped and mixed-message news stories, staying indoors excessively and not getting proper sunlight or oxygen. The multitude of complex and multi-level issues caused by this pandemic, that have nothing to do with getting any virus, is vast. More on that later …

We have heard the news and heard of the numbers of cases and positive test results and some deaths, but we do not see people dying en masse in our towns or on the streets, as we would have in the days of the black plague, and few of us know anyone who's actually died of this 'killer' disease. Yes, people have died, I am not discounting that at all, but many 'Covid deaths' have actually been cases of comorbidity and in very vulnerable people who were sick including the elderly or infirm to begin with; and the actual cause may not have been the virus. Cases of 'new virulent strains' overseas that we see on the news, may not be all they seem. We know that numbers of cases have been inflated and I've been told this first-hand from people who work in funeral homes and hospitals; dying of Covid and dying with Covid are two very different things. Regardless of that, even the official death figures show that the response from our authorities has been hugely disproportionate to the danger, which is no more life-threatening in terms of numbers than any regular seasonal flu or other diseases like TB, AIDS, malaria or cholera – all of which we just deal with rationally and the world carries on.

Incidentally, CDC/WHO figures at March 2020 (when we first went into lockdown), show that there were 70 deaths world-wide per day from coronavirus, but 2,200 per day from HIV/AIDS – 31 times more. Yet the powers that be have not tried to ban all sexual activity, even amongst gay males, prostitution and the like which are generally the communities with the highest transmission rate, according to CDC and many other official figures.[42] Imagine the outrage of even proposing that idea … oh and let's keep the abortion clinics open as a necessity?

---

[42] 'STI Epidemic amongst Gay Men Undoubtedly Contributing to Continuing High Rate of HIV Transmission'. *National AIDS Trust*, 29 Nov. 2012, https://www.nat.org.uk/press-release/sti-epidemic-amongst-gay-men-undoubtedly-contributing-continuing-high-rate-hiv. Accessed 20 May 2021.

Yet, the authorities seem to think it's ok to label Churches 'hot beds of the virus' because we – shudder – dare to sing. An erroneous claim that has not been substantiated in any way and completely lacks any insight into the tremendous spiritual, emotional, mental and physical benefits of singing and community – and not to forget, you know, the corporate worship of our Living God.

We acknowledge that life brings with it a risk of death and disease and when we assess it completely, objectively and soberly, we know that no one escapes alive. Death is a 100% given for us all (unless you happen to be Enoch or Elijah, or any other saint who the LORD might have decided to take from the earth in a different way). So we get on with it and live life. And for Christians, we know that Jesus *"came that they may have life and have it abundantly"*, John 10:10 tells us. If we consider all the possible threats to our life and health on a day-to-day basis, we could very soon be enjoying an existence like this video parodies: JP Sears – How to Be More Afraid.[43]

Right now, there are a number of issues and mandates that are in place, or coming at the rate of knots, that have been put in place in the name of **practical necessity** that are of serious concern in all of this to us as the Church, the body of Christ here on earth.

In my estimation, the clear problems are these:

- Churches ordered to completely shut their doors.
- Enforced 'self' isolation.
- Enforced social distancing and sanitisation in services and other gatherings.
- Ban on singing during services.
- Ban on Bibles in Church buildings.
- Ban on the Lord's Supper and Baptism.

---

[43] 'How to Be More Afraid!'. *YouTube*, https://www.youtube.com/watch?v=lcX9HBG4L34. Accessed 4 May 2021.

- 'Tracking and tracing' names and numbers of attendees, and ticketed services.
- **Enforced wearing of masks in services and other gatherings.**
- **Enforced virus 'PCR' testing.**
- **Enforced vaccines (covered in the next section, as it warrants detailed attention).**
- …And no doubt other unknown and unannounced mandates yet to come to light (at the time of my writing).

I've highlighted the enforced wearing of masks, virus tests and vaccinations in bold, since I believe these are 'landmark' mandates that affect all the others and as such are included as part of my overall thesis statement – and we must resist such things. Let's explore these problems in a little more depth …

Churches Ordered to Shut – Lockdowns

Firstly, when the world went into 'lockdown' (lock-up), the vast majority of Churches followed suit and shut down – submitting to the government and State demands to do so. No one forced a gun to our head, we just did it, in the name of Romans 13 and 'loving our neighbour'. In a few short weeks, since all this was first announced, we stopped gathering. Most Churches moved to an online format – streaming their services via various social media and webinar platforms.

Let me say that again – WE STOPPED GATHERING. This is momentous. Many Churches smoothed over that fact with falsely empowering and comforting words, 'we are not the building, we are the people'. But those same people would rightly balk against the notion of 'Church online' in the normal run of things. So, what has changed since March 2020? Nothing, other than some massaged rationales and consciences. Built into the very fabric of the word 'Church' is the gathering together of God's people. The word 'ekklesia' is correctly translated 'assembly' and means 'citizens called to be a governing assembly'. Much as we'd like to think that Zoom Bible studies and YouTube livestreams with hundreds of people on (or at least watching for a few seconds or more to register a 'view') is a 'gathering', it just isn't. To be clear, the Bible is clear – no assembling, no Church.

Enforced 'Self' Isolation

As part of the lockdown mandate, we were all told to 'stay home' and 'stay safe' by isolating ourselves. This imposed a crucible of 24/7 togetherness for families and sharers and 24/7 aloneness for singles and people away from their families. Being cooped up together with no breaks from other people – even the people we love, has caused a great strain on relationships and the divorce rate over the lockdown periods has risen greatly: In Wuhan and Brussels, law firms reported a 25% increase in 2020. Leading British law firm, Stewarts logged a 122% increase in divorce enquiries between July and October 2020, compared with the same period in 2019. In the US, a major legal contract-creation site announced a 34% rise in sales of its basic divorce agreement,[44] with newlyweds who'd got married in the previous five months making up 20% of sales. Domestic violence and child abuse has risen too and no doubt countless other evils that come with relational and financial strain, fear and anxiety, increased anonymity and greater ability to be hidden and unaccountable (at least from each other, all the while being tracked to the hilt online). We were told that if we had any sniff of virus symptoms (which were vague and ever-changing), or any of a plethora of vulnerabilities, that we must self-isolate. Notice the term – 'self' isolation; giving us the illusion of personal agency over this. Termed like 'self-development', it carries with it a notion of empowerment and proactivity, but there is nothing empowering or self-directed about a house arrest order from an over-zealous government, with clear penalties and fear-mongering threats if we

---

[44] Moric, Mollie. 'US Divorce Statistics During COVID-19'. *Legal Templates*, 29 July 2020, https://legaltemplates.net/resources/personal-family/divorce-rates-covid-19/.

chose to do otherwise. Even if there was a level of personal choice in this matter, the thing that rang through my mind like a loud alarm as soon as this order was announced was Proverbs 18:1: *"A man who isolates himself seeks his own desire; He rages against all wise judgment." (NKJV)*

Or in another translation: *"An unfriendly person pursues selfish ends and against all sound judgement starts quarrels." (NIV)*

The Bible is unambiguous – isolation from other people is folly, fosters selfishness and quarrelling and goes against *all* wise judgement (wisdom). So how could this manifest?... In the most insidious temptation, sin, backsliding and waning of faith and power as a Christian. A soldier on his own is terribly vulnerable to enemy attack; he needs the safety, discernment, integrity and differing roles and skills that are only present when the whole army are gathered together.

Paul tells us in 1 Corinthians 12 that we literally cannot function on our own away from the rest of the body of Christ: *"For the body is not one member, but many. If the foot shall say, Because I am not the hand, I am not of the body; is it therefore not of the body? (12:14-15) ... If the whole body were an eye, where were the hearing? If the whole were hearing, where were the smelling? (12:17) ... And if they were all one member, where were the body? But now are they many members, yet but one body. And the eye cannot say unto the hand, I have no need of thee: nor again the head to the feet, I have no need of you. (12:19-21) ... And whether one member suffer, all the members suffer with it; or one member be honoured, all the members rejoice with it." (12:26)*

I know personally that since March 2020, I have felt under more attack from the enemy and temptation and indulgence in sin than ever before in my Christian walk. I have continued to read my Bible daily, pray lots, repent, fast, evangelise and have joined pretty much every Zoom Bible study and prayer meeting going including one my dear Pastor instituted twice daily for us for months, in his wisdom and good shepherding. Yet, it has been terribly difficult to stand strong and remain encouraged and holy in my walk with the LORD and as salt and light in the world.

What about those whose spiritual disciplines are not quite as vigilant or have not been provided for so well? Are we having discussions around this? I don't know about you, but under these current circumstances there seems to have been pitifully little discussion or confession around sin and temptation in isolation. Let's face it, staring into a computer screen on a Zoom call with kids milling around in the background and the awkwardness of only one person being able to speak at a time and heard by everyone, doesn't exactly foster a good setting for the vulnerable sharing of struggles, confession and iron-sharpening-iron ministry. Even on one-to-one phone calls, there is always a temptation when asked how we are to say *"I'm fine"*. We simply cannot get around the fact that as people, we need to be in frequent face-to-face, eye ball-to-eye ball, bodily and visceral community with a range of people. That applies all the more to us Christians, with our responsibility to be a city on a hill in this dark world and with a ferocious enemy seeking to devour us and render us ineffectual.

So, the secular authorities tell us that we need isolation to ensure safety. The Bible tells us we need community for safety. Woefully, which one did we trust?

Further, in a study published in The Lancet in March 2020, entitled 'The psychological impact of quarantine and how to reduce it: rapid review of the evidence'[45], concludes that *"the psychological impact of quarantine is wide-ranging, substantial, and can be long lasting ... Most reviewed studies reported negative psychological effects including post-traumatic stress symptoms, confusion, and anger."*

---

[45] Brooks, Samantha K., Webster, Rebecca K., et al. 'The Psychological Impact of Quarantine and How to Reduce It: Rapid Review of the Evidence'. *The Lancet*, vol. 395, no. 10227, Mar. 2020, pp. 912–20. *www.sciencedirect.com*, doi:10.1016/S0140-6736(20)30460-8.

Lockdowns Don't Work

It has been proven beyond a shadow of a doubt that lockdowns simply do not work to stop the transmission of coronavirus and have had 'counter-productive' effects, to put it mildly. You can read almost fifty studies and reports from many different countries showing that lockdowns do not work and cause much devastation[46] and I'd highly recommend watching the Planet Lockdown expert interviews [47] attesting to this, as well as the Pandemics Data and Analytics (PANDA) reports showing that lockdowns contradict a century of pre-Covid science.[48]

Enforced Social Distancing and Sanitisation in Services and Other Gatherings

Further to the isolation, we were told to stay six feet apart from all other people who we don't live with. Then three feet, oh hold on, back to six feet. So even when we are allowed out or 'allowed to go back to Church', we cannot be next to each other. Think about that for a second. We currently have authority figures who do not acknowledge their creator, wielding their power to tell us if and when we can go and be the body of Christ and worship the triune God. And when they graciously grant that we can meet, they order that we must not truly commune as family members. Hey, it's all in the name of necessity, right? Anyone who seriously thinks that rich relationships and discipling can take place 'socially distanced' is either hugely naive or is used to settling for awkward, superficial interactions. And what about greeting each other with a holy

---

[46] 'Studies Showing Lockdowns Do Not Work – Planet Lockdown Documentary Film'. *Planet Lockdown,* 18 Jan. 2021, https://planetlockdownfilm.com/2021/01/studies-showing-lockdowns-do-not-work/. Accessed 4 May 2021.

[47] 'Full Interviews – Planet Lockdown Documentary Film'. *Planet Lockdown,* https://planetlockdownfilm.com/full-interviews/. Accessed 4 May 2021.

[48] 'Lockdowns Contradict a Century of Pre-Covid Science'. *PANDA,* 14 Feb. 2021, https://www.pandata.org/lockdowns-contradict-a-century-of-pre-covid-science/.

kiss? Seems like Paul's command will be a big faux pas for the foreseeable future. As someone who's spent a lot of time on my own during the lockdown period, I have really valued being able to meet up with friends and family who've not sought to distance. When I've met up with people who've insisted on the six-foot rule and OCD-like hand sanitisation measures, my interactions have been bittersweet. I've spent our time together feeling slightly like a leper with an 'unclean' sign around my neck and left feeling rather discouraged. Or is it just me?

I can't help but think of Colossians 2 when I look at the pages of seemingly erroneous C19 measures issued by governments and dutifully parroted by our ecclesiastical bodies, that we must put in place before we can open back up for sanitised and muted Church services ...

"Beware lest any man spoil you through philosophy and vain deceit, after the tradition of men, after the rudiments of the world, and not after Christ. For in him dwelleth all the fulness of the Godhead bodily. And ye are complete in him, which is the head of all principality and power: In whom also ye are circumcised with the circumcision made without hands, in putting off the body of the sins of the flesh by the circumcision of Christ". – Colossians 2:8-11   ·

"Therefore, if you died with Christ from the basic principles of the world, why, as though living in the world, do you subject yourselves to regulations – "Do not touch, do not taste, do not handle," which all concern things which perish with the using – according to the commandments and doctrines of men? These things indeed have an appearance of wisdom in self-imposed religion, false humility, and neglect of the body, but are of no value against the indulgence of the flesh." – Colossians 2:20-23 (NKJV)

Yes, Paul is addressing vain spirituality here but he puts a lot of emphases on the spirit vs the flesh. What are all these virus mandates if they're not fleshly decrees about that which is perishing, in the name of a false god called 'Safety'? What is all this doing to the psychology of our salvation?

The truth is, we are washed clean in the blood of the Lamb. We are spotless in His sight, yet the world is pummelling us with the message that we are dirty and dangerous.

"And a voice spoke to him again the second time, "What God has cleansed you must not call common."" – Acts 10:15

Ban on Singing

As you know, the Book of Psalms is the largest book of the Bible and it is our inspired hymn book. We see countless commands from Jesus, the Director of Music, to His Bride the Church, to sing – joyfully, corporately and often!

Corporate song is both delightful to the LORD and to us. It lifts us out of darkness and despair, it reaffirms our faith, is a powerful weapon against the enemy and it unites us in melody and harmony. As a singer in several choirs, I find rich worship in song the pinnacle of my joy. And if it's composed by Bach or Handel, I often feel like I'm going to burst with joy and adoration for our LORD! But yet, we've been told to put all that aside. Never mind that our God wants to hear his Church sing to Him, together, as a fragrant offering. We think that it's ok to stop singing and stray into the disobedient and dangerous waters of a mute Church – compounded by the mask wearing and distancing. But hey, playing a video recording of a hymn on YouTube is acceptable, all in the name of staying safe, remember. Brother or sister, by whose standard is this ok? Has God given us any exceptions for not singing to Him in the Scriptures? Not that I can find. I'm still looking for that asterisked 'C19 get out clause' in my Bible, are you?

Here are just a handful of Scriptures which command us (plural) to sing in our assemblies:

"But let all those rejoice who put their trust in You; Let them ever shout for joy, because You defend them; Let those also who love Your name Be joyful in You." – Psalm 5:11 (NKJV)

"Sing unto the Lord, O ye saints of his, and give thanks at the remembrance of his holiness." – Psalm 30:4

"But I will sing of thy power; yea, I will sing aloud of thy mercy in the morning: for thou hast been my defence and refuge in the day of my trouble. Unto thee, O my strength, will I sing: for God is my defence, and the God of my mercy." – Psalm 59:16-17

"Praise ye the Lord. Sing unto the Lord a new song, and his praise in the congregation of saints." – Psalm 149:1

Ban on Bibles in Church Buildings

Most Churches have removed pew Bibles, at least for a period of time. I'm not sure there's a lot to say about this other than it appears that the enemy has told us to put away our only and mightily powerful offensive weapon in the armour of God, and we've done it. I think Martin Luther and early Reformers would be turning in their graves at that one reality alone in all of this.

Yes, we can bring our own Bibles to Church. What about non-Christians coming into our Churches looking for spiritual help? In my experience as a Church staff member, I know that this happens often and we/they need access to Bibles. Is it not the Gospel that is the power of God for salvation? People need access to the Holy written Word.

Ban on the Lord's Supper and Baptism

Both of these ordinances ceased in most Churches under C19 guidance. To stop altogether – for an extended period of time, no matter what the reason – is simply disobedience to what Christ commands us. Further, where the Lord's Supper has been re-instituted in our Churches, it is often done without the wine. Again, this is disobedience to what the LORD clearly states in Matthew 26. We are putting man's spin and augmentations on what Jesus tells us. When God the Father told Moses to take two stone tablets to carve the Ten Commandments on, would it have been OK for Moses to have taken three pieces of wood instead? Maybe, maybe not. But other than to do exactly as the LORD tells us is to add our judgements to a clear command and to elevate our opinions over His.

"Go ye therefore, and teach all nations, baptizing them in the name of the Father, and of the Son, and of the Holy Ghost: Teaching them to observe all things whatsoever I have commanded you: and, lo, I am with you always, even unto the end of the world." – Matthew 28:19-20

"The cup of blessing which we bless, is it not the communion of the blood of Christ? The bread which we break, is it not the communion of the body of Christ?" – 1 Corinthians 10:16

In some places, like Melbourne, marriages have been banned too.

Tracking and Ticketing Church Attendance

No ticket, no entry. Is this really the reality of Church life? Churches have made it plain that in the name of C19 and safety guidelines, they will turn away people who have not registered to attend. Of course, most pastors are balking at the distasteful notion of a ticket – reducing the open house of God to a corporate attraction like a theme park or cinema outing. So instead, they are labelling it something more friendly and palatable like 'let us know you'll be coming in advance'. So, what if my elderly relative with Alzheimer's turns up? What about the group of homeless people walking in last minute? I'm aware that many Churches are setting aside some 'reserved tickets' for such rogue folk, but what if I don't want my every move to be monitored by people? What if I believe it's my free and inalienable right to come and worship the Lord at Church services freely – without barriers, restrictions and surveillance in place, or the threat of not being allowed in if I do not fit into a certain category of people and have not reserved my seat?

We are not a corporate body, we are a private family of believers, are we not? Everything does not need to be red-taped and overseen by the State. Further, with the 'track and trace' schemes in place, registering your attendance at your Church service leaves you completely beholden to being ordered under house arrest if someone, anywhere in the congregation, displays any symptoms of the virus. Hence, there will no doubt be many situations where whole swathes of Church congregations are once again forced to 'self' isolate, bringing with it all the problems identified above; I have seen this happen several times in local Churches. Could this be open to bungling, heavy-handed or even nefarious application? Well, if we think that the enemy may want to instil a way to lay off whole companies of the LORD's army and take them out of the battle, then the answer is: You bet.

Incidentally, the 'COVID-19 Testing, Reaching, And Contacting Everyone (TRACE) Act' passed recently in USA Congress is Bill **H.R.6666 —** 116th Congress (2019-2020).[49]

Enforced Virus 'PCR' Testing

All of the propaganda on the so-called pandemic is based on an assumption that is considered true, obvious and unquestionable: that a positive PCR test is synonymous with being sick with Covid. This assumption is completely wrong, as has been proven and spoken of by many experts.

---

[49] Rush, Bobby L., 'H.R.6666 - COVID-19 Testing, Reaching, And Contacting Everyone (TRACE) Act. 5: 116th Congress (2019-2020)'. *Congress.gov,* 1 May 2020, https://www.congress.gov/bill/116th-congress/house-bill/6666/titles.

The Real Time Reverse Transcription Polymerase Chain Reaction (rRT-PCR) test was adopted by the WHO in January 2020 as a means to detecting the SARS-COV-2 virus, following the recommendations of a Virology research group based in Berlin, supported by the Bill and Melinda Gates Foundation. However, the test was fatally flawed from the outset: The number of 'amplification cycles' should be less than 35, preferably 25-30 cycles. In the case of virus detection, >35 cycles only detect signals which do not correlate with infectious virus was determined by isolation in cell culture.

On August 29, 2020, the New York Times published an article headlined, 'Your coronavirus test is positive. Maybe it shouldn't be':[50] *"The standard [COVID PCR] tests are diagnosing huge numbers of people who may be carrying relatively insignificant amounts of the virus ... Most of these people are not likely to be contagious ..."*

Exactly one year after instituting mass PCR tests as the way to gauge the pandemic and apply draconian mandates, the World Health Organization tacitly admitted that *all* PCR tests conducted at a 35-cyle amplification threshold (Ct) or higher are *completely invalid*.

Dr Kary Mullis, who was awarded the Nobel Prize for inventing the PCR test, campaigned heavily to stop the tests from being used as a diagnostic for HIV. He stated that PCR tests are not calibrated for a brand-new viral pathogen. The exact same methodology applies on why the PCR test shouldn't be used for testing Covid 19. Despite the 'fact checkers' refuting this, here's a quote straight from the horse's mouth, Kary Mullis on PCR's ineffectiveness in testing for viruses:[51]

---

[50] Mandavilli, Apoorva. 'Your Coronavirus Test Is Positive. Maybe It Shouldn't Be.' *The New York Times*, 29 Aug. 2020. *NYTimes.com*, https://www.nytimes.com/2020/08/29/health/coronavirus-testing.html.

[51] 'Kary Mullis - Covid PCR Test Inventor - Not Meant To Be Used For Infectious Diseases'. *BitChute*, https://www.bitchute.com/video/wOSeTz57xrCF/. Accessed 4 May 2021.

"With PCR, the misinterpretation of the results are ... if they could find this virus in you at all, and with PCR if you do it well, you can find almost anything in anybody ... The PCR test is used to make a whole lot of something out of something. It doesn't tell you that you're sick."

Further, through a Freedom of Information (FOI) request, Gemma O'Doherty, an investigative journalist in Ireland, obtained documented proof[52] from the Department of Health in November, stating that the UK Government has no evidence whatsoever that a 'virus' called 'coronavirus' exists.

Given what Mullis says, and that Covid 19 has not formally been purified and identified, ***mass testing is a sham. You could say that the real pandemic is an outbreak of PCR testing.*** The test is designed in such a way that it generates as many positive outcomes as possible. ***The sole goal has been to make vaccination readiness as high as possible ... and it has worked.*** There is zero need for governments to be zealously ordering people to be tested for Covid, for many reasons. Current State guidelines in many countries are to 'get a test if you show any symptoms. Get a test if you don't show any symptoms.' Even if the test actually worked, does this make any common sense? Further, as time is going on, it is being mandated that school children be tested weekly, as well as regular testing of people in and visiting care homes, places of employment, airports and more. It is soon coming (maybe already here as you read this) that tests will be mandated for supermarkets, social and entertainment facilities and ... Church.

The only conclusion we can draw as to why our governments are still seeking to use an admittedly flawed means of testing people is to continue to generate false positives and keep pushing the lockdown, distancing and

---

[52] 'Gemma O'Doherty – It Does Not Exist, The Virus Does Not Exist'. *BitChute*, https://www.bitchute.com/video/ERaMnv3UYgga/. Accessed 4 May 2021.

vaccination agendas. What's more, the tests have been proven to be *exceedingly harmful* and may even be used to vaccinate you![53][54] Physicist and bio-materials researcher, Professor Antonietta Gatti examined various PCR test swabs and analysed their dangerous ingredients.[55] The results showed that they are made of tough materials and contain a large number of nano-particles including silver, aluminium, titanium, and glass fibres, as well as asbestos-like substances. None of which are declared on the PCR test package insert.

German lawyer, Dr Reiner Fuellmich is currently mounting high-profile legal cases in an effort to bring the perpetrators of these crimes to justice. **A team of over 1,000 lawyers and over 10,000 medical experts led by Dr Fuellmich have begun legal proceedings against the CDC, WHO & the Davos Group for crimes against humanity.** The cases are centred around the fact that the faulty PCR testing scheme has underpinned ALL restrictive and damaging measures put in place in the name of the 'coronavirus pandemic'. He believes that a global tribunal is needed because the scale of the events is so vast and complicated that it is beyond the competence of national judges. Fuellmich and his team are working towards what they call 'Nurnberg-2'.

Fuellmich calls the events of the past year the 'worst crime ever committed against humanity':[56] *"It is not about a virus, nor is it about health. The point is to take everything away from us, making us totally dependent*

---

[53] Coleman, Dr Vernon. 'The PCR Test Can Kill You – and Can Be Used to Vaccinate You'. *Vernon Coleman, 9 Feb. 2021,* https://www.vernoncoleman.com/pcrtestcankill.htm. Accessed 20 May 2021.

[54] Hartnett, John Gideon. 'PCR Test Swabs May Contain "Star-Shaped Microdevices" That Secretly Vaccinate the "Vaccine Hesitant"'. *Bible Science Forum*, 3 Feb. 2021, https://biblesciencefo-rum.com/2021/02/03/pcr-test-swabs-may-contain-star-shaped-microdevices-that-secretly-vaccinate-the-vaccine-hesitant/.

[55] Burkhart, Roger. 'The Covid-19 PCR Test - A Shot of Nanoparticles for Your Brain?' *Swiss Epidemics Act + Animal Diseases Act => Corona Lockdown*, 14 Nov. 2020, https://tsg-referendum.ch/en/the-covid-19-pcr-test-a-shot-of-nanoparticles-for-your-brain/.

[56] 'Update on Dr Reiner Fuellmich Class Action Lawsuits Against Coronavirus Fraud'. *Covid Truths*, 15 Nov. 2020, https://www.covidtruths.co.uk/2020/11/update-on-dr-reiner-fuellmich-class-action-lawsuits-against-coronavirus-fraud/.

on the 'Davos clique' ... They want to reduce the world's population and have complete control over the remaining humanity."

In April 2021, an Austrian Court ruled PCR tests as not suitable for Covid 19 diagnosis and that lockdowns have no legal basis.[57]

Enforced Mask Wearing

Let's be honest, most of us would rather not wear a mask. Sure, there are some people who genuinely do prefer and feel safer in doing so and that's fine. However, when asked, most are not so concerned about wearing one for their own safety and peace of mind as they are in doing so for the sake of others. In Churches, this is often deemed 'looking out for the weaker brother or sister', as per Paul's words in 1 Corinthians 8. We can thereby see that this simple action of wearing a mask to ensure the peace of mind and safety of others is a noble, kind and servant-hearted gesture; an example of loving your neighbour in action. The Gospel Coalition wrote a popular article which fleshes this perspective out, with the semblance of Christian wisdom, '4 Reasons to Wear a Mask, Even if You Hate It'.[58] It states that we should all wear masks for these reasons: To love your neighbour (citing Matthew 22:39), to respect authorities (citing Romans 13:1-7, of course), to honour the weak in our midst (citing Romans 14) and to use freedom for the sake of the Gospel (citing 1 Corinthians 9:19-23). It all sounds rational, pious and mature, and the article highlights this statement: *"Few things are more beautiful to witness than someone giving up their rights and freedom for the sake of another."*

But what if wearing a mask is symbol of a lie, a symbol of fear and shame and in contradiction to God's laws on assembly, worship and fellowship

---

[57] 'Austrian Court Rules PCR Test Not Suitable For COVID-19 Diagnosis And That Lockdowns Has No Legal Basis'. *GreatGameIndia*, 8 Apr. 2021, https://greatgameindia.com/austria-court-pcr-test/.

[58] McCracken, Brett. '4 Reasons to Wear a Mask, Even If You Hate It'. *The Gospel Coalition*, https://www.thegospelcoalition.org/article/4-reasons-wear-mask/. Accessed 4 May 2021.

of believers? We'll look more at this shortly. What if wearing a mask neither protects from any virus, nor provides peace of mind but actually creates more anxiety? What if they're actually more *harmful* than helpful to our health? Well, that's exactly what the real science shows. BBC News on July 14th 2020 stated that*: "The World Health Organisation Committee that reviewed the evidence for the use of face covering in public didn't back them, but after political lobbying, the WHO now recommends them."* The goal posts keep shifting and contradicting themselves. The rules keep being inconsistently applied and misapplied and Churches seem to be bearing the brunt of the stricter levels of compliance; it's a power play move.

"Masks when applied to the general population are dangerous. There are many listed dangers, even dangers that World Health Organisation admits to ... You are not helping the people around you by wearing a mask and you're not helping yourself preventing the disease by wearing a mask" – Professor Denis Rancourt PhD, Scientist

In fact, Denis Rancourt has written a paper that reviews the scientific evidence around mask wearing, called 'Masks Don't Work - A review of science relevant to COVID-19 social policy'.[59] He concludes: *"Masks and respirators do not work. There have been extensive randomized controlled trial (RCT) studies, and meta-analysis reviews of RCT studies, which all show that masks and respirators do not work to prevent respiratory influenza-like illnesses, or respiratory illnesses believed to be transmitted by droplets and aerosol particles. Furthermore, the relevant known physics and biology, which I review, are such that masks and respirators should not work. It would be a paradox if masks and respirators worked, given what we know about viral respiratory diseases: The main transmission path is long-residence-time aerosol particles (< 2.5 μm), which are too fine to be blocked, and the minimum-infective-dose is*

---

[59] Rancourt, Denis. 'Masks Don't work.' *Ontario Civil Liberties Association, Apr. 2020,* https://ocla.ca/wp-content/uploads/2020/04/Rancourt-Masks-dont-work-review-science-re-COVID19-policy.pdf. Accessed 4 May 2021.

smaller than one aerosol particle."[60] He ends his paper by saying: *"The present paper about masks illustrates the degree to which governments, the mainstream media, and **institutional propagandists** can decide to operate in a science vacuum, or select **only incomplete science that serves their interests**. Such recklessness is also certainly the case with the current global lockdown of over one billion people, an unprecedented experiment in medical and political history."* Other experts say: *"By all means people can wear masks – or not wear masks. Policy can make the decision, but what they can't do is say that it's an evidence-based decision."* – Dr Carl Henegan, Professor of Evidence-Based Medicine, University of Oxford

In a very insightful 39-minute interview with two experts that gives detailed information available on the efficacy and dangers of masks,[61] we can see that unless the mask is an N95, it provides zero protection against inhalation and exhalation of viruses. All masks raise CO_2 levels, reduce oxygen levels, and, if you are infected, increase the viral load that you are breathing. If an N95 mask has an exhalation valve, the CO_2 and contaminant levels are lower, but if you are infected the mask does not protect others from your exhalation of the virus. In the interview, Occupational Safety and Health Administration (OSHA) PPE expert Tammy Clark states: *"It was all very concerning ... Woah! We don't mask up! It's not only illegal and violates our civil liberties, it is incredibly dangerous and unsafe and unhealthy."*

Wearing a mask restricts airflow to your lungs and stresses respiratory muscles, as evidenced in several studies such as this one, published in

---

[61] 'Mask Whistleblowers Tell All'. *The Highwire*, https://thehighwire.com/videos/mask-whistleblowers-tell-all/. Accessed 4 May 2021.

2016, 'Effect of Wearing the Elevation Training Mask on Aerobic Capacity, Lung Function, and Hematological Variables'.[62] This is a problem especially for older people – exactly those who we are particularly aiming to protect and love in our Churches. In the 2020 publication, 'Physical interventions to interrupt or reduce the spread of respiratory viruses. Part 1 – Face masks, eye protection and person distancing: systematic review and meta-analysis',[63] face masks were found to have no detectable effect against transmission of viral infections. It found: *"Compared to no masks, there was no reduction of influenza-like illness cases or influenza for masks in the general population, nor in healthcare workers."*

An under-reported CDC study, which surveyed symptomatic Covid 19 patients, found that 70.6% of Covid patients reported 'always' wearing a mask and 14.4% say they 'often' wear a mask.[64] That means a whopping 85% of infected Covid patients are habitual mask wearers. Only 3.9% of those infected said they 'never' wear a face covering. To add insult to injury, there are many other face masks dangers.[65] They have been shown to increase dental cavities,[66] acne, bacterial pneumonia, suppressed immunity, anxiety and toxic inhalation of carcinogenic substances. The bottom line, as Dr Russell Blaylock has evidenced, 'Face masks pose serious

---

[62] Porcari, John P., et al. 'Effect of Wearing the Elevation Training Mask on Aerobic Capacity, Lung Function, and Hematological Variables'. *Journal of Sports Science & Medicine*, vol. 15, no. 2, May 2016, pp. 379–86.

[63] Jefferson, T., et al. 'Physical Interventions to Interrupt or Reduce the Spread of Respiratory Viruses. Part 1 - Face Masks, Eye Protection and Person Distancing: Systematic Review and Meta-Analysis'. *MedRxiv*, Apr. 2020, 2020.03.30.20047217. *www.medrxiv.org*, doi:10.1101/2020.03.30.20047217.

[64] Fisher, Kiva A. 'Community and Close Contact Exposures Associated with COVID-19 Among Symptomatic Adults ≥18 Years in 11 Outpatient Health Care Facilities — United States, July 2020'. *MMWR. Morbidity and Mortality Weekly Report*, vol. 69, 2020. *www.cdc.gov*, doi:10.15585/mmwr.mm6936a5.

[65] Manley, John C.A., '20 Reasons Mandatory Face Masks are Unsafe, Ineffective and Immoral.' *Much Ado About Corona* https://muchadoaboutcorona.ca/wp-content/uploads/2020/12/20-Reasons-Mandatory-Face-Masks-Flyer-Are-Unsafe-Ineffective-Immoral-ver2.pdf. Accessed 4 May 2021.

[66] Licea, Melkorka. '"Mask Mouth": Dentists Coin New Term for Smelly Side Effect of Wearing a Mask'. *New York Post*, 7 Aug. 2020, https://www.foxnews.com/health/mask-mouth-dentists-new-term.

risks to the healthy'.[67] There is much more we could say about amateur mask wearing – the efficacy of mask hygiene and disposal and correct fitting and wearing protocols, but I'll refrain. You get the point, I'm sure. Quite simply – masks do not work and are harmful, as a video from The New American 'The Truth About Face Masks'[68] further substantiates. Even if the masks DID work, there are issues with that too. They are acting as 'mobile quarantines'. To mandate everyone to wear them is a photo negative of quarantining the sick. Our governments are acting coercively in a power grab that is a subtle reversal of a Biblical principle of quarantining those who are contaminated. Someone who is healthy should not be treated as though they are not. Just because there are thieves out there, it does not mean the we should all either leave our wallets at home, or be punished as if we were pickpockets. Bottom line, everyone is kidding themselves, except for the people mandating mask wearing; they know what they're doing and it's not in the name of good health. We are witnessing and supporting an 'emperor's new clothes' type of lie – a big and obvious one.

Dr Robert Verkerk of the Alliance for Natural Health states: ***"Let's not kid ourselves, mandating masks has almost nothing do with science … It's political."***

So that brings us to our societal and Church response. Many people have willingly adopted the mask in their effort to care for others and to make a statement that they care: I care for you and you care for me. However, if we actually want to care, based on the real science, we should not support this pernicious, fear-based, irrational and dangerous lie. We Christians are called to truth, so let's stand in it. If we start compromising our sense of truth in the areas around this political pandemic agenda, how will this affect how we treat the truth of the Bible? Yes, the world colludes

---

[67] Blaylock, Dr Russell. 'Face Masks Pose Serious Risks to the Healthy'. *Global Research*, 24 Nov. 2020, https://www.globalresearch.ca/face-masks-pose-serious-risks-healthy/5712649.

[68] 'The Truth About Face Masks'. *YouTube*, https://www.youtube.com/watch?v=BwoQakI6WDg. Accessed 4 May 2021.

around many lies – the biggest being the denial of the one true God who will administer justice upon sinners at an appointed day and that our only refuge is in Christ, who is Himself fully God and fully man. We, however, are to shun all kinds of evil and deception and certainly not kid each other in Church or stand idly by as others swallow the lies, to their harm.

I really do not see that there is any theological justification for fear, hypocrisy, supporting lies or wanting to curry favour with man and gain approval. For those Christians who can clearly see the deception in all of this (and that merely means that they can perceive on any level that masks are ineffective), requiring conformity is binding our conscience and this is wrong and sinful for us to participate in. Further, these mandates are unconstitutional (in the USA) and are skating on thin ice regarding religious freedom, according to Article 9 of the European Convention on Human Rights. Therefore, I'd be so bold as to state that when authority is abused or mishandled in this way, the Church reserves the right to disobey and disregard, for conscience's sake. And the bottom line is that Christ is the head of the Church, not governments, nor even Church leaders.

Maybe you think, *"But it's just a mask, I don't see the problem?"* When we comply to government advice that is consistently shifting, overtly not rooted in the science that it claims to be and is about power and control rather than public safety, we are sending the message that whatever they tell us to do, we won't discern for ourselves or challenge, we'll just do it. Do you think there might be people with power and money and a desire for more control who might run with this? Masks were a trial run for more mandates – such as rushed, novel pseudo-vaccines, as we are now witnessing – and we should challenge the reasoning to avoid complete tyranny.

*"As a spine surgeon I spent 40% of my life in a mask. And I can tell you in my entire career ... nobody was talking about masks as a control mechanism for viruses.[69] The masks may look like they are not much ... What's the big deal? The big deal is, they may be soft, and they may look okay, but **this is George Orwell's boot on a human face forever if we don't get this off.**"* – Dr Lee Merritt, MD, spinal surgeon

You might want to check out this interesting article from Pulpit and Pen, entitled Masks Are an Eschatological Dry-Run for the Mark of the Beast.[70]

---

[69] Delaney, Patrick. 'Physicians: "Masks Don't Control Viruses, They Control You," "Pandemic Is Over"'. *LifeSiteNews*, 29 Oct. 2020, https://www.lifesitenews.com/news/group-of-doctors-masks-are-completely-irrelevant-to-blocking-covid-19. Accessed 4 May 2021.

[70] 'Masks Are an Eschatological Dry-Run for the Mark of the Beast'. *Pulpit & Pen News*, 17 July 2020, http://pulpitandpen.org/2020/07/17/masks-are-an-eschatological-dry-run-for-the-mark-of-the-beast/.

[When I first wrote this chapter and included this image, this was seen as fanciful by many people – "that'll never happen" they said. Well, here it is, rolled out in full effect across the whole world ...]

Lastly on this issue of masks, I'll say that there is known detrimental psychological impact around wearing masks. Mind.org[71] states three main things at play:

1. Masks are a visual reminder of the virus – like danger is everywhere and can make us feel on edge or unable to relax.
2. Seeing people cover their faces might make us feel uneasy or scared of others. People might seem threatening, sinister, or dehumanised.
3. On the other hand, we might feel very anxious or upset around people who are not wearing masks in public.

Anti-mask protesters complain that they are like muzzles – gagging us into silence, a symbol of shame and oppression and violating free speech. I agree, it is easily observed that free speech is being suppressed at the rate of knots and, sadly to say, even within the Church. Allow me a few strong words on this: Jesus and His disciples shook the world with their bold proclamations of truth. How are we meant to do the same if we're physically masked, distanced and gagged by our own fear? The righteous are as bold as lions, not timid as puppy dogs.

University College London professor Xine Yao in a BBC radio show 'Rethinking Masks'[72] published in July 2020 astutely observes *"because masks conceal our faces from one another, they frustrate our efforts to express ourselves and connect with others."*

---

[71] *'Mask Anxiety, Face Coverings and Mental Health'. Mind.org,* https://www.mind.org.uk/information-support/coronavirus/mask-anxiety-face-coverings-and-mental-health/. Accessed 4 May 2021.

[72] 'BBC Sounds - Rethink, 'Dr Xine Yao: Rethinking Masks'. *BBC,* 1 July 2020, https://www.bbc.co.uk/programmes/p08jhdlg. Accessed 4 May 2021.

In our Churches, where our desire is to connect with each other, have good fellowship, disciple, evangelise and love one another, wearing a mask is a very visual sign that says 'stay away' and stunts effective communication. Yes, there are ways around it – after the service we can gather outside and fellowship but if the weather is not great, realistically, how many people will be hanging around in the cold and wet, with no refreshments? In the past few months, I've observed people scurrying away pretty quickly after Church services. In open Churches, we might see people each week, but do not see their facial expressions and we may not have spoken to them for months. Instead of delighting in fellowship each week, it's fostering alienation between believers. That's exactly how many people I've spoken to on this issue feel and it's eroding the vibrancy of the assembly of saints.

The bottom line is that masks pose a very serious problem in Church – they are a symbol of a lie and they are potentially harmful, rather than helpful to health (especially to older and vulnerable people), as well as a threat to our spiritual strength. Further, they greatly inhibit our fellowship and prevent us from singing and celebrating the Lord's Supper. We simply cannot entertain their use if we are to be a free and loving Church family that has a heart for each other and for reaching out to the lost in earnest.

Pastor Stephen Richardson from Faith Presbyterian Church has written a great article, On mask wearing and obeying civil authorities,[73] which expounds more on five key issues with mask wearing in Church.

"Now the Lord is the Spirit; and where the Spirit of the Lord is, there is liberty. But we all, with unveiled face, beholding as in a mirror the glory of the Lord, are being transformed into the same image from glory to glory, just as by the Spirit of the Lord." – 2 Corinthians 3:17-18 (NKJV)

---

[73] Richardson, Stephen. 'On Mask Wearing and Obeying Civil Authorities'. *Canada Revival* (blog), https://canadarevival.blogspot.com/2020/08/on-mask-wearing-and-obeying-civil.html. Accessed 4 May 2021.

CHAPTER FOUR

Enforced Vaccines

The problem of vaccines is a major one, as we'll investigate. This chapter is the longest in the book and it is unique in that it digs primarily into scientific and medical issues. We explore theological and ecclesiastical issues at the end of the chapter, but they are not necessarily the primary focus. The main aim of this chapter is to show you the *clear evidence of danger* of this unprecedented and experimental medical initiative, especially since much of it is quickly disappearing from the internet and getting labelled as 'fake news'. There is much to question about the dubious message of this Covid 'vaccine' being 'safe and effective'. But over and above that, I believe there are grave spiritual dangers of accepting a forced, rushed, unsatisfactorily tested concoction of unhealthy, toxic and gene and mind-altering substances and novel technologies that are not being fully disclosed and have been **cooked up by known Satanists with an anti-Christian spiritual agenda in mind: This vaccine is designed to harm in all ways possible.**

Ok, so now I've hit you with that wild claim, let's explore it. But before that, a word of reassurance upfront … if you're a Christian, our LORD tells us:

"For I am persuaded, that neither death, nor life, nor angels, nor princi-palities, nor powers, nor things present, nor things to come, Nor height, nor depth, nor any other creature, shall be able to separate us from the love of God, which is in Christ Jesus our Lord." – Romans 8:38-39

Our lives are purchased by Jesus and hidden in Him. So if you've had the vaccine and may be reluctant to read this chapter and concerned with what you may uncover in terms of potential dangers, please be reassured that whatever happens to you, your eternal future is secure and bright! Please do pray and read this chapter and make your own informed decisions moving forward. You may want to share this information with friends and family, especially those with children. If you're not yet Christian, I refer you again to Chapter 14.

Let's get started with the manifold issues of this Covid 'vaccine'…

Motivations and Benefits

'Triangulation' is very important when it comes to research. It is de-scribed by 'The BMJ' as being 'the use of multiple theories, data sources, methods or investigators within the study of a single phenomenon.' I.e., it's important to find differing sources and investigators when looking to see the validity of a claim or set of data. This was hammered home to me during the Criminal Evidence modules of my Law degree and again high-lighted when I sat on an Ethics Committee for Medical Research in my role as Medical Research Manager and working in a legal policy setting for ten years. Personally, I view triangulation of data as critical to estab-lishing corroborating evidence, especially in light of fake-fake news and the tendency of vast numbers of people to lazily share some news report or other and take it as unbiased fact.

It's also good to apply the question, 'cui bono?' Who benefits? – when looking at the validity of a claim or set of data. This Latin legal phrase is used to imply that whoever appears to have the most to gain from a crime is probably the culprit. We can use it to question the meaningfulness, motivation or advantages of a claim, phenomenon or action. To this end, we must look at who the author of the data is and not only their credentials but their vested interests, what else they've written/spoke on and who their sponsors are. We must verify sources and contexts. **It is therefore not sufficient to simply say *"I just trust in the science"*, as many do when the topic of the vaccine comes up.**

Dear friend, discerning truth is critically important in this time we're living in, it is completely Biblical (after all, Jesus is *the* great Truth) and I say all this as a preface to some very hard to swallow realities, coming next. We believe in the unbelievable Good News of the fact that Jesus Christ died for sinners, rose from the dead and ascended into heaven; securing our salvation and a perfect future with Him in glory. We love the truth, even though the world tries to discredit and dismiss us, Satan tries to deceive and discourage us and we are ridiculed for the 'foolishness' of the Gospel. That's ok, we hold firm anyway and rejoice in persecution for our truth claims, amen?

As I write this, and things are changing so rapidly, the silver bullet of a 'Covid vaccine' is rolling out at a 'warp speed' pace (as Donald Trump labelled it) – to be distributed to at least 7 billion people on earth, or so Gates, Fauci and various government leaders are drumming into us. Gates vows (threatens), along with world leaders that *"things will not return to 'normal' until everyone's been vaccinated"*. We are told that it will be mandatory and those with 'vaccine hesitancy' are labelled as everything from 'conspiracy theory nut jobs' and 'sociopaths' or 'narcissists' to 'anti-vax Neo Nazis' and 'those with mental health issues' and 'recklessly and selfishly threatening everyone's health'.

We will get into the details of this novel 'vaccine' shortly but just think about this for a second: Vaccines normally take between 6-15 years of rigorous testing and trial for efficacy and safety and are put out for public, independent scrutiny. Yet this one – to be given to EVERYONE indiscriminately – has been rushed in a matter of mere months (or so we are led to believe); and those who express any level of questioning or concern about it are swiftly censored, castigated and condemned – and likely to be punished in the near future. Freedom of speech is fast becoming a distant fond memory and this whole situation should greatly alarm us. As Christians, we hold that Jesus Christ is the one and only way to salvation and life eternal, yet we would not want religious freedom to be shut down and Muslims, New Agers, Hindus, etc. to be silenced; we uphold the value of freedom of thought, expression and speech, as is constitutional in the USA and many other countries.

The virus hit in earnest in the West in March 2020. Trump was talking about having the military (i.e., martial law) mobilised to distribute a vaccine to the masses in as early as October 2020 – in less than eight months; if we are to believe in the sequence and timeline of the problem-reaction-solution we are being told. (Although on this subject, you may want to check out a simple and clear video on the Hegelian Dialectic,[74] which may well perfectly describe a lot of what I am trying to convey in this book, in four short minutes. Watch it now, I'll wait.)

So, the questions we need to ask are these: If government mandates are ratcheting up for the enforced, rushed, untested Covid vaccination of all people on earth – why is this, what are the issues with it, who is behind it and cui bono – who benefits and how?

The Gates Dark Web of Influence

You probably don't need me to tell you that the co-founder and former CEO of Microsoft, centi-billionaire Bill Gates Jr, is the key player pushing and funding the vaccine and associated 'vaccine passport' agenda via his organisations, the Bill and Melinda Gates Foundation (BMGF) and

---

[74] 'Problem Reaction Solution Explained'. Y*ouTube*,
https://www.youtube.com/watch?v=wWXTW4RoZHk. Accessed 4 May 2021.

GAVI – The Vaccine Alliance. He is currently (at time of writing) funding seven of the main vaccine candidates and he is the largest private funder of the World Health Organisation (WHO) – the body that we all think of as being 'independent' and beneficent. With influence and money to fuel its own agenda, it is neither. BMGF also heavily funds the following organisations: Centers for Disease Control and Prevention (CDC), UNICEF, Vaccines for Malaria Venture, PATH Vaccines Solutions, Planned Parenthood, the United Nations (UN), The World Bank Group, as well as many universities, such as Oxford, Cornell, Johns Hopkins, Washington, Emory, UCSF, food and agriculture organisations and various media organisations such as The Guardian, the BBC, The Financial Times, ABC, The New York Times and The Huffington Post. He also has 500,000 shares in the notorious genetically modified organism (GMO) agriculture company Monsanto and has bought up vast areas of land across the world, making him the biggest private owner of farmland in the USA.[75]

So, Gates has huge investments and influence in the following sectors: vaccine development and infectious disease control, health policy, abortion and family planning, GMO agricultural development and farmland, news media and idea promotion, university research, financial policy and administration ... We can see that he holds a whole lot of power and influence in all of the key sectors of our lives and society. And if you're tempted to think that he is a silent partner without any influence, think again. There are rigorous propaganda training programmes in place for 'educating' all his stakeholders in his ideologies and there have been many reports documenting this, such as the Alliance for a Green Revolution in Africa (AGRA) Watch report,[76] 'The Man Behind the Curtain: The

---

[75] Estes, Nick. 'Bill Gates Is the Biggest Private Owner of Farmland in the United States. Why?'. *The Guardian*, 5 Apr. 2021, http://www.theguardian.com/commentisfree/2021/apr/05/bill-gates-climate-crisis-farmland.

[76] 'AGRA Watch Media'. *Community Alliance for Global Justice*, https://cagj.org/agra-watch/media/. Accessed 4 May 2021.

Gates Foundation's Influence on the UN Food Systems Summit', published August 2020. Another AGRA report of 2017 stated that: *"It is ... likely that Bill Gates, who has regular access to world leaders and is in effect personally bankrolling hundreds of universities, international organizations, NGOs and media outlets, has become the single most influential voice in international development."*

The term 'conflict of interests' is a gross understatement when it comes to Bill Gates. Many claim his actions to be not only unethical and dangerous but illegal.[77] Long-time leading independent health educator, Dr Joseph Marcela notes the following:[78] *"The fact that Gates' irrational and scientifically unsound opinions are shaping pandemic responses around the globe while real medical professionals are being censored by mainstream media and social media platforms is proof positive that we're no longer operating from a base of science and medical truth. Instead, the whole world is expected to fall into line with the self-serving agenda created by Gates and his many allies in technology and medicine. In an April 30, 2020, GatesNotes post, Gates even states he "suspects the COVID-19 vaccine will become part of the routine new-born immunization schedule" - a nice little piece of predictive programming, if you ask me. Mind you, the mRNA vaccines being developed against COVID-19 will alter your genetic expression, turning your body into a viral protein factory. Is it really wise to consider using such a novel vaccine on newborns? In a sane and rational world, the answer would be a resounding no. Unfortunately, we now live in a world run by Gates' goons, and thus reason and logic have largely vanished from the equation."*

---

[77] Mercola, Dr Joseph. 'Bill Gates — Most Dangerous Philanthropist in Modern History?' *LewRockwell.com*, 22 Apr. 2020, https://www.lewrockwell.com/2020/04/joseph-mercola/bill-gates-most-dangerous-philanthropist-in-modern-history/. Accessed 4 May 2021.

[78] Mercola, Dr Joseph. 'Bill Gates Secretly Dictates Global Food Policy, Too'. *LewRockwell.com*, 22 Apr. 2020. https://www.lewrockwell.com/2020/08/joseph-mercola/bill-gates-secretly-dictates-global-food-policy-too/. Accessed 4 May 2021.

A Columbia Journalism Review[79] exposé reveals the huge and systematic influence the Gates Foundation has had on mainstream media. This image gives a good indication of the state of play, taken from the article, 'Bill Gates' Web of Dark Money and Influence – Part 2: The COVID-19 Operation'.[80]

[79] Schwab, Tim. 'Journalism's Gates Keepers'. *Columbia Journalism Review*, 21 Aug. 2020, https://www.cjr.org/criticism/gates-foundation-journalism-funding.php. Accessed 4 May 2021.

[80] Broze, Derrick. 'Bill Gates' Web of Dark Money and Influence - Part 2: The COVID-19 Operation'. *The Last American Vagabond*, 28 May 2020, https://www.thelastamericanvagabond.com/bill-gates-web-dark-money-influence-part-2-covid-19-operation/.

The Gates Eugenics Agenda

Now, we next need to ask, what are the values of this man? With all his 'philanthropic' investment and work, what is he trying to achieve with his wealth and influence? What kind of future does he want to see? What legacy is he trying to leave?

In one word, Eugenics.

What is eugenics? Eugenics refers to the use of procedures like selective breeding and forced sterilisation in an attempt to improve the genetic purity of the human race. Eugenicists believe that disease, disability, and 'undesirable' human traits – like certain races and ethnicities – can be 'bred out' of humanity. Influenced by Charles Darwin's theory of natural selection and survival of the fittest and commonly associated with the genocide in Nazi Germany under Adolf Hitler, eugenics, in the form of forced sterilization, was first used in the United States during the early 1900s.

Bill Gates and his family have a long-held 'interest' with eugenics, evidenced not least by the vast sums of money they've ploughed into it, under various guides. Gates' father held an elitist view of eugenics which led him to become the head of Planned Parenthood and facilitate the mass killing of unborn babies, amongst other 'selective breeding' regimes.

Margaret Sanger is the founder of Planned Parenthood and her goals had racist eugenics at its core. *"Eugenics is ... the most adequate and thorough avenue to the solution of racial, political and social problems."* – Margaret Sanger, 'The Eugenic Value of Birth Control Propaganda' – Birth Control Review, October 1921. Eugenics takes on many forms in our current time – under more palatable and stealth propaganda names such as 'sustainable development', 'climate control', 'population control', 'pro-choice', 'gender equality', 'Black Lives Matter' (which echoes the Marxist Black Panther movement of the 1960s) and the blanket term which has been inappropriately named 'philanthropy' by Bill Gates. Further, Bill Gates has been heavily investing in 'third culture' scientists[81] (who are 'seeking to redefine who and what we are') and biotech companies, such as Ginkgo Bioworks,[82] set up by Tom Knight, professor at MIT's Artificial Intelligence Lab. In 2007, Tom was quoted as saying, *"The genetic code is 3.6 billion years old. It's time for a rewrite."*[83] In 2020, his company partnered with Moderna to offer their expertise in creating the Moderna Covid gene shot. You can join the dots here, and we'll explore more about gene editing shortly. The Alliance for Natural Health issued a video in July 2020, 'Bill Gates on Covid Vaccines: Straight from the horse's mouth'.[84] Dr Joseph Marcela asks the question, in an eight-minute video on the WHO, 'Is Bill Gates the Most Dangerous Philanthropist in Modern History?'[85] If you feel you want a little more information on his agenda for the world, check out this Lew Rockwell article on Deconstructing the Gates Agenda[86] or the Corbett Report [87] and follow the links and references. I'll also list some primary source books on the eugenics agenda in the later Babylon chapter of this book.

---

[81] Brockman, John. 'The Third Culture'. *Edge.Org.* 9 Sept. 1991, https://www.edge.org/conversation/the-third-culture. Accessed 4 May 2021.

[82] *Ginkgo Bioworks*, https://www.ginkgobioworks.com/. Accessed 4 May 2021.

[83] Silver, Lee. 'Scientists Push the Boundaries of Human Life'. *Newsweek*, 3 June 2007, https://www.newsweek.com/scientists-push-boundaries-human-life-101723.

[84] 'Bill Gates on Covid Vaccines: Straight from the Horse's Mouth'. *YouTube*, https://www.youtube.com/watch?v=PI95pEvBkuE. Accessed 4 May 2021.

[85] Mercola, Dr Joseph. 'Bill Gates Leads Medical Tyranny Agenda'. *Mercola*, 21 Apr. 2020, https://articles.mercola.com/sites/articles/archive/2020/04/21/bill-gates-political-power.aspx. Accessed 4 May 2021.

[86] Mercola, Dr Joseph. 'Deconstructing Bill Gates's Agenda'. *LewRockwell.com*, 15 June 2020. https://www.lewrockwell.com/2020/06/joseph-mercola/deconstructing-bill-gates-agenda/. Accessed 4 May 2021.

[87] *The Corbett Report*. https://www.corbettreport.com/. Accessed 4 May 2021.

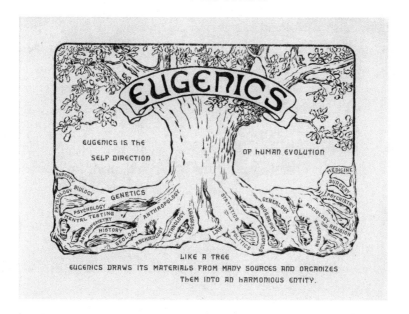

'Eugenics is the self-direction of human evolution': Logo from the Second International Eugenics Congress, 1921

Five Examples of Eugenics At Play Right Now

I have been following this stuff for almost two decades. There are scores of things I could reference to show that the eugenics agenda is rolling out in full force right now and has accelerated into top gear with the advent of Covid-19; **specifically, to depopulate or sterilise vast numbers of people across the world.** For brevity, I'll list a few key things here and let you do your own research and follow the links and documents I've referenced to discover more:

1.   **The United Nations Agenda 21**[88] – Now conflated with the updated Agenda 2030, there are 17 Sustainable Development

---

[88] 'Agenda 21: Sustainable Development Knowledge Platform'. *United Nations Sustainable Development*, https://sustainabledevelopment.un.org/outcomedocuments/agenda21. Accessed 4 May 2021.

Goals[89] that detail eugenics and depopulation in politically correct and propaganda laden language and with the vehicle being
a one-world government. Leaders of 178 nations have signed
this document. Couching their goals as ethical, positive and
good for us all and the earth, but they are far from it. Rather,
they are in alignment and furtherance of Alice Bailey's 10-Point
Charter for the New World Order (more on that later). The UN's
agenda is to destroy capitalism and private property, move us all
into 5G-controlled 'smart cities' under constant surveillance,
existing on toxic GMO non-foods and ushering in communism and technocracy to systematically remove our freedoms and depopulate the world. The UN, by the way, is an occult, esoteric body of the deep state[90] which has long been channelling the demonic realm to gain its power and insights, so
we should not be surprised by these plans. Sceptical? Read Tal
Brooke's book, 'One World'[91] or this article on the UN occultism,[92] or this article showing the UN's intimate connection with
high level occultists[93] Alice Bailey and Helena Blavatsky
and their organisations. Sustainable Development Goal number
3, 'good health and wellbeing', begins with the U.N.'s demand
that you 'vaccinate your family'. Goal 3.8 states: *"Achieve universal health coverage, including financial risk protection, access to quality essential healthcare services and access to safe,
effective, quality and affordable essential medicines and **vaccines for all**"*, with the repeated tagline 'no one left behind'.

---

[89] 'THE 17 GOALS | Sustainable Development'. *United Nations Sustainable Development* ,
https://sdgs.un.org/goals. Accessed 4 May 2021.

[90] Deep State – a type of governance made up of potentially secret and unauthorised networks of power
operating independently of a state's political leadership in pursuit of their own agenda and goals.

[91] Brooke, Tal. *One World.* CreateSpace Independent Publishing, 2015.

[92] Brooks, Carol. 'The United Nations'. http://www.inplainsite.org/html/the_united_nations.html. Accessed 4 May 2021.

[93] 'The Occult Connections to the United Nations - Part 1'. *Steemit*, 30 Jan. 2018,
https://steemit.com/christianity/@truth-be-told/the-occult-connections-to-the-united-nations-part-1.

2. **The Georgia Guidestones:**[94] these are the Freemasonic '10 Commandments of the New World Order'[95], listed on a Stonehenge-like monument in Elbert County, Georgia, USA. The themes are on sustainable development, one world religion, world government system, eugenics/transhumanism, and outright reducing the population by 80-90%. Sounds outlandish? Check them out – the first commandment states: *"Maintain humanity under 500,000,000 in perpetual balance with nature."* Erm, that's a reduction of 7.3 billion people; how exactly, without mass genocide ...? This ties in with Deagel.com's population reduction forecasts[96] (Deagel is a legitimate organisation for the U.S. government, providing news and intelligence on international military aviation and advanced technologies) – predicting massive global depopulation (50-80%) by 2025. For example, it forecasts a reduction in population from 332 million to 99 million in the USA and from 65 million to 14 million in the UK, gulp.

3. **The 2010 Rockefeller report that predicts how a pandemic will usher in totalitarian authority.**[97] Entitled 'Scenarios for the Future of Technology and International Development' – The Rockefeller Foundation published this report in May 2010 in cooperation with the Global Business Network of futurologist Peter Schwartz. The first 'scenario', called, 'Lock Step', describes

---

[94] 'Georgia Guidestones'. *Wikipedia*, 2 May 2021, https://en.wikipedia.org/w/index.php?title=Georgia_Guidestones&oldid=1020986002.

[95] 'The Georgia Guidestones: 10 Masonic Commandments'. *Scribol*, 18 May 2018, https://scribol.com/anthropology-and-history/occult/the-georgia-guidestones-10-masonic-commandments/4.

[96] *Deagel.com,* https://deagel.com/forecast. Accessed 4 May 2021.

[97] 'Scenarios for the Future of Technology and International Development'. *Rockefeller Foundation.* http://www.nommeraadio.ee/meedia/pdf/RRS/Rockefeller%20Foundation.pdf. Accessed 4 May 2021.

a world of total government control and authoritarian leadership. **It envisions a future where a pandemic would allow national leaders to flex their authority and impose airtight rules and restrictions that would remain after the pandemic faded.** The majority of this scenario has already unfolded. We will see if it continues as predicted. It's fairly resolute in its scenarios and the power and authority and measures to be imposed on us all.

4. **Bill Gates Ted Talk in 2010 – 'Innovating to Zero!'**[98] In this now infamous TED talk, Bill Gates unveils his vision for the world's energy future, describing the need for 'miracles' to avoid planetary catastrophe and the necessity to get to zero carbon emissions by 2050. At minute 4:21, he states: *"First, we've got population. The world today has 6.8 billion people. That's headed up to about nine billion. Now, if we do a really great job on new vaccines, health care, reproductive health services, we could lower that by, perhaps, 10 or 15 percent."* Is he talking depopulation here – with new vaccines? You decide. When challenged on this, Gates has defended that what he means is that when people in third world countries are healthier with vaccines, they have less children since they have confidence that more will survive and be able to provide and support parents in their older age; thereby lowering the population. Wrong: As leading economist and political advisor, Martin Armstrong states in his article 'Is Gates Stupid or Very Clever with Vaccines?'[99] – *"Either Bill Gates is amazingly ignorant, or he is engaging in sophistry to sell his population-climate change agenda. The mistake people are making here is they are judging the third world on our own. What he is saying is that vaccinating*

---

[98] Gates, Bill. 'Transcript of 'Innovating to Zero!'' *TED*, https://www.ted.com/talks/bill_gates_innovating_to_zero/transcript. Accessed 4 May 2021.

[99] Armstrong, Martin. 'Is Gates Stupid or Very Clever with Vaccines?' *Armstrong Economics*, 27 May 2020, https://www.armstrongeconomics.com/world-news/climate/is-gates-stupid-of-very-clever-with-vaccines/. Accessed 4 May 2021.

everyone will mean they have a healthier child so they will need fewer children, which is absolutely a joke. The population natu-rally declines ONLY with economic advancement ... Sorry, I cannot believe Gates is that stupid. I believe it is merely his ex-cuse for the depopulation of the earth and his father was a mem-ber of Eugenics which believed in the superiority of the Nordic-Anglo-Saxon Race genetically and were actively seeking to re-duce the population of darker skinned people where Gates has focuses – India & Africa. There is absolutely no support what-soever for his claim that vaccinating children will make them healthier so they will have less. Donate food if that is really the issue – but there is no profit in that."

5. **Gates' past history of huge damage in third world countries and law suits against him.** This article from Children's Health Defence (CHD)[100] illuminates us on some of Gates' track record in administering vaccines to the third world: *"Promising his share of $450 million of $1.2 billion to eradicate polio, Gates took control of India's National Technical Advisory Group on Immunization (NTAGI), which mandated up to 50 doses of polio vaccines through overlapping immunization programs to chil-dren before the age of five.* **Indian doctors blame the Gates campaign for a devastating non-polio acute flaccid paralysis (NPAFP) epidemic that paralyzed 490,000 children beyond ex-pected rates between 2000 and 2017.** *In 2017, the Indian gov-ernment dialled back Gates' vaccine regimen and asked Gates and his vaccine policies to leave India. NPAFP rates dropped precipitously."*

---

[100] Kennedy Jr., Robert F. 'Gates' Globalist Vaccine Agenda: A Win-Win for Pharma and Mandatory Vaccination'. *Children's Health Defense*, 9 Apr. 2020, https://childrenshealthdefense.org/news/govern-ment-corruption/gates-globalist-vaccine-agenda-a-win-win-for-pharma-and-mandatory-vaccination/.

Technocracy News' article – 'Mandatory Vaccines: Complete Control Over Your Physical Body'[101] reports, amongst other alarming cases: *"In 2014, the Gates Foundation funded tests of experimental HPV vaccines, developed by Glaxo Smith Kline (GSK) and Merck, on 23,000 young girls in remote Indian provinces.* **Approximately 1,200 suffered severe side effects, including autoimmune and fertility disorders. Seven died.** *Indian government investigations charged that Gates-funded researchers committed pervasive ethical violations: pressuring vulnerable village girls into the trial, bullying parents, forging consent forms, and refusing medical care to the injured girls. The case is now in the country's Supreme Court."*

Gates is extremely clear, in his many interviews, that his desire is that everyone on the planet is vaccinated and 'things won't return to normal' until this is the case, and we are seeing this plan roll out thick and fast. Yet he has also openly admitted, albeit in a slightly construed manner, that a Covid vaccine will kill or cause permanent side effects in around 700,000 people and seems to think that the end justifies the means.

In a CNBC News report of April 2020, he states: *"We clearly need a vaccine that works in the upper age range because they're most at risk of that ... And doing that so that you amp it up so that it works in older people, and yet you don't have side effects, if we have one in 10,000 side effects that's way more, 700,000 people who will suffer from that."*

Robert F Kennedy Jr, an avid Defender of Children's Rights and anti-vaccination activist, launched a petition sent to the White House, calling for 'Investigations into the 'Bill and Melinda Gates Foundation' for Med-

---

[101] Wood, Patrick. 'Mandatory Vaccines: Complete Control Over Your Physical Body'. *Technocracy News & Trends*, 13 Apr. 2020, https://www.technocracy.news/mandatory-vaccines-complete-control-over-your-physical-body/.

ical Malpractice & Crimes Against Humanity' – it had 655,041 signatures and growing in the summer of 2020. In May 2020, it was reported that an Italian Politician Demand Bill Gates Arrest For Crimes Against Humanity.[102]

It is interesting to note that on 18th October 2019 (before our 'virus outbreak'), the Gates Foundation, along with the World Economic Forum (WEF) and Johns Hopkins University (Gates funded), hosted 'Event 201' an exercise which plotted, in precise detail, a world lockdown and complete media response to a universal coronavirus pandemic. Attendees left with their very own stuffed toy coronavirus microbe. Cute.

 Johns Hopkins Center for Health Security @JHSP... · Oct 16, 2019 ⌄
Have you registered for the #Event201 virtual pandemic exercise yet? See the story of #Event201 play out in real-time and answer tough questions that could arise in a severe pandemic. Register today and be entered to win one of our Event201 giant microbes!
centerforhealthsecurity.org/event201/

♡ 4   ↻ 18   ♡ 15   ↑

Gates and other billionaires – David Rockefeller, Ted Turner, Oprah Winfrey, Warren Buffett, George Soros, Michael Bloomberg – have had documented secret meetings since at least 2009 and one in 2018 to discuss

---

[102] 'Italian Politician Demand Bill Gates Arrest For Crimes Against Humanity'. *GreatGameIndia*, 17 May 2020, https://greatgameindia.com/italian-politician-demand-bill-gates-arrest-for-crimes-against-humanity/.

what they deem to be the number one most pressing issue in the world – population control. Could we be seeing these plans in action, and in alignment with the Rockefeller Report's 'Lock Step', the UN's Agenda 21 and the World Economic Forum's Annual Meeting in Davos in January 2020?[103] It's very, very hard to conclude otherwise in the face of overwhelming evidence and the vastly disproportionate response to this overplayed so-called world pandemic.

If we now revisit our Covid vaccine question 'cui bono?' It's very clear to see what's going on here: If, on the one hand, Bill Gates' (and other mega-rich world leaders') plans are dominated by CO2 arguments on how to prevent climate change by reducing the population and on the other hand his desire is for a world-wide vaccine (his vaccine) to save the population from a pandemic, there would be a huge and direct conflict of interests and his investments would, in effect be cancelling each other out. This man is a savvy investor with his mind fixed on population control. He did not become a centi-billionaire by making such blunders and he is not about to sabotage his plans by funding a 'safe and effective' vaccine to cure illness or prolong and improve the lives of the masses - many of such people eugenicists label 'feeble-minded', 'imbeciles', 'morons', 'idiots' and 'useless eaters'. No, what we are seeing playing out on the world stage before our very eyes is the culmination of decades (centuries actually if you read any of the books I'll list in Chapter 10 on 'Discerning Babylon') of careful political manipulation, propaganda and world domination plans of elitist, megalomaniac billionaires and their friends to depopulate the world with the mass rollout of this new, untested, dangerous pseudo-vaccine, amongst other things … **And we need to wake up to this, now.** These people are employing the classic gaslighting techniques used by all narcissistic abusers, causing us to question and quash our unsettled consciences on this matter and conclude – surely not, they could never be lying on such a grand scale.

---

[103] 'World Economic Forum Annual Meeting Davos 2020'. *World Economic Forum,* https://www.weforum.org/events/world-economic-forum-annual-meeting-2020/. Accessed 4 May 2021

If you think this sounds more like a far-fetched movie, you'd be right because they've also been using predictive programming in Hollywood and entertainment for decades too, to desensitise us and normalise the depopulation agenda.[104] If you want your eyes further opened to indoctrination placed into movies, watch Jay Dyer's analysis of a selection of films in this Hollywood occult and predictive programming presentation of 2016.[105] Watch from minute 17:40 for the vaccine stuff from the James Bond film of 1969, 'On Her Majesty's Secret Service'. Oliver Wendell Holmes, Jr – one of most famous of the U.S. Supreme Court justices, states the position on eugenics and vaccines clearly, all the way back in the 1930s: *"It is better for all the world, if instead of waiting to execute degenerate offspring for crime or to let them starve for their imbecility, society can prevent those who are manifestly unfit from continuing their kind. The principle that sustains compulsory vaccination is broad enough to cover cutting the fallopian tubes. Three generations of imbeciles are enough."*

Eugenics and the Rushed Covid Pseudo-Vaccine

So now we've seen that the rich elites' agenda is for eugenics and why they have been so keen for a Covid vaccine to be approved and mandated for everyone to have it ASAP (except themselves, incidentally), let's take a look at some of the objective issues with its rushed rollout.

---

[104] Lance. 'Hollywood Movies and Predictive Programming'. *Liberation from the System*, 14 Feb. 2019, https://endalltyranny.wordpress.com/2019/02/14/hollywood-movies-and-predictive-programming/.

[105] Dyer, Jay. "Hollywood Occultism – Jay Dyer'. *YouTube*, https://www.youtube.com/watch?v=vI25U-kkBNs. Accessed 4 May 2021.

There were early warnings clearly sounded from a number of organisations. The Alliance for Natural Health, identified four key problems, as at May 2020:[106]

1. Patients including the elderly and frontline healthcare workers have been recruited for trials.

2. **The participants in these trials are acting as guinea pigs for the public.** They are going in blind, with no information on the safety profile of the experimental vaccines. Vaccines for RNA viruses like SARS-CoV-2 using the kinds of technologies employed by the frontrunners have never been created before at scale. Any safety issue found in one study needs to be communicated as quickly as possible to those involved with other trials. This is an ethical imperative.

3. **Leading vaccine scientists like Dr Shino Jiang have issued warnings,**[107] saying in March 2020 in the prestigious journal Nature, *"My worry is that this could mean a vaccine is administered before its efficacy and safety have been fully evaluated in animal models or clinical trials"*. Governments, health authorities and vaccine developers don't appear to be listening so the public and onside politicians must make them hear.

4. **Vaccine development is happening at such a rapid rate** – there is a genuine vaccine race ongoing with over 100 contenders[108] vying to win the prize: sign off by the World Health Organization, and roll-out following deals with the largest vaccine companies in the world.

---

[106] 'Call to Action – Help Create the New Vaccine Narrative'. *Alliance for Natural Health International*, 7 May 2020, http://www.anhinternational.org/news/call-to-action-help-create-the-new-vaccine-narrative/.

[107] Jiang, Shibo. 'Don't Rush to Deploy COVID-19 Vaccines and Drugs without Sufficient Safety Guarantees'. *Nature*, vol. 579, no. 7799, Mar. 2020, pp. 321–321. *www.nature.com*, doi:10.1038/d41586-020-00751-9.

[108] Le, Tung Thanh, et al. 'The COVID-19 Vaccine Development Landscape'. *Nature Reviews Drug Discovery*, vol. 19, no. 5, Apr. 2020, pp. 305–06. *www.nature.com*, doi:10.1038/d41573-020-00073-5.

The ANH goes on to say that people are not being told that *"The vaccine will probably be genetically engineered [the vaccines are genetically engineered - author]. In many countries in the world, you can't sell a food that contains genetically engineered plants unless you state that it contains GMOs on the label. What about vaccines that go straight into your bloodstream?"*

All of these early concerns have been shown to have been right in their assessment. The pseudo-vaccines are indeed genetically engineered and have been rolled out after conflating animal trials with phase I human trials, where they have been conducted that is.

In other words, this new injectable technology has skirted around the sometimes 10-15 years of assessment where its effects on recipients can be observed over time. It should go without saying that long-term effects of a vaccine or other drug (especially a novel one) needs to be proven over the long-term. This is common sense that is being ignored and silenced and so-called Covid vaccine experts are giving fine-sounding, highly-scientific reasons why 'long-term results' does not need to mean 'long-term'. Even if the claim that 'any vaccine injury will manifest generally within two months' is true, which is what many 'experts' claim, we need to remind ourselves that this is NOT a vaccine in the traditional sense, it's a novel gene tool, so we cannot extrapolate case data in the same way.

Concerning eugenics and vested profitable interests …

The AstraZeneca experimental vaccine was co-developed by Adrian Hill, who has long-term ties to the British eugenics movement through his work with the Wellcome Trust's Centre for Human Genetics and affiliation with the Galton Institute, formerly the U.K. Eugenics Society. Members of the Galton Institute have called for population reduction in Latin America, South and Southeast Asia and Africa, the very areas where the AstraZeneca vaccine is being promoted.

In December 2020, the Journal on Geopolitics and International Relations stated:[109] *"Mainstream media has had little, if anything, to say about the role of the vaccine developers' private company – Vaccitech – in the Oxford-AstraZeneca partnership, a company whose main investors include former top Deutsche Bank executives, Silicon Valley behemoth Google and the UK government. All of them stand to profit from the vaccine alongside the vaccine's two developers, Adrian Hill and Sarah Gilbert, who retain an estimated 10% stake in the company. Another overlooked point is the plan to dramatically alter the current sales model for the vaccine following the initial wave of its administration, which would see profits soar, especially if the now obvious push to make COVID-19 vaccination an annual affair for the foreseeable future is made reality. Yet, arguably most troubling of all is the direct link of the vaccine's lead developers to the Wellcome Trust and, in the case of Adrian Hill, the Galton Institute, two groups with longstanding ties to the UK Eugenics movement. The latter organization, named for the 'father of eugenics' Francis Galton, is the re-named UK Eugenics Society, a group notorious for its promotion of racist pseudoscience and efforts to 'improve racial stock' by reducing the population of those deemed inferior for over a century. The ties of Adrian Hill to the Galton Institute should raise obvious concerns given the push to make the Oxford-AstraZeneca vaccine he developed with Gilbert the vaccine of choice for the developing world, particularly countries in Latin America, South and Southeast Asia and Africa, the very areas where the Galton Institute's past members have called for reducing population growth."*

You may want to take a look over this detailed document to verify these associations and interests, 'Eugenics, Human Genetics and Human Failings – The Eugenics Society, its sources and other critics in Britain'. [110]

---

[109] 'COVID-19 Vaccine Developers Oxford-AstraZeneca Linked To British Eugenics Movement'. *GreatGameIndia*, 28 Dec. 2020, https://greatgameindia.com/covid-19-vaccine-eugenics/.

[110] Mazumdar, Pauline M.H. 'Eugenics, Human Genetics and Human Failings – The Eugenics Society, its sources and other critics in Britain'. http://pombo.free.fr/mazumdar1992.pdf. Accessed 4 May 2021.

Back in May 2020, Donald Trump announced plans, under a directive he called 'Operation Warp Speed',[111] to make available at least 300 million doses of a $750 million Gates-funded coronavirus injection, Oxford-AstraZeneca AZD1222 and delivered as early as October 2020, with mass roll out by January 2021. Joe Biden picked up this ball and ran with it with even faster 'warp-speed' pace with new injections from Pfizer, Moderna, Johnson & Johnson and more.

The pro-vaccine propaganda has been laid on thick from the outset, successfully coercing millions of otherwise healthy and low-risk people to go and receive an experimental injected serum in the name of 'safety' and 'playing our part' – with the carrot of a re-opening of society when enough people receive the shot dangled in front of us.

USA
TODAY

OPINION

Defeat COVID-19 by requiring vaccination for all. It's not un-American, it's patriotic.

Dr. Michael Lederman, Maxwell J. Mehlman and Dr. Stuart Youngner | Opinion contributors
Published 12:28 AM EDT Aug 10, 2020

To win the war against the novel coronavirus that has killed nearly 163,000 people in this country, the only answer is compulsory vaccination — for all of us.

And while the measures that will be necessary to defeat the coronavirus will seem draconian, even anti-American to some, we believe that there is no alternative. Simply put, getting vaccinated is going to be our patriotic duty.

---

[111] Wong, Kristina. 'Operation Warp Speed Aims to Deliver 300M Vaccine Doses by January'. *Breitbart*, 16 June 2020, https://www.breitbart.com/politics/2020/06/16/trump-administrations-operation-warp-speed-aiming-to-deliver-300-million-vaccine-doses-by-january/.

In a White House announcement in early April 2021, Joe Biden stated the following:[112] *"Every adult above the age of 18 will now be eligible to stand in the virtual line for getting vaccinated ... We aren't at the finish line. We still have a lot of work to do. We're still in a life-and-death race against this virus ... When you go home, get all your friends, tell them, "Get a shot when they can", that's how we're going to beat this."* Meanwhile, in May 2021, the White House Press Secretary, Jen Psaki, has reported that the government will be delivering more than 28 million vaccine shots to the US states. She also stressed that the government does not support the idea of a federal vaccine database or a vaccine passport. *"The government is not now, nor will we be supporting a system that requires Americans to carry a credential. There will be no federal vaccinations database and no federal mandate requiring everyone to obtain a single vaccination credential."* Biden has assured people that he will put his best foot forward to bring the country out of the pandemic soon. *"I want to have an Independence Day – an independence from the Covid,"* he said. *"How much death, disease and misery are we going to see between now and then."* So, Biden stated that he does not support a vaccine database or 'passport'. Many other government leaders across the world stated the same, but from the research I've done, which we'll look at shortly, I would say that the word 'yet' needs to be firmly added to any promises of not introducing a vaccine passport – and maybe by the time you're reading this it has already come into place. Indeed, this has been the endgame in all of this from the beginning – the merging of technology with human biology. To chip us, file us, keep every aspect of our lives (including intimate biometrics) under surveillance and control, much like the already-established, prototype social credit system in China,[113] which came

---

[112] 'All Adults in US Eligible for COVID-19 Vaccine from 19 April: President Joe Biden'. *WION*, https://www.wionews.com/world/all-adults-in-us-eligible-for-covid-19-vaccine-from-19-april-president-joe-biden-375785. Accessed 20 May 2021.

[113] 'Planning Outline for the Construction of a Social Credit System (2014-2020)'. *China Copyright and Media*, 14 June 2014, https://chinacopyrightandmedia.wordpress.com/2014/06/14/planning-outline-for-the-construction-of-a-social-credit-system-2014-2020/.

into full effect in 2020. An external passport will give way to an internal one – implanted, injected, swabbed or ingested into our bodies.

Gary D. Barnett, writer on freedom and liberty at The Future of Freedom Foundation, states: *"Mass vaccination, and likely eventual mandatory vaccination, is on the horizon, and has already been accepted by most in this country and around the world as a necessity for avoiding the so-called novel coronavirus. This false notion being pushed on the people by the State and its media is but a lie masquerading as the truth. Propaganda at this level would make Hitler proud. It will not be a godsend for the world, but will be the state's weapon of choice for mass murder for the purpose of genocide and population control. No coronavirus or RNA vaccines have ever been effective, but have been very dangerous to the health of those inoculated. In the case of this new vaccine being fast-tracked, it will be untested, and the risks due to many factors will be astronomical."* He goes on to strongly assert the following, in a later article, 'The Next Phase of This Fake Pandemic Will Be Premeditated Mass Murder by 'Vaccine'':[114] *"The stage is set, the plan is in place, and the people are still asleep. The realization that this State has declared war on the American people is unknown to most, and when the killing reaches high levels, the sheep will be told it is due to a mutated virus variant, and it is their fault for not being injected quickly enough with a poisonous 'vaccine' administered by this same criminal state. Make no mistake about it; you are the enemy of the State in this war against mankind. This manufactured pandemic began with lies, and was perpetuated by mass propaganda; so much so as to cause extreme fear and panic out of thin air. This is what real domestic terrorism looks like, and it is being executed by the United States government under the control of its masters in banking, finance, and corporate America; those at the top of the pyramid of power that make up the Council on Foreign Relations, the Trilateral Commission, the Bilderberg Group, and all the major players in science, technology,*

---

[114] Barnett, Gary D. 'The Next Phase of This Fake Pandemic Will Be Premeditated Mass Murder by "Vaccine"'. *LewRockwell.com*, 6 Apr. 2021, https://www.lewrockwell.com/2021/04/gary-d-barnett/the-next-phase-of-this-fake-pandemic-will-be-premeditated-mass-murder-by-vaccine/.

the mainstream media, medicine, and the pharmaceutical industry. This long-planned plot to depopulate the earth and take total control over all of us could be considered ingenious but for the fact that it is pure evil."

Twelve Key Dangers and Problems with Covid 'Vaccines' – What's in Them and How They Will Harm Us

Now we know the vaccine agenda, let's look at the actual dangers of it; not only to our physical health but, more importantly in my view, to our mental and spiritual health.

There have been many, many credible medical doctors who've spoken out (and swiftly been censored), urging us against a Covid vaccine and the faulty and deceptive scientism behind it. Dr Carrie Madej in her excellent presentation of August 2020, entitled "Human 2.0?' A Wake-Up Call To The World.'[115] You can also read about it and view it here,[116] in case the video gets deleted again, as it has been from many platforms. It gives a succinct but thorough explanation of the main problems – all easily verifiable and corroborated by many other doctors. Dr Madej is an Internal Medicine Specialist in McDonough, GA and has over 19 years of experience in the medical field. She states:

"This new vaccine is not like your normal flu vaccine – this is something very different, something brand new, something completely experimental on the human race. It's not just about being a different vaccine. There are technologies that are being introduced <u>with this vaccine</u>

---

[115] 'Human 2.0 – Transhumanist Vaccine – A Wake Up Call to the World – Dr Carrie Madej'. *BitChute*, https://www.bitchute.com/video/BkVkN0JDZmaz/. Accessed 4 May 2021.

[116] Madej, Carrie. 'Dr Carrie Madej: "Human 2.0"? A Wake-Up Call About the Coming Vaccine – Truth Comes to Light'. https://truthcomestolight.com/dr-carrie-madej-human-2-0-a-wake-up-call-about-the-coming-vaccine/. Accessed 4 May 2021.

that can change the way we live, who we are and what we are – and very quickly." – **Dr Carrie Madej**

Did you catch that? These experimental pseudo-vaccines may change *what we are* – from human to transhuman; part human with a technological 'extension' or augmentation and hooked up as a node in the 'global switch board' able to be controlled and sold for purposes best known to the elites. This is Satanic to its core. We have been designed and created by God and our body, heart, spirit and soul are not to be bought or manipulated and fashioned into a Frankenstein-like, sub-human abomination. Dr Madej goes on to explain that the vaccines being developed and rolled out are funded and created by these transhumanists who believe we should go to 'human 2.0' – where technology is melded and is inseparable from humans; a robotic human race if you like. Again, this has long been the desire of the elites and is part of the eugenics and totalitarian world-State agenda and believers in Christ should not be ignorant of this evil; we must stand firm against it.

The Legal Definition of a Vaccine – This One Does Not Fit

The legal definition of the term 'vaccine', according Law Insider,[117] is 'a specially prepared antigen administered to a person for the purpose of providing immunity'. The Covid 'vaccine' is therefore a misnomer, since it does not fit the legal description. Dr David Martin states the following[118] and many medical doctors and lawyers concur: *"This is not a vaccine. We need to be really clear. We're using the term 'vaccine' to sneak*

---

[117] 'Vaccine definition'. *Law Insider*, https://www.lawinsider.com/dictionary/vaccine. Accessed 4 May 2021.

[118] Shilhavy, Brian. 'Dr David Martin on Experimental MRNA COVID Vaccines: This Is NOT a Vaccine! It Is a Medical Device - Medical Kidnap'. *Medical Kidnap,* 13 Jan. 2021, https://medical-kidnap.com/2021/01/13/dr-david-martin-on-experimental-mrna-covid-vaccines-this-is-not-a-vaccine-it-is-a-medical-device/.

this thing under public health exemptions. This is not a vaccine. This is an mRNA packaged in a fat envelope, that is delivered to a cell. It is a medical device designed to stimulate the human cell into becoming a pathogen creator ... And a vaccine specifically has to stimulate both an immunity within the person who is receiving it, but it also has to disrupt transmission. And that is not what this is. They have been abundantly clear in saying that the mRNA strand that is going into the cell, it is not to stop transmission. It is a treatment. But if it was discussed as a treatment, it would not get the sympathetic ear of the public health authorities, because then people would say, well what other treatments are there?"

Let's move on to the nuts and bolts of the Covid vaccine ...

For a list of 'front runner' Covid vaccines and some degree of transparency regarding their funding, ingredients and details of planned roll out, you can check out the Genetic Engineering & Biotechnology News Covid Vaccine Front Runner website.[119] Moderna Therapeutics' mRNA-1273 Covid vaccine was the first to emerge and began testing in May 2020. It is pushing all technological frontiers in doing so, including the use of nano-technology, gene-altering 'transfection', 'hydrogel' and more. You can read more on the use of nanoparticle technology in Covid vaccine development in Science daily's report[120] and 'Nanotechnology for COVID-19: Therapeutics and Vaccine Research'.[121]

As vaccines have rolled out across the world and been given to millions upon millions of people, it is important to note that NONE of them, not a

---

[119] 'COVID-19 Front Runner'. *GEN - Genetic Engineering and Biotechnology News*, https://www.genengnews.com/category/covid-19-candidates/covid-19-front-runner/. Accessed 4 May 2021.

[120] Connor, Katherine. 'A Nanomaterial Path Forward for COVID-19 Vaccine Development'. *Science-Daily*, https://www.sciencedaily.com/releases/2020/07/200715095500.htm. Accessed 4 May 2021.

[121] Chauhan, Gaurav, et al. 'Nanotechnology for COVID-19: Therapeutics and Vaccine Research'. *ACS Nano*, vol. 14, no. 7, July 2020, pp. 7760–82. *ACS Publications*, doi:10.1021/acsnano.0c04006.

single one, has been Food and Drug Administration (FDA) or other regulatory body-approved, other than for emergency use. The drug companies' vaccine literature states so:

"The Moderna COVID-19 Vaccine is an unapproved vaccine[122] *that may prevent COVID-19.* **There is no FDA-approved vaccine to prevent COVID-19.** *The FDA has authorized the emergency use of the Moderna COVID-19 Vaccine to prevent COVID-19 in individuals 18 years of age and older under an Emergency Use Authorization (EUA)."*

"The Pfizer-BioNTech COVID-19 Vaccine is an unapproved vaccine[123] *that may prevent COVID-19. There is no FDA-approved vaccine to prevent COVID-19. 2 Revised: December 2020 The FDA has authorized the emergency use of the Pfizer-BioNTech COVID-19 Vaccine to prevent COVID-19 in individuals 16 years of age and older under an Emergency Use Authorization (EUA)."*

In the UK, the government issued a press release announcing the approval of the first Covid vaccine,[124] and states the terms of doing such: *"The decision to approve the supply of this vaccine was taken under Regulation 174 of the Human Medicine Regulations 2012, which enables* **rapid temporary regulatory approvals** *to address significant public health issues such as a pandemic."*

So, let's explore the physical components of the new experimental Covid injections and their very concerning features ...

---

[122] 'Moderna Covid Vaccine Fact Sheet for Recipients and Caregivers'. *Moderna US, Inc.,* 26 Mar. 2021, https://www.fda.gov/media/144638/download.

[123] 'Pfizer-Biontech Covid Vaccine Fact Sheet for Recipients and Caregivers'. *Pfizer Inc.,* 10 May 2021, https://www.fda.gov/media/144414/download

[124] 'UK Medicines Regulator Gives Approval for First UK COVID-19 Vaccine'. *GOV.UK,* https://www.gov.uk/government/news/uk-medicines-regulator-gives-approval-for-first-uk-covid-19-vaccine. Accessed 4 May 2021.

1. Nanobot, Hydrogel and Quantum Dot Technology – Chipping You

The Oxford English Dictionary defines Nanotechnology as 'the branch of technology that deals with dimensions and tolerances of less than 100 nanometers, especially the manipulation of individual atoms and molecules.'

Future technologists often claimed that nanobots will be flowing through your body by 2030,[125] but the Covid vaccine promises to accelerate that by a decade. Frontiers in Immunology, October 4, 2018 'Nanoparticle Vaccines Against Infectious Diseases' states: *"In the last several years, the use of nanoparticle-based vaccines has received a great attention to improve vaccine efficacy, immunization strategies, and targeted delivery to achieve desired immune responses at the cellular level ... Nanocarriers composed of lipids, proteins, metals or polymers have already been used ... This review article focuses on the applications of nanocarrier-based vaccine formulations and the strategies used for the functionalization of nanoparticles to accomplish efficient delivery of vaccines in order to induce desired host immunity against infectious diseases."*

Lipid nanoparticles are being used currently in the Covid injections, such as the Pfizer and Moderna ones. These have a high-surface area and are self-assembling and can create a kind of 'scaffolding' within your body. A Scientific American article[126] states: *"With all due respect to nature, synthetic biologists believe they can do better. Using computers, they are designing new, self-assembling protein nanoparticles studded with viral proteins, called antigens: these porcupine-like particles would be the guts*

---

[125] English, Trevor. 'Nanobots Will Be Flowing Through Your Body by 2030'. *Interesting Engineering*, 20 Nov. 2020, https://interestingengineering.com/nanobots-will-be-flowing-through-your-body-by-2030.

[126] Begley, Sharon. 'Synthetic Biologists Think They Can Develop a Better Coronavirus Vaccine Than Nature Could'. *Scientific American*, 9 Mar. 2020, https://www.scientificamerican.com/article/synthetic-biologists-think-they-can-develop-a-better-coronavirus-vaccine-than-nature-could/. Accessed 4 May 2021.

of a vaccine. If tests in lab animals of the first such nanoparticle vaccine are any indication, it should be more potent than either old-fashioned viral vaccines like those for influenza or the viral antigens on their own (without the nanoparticle) ... Its shape and composition must be such that the protein's building blocks not only spontaneously self-assemble and stick together but also turn into something that can display the viral antigens in a way the immune system will strongly respond to."

Many, many doctors, including Carrie Madej have expressed major concerns with this.[127] As soon as atheistic scientists believe that they 'can do better than nature' – better than God in actuality, we should be very worried. It's been widely documented that scientists are now able and are producing millions of nanorobots that can fit inside a hypodermic needle. A Nature medical journal, entitled 'Electronically integrated, mass-manufactured, microscopic robots'[128] gives details on this, as well as a video showing microscopic robots drawn into a syringe (see Video 7). The Gates Foundation and The Defense Advanced Research Projects Agency (DARPA) have partnered with the company Profusa to push forward the hydrogel technology used to deliver the nano-biosensor chips. A Defense One article[129] states: *"The sensor has two parts. One is a 3mm string of hydrogel, a material whose network of polymer chains is used in some contact lenses and other implants. Inserted under the skin with a syringe, the string includes a specially engineered molecule that sends a fluorescent signal outside of the body when the body begins to fight an infection. The other part is an electronic component attached to the skin. It sends light through the skin, detects the fluorescent signal and generates another signal that the wearer can send to a doctor, website, etc. It's like a*

---

[127] Madej, Dr Carrie. 'Transhumanism, Vaccines, Hydrogel, Secret Gov Programs, Nanotech & DNA'. *BitChute*, https://www.bitchute.com/video/fESnu1j68Jp3/. Accessed 4 May 2021.

[128] Miskin, Marc Z., et al. 'Electronically Integrated, Mass-Manufactured, Microscopic Robots'. *Nature*, vol. 584, no. 7822, Aug. 2020, pp. 557–61. *www.nature.com*, doi:10.1038/s41586-020-2626-9.

[129] Tucker, Patrick. 'A Military-Funded Biosensor Could Be the Future of Pandemic Detection'. *Defense One*, 3 Mar. 2020. https://www.defenseone.com/technology/2020/03/military-funded-biosensor-could-be-future-pandemic-detection/163497/. Accessed 4 May 2021.

blood lab on the skin that can pick up the body's response to illness before the presence of other symptoms, like coughing."

A 2016 Profusa press release, 'Profusa, Inc. Awarded $7.5M DARPA Grant to Develop Tissue-integrated Biosensors for Continuous Monitoring of Multiple Body Chemistries',[130] states the following: *"Profusa's vision is to replace a point-in-time chemistry panel that measures multiple biomarkers, such as oxygen, glucose, lactate, urea, and ions with a biosensor that provides a continuous stream of wireless data. Each biosensor is comprised of a bioengineered* **'smart hydrogel' (similar to contact lens material) forming a porous, tissue-integrating scaffold that induces capillary and cellular in-growth from surrounding tissue. A unique property of the smart gel is its ability to luminesce upon exposure to light** *in proportion to the concentration of a chemical such as oxygen, glucose or other biomarker ... Long-lasting, implantable biosensors that provide continuous measurement of multiple body chemistries will enable monitoring of a soldier's metabolic and dehydration status, ion panels, blood gases, and other key physiological biomarkers,"* said Natalie Wisniewski, Ph.D., the principal investigator leading the grant work and Profusa's co-founder and chief technology officer. *"Our ongoing program with DARPA builds on Profusa's tissue-integrating sensor that overcomes the foreign body response and serves as a technology platform for the detection of multiple analytes."*

This image is taken from on official Profusa presentation, 'Implantable Biosensor for Continuous Long-Term Monitoring of Body Chemistry':[131]

---

[130] 'Profusa, Inc. Awarded $7.5M DARPA Grant to Develop Tissue-Integrated Biosensors for Continuous Monitoring of Multiple Body Chemistries.' 12 July 2016, https://www.prnewswire.com/news-releases/profusa-inc-awarded-75m-darpa-grant-to-develop-tissue-integrated-biosensors-for-continuous-monitoring-of-multiple-body-chemistries-300297050.html. Accessed 4 May 2021.

[131] 'Implantable Biosensor for Continuous Long-Term Monitoring of Body Chemistry', 2016 https://www.swissre.com/dam/jcr:f8e57e3a-3913-4baf-a824-8f855163a8c6/Presentation_Frederic_Gaume.pdf

MEET THE PROFUSA SENSOR – SOLVES AN UNSOLVABLE BARRIER FOR MORE THAN 5 DECADES

- Micro hydrogel sensor – 250 microns diameter; 3 mm length
- Embedded fluorescence sensing chemistry
- Hypodermic needle placement in the subcutaneous space
- Non-invasive optical signal collection
- Clinical-grade data
- Demonstrated >24 month longevity in humans
- Multi-analyte capable

profusa

Nanotechnology News released an article in December 2020, 'DARPA funded implantable biochip can potentially be used to deploy Moderna's mRNA vaccine',[132] which stated: *"In a bid to try to battle the ongoing Wuhan coronavirus (Covid-19) pandemic, the Defense Advanced Research Projects Agency (DARPA) is funding the development of **an implantable biochip** that could be deployed as soon as next year. The chip is said to be able to deploy an **experimental new vaccine**, developed jointly by Moderna and U.S government, that could **change human DNA**. Profusa's biochip is made using a technology called 'hydrogels' that were a product of the 'In Vivo Nanoplatforms' (IVN) program that DARPA's Biological Technologies Office (BTO) launched in 2014 to develop implantable nanotechnologies. These hydrogels are soft, flexible*

---

[132] Walker, Franz. 'DARPA Funded Implantable Biochip Can Potentially Be Used to Deploy Moderna's MRNA Vaccine'. *Nanotechnology News*, 12 Oct. 2020, https://www.nanotechnology.news/2020-10-12-darpa-funded-implantable-biochip-deploy-moderna-vaccine.html. Accessed 4 May 2021.

nanomachines that are injected beneath the skin to perform monitoring. This hydrogel includes a specially engineered molecule that sends a fluorescent signal outside the body when it begins to fight infection. This signal can then be detected by a sensor attached to the skin that can then be sent to an app or even to a doctor's website."

New Medical Life Sciences claimed in April 2021 that 'Novel hydrogel-based vaccine formulation shows high efficacy against SARS-CoV-2'.[133] Despite this clear talk and obvious rollout of the hydrogel biosensor in Covid vaccines, mainstream news media and official government websites, have released campaigns to claim that this is 'fake news'. An Australian Government Department of Health information[134] page states: *"Can COVID-19 vaccines connect me to the internet? COVID-19 vaccines do not – and cannot – connect you to the internet. Some of the mRNA vaccines being developed include the use of a material called a hydrogel, which might help disperse the vaccine slowly into our cells."*

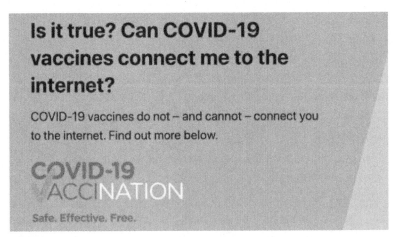

---

[133] Thomas, Dr Liji. 'Novel Hydrogel-Based Vaccine Formulation Shows High Efficacy against SARS-CoV-2'. *News-Medical.Net*, 6 Apr. 2021, https://www.news-medical.net/news/20210406/Novel-hydrogel-based-vaccine-formulation-shows-high-efficacy-against-SARS-CoV-2.aspx.

[134] 'Can Covid Connect Me to the Internet?' *Australian Government Department of Health*. https://www.health.gov.au/initiatives-and-programs/covid-19-vaccines/is-it-true/is-it-true-can-covid-19-vaccines-connect-me-to-the-internet. Accessed 4 May 2021.

This is in direct conflict with Profusa's official documentation[135] [136]on how the biosensor works and connects to a Cloud Database and overall Data Ecosystem. This is a clear example of the conflicting information, propaganda and outright lies that we're being fed around this pseudo-vaccine.

GREAT BIG WORLD - THE DATA ECOSYSTEM

Real-time Biochemistry	Data Aggregation	Patient Engagement	Patient Behavior Modification
Sensor luminescence signal	Patient: • Biovotion • geolocation; • other physiologic data (HR, HRV)	Patient Smartphone UI	Patient Action
Skin reader patch Data processing Wireless IN	Cloud DB • Data aggregation • Algorithms • Event detection • Message push	Physician/ Caregiver/ EMR/? Pad/ Smartphone	
Patient Smartphone Wireless IN Cellular or wireless OUT	External: • App searches • Climate alerts • iBeacons • Other		

An understatement would be to say that there are some serious issues to be raised with biofeedback chips and nanobots being inserted into our bodies via the Covid (or any) vaccine.

---

[135] *'Implantable Biosensor for Continuous Long-Term Monitoring of Body Chemistry'* 2016 https://www.swissre.com/dam/jcr:f8e57e3a-3913-4baf-a824-8f855163a8c6/Presentation_Frederic_Gaume.pdf.

[136] *Injectable Body Sensors Take Personal Chemistry to a Cell Phone Closer to Reality | Profusa, Inc.* https://profusa.com/injectable-body-sensors-take-personal-chemistry-to-a-cell-phone-closer-to-reality/. Accessed 2 June 2021.

People like Ray Kurzweil, futurist and Google's director of engineering, have talked extensively about 'modulation' of the brain remotely connected to machines, for the purpose of control – for our good, of course – billed as benevolent medical purposes, such as curing diabetes and brain tumours. Check his 2005 Ted Talk 'The Accelerating Power of Technology' on the use of nanobots.[137] These robots get around the 'pesky problem of our blood-brain barrier' (a vitally important thing God has put in place for a reason) to intrude in and affect our brain functioning. Again, we are told this all in the name of our good, expecting us to implicitly trust that what they're saying is truth, when indeed this may not be the case. Modulation involves control of basic thought impulses, sensations, emotions and bodily functions and reactions. Nano-sensors, implanted in the body and brain, would issue real time data-reports on body/brain functioning to 'Internet of Things'[138] ops centres. Feedback data, including instructions, would then be sent back to the nanosensors, which would impose those instructions on the brain and body. The mind boggles at what this could be used for – anything from 'harmonising' all brain thought (think one world, one brain) to the type of mind and body control manipulation that Nazi Germany and the Tavistock Institute[139] have heinously employed and at a scale that they could have only dreamt about.

This is being pushed right now, with the Covid vaccine. Make no mistake, the goal is to chip you.

---

[137] Kurzweil, Ray. 'The Accelerating Power of Technology'. *TED*, Feb. 2005, https://www.ted.com/talks/ray_kurzweil_the_accelerating_power_of_technology. Accessed 4 May 2021.

[138] Smith, Charles Hugh. '5G And Internet Of Things To Create Unprecedented Surveillance'. *Technocracy News & Trends,* 15 July 2019, https://www.technocracy.news/5G-and-internet-of-things-to-create-unprecedented-surveillance/.

[139] Estulin, Daniel. Tavistock Institute: Social Engineering the Masses. Trine Day, 2015.

Indeed, DARPA finally laid its cards on the table in April 2021 in its plans to chip humans under Covid. See this article in the Independent, 'Pentagon unveils microchip that senses Covid in the body'.[140] You can read an official paper from the National Center for Biotechnology Information in June 2020, entitled, 'Quantum dots as a promising agent to combat COVID-19',[141] as well as this from Massachusetts Institute of Technology (MIT), on the Gates-funded 'Quantum Dot tattoo' project:

""This technology could enable the rapid and anonymous detection of patient vaccination history to ensure that every child is vaccinated," says Kevin McHugh, a former MIT postdoc who is now an assistant professor of bioengineering at Rice University. The researchers showed that their new dye, which consists of nanocrystals called quantum dots, can remain for at least five years under the skin, where it emits near-infrared light that can be detected by a specially equipped smartphone."

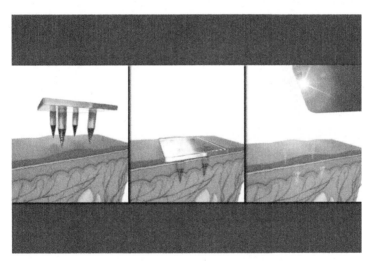

[140] Massie, Graeme. 'Pentagon Unveils Sensor That Detects Covid in the Body'. *The Independent*, 12 Apr. 2021, https://www.independent.co.uk/news/world/americas/pentagon-covid-sensor-blood-virus-b1830372.html.

[141] Manivannan, Selvambigai, and Kumar Ponnuchamy. 'Quantum Dots as a Promising Agent to Combat COVID-19'. *Applied Organometallic Chemistry*, June 2020. *PubMed Central*, doi:10.1002/aoc.5887.

The paper concludes with *"Conflicts of Interest: None declared."*

You can read further research study articles on quantum dot Covid vaccine technology here:

- Science Translational Medicine article from December 2019, called 'Biocompatible near-infrared quantum dots delivered to the skin by microneedle patches record vaccination'.[142]
- Study from September 2020, 'Quantum Dot-Conjugated SARS-CoV-2 Spike Pseudo-Virions Enable Tracking of Angiotensin Converting Enzyme 2 Binding and Endocytosis'.[143]
- This March 2021 paper, 'Support of intelligent emergent materials to combat COVID-19 pandemic'.[144]

Once you are 'chipped' and your body, blood and brain have been invaded by nano robots, this is done – permanently. You'd be connected with A.I. to the cloud and 5G – 24 hours a day, 365 days of the year. As a result, there can be constant surveillance of bodily and brain functions, giving intimate and complete biofeedback to any known or unknown source – with any known or unknown, benevolent or malevolent reasons to access it.

Furthermore, the ability of nanobots to communicate back to your body and brain anything they'd like to transmit, would bring grave ramifications for our privacy, autonomy and freedom of thought, body composition, speech and actions. This technology can gather data like blood

---

[142] McHugh, Kevin J., et al. 'Biocompatible Near-Infrared Quantum Dots Delivered to the Skin by Microneedle Patches Record Vaccination'. *Science Translational Medicine*, vol. 11, no. 523, Dec. 2019. *stm.sciencemag.org*, doi:10.1126/scitranslmed.aay7162.

[143] Gorshkov, Kirill, et al. 'Quantum-Conjugated SARS-CoV-2 Spike Pseudo-Virions Tracking of Angiotensin Converting Enzyme 2 Binding and Endocytosis'. *ACS Nano*, vol. 14, no. 9, Sept. 2020, pp. 12234–47. *PubMed Central*, doi:10.1021/acsnano.0c05975.

[144] Yalcin, Huseyin C. and Ajeet Kaushik. 'Support of Intelligent Emergent Materials to Combat COVID-19 Pandemic'. *Emergent Materials*, vol. 4, no. 1, Feb. 2021, pp. 1–2. *Springer Link*, doi:10.1007/s42247-021-00189-3.

sugar, hormone levels, heart rate, oxygen levels, but also women's menstrual cycle and fertility levels, nutrient profile, emotions, brain waves and thoughts. Is it just me who finds this exceedingly scary? Especially when the questions of who is in control of this data and wielding the power, what are they using it for and who's protecting it are left completely unanswered. This is conspicuous by its absence in the vaccine propaganda frenzy and most people, caught up in the hype, have not stopped to consider or question this.

Along with the hydrogel, nanotechnology and the vaccine itself, there is a **'Luciferase'** enzyme (yep, for real), which has bioluminescent qualities – a light source. They want to make sure that a successful chip insertion has taken place, so this is a digital code/tattoo that would confirm your vaccination; they're not taking chances with a mere certificate, or your say so. This also gives you an ID, a unique number, a brand, a barcode – making you a patented product commodity. (As an aside, many people have mused on 'COVID' … COVert ID, Certificate Of Vaccination ID?) When you do a U.S. Patent search using the term 'Moderna and Luciferase' you come up with 62 Patents.[145]

One thing that we know is that the elites want to collect our biofeedback data from biofeedback sensors and link it to cryptocurrency, shown in the patent filed by Mr Philanthropist, Bill Gates: **Patent WO/2020/060606**[146] **(did you catch the Biblically interesting number?)**, was registered on 26 March 2020. The title of the patent is 'Cryptocurrency system using body activity data'. So, what is this invention that the people at Microsoft decided to patent? The abstract of the patent application online states:

---

[145] *USPTO Patent Full-Text and Image Database*, http://patft.uspto.gov/netacgi/nph-Parser?Sect1=PTO2&Sect2=HITOFF&p=1&u=%2Fnetahtml%2FPTO%2Fsearch-bool.html&r=0&f=S&l=50&TERM1=luciferase&FIELD1=&col=AND&TERM2=moderna&FIELD2=&d=PTXT. Accessed 4 May 2021

[146] Abramson, Dustin, et al. 'Cryptocurrency System Using Body Activity Data'. https://patentscope.wipo.int/search/en/detail.jsf;jsessionid=D828876275820FF07DFFC98B7588C118.wapp2nB?docId=WO2020060606&tab=PCTDESCRIPTION. Accessed 4 May 2021.

"Human body activity associated with a task provided to a user may be used in a mining process of a cryptocurrency system. A server may provide a task to a device of a user which is communicatively coupled to the server. A sensor communicatively coupled to or comprised in the device of the user may sense body activity of the user. Body activity data may be generated based on the sensed body activity of the user. The cryptocurrency system communicatively coupled to the device of the user may verify if the body activity data satisfies one or more conditions set by the cryptocurrency system, and award cryptocurrency to the user whose body activity data is verified."

2. Transfection and Gene Editing

Here's Thermofisher Scientific's definition of Transfection:[147] *"Transfection is the process of artificially introducing nucleic acids (DNA or RNA) into cells, utilizing means other than viral infection. Such introductions of foreign nucleic acid using various chemical, biological, or physical methods can result in a change of the properties of the cell, allowing the study of gene function and protein expression in the context of the cell."*

The Moderna and other vaccines synthesize messenger RNA, or mRNA – which is an instruction manual in every living cell for creating protein – to prompt the human body to make its own medicine. So instead of injecting a piece of virus into a person to stimulate the immune system, the synthesized genes would be shot into the body whereby the genes are edited, deleted, added, to re-engineer human DNA to resist the disease.

---

[147] 'Introduction to Transfection – US'. *ThermoFisher Scientific*, https://www.thermofisher.com/us/en/home/references/gibco-cell-culture-basics/transfection-basics/introduction-to-transfection.html. Accessed 4 May 2021.

In 2015, The New York Times reported[148] on the developing vaccine technology called 'immunoprophylaxis by gene transfer' in 2015. It reported that animal tests on the synthetic DNA vaccine *"are **essentially re-engineering** the animals to resist disease."*

You can read more about what Moderna term their 'Software of Life' mRNA technology platform here.[149] Dr Tal Zaks, Chief Medical Officer at Moderna, presented a TED talk in 2017 called, 'Rewriting the Genetic Code: A Cancer Cure In the Making'.[150] He talks about the use of gene-editing vaccines tailored to each patient's immune system. He boldly asserts (threatens): *"I'm here today to tell you that we're actually hacking the software of life"*. Call me priggish but I'd rather stick with God's 'software of life', thank you.

Dr Andrew Kaufman[151] is a highly qualified Medical Doctor and university Medical and Forensics Director, as well as Assistant Clinical Professor of Psychiatry. He has made detailed claims that the Covid vaccine alters your DNA to genetically modify you. This is done by 'electroporation' – a delivery method used to introduce macromolecules such as proteins into cells,[152] either in vivo or in vitro, via the application of brief electric pulses which induce momentary and reversible permeabilization of the cell membrane, through which a foreign material such as DNA may pass. Reuters 'fact checked' his claims and declared it to be false but Dr

---

[148] Zimmer, Carl. 'Protection Without a Vaccine'. *The New York Times*, 9 Mar. 2015, https://www.nytimes.com/2015/03/10/health/protection-without-a-vaccine.html.

[149] 'MRNA Platform: Drug Discovery & Development – Moderna'. https://www.modernatx.com/mrna-technology/mrna-platform-enabling-drug-discovery-development. Accessed 4 May 2021.

[150] Zaks, Tal. *The Disease-Eradicating Potential of Gene Editing. TED*, Nov. 2017, https://www.ted.com/talks/tal_zaks_the_disease_eradicating_potential_of_gene_editing. Accessed 4 May 2021.

[151] 'Bio & Credentials - Dr Andrew Kaufman, M.D. '. https://andrewkaufmanmd.com/bio-credentials/. Accessed 4 May 2021.

[152] Ojiambo, Marie. 'Electroporation as a Drug Delivery System for COVID-19 Vaccines'. *Charles River Laboratories*, 13 Jan. 2021, https://www.criver.com/eureka/electroporation-drug-delivery-system-covid-19-vaccines. Accessed 4 May 2021.

Kaufman responded to refute this[153] – stating that they are outright lying and that the vaccines do indeed alter DNA. Dr Evenhouse,[154] the 'Disruptive Physician' has concurred: *"Any vaccine that needs to be shipped and stored at -80 degrees isn't a vaccine. It's a transfection agent, kept alive so it can infect your cells and transfer genetic material. Don't let them fool you. This is genetic manipulation of humans on a massive scale. Shut it down."*

Transfection or electroporation could in effect create genetically modified humans, like a Monsanto soy bean. GMO foodstuffs are banned in quite a few countries in the world because of their known dangers, and yet, we are proposing that we genetically engineer humans and think it's perfectly safe and good? There are no long-term studies on doing this and it's possible that this artificial genetic engineering could replicate and become a permanent part of our genome. This is a synthetic piece of RNA and this can be patented and patents have owners, just like the hydrogel and Luciferase enzyme. Suddenly our bodies are 'owned' by a vaccine company or DARPA who are patenting these things?

The gene-editing possibilities are further corroborated by the use of CRISPR technology. New Scientist states:[155] *"CRISPR is a technology that can be used to edit genes and, as such, will likely change the world. The essence of CRISPR is simple: it's a way of finding a specific bit of DNA inside a cell. After that, the next step in CRISPR gene editing is usually to alter that piece of DNA. However, CRISPR has also been adapted to do other things too, such as turning genes on or off without altering their sequence. There were ways to **edit the genomes** of some plants and animals before the CRISPR method was unveiled in 2012 but*

---

[153] Skouras, Spiro. 'Dr Andrew Kaufman Responds To Reuters Fact Check on COVID-19 Vaccine Genetically Modifying Humans'. *Natural Health News*, 21 June 2020, https://www.naturalblaze.com/2020/06/dr-andrew-kaufman-responds-to-reuters-fact-check-on-covid-19-vaccine-genetically-modifying-humans.html.

[154] '*DOC EVENHOUSE*, https://www.docevenhouse.com/. Accessed 4 May 2021.

[155] 'What Is CRISPR?' *New Scientist*, https://www.newscientist.com/definition/what-is-crispr/. Accessed 4 May 2021.

it took years and cost hundreds of thousands of dollars. CRISPR has made it cheap and easy."

Brink News Article, 'Could CRISPR Create a COVID-19 Vaccine?'[156] states: *"Policy has already begun to respond to the potential implications of **gene editing as part of a healthcare system's pandemic response mechanism**. In a bold step, suggesting a softening of European Union regulations, the European Parliament and Council of the European Union adopted a regulation introducing a temporary derogation to the GMO regulation for clinical trials on vaccines for COVID-19[157] utilizing gene editing technologies."* This means that GMO regulations have been relaxed in order to accommodate CRISPR use in clinical trials. The Ted Talk by CRISPR's inventor Jenifer Doudna, 'How CRISPR lets us edit our DNA'[158] shows how gene editing has been in place since 2015.

Craig Venter is founder of CRISPR company, 'Synthetic Genomics'. He is also the man behind the 'human genome project' and is known for leading the first draft sequence of the human genome and assembled the first team to transfect a cell with a synthetic chromosome. He has partnered with the Gates Foundation to push dubious gene drive projects.[159] Publicly, he has said that we need to 'proceed with caution' in editing human genes, but he is more than comfortable with it as a concept and his book,

---

[156] Eatwell, Emma and Victor Maertens. 'Could CRISPR Create a COVID-19 Vaccine?' *BRINK – News and Insights on Global Risk*, 6 Sept. 2020 https://www.brinknews.com/crispr-and-the-fight-against-covid-19/. Accessed 4 May 2021.

[157] 'Regulation (EU) 2020/1043 on the conduct of clinical trials with and supply of medicinal products for human use containing or consisting of genetically modified organisms intended to treat or prevent coronavirus disease'. *Office Journal of the European Union,* 15 July 2020, https://eur-lex.europa.eu/legal-content/EN/TXT/PDF/?uri=CELEX:32020R1043&from=EN

[158] 'How CRISPR Lets Us Edit Our DNA | Jennifer Doudna'. *YouTube,* https://www.youtube.com/watch?v=TdBAHexVYzc. Accessed 4 May 2021.

[159] Latham, Dr Jonathan. 'Gates Foundation Hired PR Firm to Manipulate UN Over Gene Drives'. *Independent Science News | Food, Health and Agriculture Bioscience News*, 4 Dec. 2017, https://www.independentsciencenews.org/news/gates-foundation-hired-pr-firm-to-manipulate-un-over-gene-drives/.

'Life at the Speed of Light'[160] seems to indicate more than a little excitement for it. Could we be creating human versions of the cloned 'Dolly the Sheep' (who died prematurely at only six years old and disease-ridden)? Here's what the blurb from the book says: *"Venter presents a fascinating and authoritative study of this emerging field from the inside – detailing its origins, current challenges and controversies, and projected effects on our lives.* **This scientific frontier provides an opportunity to ponder anew the age-old question 'What is life?' and examine what we really mean by 'playing God'.** *Life at the Speed of Light is a landmark work, written by a visionary at the dawn of a new era of biological engineering."* Some more quotes from him:

"A doctor can save maybe a few hundred lives in a lifetime. A researcher can save the whole world."

"We are going from reading our genetic code to the ability to write it. That gives us the hypothetical ability to do things never contemplated before."

"Now that we can read and write the genetic code, put it in digital form and translate it back into synthesized life, it will be possible to speed up biological evolution to the pace of social evolution."

"Accuracy in the genetic field will be essential. Errors in testing could be disastrous."

An article published in Proceedings of the National Academy of Sciences of USA (PNAS), titled 'Vaccinology in the post–COVID-19 era',[161] states: *"Anticipated by the work of Craig Venter [in his book, 'Life at the Speed of Light'], teleportation of DNA code through great distances was not Star Trek's fiction anymore. For the first time, a fully synthetic viral*

---

[160] Venter, J. Craig. Life at the Speed of Light: From the Double Helix to the Dawn of Digital Life. Viking, 2013.

[161] Rappuoli, Rino, et al. 'Vaccinology in the Post–COVID-19 Era'. *Proceedings of the National Academy of Sciences*, vol. 118, no. 3, Jan. 2021. *www.pnas.org*, doi:10.1073/pnas.2020368118.

vaccine was developed by in vitro cell-free synthesis of genes using the genomic sequence that had been teleported across the planet at the speed of light via the Internet. The process of teleporting the genomic sequence has the ambition to change forever the old – and dangerous – way we used to make viral vaccines by shipping viruses across the world. We use the term 'Internet-based vaccines' to describe this new way of making vaccines using the Internet to share the genomic information, without the need to transport, access, and grow the real virus."

It is clear that this field of 'science' is keen to play God and that Covid 19 has provided the seemingly plausible reason to usher it in at a rapid rate. Further, 3D printing of human and other organic DNA has been underway for years.[162] In 2015, Cambrian Genomics' founder, Austen Heinz stated, *"To think that we can't make organisms that aren't more efficient than existing ones – I don't think is correct because nature doesn't have DNA laser printers, and we do."* So, we can see the wider agenda at play here and its growing momentum. We'll explore more on this and the crazy plans that are underway with human cloning and even resurrection, in Chapter 10.

The vaccine companies and governments are telling us that these novel pseudo-vaccines will be 'safe and effective' and cannot affect our DNA but it is simply not true. Dr Carrie Madej has also stated emphatically that they will affect our DNA and genome and that they are dangerous. Further, we know that DARPA and the Bill and Melinda Gates Foundation, as we've looked at already, are heavily invested in eugenics and 'gene extinction technology' – where you can literally exterminate an entire species - as they're doing right now with mosquitos.[163] Are we next under this Covid injection frenzy?

---

[162] '3-D Printing DNA: Hacking Life's Code and Creating New Organisms'. *YouTube,* https://www.youtube.com/watch?v=PGyNyQ5IDUM. Accessed 4 May 2021.

[163] Pakpour, Nazzy, et al. 'Transfection and Mutagenesis of Target Genes in Mosquito Cells by Locked Nucleic Acid-Modified Oligonucleotides'. *Journal of Visualized Experiments : JoVE*, no. 46, Dec. 2010. *PubMed Central*, doi:10.3791/2355.

3. Adjuvants

Adjuvants are substances added to vaccines to supposedly enhance the immunogenicity of highly purified antigens that have insufficient immunostimulatory capabilities, and have been used in human vaccines for more almost a century. One of the most common adjuvants is Aluminium. A Current Medicinal Chemistry article[164] states that: *"Research clearly shows that aluminium adjuvants have a potential to induce serious immunological disorders in humans. In particular, aluminium in adjuvant form carries a risk for autoimmunity, long-term brain inflammation and associated neurological complications and may thus have profound and widespread adverse health consequences."*

Other adjuvants used include Ethyl Mercury (yes, a toxic mercury substance), Formaldehyde and Monosodium Glutamate (MSG) – all of which have been proven to be toxic and can cause or contribute to long-term health issues. The use of Polyethylene Glycol (PEG) in Covid vaccines also poses a risk. The Children's Health Defense[165] state that: *"mRNA vaccines undergoing Covid-19 clinical trials, including the Moderna vaccine, rely on a nanoparticle-based 'carrier system' containing a synthetic chemical called polyethylene glycol (PEG). The use of PEG in drugs and vaccines is increasingly controversial due to the well-documented incidence of adverse PEG-related immune reactions, including life-threatening anaphylaxis. Roughly seven in ten Americans may already be sensitized to PEG, which may result in reduced efficacy of the vaccine and an increase in adverse side effects."*

---

[164] Tomljenovic, L., and C. A. Shaw. 'Aluminum Vaccine Adjuvants: Are They Safe?' *Current Medicinal Chemistry*, vol. 18, no. 17, 2011, pp. 2630–37. *PubMed*, doi:10.2174/092986711795933740.

[165] 'Components of MRNA Technology "Could Lead to Significant Adverse Events in One or More of Our Clinical Trials," Says Moderna • Children's Health Defense'. *Children's Health Defense*, 6 Aug. 2020, https://childrenshealthdefense.org/news/components-of-mrna-technology-could-lead-to-significant-adverse-events-in-one-or-more-of-our-clinical-trials-says-moderna/.

4. Aborted Foetuses

Many of the leading Covid vaccine candidates are being developed using foetal cell lines (human 'diploid' cells) that were originally derived from the tissues of aborted babies in the 1970s and 80s. There is a clear ethical and spiritual problem with this for Christians. Back in June 2020, The Population Research Institute[166] stated that: *"Several COVID-19 vaccine frontrunners, including those being developed by Moderna, Oxford University/AstraZeneca, CanSino Biologics/Beijing Institute of Biotechnology, and Inovio Pharmaceuticals, are using a human fetal kidney cell line called HEK-293 to develop their trial vaccines. HEK-293 was originally derived from kidney tissue taken from a baby girl who was aborted in the Netherlands in 1972 and later developed into a cell line in a lab in 1973. Additionally, Janssen, the pharmaceutical division of consumer product giant Johnson & Johnson, is using the human fetal cell line PER.C6 to develop its vaccine. The PER.C6 fetal cell line was derived from retinal tissue taken from an 18-week-old baby boy who was aborted in the Netherlands in 1985 and later converted into a fetal cell line in 1995."*

Some misguided Christians think that the Covid pseudo-vaccine is a 'gift from God'. One has to ask, how likely is our God to provide a 'solution out of this pandemic' that involves using the cells of aborted babies? Especially as we can be sure He *judges* the evil practice of mass murder, no matter how culturally acceptable it is. Further, there's the fact that there really is no 'pandemic', only a carefully-engineered tranche of propaganda around an illness that has a death rate of less than 0.05%.

---

[166] Abbamonte, Jonathan. 'Which COVID-19 Vaccines Are Being Developed with Aborted Babies?' *PRI (Population Research Institute)*, 4 June 2020, https://www.pop.org/which-covid-19-vaccines-are-being-developed-with-fetal-cell-lines-derived-from-aborted-babies/.

5. The Virus Itself – Paradoxical Immune Response

You may know that coronaviruses have been around for decades in one form or another. Vaccine development has proven very difficult over the past 20 years, as the vaccines create very robust antibody response, which initially looks very promising. However, **when the patient encounters the actual wild virus, they become severely ill and often die** – this is a reaction known as 'paradoxical immune response' or 'paradoxical immune enhancement'. A 'cytokine storm' can occur, where the innate immune system causes an uncontrolled and excessive release of pro-inflammatory signalling molecules called cytokines. Coronavirus vaccines have therefore never passed animal trial stage, since many of the animals died. As a result, this caution was given in the study, 'Immunization with SARS coronavirus vaccines leads to pulmonary immunopathology on challenge with the SARS virus':[167] *"Conclusions: These SARS-CoV vaccines all induced antibody and protection against infection with SARS-CoV. However, challenge of mice given any of the vaccines led to occurrence of Th2-type immunopathology suggesting hypersensitivity to SARS-CoV components was induced. Caution in proceeding to application of a SARS-CoV vaccine in humans is indicated."*

There have been many instances of this and, according to Professor Robert F. Kennedy Jr's investigations, the same thing happened in 2014 with the dengue vaccine DENVax, which Anthony Fauci owns the patent on: *"They knew from the clinical trials that there was a problem with paradoxical immune response, but they gave it to several hundred thousand Filipino kids anyway. They got a great immune response from the vaccine, but those exposed to wild dengue got horribly sick and 600 of*

---

[167] Tseng, Chien-Te, et al. 'Immunization with SARS Coronavirus Vaccines Leads to Pulmonary Immunopathology on Challenge with the SARS Virus'. *PLOS ONE*, vol. 7, no. 4, Apr. 2012, p. e35421. *PLoS Journals*, doi:10.1371/journal.pone.0035421.

the children died. Today, the Philippine government is criminally prosecuting a bunch of the people locally who were involved in that decision."

Also, each time you transfer the virus to another animal tissue in testing, mutations occur. There's also evidence showing these animal cell lines are contaminated with coronaviruses and retroviruses, which end up contaminating the vaccines grown in them. You can read more here on the well-known hazards of coronavirus vaccines.[168]

These vaccines essentially create a phenomenon called 'antibody-dependent enhancement' (ADE) or an increased dependence on antibodies that will allow a piece of messenger mRNA to replicate indefinitely creating chunks of protein ('protein spike') inside the body. In response, it will produce antibodies, which is why Bill Gates said that our body will become an 'automatic producer of endogenous vaccines' in response to these proteins. These concerns are real. As recently as 2016, Dengavxia, intended to protect children from the dengue virus, increased hospitalisations for children who received the vaccine. A Nature Microbiology article, 'Antibody-dependent enhancement and SARS-CoV-2 vaccines and therapies'[169] states: *"One potential hurdle for antibody-based vaccines and therapeutics is the risk of exacerbating COVID-19 severity via antibody-dependent enhancement (ADE). ADE can increase the severity of multiple viral infections, including other respiratory viruses such as respiratory syncytial virus (RSV) and measles."*

The novel and experimental Covid gene tool 'vaccines' are still in clinical trial stage and have never progressed 'safely and effectively' out of trial in any previous study, yet it's been rolled out to millions upon millions of people worldwide. This concerns me, does it you?

---

[168] Mercola, Dr Joseph. 'The Well-Known Hazards of Coronavirus Vaccines'. *Mercola*, http://articles.mercola.com/sites/articles/archive/2020/05/31/is-there-a-vaccine-for-coronavirus.aspx. Accessed 4 May 2021.

[169] Lee, Wen Shi, et al. 'Antibody-Dependent Enhancement and SARS-CoV-2 Vaccines and Therapies'. *Nature Microbiology*, vol. 5, no. 10, Oct. 2020, pp. 1185–91. *www.nature.com*, doi:10.1038/s41564-020-00789-5.

6. No Indemnity or Recourse for Damages Done By Vaccines

Rigorous vaccine testing procedures that were introduced on the back of the horrific Thalidomide disaster are now being recklessly thrown aside to roll out a Covid vaccine under major amendments to medical laws across the world. Further, a major part of these amendments is a waive of all liability and indemnity for producers and administrators of any kind of medical product to do with countering Covid – vaccine included. So, if you have an adverse reaction, or worse, from having an experimental mRNA pseudo-vaccine, you or any of your family members cannot sue. This alone should set off alarm bells!

On 17th March 2020, the US Congress issued a Declaration pursuant to section 319F-3 of the Public Readiness and Emergency Preparedness Act to provide liability immunity for activities related to medical counter-measures against COVID-19.[170] This liability immunity was extended further on April 15th 2020. In the UK, the government amended The Human Medicine Regulations 2012[171] to do the following:

- Authorise **temporary supply of an unlicensed product**
- Waive civil liability and immunity
- Expand the workforce eligible to administer vaccinations (including by non-medically trained people)
- Promote vaccines heavily
- Make provisions for wholesale dealing of vaccines

---

[170] Azar II, Alex M. (Health and Human Services Department). 'Declaration Under the Public Readiness and Emergency Preparedness Act for Medical Countermeasures Against COVID-19'. *Federal Register*, 17 Mar. 2020, https://www.federalregister.gov/documents/2020/03/17/2020-05484/declaration-under-the-public-readiness-and-emergency-preparedness-act-for-medical-countermeasures.

[171] 'The Human Medicines Regulations 2012'. *Legislation.gov.uk,* https://www.legislation.gov.uk/uksi/2012/1916/contents/made. Accessed 4 May 2021.

UK Health Secretary Matt Hancock said, parroting Gates' and Trump's threats: *"A safe and effective vaccine is our best hope of defeating coronavirus and returning to life as normal."*

Dr Mike Yeadon, who writes for Lockdown Sceptics[172] is the former CSO and VP, Allergy and Respiratory Research Head with Pfizer Global R&D and co-Founder of Ziarco Pharma Ltd and he holds a wildly different point of view. Regarding the UK Health Regulations proposed amendments, he wrote a letter to the Health Secretary in September 2020:

"Dear Mr Hancock,

I have a degree in Biochemistry and Toxicology and a research-based PhD in pharmacology. I have spent 32 years working in pharmaceutical R&D, mostly in new medicines for disorders of lung and skin. I was a VP at Pfizer and CEO of a biotech I founded (Ziarco – acquired by Novartis). I am knowledgeable about new medicine R&D. I have read the consultation document. I have rarely been as shocked and upset.

All vaccines against the SARS-Cov-2 virus are by definition novel. No candidate vaccine has been in development for more than a few months. If any such vaccine is approved for use under any circumstances that are not EXPLICITLY experimental, I believe that recipients are being misled to a criminal extent. This is because there are precisely zero human volunteers for whom there could possibly be more than a few months' past-dose safety information.

My concern does not arise because I have negative views about vaccines (I don't). Instead, it's the very principle that politicians seem ready to

---

[172] Yeadon, Dr Michael. 'Lies, Damned Lies and Health Statistics – the Deadly Danger of False Positives'. *Lockdown Sceptics*, 20 Sept. 2020. https://lockdownsceptics.org/lies-damned-lies-and-health-statistics-the-deadly-danger-of-false-positives/. Accessed 4 May 2021.

waive that new medical interventions – at this incomplete state of development – (which) should not be made available to subjects on anything other than an explicitly experimental basis. That's my concern.

And the reason for that concern is that it is not known what the safety profile will be, six months or a year, or longer after dosing. You have literally no data on this and neither does anyone else. It isn't that I'm saying that unacceptable adverse effects will emerge after longer intervals after dosing. No: it is that you have no idea what will happen yet, despite this, you'll be creating the impression that you do.

Several of the vaccine candidates utilise novel technology which have not previously been used to create vaccines. There is therefore no long-term safety data which can be pointed to in support of the notion that it's reasonable to expedite development and to waive absent safety information on this occasion.

I am suspicious of the motives of those proposing expedited use in the wider human population. We now understand who is at particularly elevated risk of morbidity and mortality from acquiring this virus. Volunteers from these groups only should be provided detailed information about risk / benefit, including the sole point I make here. Only if informed consent is given should any EXPERIMENTAL vaccine be used.

I don't trust you. You've not be straightforward and behaved appallingly throughout this crisis. You're still doing it now, misleading about infection risk from young children. Why should I believe you in relation to experimental vaccines?

Dr Michael Yeadon"

Dr Yeadon has by no means been a lone medical voice with serious concerns and suspicions about the Covid vaccine, there are many, as we can see next. The Alliance for Natural Health and its Founder and Scientific

Director, Dr Robert Verkerk, has serious enough concerns about a vaccine that it has created a 10-Point Vaccine Transparency Manifesto,[173] which it's petitioned UK government with ...

The 10-point Vaccine Transparency Manifesto – Key Areas of Transparency Needed:

1. Full disclosure of raw data from studies and trials to allow independent analysis.
2. Full transparency in relation to safety and efficacy trials.
3. Full transparency over the vaccine platform(s) and technology used for commercial vaccines.
4. Conduct of comprehensive studies evaluating the independent risks from adjuvants (additives).
5. Full disclosure of vaccine composition in commercial formulations.
6. Full transparency of all adverse event data in all studies and post-marketing surveillance.
7. Clarification of eligibility and criteria for no-fault vaccine injury payments or compensation.
8. Clarification of nature and extent of government indemnity of manufacturers in the event of vaccine injury.
9. Public dissemination of extent of naturally-acquired (herd) immunity prior to vaccine roll-out and individual consent.
10. Involvement of elected representatives in due democratic process should mandatory vaccination be contemplated by authorities.

Moreover, consent forms given before experimental injection have minimal information, like this Covid-19 vaccination consent form from the NHS in the UK.[174] It gives this chipper little scant warning: *"Like all*

---

[173] 'The 10-Point Vaccine Transparency Approach'. *Alliance for Natural Health International*, 29 Apr. 2020, http://www.anhinternational.org/news/the-10-point-vaccine-transparency-approach/.

[174] 'NHS Covid Vaccine Consent Form'. *HealthPublications.gov.uk*, https://assets.publishing.service.gov.uk/government/uploads/system/uploads/attachment_data/file/963182/Easy_read_Covid-19_vaccination_consent_form_for_adults.pdf. Accessed 4 May 2021.

medicines, vaccines can cause side effects. Most of these are mild and short-term, and not everyone gets them." Someone told me that they received a more detailed leaflet about the Pfizer vaccine[175] *after* vaccination. We need to remember that Pharma companies have a long, dubious history of lying to the public and cutting corners in bringing their drugs and vaccines to market. Here are just some of the leading Covid experimental vaccine creators' recent criminal and civil legal settlements:

Pfizer paid out $2.3 billion in legal settlements in 2009:[176]

The criminal fine was $1.3 billion, and the additional $1 billion was for civil allegations under the False Claims Act. Pfizer falsely promoted Bextra, antipsychotic drug Geodon, antibiotic Zyvox, and antiepileptic Lyrica. The company was also accused of paying kickbacks related to these drugs and submitting false claims to government health care programs based on uses that weren't medically accepted. Bextra was pulled from the market in 2005 after it was deemed unsafe.

Johnson & Johnson paid out $2.2 billion in 2013:[177]

Criminal fines and forfeiture totalled $485 million, and civil settlements amounted to $1.72 billion. In the early 2000s, Risperdal was approved to treat schizophrenia. However, the company's sales representatives were promoting the drug to physicians as a treatment for elderly dementia patients for anxiety, agitation, depression, hostility, and confusion. There were also allegations that Risperdal was marketed for other unapproved

---

[175] 'Pfizer-Biontech Package leaflet: Information for the recipient COVID-19 mRNA Vaccine BNT162b2 concentrate for solution for injection.' GOV.UK, https://assets.publishing.service.gov.uk/government/uploads/system/uploads/attachment_data/file/967860/Temporary_Authorisation_Patient_Information_BNT162_7_0_UK_.pdf. Accessed 4 May 2021.

[176] 'Justice Department Announces Largest Health Care Fraud Settlement in Its History'. 2 Sept. 2009, *The United States of Department of Justice*, 2 Sept. 2009, https://www.justice.gov/opa/pr/justice-department-announces-largest-health-care-fraud-settlement-its-history.

[177] 'Johnson & Johnson to Pay More Than $2.2 Billion to Resolve Criminal and Civil Investigations'. *The United States of Department of Justice*, 4 Nov. 2013, https://www.justice.gov/opa/pr/johnson-johnson-pay-more-22-billion-resolve-criminal-and-civil-investigations.

uses, such as prescription to children and individuals with mental disabilities. Invega and Natrecor were also included in these lawsuits as having been illegally marketed for off-label and unapproved uses.

AstraZeneca paid out $520 million in 2010:[178]

Seroquel is an antipsychotic drug manufactured by AstraZeneca that was approved in 1997 by the FDA for treatment of psychotic disorders. In 2000, that approval was proposed to be narrowed to short-term treatment of schizophrenia only. In 2004, it was narrowed to short-term treatment of acute manic episodes associated with bipolar disorder. It was later approved for bipolar depression. However, during this time, the manufacturer was marketing the drug for additional uses like treatment of aggression, Alzheimer's, anger management, anxiety, attention deficit hyperactivity disorder, bipolar maintenance, dementia, depression, mood disorder, post-traumatic stress disorder, and sleeplessness – even though the FDA hadn't approved Seroquel for those uses. In addition, AstraZeneca paid kickbacks to doctors for authoring articles about the drug being used in ways that weren't approved.

Want some of my experimental health drink? I made it in a hurry, I have a criminal history of fraud, I wont tell you the ingredients & you can't sue me if anything goes wrong. If you have a problem with any of that you are an ANTI-DRINKER.

---

[178] 'Pharmaceutical Giant AstraZeneca to Pay $520 Million for Off-Label Drug Marketing'. *The United States of Department of Justice*, 27 Apr. 2010, https://www.justice.gov/opa/pr/pharmaceutical-giant-astrazeneca-pay-520-million-label-drug-marketing.

7. Adverse Reactions and Deaths

Since the rollout of the experimental injection at the end of 2020, there have been many adverse reactions and even deaths within the first few months. In the USA, these are reported to the Vaccine Adverse Event Reporting System (VAERS), managed by the CDC and FDA. In the UK it is via a 'Yellow Card' system – and there are similar reporting systems around the world. A VAERS report as of March 19, 2021 showed 2050 deaths and 44,606 injuries following Covid vaccines. In the following image, data taken from the National Vaccine Information Center's search engine of VAERS raw data, shows the following adverse event stats in early April 2021:[179]

From the 4/1/2021 release of VAERS data:

Found 56,869 cases where Vaccine is COVID19

Table		
↓	↑ ↓	
Event Outcome	Count	Percent
Death	2,342	4.12%
Permanent Disability	941	1.65%
Office Visit	8,743	15.37%
Emergency Room	29	0.05%
Emergency Doctor/Room	8,946	15.73%
Hospitalized	4,961	8.72%
Hospitalized, Prolonged	11	0.02%
Recovered	21,678	38.12%
Birth Defect	57	0.1%
Life Threatening	1,484	2.61%
Not Serious	20,950	36.84%
TOTAL	† 70,142	† 123.34%

† Because some cases have multiple vaccinations and symptoms, a single case can account for multiple entries in this table. This is the reason why the Total Count is greater than 56869 (the number of cases found), and the Total Percentage is greater than 100.

---

[179] Search Results from the VAERS Database, https://www.medalerts.org/vaersdb/find-field.php?TABLE=ON&GROUP1=CAT&EVENTS=ON&VAX=COVID19. Accessed 4 May 2021.

Here are some of the report write ups from deaths following a Covid vaccine,[180] taken from VAERS datasets:

"Resident in our long-term care facility who received first dose of Moderna COVID-19 Vaccine on 12/22/2020, only documented side effect was mild fatigue after receiving. She passed away on 12/27/2020 of natural causes per report. Has previously been in & out of hospice care, resided in nursing home for 9+ years, elderly with dementia. Due to proximity of vaccination, we felt we should report the death, even though it is not believed to be related." – VAERS ID: 914621

"Injection given on 12/28/20 - no adverse events and no issues yesterday; Death today, 12/30/20, approx.. 2am today (unknown if related - Administrator marked as natural causes)" – VAERS ID: 914895

"Death by massive heart attack. Pfizer-BioNTech COVID-19 Vaccine EUA" – VAERS ID: 914917

"Resident received vaccine in am and expired that afternoon." – VAERS ID: 915920

"At the time of vaccination, there was an outbreak of residents who had already tested positive for COVID 19 at the nursing home where patient was a resident. About a week later, patient tested positive for COVID 19. She had a number of chronic, underlying health conditions. The vaccine did not have enough time to prevent COVID 19. There is no evidence that the vaccination caused patient's death. It simply didn't have time to save her life." – VAERS ID: 917790

"Prior to the administration of the COVID 19 vaccine, the nursing home had an outbreak of COVID-19. Patient was vaccinated and about a week later she tested positive for COVID-19. She had underlying thyroid and

---

[180] Search Results from the VAERS Database, https://www.medalerts.org/vaersdb/find-field.php?EVENTS=on&PAGENO=1&PERPAGE=10&ESORT&REVERSESORT&VAX=%28COVID19%29&VAXTYPES=%28COVID-19%29&DIED=Yes. Accessed 4 May 2021.

diabetes disease. She died as a result of COVID-19 and her underlying health conditions and not as a result of the vaccine." – VAERS ID: 917793

"Found deceased in her home, unknown cause, 6 days after vaccine." – VAERS ID: 920815

"Complained Right arm/back hurt - took Tylenol 1-3-2021 Complained Right arm hurt, dizzy 1-4-2021 Felt better - did laundry, daughter found her deceased at 3:30 pm. Dr. at hospital said it was 'cardiac event' according to death certificate." – VAERS ID: 933846

Some things are interesting and shocking to note from these handful of reports: People who have had the vaccine, then test positive for Covid 19 and then die are subsequently reported as dying from Covid, not the vaccine. This is the reverse of what we've seen under Covid death reporting that people dying with Covid and other health conditions are reported as Covid deaths. Here, people who've died having had the vaccine are being reported as something else. There is a different standard for each it would seem. Also, should the vaccine not protect against Covid 19? The UK government's website page 'Coronavirus vaccine – weekly summary of Yellow Card reporting'[181] gave these Covid vaccine adverse events figures for March 2021: *"As of 28 March 2021, for the UK, 43,491 Yellow Cards have been reported for the Pfizer/BioNTech, 116,162 have been reported for the Oxford University/AstraZeneca vaccine, and 418 have been reported where the brand of the vaccine was not specified."*

On 4th December 2020, CNN reported[182] the following: *"One of the things we want to make sure people understand is that they **should not be unnecessarily alarmed if there are reports, once we start vaccinating, of***

---

[181] 'Coronavirus Vaccine - Weekly Summary of Yellow Card Reporting'. *GOV.UK*, https://www.gov.uk/government/publications/coronavirus-covid-19-vaccine-adverse-reactions/corona-virus-vaccine-summary-of-yellow-card-reporting. Accessed 4 May 2021.

[182] Bonifield, John. 'Why Vaccinate our most Frail? Odd Vote out Shows the Dilemma'. *CNN*, 4 Dec. 2020, https://lite.cnn.com/en/article/h_f57704265a0db9708053b6eb5320dd44. Accessed 4 May 2021.

someone or multiple people dying within a day or two of their vaccina-tion who are residents of a long-term care facility. That would be some-thing we would expect, as a normal occurrence, because people die fre-quently in nursing homes. "

Right, so now we've been told to expect deaths immediately following vaccination, it's all ok? I myself know of at least five people who have had the experimental shot and died within a day or two and have heard of many more in care homes, from nursing and support worker friends.

The vaccine has now been declared 'safe and effective' for children, roll-ing out for 12–15-year-olds initially and then younger. Schools across California, such as Gilroy High School in Santa Clara are being used as vaccine centres.[183] Human rights attorney Leigh Dundas has given a loud and clear public warning[184] about this: *"You cannot mandate it, nor can you sidestep informed consent, particularly with children. There is a rea-son kids cannot smoke, drive, drink, have sex, vote or die for this country. Hear me loud and hear me clear: We will not be morphing our school campuses into Covid vaccine centers for delivery of an experimental med-ical protocol that killed every damn ferret in the last animal study. "*

As at 31st May 2021, CDC VAERS figures reported a death toll of 4,863 people (both adults and children), who were recorded as dying after re-ceiving one of the experimental Covid injections. **Staggeringly, these deaths from the Covid vaccine exceed the total number of deaths re-ported to VAERS following vaccination for the past *23 years*.** There's also a whopping 262,521 injuries – including 3,299 Permanent Disabili-ties, 34,475 Emergency Room visits, and 14,986 Hospitalisations.[185] Sim-

[183] 'Santa Clara County Opens New COVID Vaccine Site At Gilroy High School'. *CBS SF Bay Area,* 24 Feb. 2021, https://sanfrancisco.cbslocal.com/2021/02/24/santa-clara-county-opens-new-covid-vac-cine-site-at-gilroy-high-school/.

[184] 'Human Rights Attorney Leigh Dundas Warns That Covid-19 Tyranny Is Becoming'. *A Final Warn-ing,* 29 Apr. 2021, https://AFinalWarning.com/515184.html. Accessed 4 May 2021.

[185] Shilhavy, Brian. 'CDC: Death Toll Following Experimental COVID Injections Now at 4,863 – More than 23 Previous Years of Recorded Vaccine Deaths According to VAERS'. *Health Impact News,* 30

ilarly, EudraVigilance – the European Database of Adverse Drug Reactions show that for Covid 19 'vaccines' there were reports of 10,570 dead and 405,259 Injuries, as at 8th May 2021.[186]

8. Many Medical Doctors' Concerns

Here are just a handful of very experienced, highly qualified and credible (although heavily smeared and censored) medical professionals who are disturbed by the rushed mass Covid vaccination being pushed upon us:

- Dr Judy Mikovits[187] – is a Christian doctor renowned for her ground-breaking research in molecular biology and virology. Her 1991 doctoral thesis revolutionised the treatment of HIV/AIDS. She is author of the book 'Plague of Corruption'[188] and creator of the 'Plandemic' documentary, in which she states: *"Most people don't realize the vaccines do not prevent infection. You're injecting the blueprint of the virus and letting a compromised system try to deal with it. And worse, it doesn't go in the cells that a natural infection would, that have lock and key receptors, gatekeepers, so that only certain cells can be infected, like the upper respiratory tract for a coronavirus. Now you're making it in a nanoparticle which means it can go in every cell without that receptor. So, can you imagine the damage of bypassing God's natural immunity and allowing the blueprint for coronavirus that also has*

May 2021, https://healthimpactnews.com/2021/cdc-death-toll-following-experimental-covid-injections-now-at-4863-more-than-23-previous-years-of-recorded-vaccine-deaths-according-to-vaers/.

[186] Shilhavy, Brian. '10,570 DEAD 405,259 Injuries: European Database of Adverse Drug Reactions for COVID-19 "Vaccines" - Medical Kidnap'. *Medical Kidnap,* 14 May 2021, https://medical-kidnap.com/2021/05/14/10570-dead-405259-injuries-european-database-of-adverse-drug-reactions-for-covid-19-vaccines/.

[187] 'Watch The Banned Video Plandemic'. *Dr Judy A Mikovits,* https://drjudyamikovits.com/. Accessed 4 May 2021.

[188] Mikovits, Judy, Kent Heckenlively, and Robert F. Kennedy Jr. *Plague of Corruption.* Skyhorse, 2020. *Open WorldCat*

components of HIV in some strains, meaning you can infect your white blood cells. So now you're going to inject an agent into every cell of the body. **I just can't even imagine a recipe for anything other than what I would consider mass murder on a scale where 50 million people will die in America from the vaccine.** *The numbers from the XMRV's (xenotropic murine leukemia virus-related virus) and the vaccine injuries for the (past) 40 years support that."*

- Dr Sherri Tenpenny[189] – is a Christian osteopathic medical doctor, board certified in three medical specialties, she is widely regarded as the most knowledgeable and outspoken physician on the adverse impact that vaccines can have on health and has been a leading and courageous voice exposing the Covid vaccine dangers. She has studied the vaccine problems for over 20 years – read thousands of mainstream medical scientific papers and has put in over 40,000 hours of study on these issues. That's quite a lot, wouldn't you agree? Watch any of Sherri Tenpenny's excellent interviews here.[190] She believes the vaccine is designed to harm, calling them 'well-designed killing machines' and concurring with Dr Mikovits' death predictions. She has stated, ***"This is not 'just another vaccine' and this is not 'just like getting a flu shot'. The ingredients are experimental and the mRNA is coded to produce a protein that CAN modify your genes."*** She has made clear claims that it can and will cause full blown autoimmune disease anywhere from 2-20 years after injection, that it permanently alters the host's immune system and even ventures to say that the experimental injections will begin the depopulation process from summer 2021.

---

[189] VaxxterAdmin2. 'Coronavirus Pt. 6: The COVID Vaccines – Part 1 - UPDATED 3-30-2021'. *Vaxxter*, 28 Dec. 2020, https://vaxxter.com/the-covid-vaccines-part-1/.

[190] 'Media - Podcasts & Interviews | Dr Sherri Tenpenny'. *Dr Sherri Tenpenny*, https://www.drtenpenny.com/podcasts-interviews. Accessed 4 May 2021.

- Dr Mike Yeadon[191] – Pfizer's former Vice President and Chief Science Officer, mentioned prior, says that taking the Covid injection is like 'playing Russian roulette with your life' and has stated the following in a telephone interview with Life Site magazine: *"Look out the window, and think, "why is my government lying to me about something so fundamental?" Because, I think the answer is, they are going to kill you using this method. They're going to kill you and your family. Since no benign reason is apparent, the use of vaccine passports along with a 'banking reset' could usher in a totalitarianism unlike the world has ever seen. Recalling the evil of Stalin, Mao, and Hitler,* **'mass depopulation' remains a logical outcome.***"* Dr Yeadon has also heavily criticised the notion of 'new strains' of the virus and says that it's like a boy taking his baseball cap off, turning it around and putting it on backwards and expecting his parents not to recognise him; i.e., that our bodies are more than capable of recognising and handling any 'new strains' of the virus in the same way it dealt with the previous ones, however that might be.

- Professor Delores Cahill[192] – Irish Molecular Biologist & Immunologist who has been heavily censored and banned for her activism against Covid mandates, which she claims are criminal and is working to bring perpetrators to account. She has also stated on video that many people will die a few months after the first mRNA was released.[193] She has set up the World Freedom Alliance[194] to resist the medical tyranny and take back our freedoms, including the freedom to travel without PCR test and vaccines.

---

[191] Yeadon, Dr Mike. 'EXCLUSIVE - Former Pfizer VP: "Your Government Is Lying to You in a Way That Could Lead to Your Death."' *LifeSiteNews*, 7 Apr. 2021, https://www.lifesitenews.com/news/exclusive-former-pfizer-vp-your-government-is-lying-to-you-in-a-way-that-could-lead-to-your-death. Accessed 4 May 2021.

[192] 'News/Videos'. *DoloresCahill*, https://dolorescahill.com/pages/video. Accessed 4 May 2021.

[193] 'Prof. Dolores Cahill: Why People Will Start Dying A Few Months After The First Mrna Vaccination'. *Coronavirus News*, 18 Jan. 2021, https://coronanews123.wordpress.com/2021/01/18/professor-dolores-cahill-why-people-will-start-dying-a-few-months-after-the-first-mrna-vaccination/.

[194] *World Freedom Alliance*, https://worldfreedomalliance.org/. Accessed 4 May 2021.

- Dr Simone Gold and America's Frontline Doctors (AFLD)[195] – is a Christian doctor and Covid whistle blower. Dr Simone Gold's presentation video, 'The Truth About Covid 19' has been viewed and applauded by millions and AFLD have been very front-footed in speaking out about and fighting the medical misinformation, Covid vaccine lies and violations of our freedoms. Their 'White Paper On Experimental Vaccines For COVID-19' gives the following eleven reasons why we should all be concerned with the experimental new vaccine:

  1. Brand new technology
  2. Failure of previous coronavirus vaccines
  3. No animal studies
  4. Known complications
  5. Unknown complications
  6. Pharmaceutical companies are immune from all liability
  7. An experimental vaccine is not safer than a very low infection rate
  8. No proof the vaccine stops transmission of the virus
  9. Unknown mortality or hospital admission benefit
  10. The vaccine lasts unknown duration
  11. The data has not been independently peer-reviewed and published.

- Dr Barbara Loe Fisher[196] – co-founder of National Vaccine Information Centre (NVIC), stated back in 2013, *"If the State can tag, track down and force citizens against their will to be injected with biologicals of known and unknown toxicity today, there will be no limit on which individual freedoms the State can take away in the name of the greater good tomorrow."*

---

[195] *America's Frontline Doctors*, https://www.americasfrontlinedoctors.org/. Accessed 4 May 2021.

[196] 'Barbara Loe Fisher Profile - About Us - NVIC'. *National Vaccine Information Center (NVIC)*, https://www.nvic.org/about/barbaraloefisher.aspx. Accessed 4 May 2021.

153

- Dr Meryl Nass[197] – biological warfare epidemiologist with special interests in vaccine-induced illnesses, who has been outspoken in asserting that Covid was a manufactured and released bioweapon.

- Dr Joseph Mercola [198] – natural health award-winning thought leader, osteopathic physician and best-selling author, who has written a book called 'The Truth About COVID-19: Exposing the Great Reset, Lockdowns, Vaccine Passports and the New Normal'.

- Dr Andrew Wakefield[199] – who's been heavily and unfairly smeared for his anti-vaccination activism around vaccines and child autism, but vindicated by *The BMJ*,[200] which has stated, *"this is not the first time Wakefield's research has been confirmed by independent researchers around the world"*. In an interview, he has stated,[201] *"The potential for this to go horribly wrong is enormous. You have cells in your own body that are producing protein to which your immune system is going to mount an immune response. That's called an autoimmune disease ... If it causes a problem – a year, two years, five years down the line – and it's already been given to billions of people worldwide, it's too late. You can't take it out. You can't switch it off. You can't stop it. It's in there. It's rather like Jurassic Park that is about to escape the island."*

---

[197] 'Dr Meryl Nass Why Is Protecting Covid19's Origin so Important'. *BitChute*, https://www.bitchute.com/video/jQIGNkVF6bAi/. Accessed 4 May 2021.

[198] Mercola, Dr Joseph. 'Will New COVID Vaccine Make You Transhuman?' *Mercola*, 12 Sept. 2020, http://articles.mercola.com/sites/articles/archive/2020/09/12/coronavirus-vaccine-transhumanism.aspx. Accessed 4 May 2021.

[199] *Vaxxed - From Cover Up to Catastrophe*, https://vaxxedthemovie.com/who-is-dr-andrew-wakefield/. Accessed 4 May 2021.

[200] Miller, Clifford G. 'Wakefield's Lancet Paper Vindicated – [Yet Again]'. *The BMJ*, May 2021, https://www.bmj.com/rapid-response/2011/11/02/wakefield%E2%80%99s-lancet-paper-vindicated-%E2%80%93-yet-again.

[201] Dr Andrew Wakefield Warns about Risks of Coronavirus Vaccines. *BitChute*, https://www.bitchute.com/video/LKg4uU0QOFvj/. Accessed 4 May 2021.

- Professor Denis Rancourt[202] – former Professor of physics at the University of Ottawa, Canada, known for applications of physics education research and an interest in nanoparticles.
- Professor Robert F Kennedy Jr[203] – Chairman of the Children's Health Defense, American environmental lawyer and activist, author and vocal anti-vaccinationist, who has openly stated that we are experiencing medical tyranny, akin to how the Nazi regime started.
- Dr Vernon Coleman[204] – Medical Doctor of 50 years and best-selling author of over 100 books.

I think Dr Vernon Coleman's experience and perspective is worth taking a more detailed look at ... Vernon Coleman is a general practitioner principal of over 50 years and a former Professor of Holistic Medical Sciences at the International Open University in Sri Lanka. He has an honorary DSc, has given evidence to the House of Commons and the House of Lords in the UK and is a Sunday Times bestselling author of over 100 books which have sold over two million copies in the UK alone. He has appeared as TV doctor for BBC TV programmes and has written many articles for mainstream UK newspapers.

All this to say, he's hardly a fringe or crackpot dissenter. Yet he has been very clearly vocal that he believes that the coronavirus is a big

---

[202] 'COVID-19 And Face Masks- Interview with Denis Rancourt' Jul 17, 2020. *BitChute*, https://www.bitchute.com/video/fHonKDvyQQnG/. Accessed 4 May 2021.

[203] 'COVID Archives • Children's Health Defense'. *Children's Health Defense*, https://childrenshealthdefense.org/defender_category/covid/. Accessed 4 May 2021.

[204] Vernon Coleman - Author, Columnist & Leading Campaigning Journalist, https://www.vernoncoleman.com/main.htm. Accessed 4 May 2021.

hoax[205] designed to mass vaccinate us, with fatal implications. Here's his expert opinion from 'Fact Sheet on Vaccines: The Truth':[206]

"The pro-vaccine establishment likes to demonise those who dare to question vaccination – dismissing them as 'anti-vaxxers'. UK Prime Minister Boris Johnson has declared that anyone who questions vaccination is a 'nut'. I have been demonised as an 'anti-vaxxer' simply because I have published criticisms showing how and when vaccines can be dangerous and ineffective. I believe it is important to study the risk/value ratio for any medicine. If you're giving a drug to a patient who is dying then risks and side effects are less significant than if you're giving a drug for a relatively minor illness. Sadly, many modern vaccines are neither safe nor effective. Pro-vaxxers steadfastly and obsessively believe that all vaccinations are safe and effective all the time. This is patently not true. The World Health Organisation has admitted that the vaccines pushed by the WHO and Bill Gates have caused a polio outbreak in Sudan with several children now paralysed as a result. Making a vaccine in a few months instead of many years massively increases the dangers. Some serious side effects do not appear for years after vaccination. Giving a relatively untested vaccine to seven billion people (as is planned with the Covid-19 vaccine) may result in hundreds of thousands dying or being made seriously ill. GlaxoSmithKline (one of the drug companies making a Covid-19 vaccine) has been fined many times. For example, after pleading guilty to federal criminal offences GSK agreed to pay a fine of $3 billion. The largest health care fraud in US history. The company was fined $490 million for bribery in China."

It's worth watching four of his short videos on the Covid vaccine, published back in June and July 2020 here:

---

[205] 'Why the Coronavirus Hoax Is a Hoax (Leaflet to Print out and Distribute). https://www.vernoncoleman.com/leaflettoprint.htm. Accessed 4 May 2021.

[206] 'Fact Sheet on Vaccines: The Truth', https://www.vernoncoleman.com/vaccinesthetruth.htm. Accessed 4 May 2021.

This Couldn't Possibly Happen, Could it?[207] (Transcript[208])
'Just a Little Prick' – Part 1[209]
'Just a Little Prick' – Part 2[210]
How Many Billion Could the Covid-19 Vaccine Kill or Damage?[211]

Many doctors have signed the Great Barrington Declaration,[212] written by infectious disease epidemiologists and public health scientists who have grave concerns about the damaging physical and mental health impacts of the prevailing Covid 19 policies. Many more doctors also have grave concerns and about the vaccine but are simply afraid to speak out – evidenced by many anonymous whistle blowers coming forward, such as a UK NHS nurse exposing Covid vaccine policy.[213] More doctors still would see the dangers about the novel Covid injection if they had the time, steel and inclination to look into it in detail. The medical and governmental authorities are sending out updates and propaganda at such a ferocious pace and things are changing so quickly that many doctors just do not have the opportunity, nor encouragement, in the course of their everyday work to see the wood for the trees. I know this first hand from my time managing medical research.

To finish off this section on many medical doctors' concerns about the Covid pseudo-vaccine, a United Health Professionals (UHP) international

---

[207] 'This Couldn't Possibly Happen. Could It?'. *YouTube*, https://www.youtube.com/watch?v=0p0qXvgsc4g. Accessed 4 May 2021.

[208] 'This Couldn't Possibly Happen. Could It?'. https://www.vernoncoleman.com/couldit.htm. Accessed 4 May 2021.

[209] *'Just a Little Prick (Part One)'. YouTube*, https://www.youtube.com/watch?v=jVa8maJb5JU. Accessed 4 May 2021.

[210] *'Just a Little Prick (Part 2)'. YouTube*, https://www.youtube.com/watch?v=p5ANr7MvS48. Accessed 4 May 2021.

[211] 'How Many Billion Could the Covid-19 Vaccine Kill or Damage?'. *YouTube*, https://www.youtube.com/watch?v=jyE9cJ0w1hk. Accessed 4 May 2021.

[212] 'Great Barrington Declaration and Petition'. *Great Barrington Declaration*, https://gbdeclaration.org/. Accessed 4 May 2021.

[213] 'UK Column News - 14th April 2021'. *UKColumn*, 14 Apr. 2021, https://www.ukcolumn.org/ukcolumn-news/uk-column-news-14th-april-2021.

urgent message document was issued to the governments of thirty countries in August 2020, called 'STOP the Terror, Madness, Manipulation, Dictatorship, Lies and the Biggest Health Scam of the 21st Century'.[214] It has 36 pages of medical signatories and made strong and clear demands for the following things, backed up with pages of scientific references:

- Stay home, save lives – was a pure lie.
- Remove the following illegal, non-scientific and non-sanitary measures: lockdown, mandatory face masks for healthy subjects, social distancing of one or two meters.
- The lockdown not only killed many people but also destroyed physical and mental health, economy, education and other aspects of life.
- The natural history of the virus is not influenced by social measures (lockdown, face masks, closure of restaurants, curfews).
- When the State knows best and violates human rights, we are on a dangerous course.
- Exclude your experts and advisers who have links or conflicts of interest with pharmaceutical companies.
- Stop the vaccination campaigns and refuse the scam of the pseudo-health passport which is in reality a politico-commercial project.

A follow up document was issued by UHP[215] in February 2021.

---

[214] 'United Health Professionals 'STOP the Terror, Madness, Manipulation, Dictatorship, Lies and the Biggest Health Scam of the 21st Century' *International Alert Message*, 26 Aug. 2020, https://www.globalresearch.ca/wp-content/uploads/2021/02/Health-Professionals.pdf. Accessed 4 May 2021.

[215] 'International Alert Message about COVID-19. United Health Professionals'. *Global Research*, 16 Mar. 2021, https://www.globalresearch.ca/international-alert-message-about-covid-19-united-health-professionals/5737680.

9. The Vaccine Propaganda & Censoring Onslaught

The mass mainstream media are pummelling us with their propaganda narrative, which is causing fear and rewarding compliance to and virtue signalling of the control and ever-changing, non-sensical directives – all in the name of peace, safety and science (scientism). People genuinely seeking to look into both sides of the vaccine argument and weight up risk-benefit factors are labelled 'anti-vaxxers' and voices expressing concern with this rushed experimental shot are censored and silenced.

The propaganda has one goal – to move us into a 'Great Reset' to bring in the transhuman eugenics agenda and a one world government, one world religion, one world currency 'cashless society' … more on that later.

The main messages we are being told about a Covid vaccine can be distilled down to these:

- All vaccines (including the Covid pseudo-vaccine) are 'safe and effective'. (FALSE)
- Fast tracking a vaccine does not mean a compromise on safety or efficacy trials. (FALSE)
- We must all be vaccinated and life can return to normal … a new normal. (DECEPTION)
- Anyone who questions anything about the standard Covid narrative and its arbitrary rules is a dangerous 'conspiracy theorist' loony and must be ignored and shut down. (FALSE)
- Those pesky, selfish, reckless, uncaring, psychopathic, science-denying 'anti-vaxxers' are a threat to everyone, with their fake news stories. They must be censored, silenced and made to comply. After all, we're 'all in this together' and have to get through it with everyone's help and submission to the safety rules and vaccination programme. We must not abide rogue dissenters who are endangering the collective. (DECEPTION)

From early 2020, we have constantly been sent thinly-veiled threatening and predictive programming messages such as this early one from The Atlantic article:[216] *"All hopes of extinguishing COVID-19 are riding on a still-hypothetical vaccine. And so a refrain has caught on: We might have to stay home – until we have a vaccine. Close schools – until we have a vaccine. Wear masks – but only until we have a vaccine. During these months of misery, this mantra has offered a small glimmer of hope. Normal life is on the other side, and we just have to wait – until we have a vaccine. Rather than a onetime deal, a Covid-19 vaccine, when it arrives, could require booster shots to maintain immunity over time. You might get it every year or every other year, much like a flu shot."*

And this headline, castigating religious laws as putting everyone in danger: 'How the United States Became a Country Where Religious Liberty Could Be Complicit in Greater Suffering During a Pandemic'.[217] We can see as time has gone on that this, of course, has panned out exactly as the powers that be have planned. Notice how the following article from the UK's Daily Mail in July 2020[218] uses such emotive and scathing language about Dr Andrew Wakefield, the UK doctor who was stripped of his medical licence for his views on vaccines and autism – which have been upheld in their evidence.[219] Him and other vaccine sceptics are condemned as 'science-deniers', gullible, fear-mongers and terrifying.

---

[216] Zhang, Sarah. 'A Vaccine Reality Check'. *The Atlantic*, 24 July 2020, https://www.theatlantic.com/health/archive/2020/07/covid-19-vaccine-reality-check/614566/.

[217] Hamilton, Marci A. 'The Biggest Threat to Herd Immunity Against COVID-19 May Be the Religious Freedom Restoration Act(s) and State Religious Exemptions'. Justia – *Verdict,* 25 Aug. 2020, https://verdict.justia.com/2020/08/25/the-biggest-threat-to-herd-immunity-against-covid-19-may-be-the-religious-freedom-restoration-acts-and-state-religious-exemptions. Accessed 4 May 2021.

[218] Leonard, Tom. 'Disgraced British Doctor Is Leading Movement against Covid Vaccine'. *Mail Online*, 16 July 2020, https://www.dailymail.co.uk/news/article-8531689/Disgraced-British-doctor-leading-movement-against-covid-vaccine.html.

[219] Ibid.

Could this conspiracy theory kill thousands? Disgraced British doctor Andrew Wakefield, who lost his licence for saying the MMR jab caused autism, is already at heart of a movement that says the pandemic is a hoax and NO ONE should have vac

By TOM LEONARD IN NEW YORK FOR THE DAILY MAIL

PUBLISHED: 22:13, 16 July 2020 | **UPDATED:** 12:51, 17 July 2020

       9.6k shares **3.9k** View comments

Speaking in the measured, authoritative tones of an expert, Andrew Wakefield delivered his considered judgment on the **coronavirus** pandemic.

It was, said the disgraced British former doctor, one big hoax: a cynical plot by pharmaceutical giants — aided by governments, scientists and the media — to force the world to be unnecessarily and dangerously vaccinated.

People must fight it — even, he suggested, to the death.

'It is a very, very alarming time,' he told a recent online 'Health Freedom Summit'.

The article goes on to state:

"These are terrifyingly gullible times – the perfect environment for Wakefield, who is still shamelessly preaching the same dangerous anti-vaccine message a decade after it was discredited by British medical authorities."

"Convincing his disciples that he was the victim of a conspiracy by the pharmaceutical industry, medical establishment and media, Wakefield now neatly argues that the same shadowy cabal are lying to the public about coronavirus."

"Having terrified one generation of parents – leading, some believe, to a spike in measles among children and a number of deaths in countries where a minority have promoted his claims – Wakefield is spreading fear

and misinformation again. And the anti-vaxxers are proving alarmingly successful, say experts who fear these science-deniers could seriously undermine efforts to tackle coronavirus effectively."

These are classic propaganda techniques that I even remember being taught back in the 1990s in 'Politics of the Media' modules of my university Law degree course. It's very predictable and would be deathly boring if it wasn't so alarmingly effective on the mass populace.

"Political language ... is designed to make lies sound truthful and murder respectable, and to give an appearance of solidity to pure wind." – George Orwell, 'Politics and the English Language' (1946)

And that was just some of the propaganda months before the novel pseudo-vaccine was rolled out and paved the way for millions upon millions of people to accept it willingly and immediately. Now that the Covid shot is here and the plans to vaccinate the whole world are being executed (no pun intended) at 'warp speed', the manipulation and psychological warfare tactics have elevated to a whole new level.

Coercion from 'health care' organisations

A training document was published in December 2020 by NHS England and NHS Improvement Behaviour Change Unit, in partnership with PHE and Warwick Business School, called 'Optimising Vaccination Roll Out – Dos and Don'ts for all messaging, documents and 'communications' in the widest sense', which has subsequently been removed from the internet. (You can access the less coercive UK government 'Covid 19 vaccination uptake plan'[220] here.) It details how to engage and persuade various groups of people who might be 'vaccine undecided' – such as leaders and managers, health care workers (both immunisers and recipients), care home residents, over 65s and young people. This is an extract from the procedures for engaging with young people about the vaccine:

---

[220] 'UK COVID-19 Vaccine Uptake Plan'. *GOV.UK*, https://www.gov.uk/government/publications/covid-19-vaccination-uptake-plan/uk-covid-19-vaccine-uptake-plan. Accessed 4 May 2021.

*"Acknowledge conspiracy theories, identify which ones have most traction through social media and counter through clear evidence based, unemotional messaging, including from trusted sources. Don't be dismissive, the conspiracies are resonating because trust has been lost. Messages that will land well: "There are many conspiracy theories across social media. **Our leading scientists and medical experts recommend vaccination because of the robust evidence that it works.**" Note: NHS messages will be more trusted than Government messages. Highlight popular 'normal life' activities that young people can engage in again once vaccinated – socialising, sports and exercise, work, lectures, events, etc. Don't focus on 'we're in this together' – young people feel unfairly treated by 'us'. Messages that will land well: "**The more young people vaccinated, the safer it will be and the less likely will be future lockdowns.**" "**If you want to be able to do what you want, then having the vaccine is the fastest and safest way to achieving this.**" Explain implications of not being vaccinated for seeing loved ones by **focusing on the potential regret one might feel if they were not vaccinated and were to subsequently infect others.** Don't dispel or ignore the naysayers and conspiracy theorists. Messages that will land well: "The vaccine is not 100% effective, so if only your older relative has **it, you could still give them the virus if you are not vaccinated.**""*

I have emboldened the most emotionally laden and manipulative language used and find it quite shocking. The essence of the message is, 'if you don't get vaccinated, you can forget normal life and you'll probably kill grandma.'

The WHO produced a very detailed, derogatory 53-page report called 'Best practice guidance – How to respond to vocal vaccine deniers in public'[221] – even the name 'vaccine denier' is a slanderous, weaponised one, making the assumption that anyone with a 'very negative attitude

---

[221] Schmid, Philipp, et al. *'Best practice guidance – How to respond to vocal vaccine deniers in public'. World Health Organization.* https://www.euro.who.int/__data/assets/pdf_file/0005/315761/Vocal-vaccine-deniers-guidance-document.pdf. Accessed 4 May 2021.

towards vaccination' is a rigid 'science denier', as set out in their definition of the term: *"'Vaccine deniers' refers to a subgroup at the extreme
end of the hesitancy continuum; people who have a very negative attitude
towards vaccination and are not open to a change of mind no matter the
scientific evidence. Vaccine deniers may even counter-react to evidence-
based arguments. The vaccine denier has characteristics that are similar
to other types of science deniers and to religious and political fanatics in
that they adhere to a belief that is impossible to challenge, even if challenge is the fundamental tenet of scientific progress."*

Many self-proclaimed and dubious pro-vaccine 'expert blogs', such as
Science-Based Medicine[222] have popped up to try and slander and silence
people questioning the official vaccine narrative. Five other coercive
measures to get the general public to go and get the experimental Covid
shot and voiced well in an Off-Guardian article,[223] include:

1. Bribery – 'no vaccine, no gym/ work/ school/ travel/ restaurants'.
2. Celebrity endorsements – such as the Queen Elizabeth, Dolly Par-
   ton, Britney Spears, Jeff Goldblum, Ryan Reynolds.
3. Forced scarcity – 'there's dwindling stock – get yours while you
   still can!'
4. Fake popularity and peer pressure – 'everyone's getting it!'
5. Resistance is useless – 'mandatory vaccines and passports are inevitable'.

**Whatever happened to 'my body, my choice'? And why do we have
celebrities, news reporters, teenagers and pastors telling us to 'go get
jabbed' and that this experimental injection is safe, yet doctors with**

---

[222] Gorski, David. 'The Efforts of Antivaxxers to Portray COVID-19 Vaccines as Harmful or Even
Deadly Continue Apace…' *Science-Based Medicine.* 18 Jan. 2021, https://sciencebasedmedi-
cine.org/the-efforts-of-antivaxxers-to-portray-covid-19-vaccines-as-harmful-or-even-deadly-continues-
apace/.

[223] Knightly, Kit. '5 Ways They're Trying to Trick You into Taking the Covid "Vaccine"'. *OffGuard-
ian,* 4 Mar. 2021, https://off-guardian.org/2021/03/04/5-ways-theyre-trying-to-trick-you-into-taking-the-
covid-vaccine/.

40,000+ hours of research and who are speaking clearly, boldly, scientifically and with dignity are 'dangerous' and not to be listened to?

One of the leading propaganda organisations is the international NGO The Center for Countering Digital Hate[224] (CCDH). It has produced pernicious and slanderous reports such as 'The Anti-Vaxx Playbook'[225] and 'The Disinformation Dozen'[226] Here are some excerpts from the 'Anti-Vaxx Playbook':

*"**The master narrative:** Online anti-vaxxers have organised themselves around a 'master narrative' comprised of three key messages: Covid is not dangerous, the vaccine is dangerous and vaccine advocates cannot be trusted.*

*… **Covid vaccines contain toxic chemicals**: Anti-vaxxers have identified chemicals present in Covid vaccines that they claim are dangerous, singling out the polyethylene glycol (PEG) present in mRNA vaccines in particular.*

*… **Covid vaccines will change your DNA:** Anti-vaxxers have traded on the novelty of mRNA vaccines and ignorance of how they work to promote the false claim that they will permanently alter the DNA of recipients. In reality, mRNA vaccines never enter the nucleus of a cell, and scientists believe that its integration into the human genome is not a practical or theoretical concern.*

*… **Vaccine advocates cannot be trusted:** Attacks on the integrity and motivation of vaccine advocates have always been a key feature of the anti-vaccination movement, and they are now applying this technique to advocates of a Covid vaccine. Analysis of leading anti-vaxxers shows there are three main strands to these attacks: that politics is being put first, that*

---

[224] *Center for Countering Digital Hate – CCDH.* https://www.counterhate.com. Accessed 4 May 2021.

[225] 'The Anti-Vaxx Playbook'. *CCDH*, https://www.counterhate.com/playbook. Accessed 4 May 2021.

[226] 'The Disinformation Dozen'. *CCDH*, 24 Mar. 2021. https://www.counterhate.com/disinformationdozen. Accessed 4 May 2021.

profit is being put first, and that leading vaccine advocates are in any case unaccountable to the public they wish to vaccinate.

*... **Anti-vaxxers' symbolic use of Bill Gates:** Anti-vaccine campaigners have collaborated with alternative health entrepreneurs and conspiracists to ensure that global health philanthropist Bill Gates has become a symbolic figure that represents all of their attacks on the trustworthiness of vaccine advocates. These attacks are not aimed at influencing the ongoing debate over a Covid vaccine, in which the role of Bill Gates takes a back seat to more practical issues. The real utility of this campaign of vilification is to create a symbol and associated memes that aid the communication of interrelated beliefs about Covid, vaccines and conspiracies ... Bill Gates has come to represent a complex of anti-vaxxer talking points and conspiracy theories. Virtually every element of the online anti-vaxx movement has found ways of featuring him in their narratives, in a variety of contexts and tones."*

These claims this report makes are largely true: It's taking legitimate concerns that conscientious, health-minded, critical thinkers (AKA 'anti-vaxxers') are voicing and condemning them, without any clear refutation at all! It's kind of like a child hitting his brother, the brother telling his friend and then the child complaining to his mother that his brother told his friend that he hit him ... and expecting the mother to sympathise. (You might have to read that again!)

The CCDH 'Disinformation Dozen' report states: *"The Disinformation Dozen are twelve anti-vaxxers who play leading roles in spreading digital misinformation about Covid vaccines. They were selected because they have large numbers of followers, produce high volumes of anti-vaccine content or have seen rapid growth of their social media accounts in the last two months."*

Countering the 'Anti-Vaxx' slander and misinformation

Members of the 'disinformation dozen', such as Ty and Charlene Bollinger, Dr Sherri Tenpenny, Dr Robert Kennedy Jr and Dr Joseph Mercola have not taken this smear campaign lying down, however, and have launched their counter-campaign,[227] to 'fight the war on Covid misinformation', stating the following '12 Vaccine Truths':

1. Vaccine makers (as well as health care professionals and practices who administer vaccines) have ZERO LEGAL LIABILITY for injuries or deaths caused by vaccines per the 1986 National Childhood Vaccine Injury Act (NCVIA).
2. The NCVIA was in response to failing vaccine manufacturers overrun with injury and death lawsuits from vaccines, namely DPT.
3. The United States Supreme Court declared vaccines to be 'unavoidably unsafe'. The Vaccine Injury Compensation Program (VICP) has awarded MORE THAN $4,000,000,000 to date, accounting for only a fraction of cases filed and injuries reported.
4. Conflict of Interest: The vaccine manufacturers, themselves, are in charge of overseeing the safety studies. They have ZERO incentive to call out any safety issues.
5. Multiple vaccines contain human fetal cells (MRC-5 and WI-38) derived from abortions. The full health implications of the use of fetal cell lines in vaccines is unknown.
6. Vaccines contain carcinogenic, mutagenic and neurotoxic ingredients that have not been tested for impairment of fertility. There are no safety studies on synergistic toxicity.
7. There has been an increase of over 1,350% in vaccines given to U.S. children from 1962 to today. In lockstep with the increased vaccination schedule, there has been an increase in infant mortality, an explosion of chronic diseases and neurological issues, and an overall decline in the health of our children, especially evident in the last 30 years when the vaccine schedule spiked after liability was removed from vaccine manufacturers (see #1). All of this while under the watchful eye of our public health agencies.

---

[227] *DIS-INFORMATION DOZEN*, https://www.dis-informationdozen.com/. Accessed 4 May 2021.

8. Vaccine mandates violate bodily autonomy via coercion. Holding education and employment hostage to the consumption of a liability free pharmaceutical is not consent, it is coercion.

9. COVID shots do not meet the traditional definition of a vaccine. They utilize mRNA technology, never before used in humans. Some have reported testing positive for COVID after injection.

10. COVID shots are experimental (due to Emergency Use Authorization), having been tested on human subjects only since Fall 2020. They have not been FDA approved. The only way to invoke the EUA was to show that there were no other available safe treatments for COVID. We now know that safe and effective treatments were censored and smeared by authorities so they could maintain the emergency status for the vaccines.

11. COVID shots have not been shown to prevent disease in the recipient, nor to prevent transmission of infection, which is why the CDC states people still need to wear a mask and social distance.

12. As evidenced by the CDC reporting system, COVID vaccines may have caused deaths in some and severe injuries in many. Mainstream media has not been forthcoming with these reports.

Coercion from within the Church

Long before the Covid injection began rolling out, governments were recruiting 'Clergy Response Teams' (CRTs) and 'Places of Worship Task Forces'[228] (PWTF) to massage the views of Christians and Churchgoers and to persuade them that not only is this experimental vaccine 'safe and effective' but that taking it is the most loving, Christlike thing to do. Sadly, many Christians have lacked discernment and Biblical wisdom and have fallen for this hook, line and sinker. I discuss CRTs more in Chapter

---

[228] 'New Taskforce Developing Plan to Reopen Places of Worship'. *GOV.UK*, https://www.gov.uk/government/news/new-taskforce-developing-plan-to-reopen-places-of-worship. Accessed 4 May 2021.

10 on Babylon and the dangers of following 'another gospel' in Chapter 9 on 'good impressions of the sinful nature'.

A UK Catholic priest reported on the Covid Church propaganda,[229] *"We have been asked to encourage parishioners to accept the opportunity to be vaccinated, and at the same time to strongly counter misinformation on social media regarding the vaccine."*

Franklin Graham has said, 'taking the vaccine is consistent with Scripture'[230] and is urging pastors to encourage their congregations to trust in the vaccines: *"I think if there were vaccines available in the time of Christ, Jesus would have made reference to them and used them."* Pastor Sam Adams of Independence Baptist Church in Florida preached an excellent sermon entitled 'Covid-Vax: What Would Jesus Do?',[231] which responded to Graham's statement. He said, *"we explain in this message why we think Jesus would instead tell us not to listen to Franklin Graham"* … along with some stronger assertions. It's well worth listening to.

Many Churches have been closed for almost a year, but those Churches are now opening up as vaccination centres.[232] For example, in the Baptist denomination, one thousand people received the Moderna vaccine at Olive Baptist Church in Florida in on 6th January 2021. On 23rd January 2021, New York announced the selection of eight Churches state-wide to host vaccination hubs with as many as 300 such sites planned. In South Carolina, the Fetter Health Care Network has been vaccinating at Mount

---

[229] Haynes, Michael. 'UK Priest, Bishops Reveal Gov't Has Asked Clergy to Push COVID Vaccines'. *LifeSiteNews*, https://www.lifesitenews.com/news/uk-priest-bishops-reveal-govt-has-asked-clergy-to-push-covid-vaccines. Accessed 4 May 2021.

[230] White, Leslie. '"It's Consistent With Scripture": Franklin Graham Urges Christians to Take the COVID-19 Vaccine'. *Beliefnet News*, 19 Mar. 2021, https://www.beliefnet.com/columnists/news/2021/03/its-consistent-with-scripture-franklin-graham-urges-christians-to-take-the-covid-19-vaccine.

[231] Adams, Pastor Sam. 'Covid-Vax: What Would Jesus Do'. *SermonAudio*, https://www.sermonaudio.com/sermoninfo.asp?m=t&s=4621149377560. Accessed 4 May 2021.

[232] Hampton, Jeff. 'Public Health Officials Find Churches Are Ideal Sites for COVID Vaccine Clinics'. *Baptist News Global*, 3 Feb. 2021, https://baptistnews.com/article/public-health-officials-find-Churches-are-ideal-sites-for-covid-vaccine-clinics/.

Moriah Missionary Baptist Church. The Pastor at Westward Ho! Baptist Church in the UK said,[233] *"We feel it's a privilege to serve the community in this way, in the name of Jesus. For us it's about loving our neighbours – letting thousands of our 'neighbours' in this area have the benefit of a clean, warm, accessible, local place to visit for their life-saving vaccination."* Knowing what we know about the 'pandemic' transmission and death rates and the true nature of the experimental vaccine, this really is the height of naiveté and lack of discernment, to put it in the best light.

Here are some very sad and troubling examples of website and articles targeting Christian 'vaccine hesitancy' and encouraging congregation members to get vaccinated: 'The Spiritual Problem at the Heart of Christian Vaccine Refusal'[234] states that *"all too many Christians are adopting a posture that declares "Don't tell me what to do" far more than it asks "How can I serve you?""* – postulating that vaccine refusal is defiance and a lack of loving your neighbour.

The website 'Christians and the Vaccine',[235] from an organisation called 'Redeeming Babel' (interesting name), also appeals to 'looking to others' interests above our own' and has so much dangerous propaganda in it that there's too much to mention here. For example, the presenter, Curtis Chang, talks about the importance of not listening to lies and then proceeds to give inaccurate statements about Pastor John MacArthur's stance on the vaccine. It also advocates that pastors should encourage their congregation to take the vaccine. In the FAQ section and in answer to the question, 'Is the Covid vaccine safe?' it merely says, with no references to any supporting materials, *"The COVID-19 vaccines are safe and effective. They were tested rigorously in tens of thousands of participants in*

---

[233] 'Baptist Church Buildings Used as Vaccination Centres'. *Baptist Times, 20 Jan. 2021,* https://baptisttimes.co.uk/Articles/600753/Baptist_Church_buildings.aspx. Accessed 4 May 2021.

[234] French, David. *The Spiritual Problem at the Heart of Christian Vaccine Refusal.* https://frenchpress.thedispatch.com/p/the-spiritual-problem-at-the-heart. Accessed 4 May 2021.

[235] *Christians and the Vaccine,* https://www.christiansandthevaccine.com. Accessed 4 May 2021.

the clinical trials before receiving approval from the FDA. Over 100 million doses have been administered under the most intensive vaccine safety monitoring in history." Like the most dangerous heresies, it mixes rational truth with lies and a twisting of Scripture. Interestingly, Curtis Chang has won an Obama White House Award for social innovation and is a former Rockefeller Fellow.[236] This says a lot. As a side note, it is important keep in mind that the globalist elite think tank, the Council on Foreign Relations (CFR) has paid 'experts' in all fields of society, including the 'Church'. More on this in Chapter 10.

The Elim Church in the UK has given this guidance on the Covid shot:[237] *"Whilst respecting that receiving a Covid-19 vaccine is an issue of individual conscience, the Elim National Leadership Team views the provision of current coronavirus vaccines as an answer to prayer and an extension of God's common grace. We recognise that some believers have expressed concerns about the Covid-19 vaccination programme and we do not wish to minimise these convictions. That said, we would highlight the need to seek good sources in light of the prevalence of misinformation that is currently circulating and advise you not to neglect the specific advice of your medical professionals. For our part, having weighed the ethical considerations and the risk to life, we see no moral objection for Christians to accept a vaccine against Covid-19, which has devastated so many. We regard vaccination as one of the best ways to control the pandemic, lessen the pressure on the NHS, save lives and ultimately express our Christian duty of loving one's neighbour and protecting the vulnerable ... As a pastor within Elim, we would encourage you to seek all the ways possible to be 'good news' to your community. Taking this into consideration, using our Churches as vaccination centres is certainly a good extension of our mission to the communities we serve."*

---

[236] 'Curtis Chang'. *Duke Divinity School,* https://divinity.duke.edu/faculty/curtis-chang. Accessed 4 May 2021.

[237] 'Coronavirus (COVID-19) Guidance'. *Elim Pentecostal, 18 Apr. 2021.* https://www.elim.org.uk/Articles/569121/Coronavirus_COVID_19.aspx. Accessed 4 May 2021.

Hold on, so as Christians, there is now more than one message of 'good news'? This sounds dangerously like another gospel and the Apostle Paul addresses this chapter and verse in several of his epistles. Perhaps the most horrific example of vaccine propaganda form within the Church that I have found and promoting an open 'other Gospel' is this website from the 'Give Hope' campaign[238] by the Christian charity 'Your Neighbour'. It has a selection of warm and unassuming videos, strongly encouraging people to get the vaccine, from a diverse range of people with differing demographics. In a video targeting black and minority ethnic groups, The Bishop of Dover, Rose Hudson-Wilkin said, *"When you are offered the opportunity to get your Covid vaccination, I want you to take it. There are distracting voices in our black and minority ethnic communities spreading doubt and alarm. And while I understand the fear and concern, listening to those voices alone will rob us of the need to live flourishing lives with our families and friends. These vaccines offer us a path through the pandemic, giving us hope, strength and the chance of safety. If the vaccine was good enough for Her Majesty, then it is good enough for us."*

In the flagship short video, Yinka Oyekan, from the Baptist Union, says, *"While our Churches may look different, there's one thing we are all agreed upon. We have to do everything in our power to give hope – and stop Covid."* Stephen Cottrell, Archbishop of York echoed this, stating, *"One thing we can all do is ensure we take the vaccine when we are offered it – this is one of the best and fastest routes out of this terrible pandemic."*

The Give Hope tagline is: *"When it comes to **sharing the good news of the Covid vaccines**, the best way to give hope to your neighbours is through a kind and constructive conversation. It's as simple as H - O - P - E."*

---

[238] 'Vaccine Give Hope'. *YourNeighbour.Org | Equipping Churches in the Covid-19 Crisis*, https://yourneighbour.org/vaccine-give-hope. Accessed 4 May 2021.

When it comes to sharing the good news of the Covid vaccines, the best way to give hope to your neighbours is through a kind and constructive conversation. It's as simple as H – O – P – E.

Have a conversation

Using VaxChat - your quick vaccine chat guide

1. Why might you **want** to have the vaccine?

2. **How** might you go about it?

3. What are the three best **reasons** for having it?

4. **How important** is it for you to have the vaccine & why? [summarise what was said]

5. So, what do you think you'll **do**/might do?

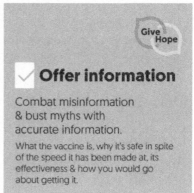

Offer information

Combat misinformation & bust myths with accurate information.

What the vaccine is, why it's safe in spite of the speed it has been made at, its effectiveness & how you would go about getting it.

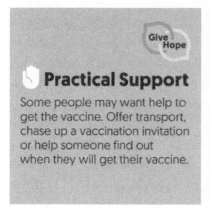

Practical Support

Some people may want help to get the vaccine. Offer transport, chase up a vaccination invitation or help someone find out when they will get their vaccine.

Engage & share

Engage with others & share opportunity.

Give HOPE to your neighbours & people in your community - share on social media & in your WhatsApp groups to friends & family.

This is exceedingly dangerous teaching that is coming from within our Churches – whether intentional or not. We need to remind ourselves of Galatians 1:6-7: *"I am astonished that you are so quickly deserting him who called you in the grace of Christ and are **turning to a different gospel** – not that there is another one, but there are some who trouble you and want to distort the gospel of Christ."*

The bottom line is that we are being coerced and fed lies and propaganda from all angles about this novel injection and sadly from our Churches too. I do not believe it is too strong to say that we are on the verge of great apostasy if this continues. Never mind the fact that trusting Christians who are failing to discern the spirits and are regurgitating the 'safe and effective' line have no idea what danger they are promoting. Thankfully, there are a few pastors who are preaching squarely into the truth of the matter, like Pastor John Weaver who says the Covid shot is a mass genocide plan and we're in the middle of a 'vaccine holocaust'.[239] Also, Pastor Matthew Trewhella of DefyTyrants.com has preached strongly on 'the shot and the tyranny of man'.[240]

10. 'Vaccine Passports' – Papers Please

In January 2021, Joe Biden signed a White House executive order to begin testing the feasibility of Covid-19 'vaccine passports'[241] for domestic and international travel. In February 2021, however, Israel was the first in the world to roll out a fully-fledged Covid vaccine passport system, called 'Green Pass'. This 'allows' people who have had both doses of the injection to return to bars, restaurants, gyms, theatres, sporting events … and 'houses of worship' – i.e., Churches. Mainstream media reported that countries around the world were supposedly observing its implementation and efficacy and how we can all 'learn from its great success'. In April 2021, the UK said that it was 'looking into creating a similar system there'. In May 2021, after much pressure, Israel announced that it was scrapping the Green Pass but it is clear that there is a worldwide agenda to have vaccine passports in place sooner or later, and that their imple-

---

[239] 'Listen: Pastor WARNS Christians about COVID Vaccine GENOCIDE Plot (Other Pastors: Follow This Example) – Vaccines and Christianity'. *Vaccines and Christianity, 22 Apr. 2021*, https://www.vaccinesandchristianity.org/2021/04/22/listen-pastor-warns-christians-about-covid-vaccine-genocide-plot-other-pastors-follow-this-example/. Accessed 4 May 2021.

[240] 'FINALLY! – A Sermon against the COVID Vaccine – Vaccines and Christianity'. *Vaccines and Christianity*, 6 Apr. 2021, https://www.vaccinesandchristianity.org/2021/04/06/finally-a-sermon-against-the-covid-vaccine/. Accessed 4 May 2021.

[241] 'Executive Order on Promoting COVID-19 Safety in Domestic and International Travel'. *The White House*, 21 Jan. 2021, https://www.whitehouse.gov/briefing-room/presidential-actions/2021/01/21/executive-order-promoting-covid-19-safety-in-domestic-and-international-travel/.

mentation was planned long before the pandemic began. The initial proposal for vaccine passports was first published on 26 April, 2018 by the European Commission. Ignored by the mainstream media it quietly proposed 'Strengthened Cooperation Against Vaccine Preventable Diseases'[242] for Europeans, to *"examine the feasibility of developing a common vaccination card/passport, compatible with electronic immunization information systems and recognized for use across borders."*

The UK government has actually been rolling out both COVI PASS – Biometric RFID enabled Coronavirus Digital Health Passports[243] and also the V-health Passport[244] since mid 2020, to monitor nearly every aspect of people's lives, in the name of more rigorous public health management through military grade tech.

The Rockefeller Foundation and the Clinton Foundation have developed a series of COVID apps,[245] designed to tightly control our post-Covid life. The initiative was launched by non-profit trust Commons Project Foundation, which is part of the World Economic Forum. The Commons Project[246] include COVID apps, including CommonHealth and CommonPass.[247] Incidentally, it was the Rockefeller Foundation that produced the 'Lockstep Scenario', detailed in its 2010 'Scenarios for the Future of Technology' report. This was a precise planning exercise that shows how

---

[242] 'Strengthened Cooperation against Vaccine Preventable Diseases'. *Official Journal of the European Union.* https://eur-lex.europa.eu/legal-content/EN/TXT/PDF/?uri=CELEX:32018H1228(01). Accessed 4 May 2021.

[243] 'COVI PASS - UK Introduces Biometric RFID Enabled Coronavirus Digital Health Passports'. *GreatGameIndia*, 27 May 2020, https://greatgameindia.com/covi-pass-biometric-rfid-enabled-coronavirus-digital-health-passports/.

[244] 'V-Health Passport - The Peoples Passport'. *V-Health*, https://v-healthpassport.co.uk/. Accessed 4 May 2021.

[245] 'How Your Post COVID Life Will Be Controlled By Rockefeller & Clinton Foundation Funded Apps'. *GreatGameIndia*, 9 Oct. 2020, https://greatgameindia.com/rockefeller-clinton-covid-apps/.

[246] *The Commons Project,* https://thecommonsproject.org. Accessed 4 May 2021.

[247] 'CommonPass'. *The Commons Project*, https://thecommonsproject.org/commonpass. Accessed 4 May 2021.

global elites can manipulate and influence public policies during a pandemic. And, of course, Bill Gates has been using biometric ID vaccination records in Africa since 2019, with his 'TrustStamp' scheme – a partnership between his company GAVI and Mastercard. Let's also not forget his filed Patent WO2020060606 for using biometric ID data to mine cryptocurrency.[248]

Then there's the US-based, White House-backed 'Good Health Pass Collaborative':[249] *"The Good Health Pass Collaborative is an open, inclusive, cross-sector initiative, bringing together leading companies and organizations from the technology, health, and travel sectors. Our members are creating a blueprint for interoperable digital health pass systems and building a safe path to restore international travel and restart the global economy."*

IBM has produced its 'Digital Health Pass',[250] linked to a person's digital wallet and blockchain, dependent on PCR test results and vaccine status. It was first rolled out in New York in March 2021 and is dubbed as *"[a] smart way to return to society: Digital Health Pass is designed to enable businesses to verify health credentials for employees, customers, fans and travellers entering their site based on their own criteria."* This is particularly concerning, since IBM was the company that produced the Nazi Germany Holocaust punch cards, so it's not this company's first rodeo. The cards had standardised perforations representing specific individual traits such as gender, nationality and occupation and were used to keep track of prisoners in the concentration camps. How quickly we seem to forget history. To top it all, in March 2021, China urged the WHO to let

---

[248] 'Bill Gates Will Use Your Microchipped Body to Mine Cryptocurrency'. *Biohackinfo News*, 20 Apr. 2020, https://biohackinfo.com/news-microsoft-patent-wo2020060606-human-biometrics-crypto-mining/. Accessed 4 May 2021.

[249] *Good Health Pass,* https://www.goodhealthpass.org/. Accessed 4 May 2021.

[250] 'Digital Health Pass'. *IBM*, https://www.ibm.com/products/digital-health-pass. Accessed 4 May 2021.

it run the world database for vaccine passports.[251] I think the writing's on the wall as to where this is all headed, if not already here by the time you're reading this. Whilst mainstream media tried to paint Israel's pioneering rollout of the vaccine passport as exemplary and generally a very good thing, for the safety of all news on the ground in Israel shows a very different picture.[252] Many people there are suffering, distressed and marginalised by this 'medical segregation' and tyranny. A 'no vaccine, no Church' mandate was implemented first in Israel and the rest of the world is following suit. This is, indeed, a Romans 13 issue.

In her 2008 book, 'End of America', Naomi Wolf outlines the 10 steps that those in power use to close down democracies and bring in authoritarianism. Sadly, she observes that as governments use the pandemic to justify the suppression of civil rights, America (and the rest of the world) is now in the throes of 'Step Ten'. In an interview, she stated: *"I cannot say this forcefully enough: This is literally the end of human liberty in the West if this plan unfolds as planned."*[253]

Former Pfizer Vice President and Chief Science Officer, Dr Mike Yeadon made these remarks about the Covid passport on the America's Front Line Doctors website[254] in April 2021, which chillingly sums up the situation:

"Those who think vaccine passports are good or at least ok, I'm addressing you. If you were a vulnerable person and have been vaccinated,

---

[251] Martel, Frances. 'China Urges W.H.O. to Let It Run Global "Vaccine Passport" System'. *Breitbart*, 10 Mar. 2021, https://www.breitbart.com/asia/2021/03/10/china-urges-who-let-it-run-global-vaccine-passport-system/.

[252] Zonshine, Idan. 'Protest against Vaccine Coercion, Green Passports in Tel Aviv'. *The Jerusalem Post - JPost.com*, 24 Feb. 2021, https://www.jpost.com/israel-news/protesters-demonstrate-against-vaccine-coercion-green-passports-in-tel-aviv-660106. Accessed 4 May 2021.

[253] Haines, Tim. 'Naomi Wolf: Mandatory Vaccine Passport Could Lead To The End Of Human Liberty In The West'. *RealClear Politics*, 29 Mar. 2021, https://www.realclearpolitics.com/video/2021/03/29/naomi_wolf_mandatory_vaccine_passport_could_lead_to_end_of_human_liberty_in_the_west.html. Accessed 4 May 2021.

[254] 'Former Pfizer VP Issues Warning: 'This Is Israel Now, UK in Just a Few Weeks' *America's Frontline Doctors*, 13 Apr. 2021, https://www.americasfrontlinedoctors.org/frontline-news/former-pfizer-vp-issues-warning-this-is-israel-now-uk-in-just-a-few-weeks. Accessed 4 May 2021.

you're protected. You don't need to know others' immune status. Note, even if they've been vaccinated, that doesn't guarantee they can't carry a single virus particle and donate it to you. So it doesn't help you or make your safer to know everyone else has been vaccinated. If you've declined vaccination, for example, because you're not at risk from this virus, noting younger people are at MORE risk from influenza than from Covid-19, you also don't need to know anyone else's immune status.

Vaccination protects those who need it. Vaccine passports protect nobody. But vaxpass is useful to our overlords. It'll be the world's first common format database, operable anywhere from Bolton to Bogota, containing your unique digital ID and an editable health status flag (initially about vaccination status).

*Who controls that database and any algorithm governing what it permits and denies has absolutely **totalitarian control** over every aspect of your life? Imagine a future in which a valid Vaxpass is required to enter a sport ground or museum. Invalid Vaxpass, no entry. Now imagine the rules are hardened up (they will be). Now you can't enter large shopping malls or hotels without a valid pass. Further? Sure, why not. The algorithm is tweaked and now you cannot enter large supermarkets or any public transport. A tyrannical step might be a Visa/MasterCard tweak that requires a valid Vaxpass BEFORE a terminal will open up for a purchase transaction. Now you can't even buy a bottle of water. Or fuel. Or anything.*

Ping! Your Vaxpass orders you to report for your top up vaccine. If you don't, your pass expires. Do you think you've got a choice? Ping! You're reminded to bring your grandson in, too, as his mother hasn't. If you don't, your pass becomes invalid, as does the baby's mother's pass. Still think you've got a choice? The fact that I can easily come up with examples must tell you at least that the potential for utterly totalitarian control of the entire population forever lies like a worm at the centre of this beyond-Orwellian future.

It's not speculative. We're told this system is about to happen. You'll **be coerced to be vaccinated or you'll rapidly be marginalised.** *Once you're vaccinated, the limited freedoms they allow you can be withdrawn at any moment. Don't kid yourselves that 'no one would be this evil'. I refer you to numerous examples during the last century. There are plenty of evil people and the only difference here is SCALE and the irreversible nature of it. Now you've seen what is so easy to do to take complete control of a whole society, you MUST object and find ways to prevent a vaccine passport system from coming into being. By any and all means necessary.*

Finally, to those who say this is all a series of unfortunate and incompetent errors, please watch this documentary.[255] *Long before you get to the end, you'll realise, as I did with mounting horror, that this is absolutely not incompetence. It's rehearsed and exercises like this have been war gamed for years if not decades. It'll perhaps change your thoughts as to the origins of this mess and crimes. But please, one thing: do not say you weren't warned."*

No Vaccine, No Job, No Church?

In less than three months since the experimental injections were foisted on society at large across the world, we have 'no vaccine, no job/Church' mandates coming out thick and fast. A US Catholic bishop has stated that all choir members and Communion ministers must be fully vaccinated:[256] *"Choirs can be permitted only when all members have been vaccinated and preferably wearing masks and congregational signing should be masked and kept to a minimum."* And another one requiring the same in

---

[255] 'Paul Schreyer: Pandemic Simulation Games – Preparation for a New Era?' *YouTube*, https://www.youtube.com/watch?v=d3WUv5SV5Hg. Accessed 4 May 2021.

[256] 'Choirs, Holy Water and Altar Servers Will Return April 1' *Arkansas Catholic, 2* Apr. 2021, https://www.arkansas-catholic.org/news/article/6909/Choirs-holy-water-and-altar-servers-will-return-April-1. Accessed 4 May 2021.

New Mexico.[257] Saudi Arabia is now only allowing 'immunised' pilgrims to Mecca.[258]

Employers in some sectors, such as frontline care work, are mandating the vaccine as a job requirement.[259] Officials in Rock County, USA nursing home issued a memo in December 2020 informing staff that having the injection was 'a requirement for all staff' and those who did not comply would be laid off[260] for 'failing to perform the essential functions of the job'. The health minister in Sweden has stated that vaccine passports will 'probably be required' for shopping, eating out, travel, meeting loved ones.[261] This is slavery and is demonic in nature. Our LORD calls us to stand firm, submit to Him and resist the devil.

An against the grain, breath of fresh air response in all of this has been from the Marcionite Church, which has forbidden taking RNA/DNA vaccinations for its members,[262] for seven years! Church spokesman, Darren Kelama, says that Scripture has played a role in their decision: *Or do you not know that your body is the temple of the Holy Spirit who is in you, whom you have from God, and you are not your own? For you were*

---

[257] 'Memo from Msgr. Raun- Tuesday February 23rd, 2021'. *St. Thomas Aquinas Church*, http://www.stanm.org/blog/2021/02/24/memo-from-msgr-raun-tuesday-february-23rd-2021. Accessed 4 May 2021.

[258] 'Saudi Arabia to Allow Only "immunised" Pilgrims to Mecca'. *WION*, https://www.wionews.com/world/saudi-arabia-to-allow-only-immunised-pilgrims-to-mecca-375572. Accessed 4 May 2021.

[259] Roach, April. 'Employers plan 'No Jab, No Job' Contracts after Vaccines Minister said it was 'Up to Businesses what they do'. *Evening Standard,* 17 Feb. 2021, https://www.standard.co.uk/news/uk/no-jab-no-job-covid-vaccine-contracts-b920069.html.

[260] Delaney, Patrick. 'Nursing Home Fires Workers for Refusing COVID-19 Vaccination'. *LifeSiteNews,* 25 Jan. 2021, https://www.lifesitenews.com/news/nursing-home-fires-workers-for-refusing-covid-19-vaccination. Accessed 4 May 2021.

[261] McLoone, David. 'Sweden Vaccine Passports Will "Probably Be Required" for Shopping, Eating out, Travel, Meeting Loved Ones'. *LifeSiteNews*, 8 Feb. 2021, https://www.lifesitenews.com/news/sweden-vaccine-passports-will-probably-be-required-for-shopping-eating-out-travel-meeting-loved-ones. Accessed 4 May 2021.

[262] Marcionite Christian Church. 'Marcionite Church Forbids RNA/DNA Vaccinations for Members'. *Press Release Distribution (PRLog)*, 31 July 2020, https://www.prlog.org/12832383-marcionite-Church-forbids-rnadna-vaccinations-for-members.html. Accessed 4 May 2021.

bought at a price; therefore glorify God in your body and in your spirit, which are God's." – 1 Corinthians 6:19-21 (NKJV). He says: *"Our understanding is that DNA vaccines inject synthesized genes, altering the human genetic makeup forever in unknown ways. And the RNA vaccines have the potential to trigger autoimmune reactions wherein the body attacks itself. Permanently altering a perfect creation of God using the cover story of a virus like Covid, which is about as dangerous as the flu, is not a risk we're willing to take."* Also, Pastor David Lynn at Christ's Forgiveness Ministries [263] in Toronto, Canada has issued this statement on their website: *"Our position on COVID-19 vaccinations, vaccinations, blood, and other medicines are as follows: We do not support, endorse, or believe that CFM members or anyone else should take the Covid 19 vaccine nor be forced to insert, inject, inhale, digest, or swallow any electronic/chemically triggered device, food, medication, drug, pill, vaccination and/or DNA or RNA altering substance against their will, as it can alter God's design and purpose in their lives, force exposure to potential unwanted side effects and even premature death, and cause believers to violate their conscience and relationship with God, bringing constant emotional, mental, and spiritual frustration and turmoil concerning the well-being of their soul (Romans 14:5, 22-23; Romans 2:15, Hebrews 10:22, 1 Timothy 1:5,19-22, 1 Timothy 3:9)."* I say, Amen!

11. The Irony is That No Vaccine is Actually Necessary

As a Nutritionist, Optimum Health Coach and former Medical Research Manager with over 20 years' experience, I know perfectly well that a vaccine is not by any means the be all and end all of how to solve any kind of virus or health issue. Rather, boosting our natural immunity, reducing

---

[263] 'Christ's Forgiveness Ministries.' *Christ's Forgiveness Ministries.*, https://christsforgivenessministries.org/. Accessed 5 May 2021.

stress and lifestyle toxins and eating well is the truly tried and tested 'safe and effective' (and I would argue, Biblical and holy) method and crucially important to consider and act upon. Vaccines should not be prioritised over nutrition, lifestyle and social determinants of health. It is not what God mandates and it's not wise. This is clearly a case of man's precepts and a love of money and power by a few at the top, led by Gates and his mates, over sound common health sense that's been used for millennia.

Alternative safe and effective Covid remedies[264] can include a combination of:

- Curcumin – an anti-inflammatory antioxidant compound found in turmeric that has been successfully used to treat cancer, infectious diseases and coronaviruses.
- Heavy doses of Vitamin C, as well as Vitamin D3 (get out in the sun, lots), or more generally the use of micronutrients essential to fight infections, such as Zinc and vitamins A, B, C, D, and E.
- Colloidal silver products are great for boosting the immune system and fighting bacteria and viruses.
- Infrared light and saunas.
- Boosting gut health with prebiotic and probiotic foods.
- Getting enough alkaline minerals such as Potassium, Magnesium, Calcium and Sodium to support immunity, heart function and the sympathetic and parasympathetic nervous systems to reduce stress.
- Eating healthy fats – grass fed butter, coconut oil, avocados.
- Possible use of correct doses of Hydroxychloroquine.[265]

---

[264] 'Coronavirus – No Vaccine Is Needed to Cure It'. *Global Research*, 19 Dec. 2020, https://www.globalresearch.ca/coronavirus-no-vaccine-needed-cure/5708327.

[265] Sherav, Vera. 'Dr Meryl Nass Discovers Hydroxychloroquine Experiments Were Designed to Kill COVID Patients – How Many Were Murdered?' *Vaccine Impact*, 21 June 2020, https://vaccineimpact.com/2020/dr-meryl-nass-discovers-hydroxychloroquine-experiments-were-designed-to-kill-covid-patients-how-many-were-murdered/.

- Nebulised Hydrogen peroxide.[266] [Update – Dr Mercola, who has been very vocal about the efficacy of nebulised H2O2, has been threatened and has removed many of his articles about Covid, including this one! He states: *"Unfortunately, threats have now become very personal and have intensified to the point I can no longer preserve much of the information and research I've provided to you thus far. So, effective immediately, much of the information on my website will be permanently removed."* Read more on his website – exceedingly concerning.]

The world has gone into lockdown, economic meltdown and social breakdown over something that is easily addressable with some simple diet and lifestyle disciplines. I'll say it again – this is deception of the highest magnitude and with the most grievous consequences. We simply must resist this.

12. The Spiritual Dangers of Transhumanism

DNA and RNA genetic modification and nanobot technology being melded into humans is an abomination to God, as is human and animal hybrid experimentation[267] as is eugenics – all of which are being enforced in the name of developing science, vaccines and pushing the frontiers of life, right now. They have deep spiritual implications and are occult to their core. Our genome is uniquely designed by our Maker and it's not to be tampered with by Satan. Our redeemed life was bought by the precious blood of the Lamb and our bodies are His.

---

[266] Mercola, Dr Joseph. 'Why Valuable COVID Info Will Be Removed From Mercola.Com'. *CNBS News*, 5 May 2021 https://www.cnbsnews.live/global-issues/why-valuable-covid-info-will-be-removed-from-mercola-com/.

[267] 'China's Secret Human Animal Hybrid Experiments'. *GreatGameIndia*, 5 Apr. 2021, https://greatgameindia.com/china-secret-human-animal-hybrid-experiments/.

"You were bought at a price; do not become slaves of men." – 1 Corinthians 7:23 (NKJV)

God makes humans, animals and all species distinct and separate. The people behind the vaccine do not trust in the God of the Bible, they think that they can be as gods – like their father the devil. We, as Christians must have no part in this.

"And God said, Let the earth bring forth grass, the herb yielding seed, and the fruit tree yielding fruit after his kind, whose seed is in itself, upon the earth: and it was so. And the earth brought forth grass, and herb yielding seed after his kind, and the tree yielding fruit, whose seed was in itself, after his kind: and God saw that it was good ... And God created great whales, and every living creature that moveth, which the waters brought forth abundantly, after their kind, and every winged fowl after his kind: and God saw that it was good ... And God said, Let the earth bring forth the living creature after his kind, cattle, and creeping thing, and beast of the earth after his kind: and it was so. And God made the beast of the earth after his kind, and cattle after their kind, and every thing that creepeth upon the earth after his kind: and God saw that it was good. And God said, Let us make man in our image, after our likeness". – Genesis 1:11-12, 21, 24-26

Living beings were created 'according to their kind' and we were made in God's likeness. A blurring of these distinctions must never be sanctioned or submitted to. Once we can see these clear and very serious problems with a Covid 'vaccine', we can also see that enforced mass vaccination is **binding to our consciences**.

Our Laws and Freedoms – Why We Must Resist the Vaccine ... Now

To enforce a vaccine upon us (or force the Church to close, wear masks, stop singing, etc.) goes against many key laws and freedoms set in place centuries or decades ago and still valid today. Therefore, it is not only immoral and abominable but it's illegal, unconstitutional and anti-Christian.

The Nuremberg Code

The Nuremberg Code[268] aimed to protect human subjects from enduring the kind of cruelty and exploitation the prisoners endured under Nazi concentration camps. The 10 elements of the code are concerned with human experimentation and are as follows:

1. Voluntary consent is essential.
2. The results of any experiment must be for the greater good of society.
3. Human experiments should be based on previous animal experimentation.
4. Experiments should be conducted by avoiding physical/mental suffering and injury.
5. No experiments should be conducted if it is believed to cause death/disability.
6. The risks should never exceed the benefits.
7. Adequate facilities should be used to protect subjects.
8. Experiments should be conducted only by qualified scientists.
9. Subjects should be able to end their participation at any time.
10. The scientist in charge must be prepared to terminate the experiment when injury, disability, or death is likely to occur.

An enforced Covid vaccine contravenes at least 8 of these statutes.

In Nazi Germany, the defence offered by almost all of the people convicted of medical war crimes at Nuremberg was notable and predictable: *"I was only following orders."* Or, *"I was only doing my job."* Also no-

---

[268] *The Nuremberg Code*, http://www.cirp.org/library/ethics/nuremberg/. Accessed 4 May 2021.

table is that, since the Covid plandemic legally constitutes a state of emergency /state of war /medical martial law, there is a possibility that similar severe penalties could be brought on those who commit similar war crimes during this time and using similar lame excuses. Indeed, the legal cases have begun …

Dr Reiner Fuellmich, German defence lawyer who has successfully mounted criminal cases against the likes of Deutsche Bank and Volkswagen, is part of the German Corona Investigative Committee, which is bringing crimes against humanity charges against the world's lockdown and other Covid mandates promoters[269] – using the Nuremberg Code and targeting the World Economic Forum. The Committee's case and investigations centre around the question: *"Is there a corona pandemic or is there only a PCR-test pandemic? Specifically, does a positive PCR-test result mean that the person tested is infected with Covid-19, or does it mean absolutely nothing in connection with the Covid-19 infection?"*

This Corona Fraud Scandal is the biggest tort case ever mounted and has unfolded into probably the greatest crime against humanity ever. There are over one thousand lawyers and over 10,000 medical experts involved in bringing legal proceedings against the CDC, WHO & the Davos Group for crimes against humanity committed under the Covid 19 mandates.

International bioweapons policy expert, Dr Francis Boyle, who believes unequivocally that Covid 19 was released intentionally as a bioweapon, advocates using this statement[270] if someone tries to force you to be injected under Covid:

---

[269] 'Dr Reiner Fuellmich Is Currently Preparing the Largest Class Action Lawsuit in History'. *BitChute*, https://www.bitchute.com/video/CmqSEvg8psGV/. Accessed 4 May 2021.

[270] Alatalo, Jerry. 'Boyle: Nuremberg Code On Medical Experimentation Is International Law.' *THE ONENESS of HUMANITY*, 21 Jan. 2021, https://onenessofhumanity.wordpress.com/2021/01/21/boyle-nuremberg-code-on-medical-experimentation-is-international-law/.

*"**NOTICE:** By authority of the Nuremberg Code on Medical Experimentation, I do hereby exercise my right to refuse to submit to or to administer the COVID-19 vaccine. The United States/UK Government has prosecuted, convicted and executed Medical Doctors who have violated the Nuremberg Code on Medical Experimentation. Aiders and abettors of Nuremberg Crimes are equally guilty and have also been prosecuted, convicted, and executed."*

USA Constitution Bill of Rights – First Amendment (1791)

The First Amendment states[271]: *"Congress shall make no law respecting an establishment of religion, or prohibiting the free exercise thereof; or abridging the freedom of speech, or of the press; or the right of the people peaceably to assemble, and to petition the government for a redress of grievances."* Many of the Covid mandates directly contravene the First Amendment. It was dissenting Protestants that had a major impact on America's constitutional Bill of Rights and fought and gave their lives to have these religious freedoms put in place and upheld. Are we about to let that all slide away from us, uncontested?

Magna Carta – Clause 1 (1215)

Four of Magna Carta's clauses are still part of English law today.[272] The first clause is one such and guarantees the freedom of the English Church. It was specifically included to stop the king from interfering in Church worship and decisions: *"Clause 1: FIRST, THAT WE HAVE GRANTED TO GOD, and by this present charter have confirmed for us and our heirs in perpetuity, that the English Church shall be free, and shall have its rights undiminished, and its liberties unimpaired. That we wish this so to be observed, appears from the fact that of our own free will, before the outbreak of the present dispute between us and our barons, we granted and confirmed by charter the freedom of the Church's elections – a right*

---

[271] The Bill of Rights: Amendments 1-10 to the U.S. Constitution, https://constitution.com/bill-rights/.

[272] *Magna Carta. The British Library*, https://www.bl.uk/magna-carta. Accessed 4 May 2021.

reckoned to be of the greatest necessity and importance to it – and caused this to be confirmed by Pope Innocent III. This freedom we shall observe ourselves, and desire to be observed in good faith by our heirs in perpetuity."

The Human Rights Act 1998

Article 9 of the Human Rights Act[273] addresses freedom of thought, belief and religion …

"Freedom of thought, conscience and religion:

1. *Everyone has the right to freedom of thought, conscience and religion; this right includes freedom to change his religion or belief and freedom, either alone or in community with others and in public or private, to manifest his religion or belief, in worship, teaching, practice and observance.*
2. *Freedom to manifest one's religion or beliefs shall be subject only to such limitations as are prescribed by law and are necessary in a democratic society in the interests of public safety, for the protection of public order, health or morals, or for the protection of the rights and freedoms of others."*

There are no doubt countless other individual countries' laws that I could list here.

---

[273] *Article 9: Freedom of Thought, Belief and Religion | Equality and Human Rights Commission.* https://www.equalityhumanrights.com/en/human-rights-act/article-9-freedom-thought-belief-and-religion. Accessed 4 May 2021.

Remaining Positive About Not Taking the Covid Shot

When resolving to not take this Satanic witches' brew injection, we need to stay resilient and positive and not be paralysed by fear. There is no need to fear condemnation – you are not condemned by Jesus, so don't let anyone else condemn you. Don't worry about 'what the cool kids might say about it and powerful men might do to us', as Doug Wilson says.[274]

Powers that be and civilians alike are going to try to discredit you and try and silence you, so brace yourself and hold on. You'll no longer be granted access to a theme park to ride a rollercoaster, or aeroplanes to travel to exotic places, without your virtual vaccine papers, so you may as well enjoy the thrill of the ups and downs and scares and new realms of real life when people, more than ever, openly oppose you, even your Christian brothers and sisters whose eyes are shut and are in error. We are promised rich joy and peace in all circumstances when we follow the LORD closely. I know this to be very true in the midst of much opposition. If you're concerned about not being able to buy or sell or get food, what a great opportunity it is for upgraded faith in our LORD! Could be that the Church in the wilderness may be fed again by manna from heaven, or by ravens as we oppose the modern-day prophets of Baal?

"As far as the Lord is concerned, the time to stand is in the darkest moment. It is when everything seems hopeless, when there appears no way out, when God alone can deliver." – David Wilkerson

---

[274] *The Fiasco of No Fear - Doug Wilson. YouTube*, https://www.youtube.com/watch?v=0hDDfiiuhIg. Accessed 4 May 2021.

If you want a clear, concise list of reasons NOT to get the experimental jab, read Australian physicist, Dr John G. Hartnett's article '18 Reasons I Won't Be Getting a Covid Jab'.[275]

What if I've Had the Vaccine?

If you acted rashly and went ahead with the injection, or the first part of the injection, or are partaking in its administration in any way, please pray. Here is a very good vaccination-specific prayer.[276]

Medical experts, like Dr Sherri Tenpenny, are widely stating that there is no 'detoxing' from this vaccine, as it's part of your DNA make-up once you take it. Just like you can't detox from things like Down's syndrome. However, it may be possible to calm the negative autoimmune effects. A ketogenic diet, plenty of Vitamin D, Vitamin C and Zinc are some good recommendations. Please see Chapter 13 (section ten), for more health suggestions that may help.

Many of the vaccine companies say that they only 'offer protection' for a period of six months at most, thus requiring that you have regular 'boosters'. Knowing what you know now, would you really want repeated injections of this type? Remember, chips and bots are an inevitability in this thing. This is not conspiracy theory; it is conspiracy fact.

---

[275] Hartnett, John Gideon. '18 Reasons I Won't Be Getting a Covid Jab'. *Bible Science Forum*, 13 Apr. 2021, https://bibliescienceforum.com/2021/04/13/18-reasons-i-wont-be-getting-a-covid-jab/.

[276] 'Prayer of Repentance for Any Spiritual Contamination in the Development and Use of Vaccines'. *Aslan's Place*. 12 Jan. 2021, https://aslansplace.com/language/en/vaccines/. Accessed 4 May 2021.

A Never-Ending Story

The 2010 Rockefeller 'Lock Step Scenario' report[277] states that: *"Even after the pandemic faded, this more authoritarian control and oversight of citizens and their activities stuck and even intensified. In order to protect themselves from the spread of increasingly global problems – from pandemics and transnational terrorism to environmental crises and rising poverty – leaders around the world took a firmer grip on power."*

Our governments are following carefully laid out plans issued by the elites and those plans do not make provision for a return to greater societal freedom; they plan for our demise, I am very sorry to say. They have seen their worldwide success in playing the Covid card since early 2020. They have also successfully played the 'dangerous new strain' card and even the 'Covid transmission to animals, so we need to vaccinate them' card. Vaccine deaths can be plausibly passed off as the virus, so why fix what isn't broken? As long as it works and people are taken in by it all, it will be an ongoing saga. And if enough people start to wake up, they have other cards up their sleeve which will be played – cyber-attacks, new bio-weapons, fake terrorism and the like. Make no mistake, this is warfare. In warfare, you stand and fight, not sit and wait for the enemy's next move and welcome the attack.

Prayer Suggestion – Psalm 109. Note: We can pray such imprecatory Psalms because we are in Christ and in agreement with Him. These Psalms leave vengeance up to God and indeed, Jesus bore the vengeance that they ask for. We can pray them against the demonic principalities and powers and corrupt world systems, as well as our own sinful nature and enemies.

---

[277] 'Scenarios for the Future of Technology and International Development.' *Internet Archive* (The Rockefeller Foundation and Global Business Network), May 2010, http://archive.org/details/pdfy-tNG7MjZUicS-wiJb.

CHAPTER FIVE

The Four Types of Governance and Church-State Relations

"Owe no one anything except to love one another, for he who loves another has fulfilled the law." – Romans 13:8 (NKJV)

When most people hear the word 'government', what they think of is city hall, the White House or the Houses of Parliament. But that is not the basic definition of government in the Bible. Rather, it refers to a sphere of delegated authority.

God's governance is supreme; that goes without saying and is revealed to us through the Scriptures. There are four types of government authorities as ordained by God – four mechanisms through which He has chosen to rule:

1. Church government
2. Family government
3. Civil government
4. Self-government

Many people ask the questions: What is the remit and level of authority of the State over the Church? What about Church authority over the State? What about individual and family authority? What's the line for civil disobedience? What examples do we see in the Bible as good precedent?

Civil government does not trump all the others. Each has its own function and jurisdiction given and delegated by God. If any one of them oversteps their authority, we have to pull the tripwire and disobey. Author of the very good book, 'The Great Reckoning: Surviving a Christianity That Looks Nothing Like Christ', Stephen Mattson, notes:[278] *"Christians must choose which kingdom they will serve: a kingdom of this world or the Kingdom of God. Because eventually, you'll be forced to choose which one has the highest priority in your life. When your desire to 'respect governing authorities' directly opposes God's great command to 'love your neighbour as yourself', what will you do? God has already told us which directive is more important, but Christians too often prefer listening to their partisan politicians over their Prince of Peace. God help us."* That said, 2 Samuel 23:3-4 (NKJV) reminds us that Civil government and rule is a blessing from God and not a necessary evil: *"The God of Israel said, The Rock of Israel spoke to me: 'He who rules over men must be just, Ruling in the fear of God. And he shall be like the light of the morning when the sun rises, A morning without clouds, Like the tender grass springing out of the earth, By clear shining after rain.'"* To expand on this, and to present a balanced argument, Pastor John Piper gives this charitable view about obeying governments: *"I think Paul ... would say, "Listen, here is what I am doing. Number one, Caesar is going to read this, and I will want to make sure that the ruling authorities in Rome know that Christians are not anarchists. We are basically law-abiding citizens and we believe that he has his position by God." That is the first thing. And the second thing, I think he wants to say to Christians, "Don't get*

---

[278] Mattson, Stephen. 'Misusing Romans 13 to Embrace Theocracy'. *Sojourners*, 10 Dec. 2019, https://sojo.net/articles/misusing-romans-13-embrace-theocracy.

your back up so easily, because being wronged by a government sends nobody to hell, but being rebellious and angry and bitter and spiteful does send people to hell. And so it is a much greater evil for you to be rebellious than of the government to mistreat you. Much greater evil for you that is. " However, in another sermon on Romans 13, John Piper states:[279] *"Paul simply does not have in view the problem of evil governments. Instead he has in view a good government in which doing good deeds will generally find approval and doing evil will generally be punished. If this is correct, then it will no longer be possible to insist that Christians should always be subject to the governing authorities. As long as authorities punish only what is evil and praise only what is good, submission to God will always conform to submission to the authorities. But if the authorities ever begin to punish the good and reward the bad (as has repeatedly happened in Church history), then submission to God will bring us into conflict with the authorities. So the command to be subject in verses 1 and 5 is not absolute; it depends on whether subjection will involve us in doing wrong. The ultimate criterion of right and wrong is not whether a ruling authority commands it, but whether God commands it. The fact that God has ordained all authority does not mean all authority should be obeyed. It is right to resist what God has appointed in order to obey what God has commanded."*

We'll look at each of the four types of governance in turn and some examples of when disobedience is permitted and necessary. American historian and activist, Howard Zinn reminds us that, *"historically, the most terrible things: war, genocide and slavery, have resulted not from disobedience, but from obedience."*

---

[279] Piper, John. 'The Limits of Submission to Man'. *Desiring God*, 5 July 1981, https://www.desiringgod.org/messages/the-limits-of-submission-to-man.

1. Church Government

Both Church and State are under God's ultimate authority, **but the Church is separate to the State and trumps it.** Where there is a conflict between God's ordinances and civil ones, we must obey God, as made very clear in the Bible and particularly so in Acts 5: *"And when they had brought them, they set them before the council. And the high priest asked them, saying, "Did we not strictly command you not to teach in this name? And look, you have filled Jerusalem with your doctrine, and intend to bring this Man's blood on us!" But Peter and the other apostles answered and said: "We ought to obey God rather than men. The God of our fathers raised up Jesus whom you murdered by hanging on a tree. Him God has exalted to His right hand to be Prince and Savior, to give repentance to Israel and forgiveness of sins." –* Acts 5:27-31 (NKJV)

The US First Amendment legally protects the separation between Church and State, as do many other countries' laws, as we looked at in Chapter 4. 'The Religious Roots of the First Amendment'[280] by Professor of Church History and ex-lawyer, Dr Nicholas P. Miller explains how it was dissenting Protestants that had a major impact on America's constitutional Bill of Rights. However, …

501(c)(3) Corporations

It is important to note that many US Churches are registered as Tax Exempt 'not-for-profit' organisations (for corporations, trusts and unincorporated associations) under Internal Revenue Code section 501(c)(3), which has a major negative impact on their First Amendment protections. Similar legal entity status restrictions can apply in other countries too. Pastor Sam Adams of Independence Baptist Church, Florida has spoken

---

[280] Miller, Nicholas Patrick. The Religious Roots of the First Amendment: Dissenting Protestants and the Separation of Church and State. Oxford University Press, 2012.

and written fervently on this topic:[281] *"501(c)(3) status ... is a trap used by the government to control the Churches and silence the preachers of America from influencing our government and society, and from crying out against wicked government policies, politics and politicians. For over a hundred years after the adoption of the Bill of Rights, the Church stood rightly as the 'watchdog' over the government, holding government accountable to the Word of God (Psalm 149:5-9). Legislation in Christian America back then had to pass the 'pulpit test'; if it wouldn't preach well from the pulpits it would surely not pass in the legislature. Sadly, those days are now long gone and the Churches have in many ways been effectively silenced. They have become incorporated, they have acknowledged another lawgiver and another ruler, and thus they have, to their shame, become state churches ... When a Church incorporates, it is then seen in the eyes of the law (by the courts) as a corporation, not a Church. Incorporated 'churches' have no First Amendment rights; they have willingly given up First Amendment protection in exchange for corporate privileges and government subsidies, just as Jacob's older brother Esau traded his birth-right for a mess of pottage. 501(c)(3)s have made an agreement with the government not to 'carry on propaganda' (not defined in the IR Code, but defined in the Bob Jones University case as speaking out against 'prevailing Federal public policy') or to 'attempt to influence legislation'. If an issue such as homosexual rights or child pornography or abortion rights is being considered in Congress, pastors of 501(c)(3) incorporated Churches are not allowed to tell their people to call their congressmen to voice their views, as that is attempting to influence legislation. The day will soon come that the 'propaganda' forbidden by 501(c)3 will include preaching the Gospel that the only way to heaven is through the Lord Jesus. Actually, under current 'hate crime' legislation, that day is already upon us ... NO MAN CAN SERVE TWO MASTERS. Neither can the Church."*

---

[281] *Church Incorporation and Tax Exemption - Independence Baptist Church.* 10 June 2020, https://independencebaptist.com/church-incorporation-and-tax-exemption/.

This is to be factored in when looking at Church authority, since 501(c)(3)s are essentially waiving much of their authority and separation from State.

The Church's Limited Role In Society

The Church does not have a Biblical mandate to rule over the State and try to conquer every area of society, despite what some charismatic Christian movements teach. The New Apostolic Reformation, for example, teaches 'dominion theology' and the 'seven mountain mandate'. Other more conservative teachers, such as R.J. Rushdoony, teach 'Christian reconstructionism' – all are wrongly asserting that Biblical Christianity should and will rule all areas of life and society. Jesus told us that His Kingdom is not of this world (John 18:36) and that we should pray 'Thy Kingdom come'. Our mandate to advance Jesus' Kingdom in the world is by evangelising the lost, making disciples and praying. We can expect Jesus' Kingdom to rule the whole of creation upon His glorious second coming, but not before.

"And the seventh angel sounded; and there were great voices in heaven, saying, The kingdoms of this world are become the kingdoms of our Lord, and of his Christ; and he shall reign for ever and ever." – Revelation 11:15

Church Leadership Authority

Within our Churches, the leadership of pastors, elders, deacons and teachers is essential for the spiritual health of the body of Christ. Believers are to honour and respect leaders and to submit to one another and walk in humility – as per Ephesians 4:11–16, Hebrews 13:17 and 1 Peter 5:1–11. If, however, the Church starts imposing unbiblical rules, we have a right and duty to resist those rules – in the name of our God-given personal or family governance. For example, if we are told that women must wear skirts, or no jeans or trainers are allowed in Church, or that we all must be vegetarian, or that all children must be home-schooled then Church authority is overstepping its mark. This is cult-like behaviour. Even some wise things must not be legislated in Church – like we must read our Bibles every morning, or we must not listen to certain types of worldly music or eat unhealthy foods. There are any number of things that could be discussed in discipleship and advised to be wise or unwise – but there is room for difference in opinion and each person must be fully convinced in his or her own mind on a particular issue, for the sake of their good conscience; the Church must not mandate in areas which Scripture does not. We are reminded in Romans 14:10 that we will each stand before God on our decisions and actions.

I've already stated that, in my view as I have presented, a Church ordering its members to wear a mask or be vaccinated is overstepping its remit of authority – irrespective of whether or not it's following legal orders from civil governments. This would be the case even if those mandates were *good*, let alone *bad*, as they actually are, as we have covered extensively.

2. Family Government

God has entrusted husbands with the leadership of the family unit, under the headship of Christ. A husband is to love his wife as he loves himself. A wife is to submit to the leadership of her husband, coming alongside him as an 'ezer kenegdo' – a suitable (and in many ways more-equipped) helper. Parents are responsible for training their children, and children are to honour and obey their parents. (See Ephesians 5:21-6:4 and Proverbs 6:20-21.) But if a father wields excessive and abusive power over his family, or a husband tells his wife to commit adultery or steal, the wife has permission to override the family authority structure and follow God, not submitting to the wrongful behaviour. Similarly, if a mother encourages her children to follow a false religion, the children are allowed and encouraged to disobey her and follow the one true Living God.

3. Civil Government

State authority includes our national leaders and governments and local officials in positions of power over us for civil and legal matters. The office of Civil government is ordained by God and put in place to protect the rights of persons, property and privacy (have another read through Deuteronomy if you're in any doubt about the laws concerning rights). Whilst there have been many examples of authorities that have indeed been concerned with upholding Biblical Christian principles, most State authorities are secular and not overly committed to what God states as true and right – at least in some areas, if not all. That is ok and whilst we need to be watchful and mindful that there will be conflicts in opinion and values at times, in general we are to submit to our State authorities and to live honourably within our communities – as per the spirit of Romans 13, 1 Peter 2:13 and even Ecclesiastes 8:2-3 (NKJV): *"I say, "Keep the king's commandment for the sake of your oath to God. Do not be hasty to go from his presence. Do not take your stand for an evil thing, for he does whatever pleases him.""*

However, it comes as news to a lot of Christians that governments are NOT set in place over Church; their authority does not trump God's. God's Word is the highest level of authority. Ideally, although not often, governments yield to Jesus and then those men are set in authority to establish societal order, in line with Jesus' teachings. Either way, where civil authorities overstep their bounds, we are bound as Christians to remember that there is no absolute authority but God's, as set out in Scripture, and *we are called to submissive disobedience*.

As Samuel Rutherford stated in his book, 'Lex, Rex',[282] *"Truth to Christ cannot be treason to Caesar"*. Elijah is a fabulous example of this. Just look at his bold confrontation of King Ahab for not upholding the

---

[282] Rutherford, Samuel. *Lex, Rex: The Law and the Prince*. Sprinkle Publications, 1955. (Original work published 1644).

LORD's commands: *"Then Elijah said, "As the Lord of hosts lives, before whom I stand, I will surely present myself to him [Ahab] today." So Obadiah went to meet Ahab, and told him; and Ahab went to meet Elijah. Then it happened, when Ahab saw Elijah, that Ahab said to him, "Is that you, O troubler of Israel?" And he answered, "I have not troubled Israel, but you and your father's house have, in that you have forsaken the commandments of the Lord and have followed the Baals. Now therefore, send and gather all Israel to me on Mount Carmel, the four hundred and fifty prophets of Baal, and the four hundred prophets of Asherah, who eat at Jezebel's table.""* – 1 Kings 18:15-19 (NKJV)

We also need to bear in mind that not *every single government* or authority is instituted and approved of by God. Really? Take a look at this proof text: ***"They have set up kings, but not by me: they have made princes, and I knew it not****: of their silver and their gold have they made them idols, that they may be cut off."* – Hosea 8:4

Further, *all* authorities are subject to God's laws. If they disobey God's laws and sanction and encourage evil, they can expect judgement.

*"Only fear the Lord, and serve Him in truth with all your heart; for consider what great things He has done for you. **But if you still do wickedly, you shall be swept away, both you and your king.**"* – 1 Samuel 12:24-25 (NKJV)

Given that *we* are subject to God's laws and *the authorities* are also subject to God's laws, if the authorities disobey or command disobedience to God's laws, *we must resist them, in order to obey God.* They are, therefore, the ones *initiating unlawful disobedience* and resistance and we are forced to *respond with lawful disobedience* to them. In our current day and age, as with examples we see throughout history and documented in the Bible (such as Herod's ordering of the killing of babies), there are certain State values that are overtly anti-Christian and the Church has indeed resisted. Some of the most prominent ones being pregnancy 'pro-choice' policy, the desecration of one-man-one-woman marriage and the sanctity and distinctness of gender. Right now, the Church is fighting in the face of condemnation and a temptation of weak or deceptive leaders to capitulate to worldly precepts in several key areas; 'gay marriage' (or 'gay mirage' as many stalwarts call it) and 'transgender rights' issues are big ones. Further, since the full passing of the Equality Act in February 2021[283] in the United States, there will be increasing infringements on religious freedoms and heat and hatred towards the Christian worldview. Here is some of the kind of deceptive propaganda that the mainstream media are pumping out about sexual orientation equality,[284] alongside that of Covid. From USA Today: *"After decades of fighting for acceptance and equal treatment under the law, the LGBTQ community has achieved monumental progress and greater representation in media, government, and public affairs than ever before. But with this increased visibility and awareness has come a backlash, particularly at the expense of transgender and nonbinary youth, who continue to face an onslaught of vitriolic rhetoric, legislative attacks, and outright misinformation campaigns each and every day. The rhetoric being used to promote these bills is already doing much harm. When LGBTQ young people see clips of elected officials berating transgender people or hear about policies that would prevent them from living openly as their true self, it can be extremely difficult to process, contribute to internalized stigma, and negatively impact one's mental health and sense of self. Feeling like you need to defend your existence, especially when these violent attacks are coming from those in positions of power, can be incredibly painful and terrifying. And many young people may find they don't have the strength, support, or resources to do so. LGBTQ young people want nothing more than to be loved and accepted for who they are, and studies show that affirming trans youth has positive effects on mental health and decreases suicide risk. This is not just the opinion of LGBTQ organizations – multiple medical, scientific, research, and academic experts and communities urge*

---

[283] Cicilline, David N. *Text - H.R.5 - 116th Congress (2019-2020): Equality Act.* 20 May 2019, https://www.congress.gov/bill/116th-congress/house-bill/5/text.

[284] Paley, Amit. 'Pass the Equality Act: Discriminatory Rhetoric and Laws Are Devastating to LGBTQ Youth'. *USA TODAY,* 26 Feb. 2021, https://www.usatoday.com/story/opinion/voices/2021/02/26/equality-act-discrimination-lgbtq-youth-rand-paul-column/6833817002/. Accessed 4 May 2021.

that affirming a young person's gender identity is essential to their health and wellness."

Legislation to ban 'conversion therapy' is being pushed in Canada[285] and the UK, with activists targeting Bible-believing Churches[286]. Conversion therapy means *"a practice, treatment or service designed to change a person's sexual orientation to heterosexual or gender identity to cisgender, or to repress or reduce non-heterosexual attraction or sexual behaviour."* This would effectively outlaw Gospel freedom to pray and witness to gay and trans people, cutting across the ordinary work of Churches and could even affect Christian parenting. That's right – sin and evil needs to be affirmed and accepted in law says our authorities, on pretty much all areas of morality. This is a clear Romans 13 issue. Other examples of government imposition on the Church that are being proposed and ushered in right now in various places are the re-writing of the Chinese Bible to make it pro-communist[287] and mandating multi-faith services in Churches.

In Melbourne in August 2020 under Covid rules, weddings were banned,[288] along with a whole host of other heavily oppressive rules ... all because 147 people died in the State of Victoria (in a total population of 6.359 million and almost all of those deaths were of people over 70 with comorbidities – the same as everywhere else in the world). Meanwhile, in March 2020, Denmark's parliament unanimously passed an emergency

---

[285] Bill C-6: An Act to amend the Criminal Code (conversion therapy)'. *Government of Canada – Department of Justice*, 27 Oct. 2020, https://www.justice.gc.ca/eng/csj-sjc/pl/charter-charte/c6b.html.

[286] An Open Letter to the Rt Hon Liz Truss'. *Ban Conversion Therapy*, 9 July 2020. https://www.ban-conversiontherapy.com/the-letter. Accessed 1 May 2021.

[287] McLean, Dorothy Cummings. 'Chinese Government to Rewrite Bible to Make It More Communist'. *LifeSiteNews*, 18 Jan. 2019, https://www.lifesitenews.com/news/chinese-communists-to-re-write-christian-scriptures-to-make-them-more-chines. Accessed 4 May 2021.

[288] 'Melbourne, Australia Imposes Curfew, Wedding Ban, Business Shutdown'. *Breitbart*, 3 Aug. 2020, https://www.breitbart.com/europe/2020/08/03/melbourne-australia-imposes-curfew-wedding-ban-business-shutdown-amid-virus-surge/.

coronavirus law[289] and the UK passed its Coronavirus Act,[290] both of which gives health authorities powers to force testing, treatment and quarantine with the backing of the police. The Coronavirus Act gives new powers to detain 'potentially infectious persons' and put them in isolation facilities. This provision impacts on our right to liberty – protected by Article 5 of the Convention of Human Rights. The Act also allows for 'the extension and removal of time limits in mental health legislations', including mental health sectioning detainment.

In December 2020, Emmanuel Macron presented his 'Global Security Bill'[291], which grants dictatorial provisions to governments akin to the 1933 Nazi Enabling Act, which 'enabled' Hitler's government to issue decrees independently of the Reichstag and the presidency and gave him a clear path in his genocide of the Jews. The Bill grants police vast new powers to carry out video-surveillance of the population. Access to security cameras in stores or public institutions as well as apartment complexes will be granted not only to national but also municipal police. Moreover, the bill authorises police to deploy drones with facial recognition technology to overfly and monitor public protest marches.

In our world today, the sobering reality is that governments have intruded on all areas of life in which they have no jurisdiction to; areas governed by God only, such as marriage. Their job should be to protect life, liberty and property. They are doing the opposite – harming all in a very prolific, dangerous and covert or deceptive way. We live in a society where mass genocide labelled 'abortion' is normalised and a nice NHS nurse can guide you through the 'safe and legal' abortion pill by post procedure –

---

[289] 'Denmark Rushes through Emergency Coronavirus Law', *The Local DK*, 13 Mar. 2020, https://www.thelocal.dk/20200313/denmark-passes-far-reaching-emergency-coronavirus-law/. Accessed 4 May 2021.

[290] *Coronavirus Act 2020*, https://www.legislation.gov.uk/ukpga/2020/7/contents. Accessed 4 May 2021.

[291] Torres, Anthony and Alex Lantier. 'Macron Prepares "Global Security" Law Banning the Filming of French Police'. *World Socialist Web Site*, 18 Nov. 2020, https://www.wsws.org/en/articles/2020/11/19/macr-n19.html. Accessed 1 May 2021.

no need to come in to a clinic, just send off for a pack from the comfort of your own home to terminate a life. Not to get too emotive but a brief look at the British Pregnancy Advisory Service's[292] smooth and encouraging propaganda on this has made me feel physically sick and deeply saddened. O LORD God, have mercy upon us.

A key point to remember is that what's against the law doesn't define sin and what's lawful does not always mean that something is not sinful. Many faithful believers have been accused of lawlessness and punished for crimes such as treason. Remember that Elijah, when he righteously stood against the prophets of Baal and King Ahab, was unjustly called 'the troubler of Israel'.

4. Self-Government

We are told that we are to be 'slaves of righteousness' and this means that we submit to God and then, in general, to family, Church and State authority too. That said, we serve a God who has granted us free will choice on many matters. This is what makes us diverse as believers and we have a freedom in Christ which allows us to follow our own personal convictions and decisions – hopefully based upon our love of God, renewal of our mind through reading the Bible and prayer. Those convictions and choices may be wise or unwise, Godly or sinful and we are to disciple each other and rebuke if needs be. In the process of growing and discerning, we are allowed to fail, remembering the grace of God, but not making that an excuse to sin. Keeping all of this in mind, God has given us a limited degree of self-governance and in some areas that overrides the other form of authority. For example, if Church, State or family command us to marry a certain person, or worship an idol, we can disobey with Biblical sanction.

---

[292] 'Coronavirus Essential Service Information'. *British Pregnancy Advisory Service,* https://www.bpas.org/. Accessed 4 May 2021.

CHAPTER SIX

Thesis Conclusions on Romans 13 Resistance

From what we've examined, can we view Romans13:1-7 as a blanket clause to submission? No! It should not be used as a blunt instrument. Gordan Runyan in his brilliant little book from 2012, 'Resistance to Tyrants – Romans 13 and the Christian Duty to Oppose Wicked Rulers',[293] argues that tyrants are *not* the subject of Romans 13:1-7 at all, as we saw John Piper allude to earlier. He teaches that government has a holy purpose, a mandate for its righteous mission that God has ordained. But that simply because a thing *exists* in the created world, as an expression of God's providential rule, it does not necessarily make the individual expression good and approved of by God. He says that if we do not believe this, it poses serious theological problems for us: like Paul being a false preacher for one, since he says that if we do good, we need have no fear of the sword. Yet, there have been countless people who have acted for good and have been met with the magistrate's sword,

---

[293] Runyan, Gordon. Resistance to Tyrants – Romans 13 and the Christian Duty to Oppose Wicked Rulers. CreateSpace Independent Publishing Platform, 2013.

for simply following Christ. Therefore, we can see that whilst the *institution* of Civil government is good, just like the institution of marriage and headship is good, *individual* civil authorities may be tyrants, as may individual husbands. In such cases where they are not acting in accordance to their God-given charge, we have a duty to disobey; not so much for our own interests and safety but more for the principle of upholding righteousness and standing firm against evil.

Runyan states, *"While you wait for the moment the government tells you to renounce Christ, your neighbours and fellow citizens are being trampled by the unrestrained, unjust use of power."* He asks us to ask these pertinent questions, which are essential to what we are facing under the Covid dictates: *"Where is that line? Where shall we distinguish between rulers who are on the right path, though failing badly at times, and those who have forsaken the way altogether and now deserve only righteous opposition? Are we ruled by good powers acting poorly (as with King David in the Bathsheba incident), or evil powers waxing worse and worse? The line is maybe not as bright as we'd like it to be, but, frankly, that is no excuse for acting like no one can possibly see it, ever."*

I would go as far as to say that our world leaders, which are increasingly acting as one voice and one unit (in line with their desire for a 'one world government') crossed this line a long time ago, which is maybe why many cannot recognise the true despotism under Covid. But make no mistake, if we were in any doubt about the line of tyranny being crossed before, it certainly has been under the guise of the 'pandemic', as well as all the other despotic laws that have been passed over the past few years, that we examined earlier in this chapter. Are we in agreement on that? If not, on what basis, may I humbly ask, are you disagreeing?

The fact that many Christians are now signing petitions and writing to their Members of Parliament and Congressmen on the issues of lockdowns, vaccine passports and restrictions of singing groups means that they are *not* now 'joyfully submitting' in good conscience to the Covid mandates. They see an issue with what governments are

enforcing. **If the governments respond positively and acquiesce to requests to relax their control, all well and good. If they don't, what then? The issue still stands. Will that Christian stand against that which he deems as troubling enough to petition in protest about?**

Passive, dejected, begrudging or complaining submission, with bad conscience, is not the type of submission that the Apostle Paul is advocating – where we resign to having no real option but to go along with it for the sake of keeping our head down and just surviving. No, that is *not* an option for the Christian. Submission should be given to the civil authorities voluntarily, positively, assuredly, cheerfully, and in good conscience. If we cannot do that, we MUST resist – also cheerfully and in good conscience.

In Chapters 3 and 4, we have examined many of the clear problems that the Covid 19 mandates have posed for the Church. There are physical, mental, emotional and human rights and freedoms dangers that are a problem for everyone, but also spiritual and ecclesiastical dangers specifically for us as the Body of Christ – seeking to be the light in this world and shine Jesus' Gospel of salvation. There is a lot more I could have said and expounded upon about the problems, but I don't want this book to be any lengthier than it needs to be. We have enough evidence to see that the rules and regulations brought in under the guise of this virus are to be seriously questioned and I have presented a full case to support my original thesis statement:

The Church must resist rules being imposed on her by the State in the name of 'peace and safety' under Covid 19+ (lockdown restrictions, masks, virus testing, vaccinations) since adherence is aiding and abetting deceptive lies, is a dangerous misapplication of Romans 13 and granting authority that belongs to the Living God only; thereby partaking in State idolatry.

In Chapter 2, we looked at the Romans 13 text, on being subject to the governing authorities, in some detail. To recap, in Romans 13:1-7, we can clearly see that people in authority and governmental positions have two key responsibilities. These people are:

1. In place to **do good as servants of Jesus.**
2. To **administer justice against evil behaviour.**

Ephesians 5:11 tells us to *"have no fellowship with the unfruitful works of darkness, but rather reprove them."*

We looked at two main scenarios where problems with this could arise and have arisen since the pandemic mandates have come into effect:

1. If the authorities **don't do good and we submit** (with good and gracious conscience but with concern, or from the seared conscience of fear, cowardice or apathy).
2. If the authorities **don't do good and we don't submit** (from a good or possibly seared conscience).

I have shown that both of these scenarios apply under Covid 19 – that **our State authorities are not doing good** and largely the Western Church has submitted to the authorities' orders to shut. Of course, there are smaller house Churches and fellowship groups and less formalised gatherings that may have continued but when I say 'the Church' in this context, I am referring predominantly to Christian gatherings in physical Church buildings and that are recognised as public places of worship. Some Churches, however, have already firmly and openly, or more quietly and discreetly, resisted and disobeyed some or all of the mandates. There are two very notable examples of this that emerged into prominence in 2020: First, Grace Community Church in Los Angeles, under Pastor John MacArthur who has received a lot of media and police attention and State threats for his civil disobedience. Second, Grace Life Church in Edmonton, Canada, whose pastor, James Coates, was jailed in February 2021 for refusing to comply with Covid 19 mandates issued by Alberta Health Services. More on this later.

The arbitrary and dangerous Covid rules are being imposed on us and will continue to be long into the future, albeit under new and 'mutating' guises. Forced vaccinations are unconstitutional, illegal and immoral. They are BAD, not good. **The dictates are wrong on the orders, wrong on the process and wrong on the facts. Complying is not granting moral authority to good powers that be, it's responding to pre-emptive coercion. Are we still able to hold to Romans 13:1 with integrity and good conscience? No, I do not believe we can, given the copious evidence.** Further, we are not to make an idol out of seven verses in the Bible. We are to weigh up the Romans 13 verses in light of the *whole* counsel of God.

US Presbyterian minister, Gavin Beers, asked an important question: 'what is public worship?'[294] Here's his answer: *"**Public worship is the highest form of Christian service!** It is the holy convocation of saints with the peculiar promise of His presence and blessing. This is issued by a divine call through the Church not the State."* Yet governments have said that Church worship is inessential and needs to be suspended. By submitting to this and shutting its doors, the Church has tacitly agreed. Sadly, with our feet we have said that the highest form of Christian service is inessential. We need to repent and rectify this.

My thesis conclusions, therefore, are that the various Covid mandates pose serious problems to our spirit, soul, heart and body and is anti-Christian. I am fully convinced in my mind and conscience and I am hoping and praying that you are persuaded of the same at this point – that they should be resisted. As such, neither governments, nor the Church, nor any other authority or person may judge us in this and place a stumbling block in our way. Such stumbling blocks include the mandate that we must be vaccinated or produce some kind of passport or biometric record, or lockdown our Churches again.

---

[294] 'Our Compromise: A Follow up on Covid-19 and the Church'. *Our Compromise*, https://canadarevival.blogspot.com/2020/05/our-compromise-follow-up-on-covid-19.html. Accessed 5 May 2021.

If the government is a terror to the good, it is *they* who are the problem not those who disobey them. People have expressed concern about division being sown. **But the responsibility for division lies with those who err from the truth not with those who speak and/or write against error.**

As well as Romans 13:1-7, we can look to later verses in the chapter too, Romans 13:9-10 (NKJV) for scriptural guidance: *"For the commandments, "For the commandments, "You shall not commit adultery," "You shall not murder," "You shall not steal," "You shall not bear false witness," "You shall not covet," and if there is any other commandment, are all summed up in this saying, namely, "You shall love your neighbor as yourself." Love does no harm to a neighbor; therefore love is the fulfilment of the law."*

Loving our neighbour means not doing any wrong or harm to him, such as murder, stealing or coveting. I have clearly shown that the 'wrongs' being mandated by the authorities under Covid tally up with these examples Paul gives. Much has and is being stolen from us and the rest is unfolding before our eyes, if we are willing to look (I refer you back to the eugenics section and VAERS data in Chapter 4). To go along with such evil is to be complicit to it.

The hour has arrived where secular authorities are telling us that *we all* need to be vaccinated and therefore subject to all of the dangers we've explored in much detail; the most important one being the spiritual dangers of transhumanism. If you want to work – be vaccinated. If you want to travel – be vaccinated. If you want to buy food – be vaccinated. If you want your kids to go to school – they and you must be vaccinated. If you want to go to Church and worship God – you must be vaccinated. This is straight from Satan and needs to be 'returned to sender'.

If you are a Christian leader, this presents a major challenge for you. Friend, it is a big weight to bear and probably not one you expected to have to deal with. But let's remember, you have been appointed by God as the shepherd over your flock at this specific time and season and our

LORD will equip you with all you need to deal with this. You have an opportunity and privilege to be the person appointed at this crucial time. The LORD was ready and willing to equip Moses to lead the Israelites in His ways and was not happy when Moses doubted God in this, so He passed the responsibility onto Aaron instead.

"Then Moses said to the Lord, "O my Lord, I am not eloquent, neither before nor since You have spoken to Your servant; but I am slow of speech and slow of tongue." So the Lord said to him, "Who has made man's mouth? Or who makes the mute, the deaf, the seeing, or the blind? Have not I, the Lord? Now therefore, go, and I will be with your mouth and teach you what you shall say." But he said, "O my Lord, please send by the hand of whomever else You may send." So the anger of the Lord was kindled against Moses, and He said: "Is not Aaron the Levite your brother? I know that he can speak well. And look, he is also coming out to meet you. When he sees you, he will be glad in his heart. Now you shall speak to him and put the words in his mouth. And I will be with your mouth and with his mouth, and I will teach you what you shall do."
– Exodus 4:10-15 (NKJV)

It is my belief that if we keep going with these tyrannical mandates in our Churches there will be no Church as we know it left (although always a small and faithful remnant, of course). All these restrictions are slowly rendering our Churches impotent and it's hard to detect the full extent whilst we're in the thick of it. We are not told by the LORD to turn a blind eye to evil. We are told to wake up and read the times but do not fear. The noose is around our neck and it's tightening by the day and we simply cannot afford to be blind to this or ignore it. How long can we be distanced from each other? Not see each other smile? Not sing praises to our LORD? Not approach people to share the Gospel and hand out tracts? Not fellowship in groups larger than six, or three or at all, depending on whatever arbitrary rule is in place at the time? And, if we receive a transhuman vaccine, how long can we remain spiritually, mentally and physically healthy, strong and effective soldiers in the army of the Living God? Let's remember, we'll stand before God one day on these matters.

211

My question to you and one which every Christian must consider is this: At what point are we going to resist tyranny? What is it going to take for our Churches to say 'No, we are not submitting to this'? Or will we submit to anything and everything that our secular governments impose on us – clinging onto a misapplication of Romans 13:1 for dear life as a justification for flabby faith, wilful deception facilitated by our television screens, and cowardice? Strong words, but perilous times.

If the Church obeys the State at all costs and whatever the request, this is Statism – a gross idolatry of elevating State above God. If we harbour a sentimental notion that withstanding persecution for our faith means submitting to authorities until the time when they hold a sword to our necks and ask us to denounce Christ, I'm afraid that too is an error in judgement. Our faith and courage are often tested little by little in this regard and bold courage is a muscle that needs to be trained and exercised. Jeremiah 12:5 (NKJV) attests to this: *"If you have run with the footmen, and they have wearied you, Then how can you contend with horses? And if in the land of peace, In which you trusted, they wearied you, Then how will you do in the floodplain of the Jordan?"*

If we have not stood up and said 'no' to the minor atrocities, it is unlikely we'll have the fortitude to do it in the bigger things. And the vaccine is a 'bigger thing', as I have presented. Masks are the smaller step that we should also be resisting, for reasons given in the previous section and should be considered part of our training in resisting arbitrary, deceitful, dangerous, tyrannical regulations that are designed to subdue, harm and immobilise. Further, I have presented enough clear and unequivocal evidence to show that partaking in the tyrannical Covid rules cannot be justified under the pretences of 'loving your neighbour', or 'we just want to focus on Jesus' (more on this in Chapter 12). They are more about *appearing* to love your neighbour by condoning and going along with spurious mandates: merely tokenism, groupthink and virtue signalling.

"Wherefore the Lord said, Forasmuch as this people draw near me with their mouth, and with their lips do honour me, but have removed their heart far from me, and their fear toward me is taught by the precept of men". – Isaiah 29:13

Can we raise these questions in our Churches and have honest conversations? Pray for our leaders. Connect and dialogue with other Church leaders. Keep lines of communication open. Fast and pray at home about this situation. Praise and sing at home. Attend prayer meetings. Repent. Keep evangelising often. Think over what issues are before us and when we will stand up and resist. Prepare for persecution. Count the cost. Time is short dear friend. We will delve deeper into how the Church can respond and reclaim authority in later chapters. An adjunct to this – can the LORD deliver His people from trials? Absolutely. All of what I have highlighted and the dangers we see should not be a cause for us to be people 'whose own strength is their god' as Habakkuk observes in his initial complaint to God (Habakkuk 1:11), nor mistrust the power and willingness of God to rescue us from these 'giants in the land' – vaccine, mask or anything else. But, invariably, in the most inspiring stories of the Bible, the LORD's people could see, squarely, the danger ahead of them and rallied together against it. They were under no illusion and they prioritised dealing with that most pressing danger, in the power of the Spirit. When we see clearly, we can pray accurately, gird our loins, wait expectantly on our LORD and trust His strengthening of us to take the correct action. Imagine if David failed to see Goliath as the biggest threat and instead saw his brother Eliab's disapproval of him leaving his sheep, or Saul's rebuke as the issue? Are we seeing the big picture here, or majoring on the minors? Seeing and speaking up about the real dangers in this world so often goes against the prevailing wisdom (folly) of the surrounding secular societies and as Christians we have a duty to watch, pray and act in the LORD's will, with courage. Our ability and willingness to see the vaccine, the deceptive agendas at play in the name of Covid 19 and the totalitarian tyranny as the real threat, rather than a virus that is killing less than 0.02% of the population, is key to our proper understanding and correct action and appeal to our LORD to deliver us from it.

Lawful Romans 13 Resistance – Civil Disobedience in Covid

Many Christians object to the notion of civil disobedience, mistakenly thinking that we are required by God to submit to all of the Covid rules and laws. Don't we just have to yield to them, whether we agree or not? After all, since we're not being asked to deny our faith in Jesus (yet, anyhow), surely it is right to submit and obey as good, gracious and mature Christians, being charitable to our 'weaker brother'? I have clearly shown that we need to move on from these questions. The answer is that no, we can no longer legitimately submit to everything our rulers are imposing on us. Church leaders are working on the assumption that 'things will get back to normal soon' and we can re-open Churches without restrictions 'when it's all over' – the virus that is. But what if governments state that we must shut Church every flu season with more lockdowns, or not to have the Lord's Supper as there's too much risk of spreading disease? You can be sure that they're going to keep control over us with the 'new and more virulent strain' tactic again and again. What do we do then? The State will of course come up with plausible, flowery, nice sounding, necessitous, 'let's keep everyone safe' and 'we're all in it together', 'greater good' reasons for mandating Church closure or heavy restrictions ... so what will we do?

To recap, most professing Christians are wrongly concluding that the Covid rules are not a huge deal and have gone along with everything imposed by governments so far, despite the evidence I've presented in Chapters 3 and 4 as to the agenda being rolled out under the pretence of a pandemic. This is a sad and hazardous, albeit honest (in some cases) miscalculation and the decisions Church leaders are making at present not only have more dangerous implications than we tend to appreciate for the body of Christ now, but are setting the stage for further totalitarian control: namely the enforcement of more dangerous pseudo-vaccines, as we are seeing, and proposed one

world religion – both of which are spiritual power plays of the devil that we should be standing firm against.

Whilst it is true that God has *allowed* every ruler that is in place, we should be aware, from reading Scripture, that some rulers are evil and God is wanting to test our faith and resolve and see if we will obey Him or them. Christians are to be both a barometer and a benefit to the pagan rulers. We cannot rely on them for moral and godly piety. **We, the Church, are the gatekeepers of truth and righteousness and we cannot devolve this responsibility to the pagan authorities.** They do not get to set the boundaries on their level of authority – our LORD does and the Church has a duty to monitor their authority. Left unchecked, unfiltered and unchallenged by the Church, they will reign untold tyranny, as per Psalm 2, which is happening now.

It could be argued that God has tried us to see what is in us, and we have been found out. We aren't the lion hearts we thought we were. We are strong on theology and confessions and ecclesiastical procedure, but we aren't so strong in the day of adversity (Proverbs 24:10). Each of our Christian journeys began with someone telling us of the sufferings of Jesus who was wounded for our transgressions and bruised for our iniquities. He suffered unspeakably and gave Himself for us. Are we not willing to give even a little of ourselves for Him? How often have we been warned that the servant is not above His Master, that as they hated Him so they will hate us, that friendship with the world is enmity with God? We want to be liked by a world that does not like Him. We can be readily inclined to curry the world's favour and yet behave as if it were a little thing to have Jesus' favour.

The Book of Judges is a *whole book of the Bible* dedicated to depicting and advocating Christian leaders resisting evil governing powers – often using force and violence too. Many of the rulers were terrible; 'they did evil in the sight of the LORD'. Was the LORD commending His people to obey them? No, they should have said 'our king is Jesus' and followed Him instead. God raised up the Judges to take a bold and positive stand against the tyrannical worldly authorities, and commended them for it! What's more, many of them appear in the Hebrews 11 'Faith Hall of Fame'.

*"And what more shall I say? For the time would fail me to tell of Gideon and Barak and Samson and Jephthah, also of David and Samuel and the prophets: **who through faith subdued kingdoms, worked righteousness, obtained promises, stopped the mouths of lions, quenched the violence of fire, escaped the edge of the sword, out of weakness were made strong, became valiant in battle, turned to flight the armies of the aliens.** "* – Hebrews 11:32-34 (NKJV)

Notice the nature of the commendation here – all about standing firm against evil and upholding justice, in the political and civil realms! And what about Moses? The government of Egypt turned tyrannical against the Israelites over a long period of time and the LORD sent Moses to oppose the government, even to its complete destruction.

"By faith he [Moses] forsook Egypt, not fearing the wrath of the king: for he endured, as seeing him who is invisible." – Hebrews 11:27

We are the best of citizens when we *obey* authorities – and we do so willingly and joyfully and because our consciences are clear before God and governments. Equally, we are the best citizens when we *disobey* authorities because the laws are so woefully evil that prayerfully, humbly and reverently we make a bold statement for Christ by our civil disobedience. We are being salt and light in the world to preserve and illuminate, we are calling leaders to recalibrate and reassess their judgements and repent in line with God's Word. Resistance to tyranny is not the same as resistance to the established civil order – there is a clear distinction between the two.

This is not a radical position we're taking here; it's rational, Biblical and in-context. The same Apostle Paul who wrote Romans 13, would have been a hypocrite if he meant that we are to obey our governments in all things, since he disobeyed and ignored various laws which caused him to

216

be punished, imprisoned, persecuted and beheaded. In Daniel 6, Daniel disobeyed by praying. In Daniel 3, Shadrach, Meshach, and Abednego disobeyed. In Exodus 1, the Egyptian midwives disobeyed. In Joshua 2, Rahab disobeyed. In 1 Samuel 14, the people disobeyed by resisting king Saul. The Biblical accounts of the prophets (such as Jeremiah) are filled with moments of non-violent resistance to illegitimate uses of power by Israelite kings. Therefore, Romans 13 does not give unlimited power to governments; this would be eisegesis[295]. We are mindful not to take scriptures in a vacuum but rather we remember to allow Scripture (as a whole) to interpret scripture (a specific text). The reality is that the message we are being sent from the State is that it is not safe for us to follow the Bible, instead we will tell you how and when to worship for your safety. There is a lion in the street, say the governments; you must disobey your God for other people's safety as well as your own. This is political theology! When will our leaders say 'enough'? What will it take? The matter at hand here is one of utmost importance; the sovereignty of the LORD and His Church. And bear in mind, the 'no vaccine, no Church' mandate is heading our way like a freight train and, along with it, the totalitarian dictatorship world State, akin to that in 1984, with the vaccine and our beloved 'modern metal image' devices (see the allegory at the beginning) as our 'Brave New World' 'soma' wonder-drug.

We should show compassion for leaders. They have such a hard job on their hands and we must pray for them and support and encourage them, but also lovingly challenge these issues. Karl Barth in his book, 'Church and State',[296] written in the eve of the Nazi war regime in 1939, interestingly notes: *The anti-Christian State is not yet truly anti-Christian, since it limits itself to using methods of oppression which take the Church into account. What is most to fear is not open violence or persecution, but to*

---

[295] The interpretation of a text, especially a Biblical text, using one's own ideas and preconceived notions.

[296] Barth, Karl. *Church and State*. https://ia803001.us.archive.org/16/items/ChurchAndState-KarlBarth/Church%20and%20State%20-%20Karl%20Barth.pdf, (Original work published 1939).

the contrary, the temptation in which the State invites believers to construct alongside the Church of Jesus Christ a new, better or more beautiful Church – heretical, because it accommodates itself to the world or the nation. It is difficult to withstand the exterior pressure, but it is even more difficult to resist dissimulated interior lies. If the Church should become confessional, it will experience long and painful downfalls: it will be abandoned by many believers who expected courageous decisions. Painful splits will occur. When peace reigns there will be no doubt – in national and in free Churches – of the strength of attachment at the moment at which it occurs: many of the first will become last, though many of the last will become first".

We need to remember that not all resistance is sin. There is a righteous resistance and submissive disobedience that is godly. I myself have experienced a righteous indignation and resistance during a short work spell at a notorious televangelist TV channel several years ago, where I witnessed all manner of hideous perversions of the Gospel. I stood up to false teachers there, in the face of unanimous Christian silence and apathy; an act that was castigated at the time but lauded years later. That one act (which took courage and undertaken with huge fear and trembling) caused a series of events, not least many other staff members walking out, that resulted in a major overturn in the way things are now run for the better in the organisation. Praise the LORD!

In the moment, it is more than likely that righteously disobedient Christians will be called the disruptive ones – even (especially?) from within the Church. This requires courage and conviction of conscience – to do good and stand against evil, even when it is unpopular and costly. Martin Luther King, Jr. 'Letter from a Birmingham Jail'[297] April 16, 1963, writes: *"One may well ask: "How can you advocate breaking some laws and obeying others?" The answer lies in the fact that there are two types of laws: just and unjust. I would be the first to advocate obeying just laws.*

---

[297] King Jr., Dr Martin Luther. 'Letter from Birmingham Jail', *Letter From Jail, (Original work published 16 April 1963),* https://letterfromjail.com/. Accessed 4 May 2021.

*One has not only a legal but a moral responsibility to obey just laws. Conversely, one has a moral responsibility to disobey unjust laws. I would agree with St. Augustine that "an unjust law is no law at all. One who breaks an unjust law must do so openly, lovingly, and with a willingness to accept the penalty. I submit that an individual who breaks a law that conscience tells him is unjust, and who willingly accepts the penalty of imprisonment in order to arouse the conscience of the community over its injustice, is in reality expressing the highest respect for law. Of course, there is nothing new about this kind of civil disobedience. It was evidenced sublimely in the refusal of Shadrach, Meshach and Abednego to obey the laws of Nebuchadnezzar, on the ground that a higher moral law was at stake. It was practiced superbly by the early Christians, who were willing to face hungry lions and the excruciating pain of chopping blocks rather than submit to certain unjust laws of the Roman Empire. To a degree, academic freedom is a reality today because Socrates practiced civil disobedience. In our own nation [USA], the Boston Tea Party represented a massive act of civil disobedience. We should never forget that everything Adolf Hitler did in Germany was 'legal' and everything the Hungarian freedom fighters did in Hungary was 'illegal'. It was 'illegal' to aid and comfort a Jew in Hitler's Germany. Even so, I am sure that, had I lived in Germany at the time, I would have aided and comforted my Jewish brothers. If today I lived in a Communist country where certain principles dear to the Christian faith are suppressed, I would openly advocate disobeying that country's anti-religious laws ... **Lukewarm acceptance is much more bewildering than outright rejection.**"*

The bottom line to keep foremost in our minds here on the issue of our decisions to obey or disobey our civil and State governments under Covid: As John Knox famously said, ***"resistance to tyranny is obedience to Christ"***.[298] Submission to tyranny is consent to evil and disobedience

---

[298] Resistance is different to *rebellion*, which is akin to witchcraft, as 1 Samuel 15:23 tells us.

to Christ. **We are to submit to persecution for well-doing, not submit to wrong-doing to avoid persecution and for comfort.**

David Lipscombe, a minister in the 1800s, wrote a great book, 'Civil Government. Its Origin, Mission, and Destiny, And The Christian's Relation To It'[299] and it still offers such relevant and wise advice for our situation: *"Our relationship to God is the first, highest, most sacred relationship into which we can enter – its duties and obligations to be observed first – all other relations and duties are secondary, and are modified and controlled by this duty we owe to God. In other words, all the commands regulating these minor and secondary relationships are modified, limited, and even annulled and abrogated by the great commandment of the Lord. It limits and modifies all – it is limited and modified by none ... Christ is equally as specific in reference to the civil ruler as he is in reference to the other relationships of an earthly and secondary nature. Speaking to his twelve apostles of the certainty of their coming in conflict with the governors and rulers of the world, tells them, "Fear not them (the civil rulers) who kill the body, but are not able to kill the soul; but rather fear him (God) who is able to destroy both soul and body in hell," Matthew 10:28. Here he admonishes us by the consideration of the more weighty importance of both soul and body, than of the body alone, to fear (and obey) God rather than the civil ruler. The great importance of obeying God rather than the civil ruler, and in violation of his rules, commands, and the extent to which we are to carry this principle, is set forth in the 10:39 and 16:25 of Matthew, "Whoever will save his life shall lose it, and whoever will lose his life for my sake shall find it." That is, the civil rulers will require you to do things contrary to the will of God, and if you refuse to do those things, they will kill you. But whoever will save his life by doing the requirements of the civil ruler, and violating the law of God, shall lose his life (or soul forever) but whoever will die rather than violate God's commandment at the behest of the civil ruler, shall save his soul*

---

[299] Lipscomb, David. Civil Government. Its Origin, Mission, and Destiny, And The Christian's Relation To It. Stone-Campbell Books, 1883.

unto life eternal. Instruction could not be clearer or more positive. The salvation of the soul in heaven is made to depend upon our setting at defiance the human law in order to obey the Divine. No power, then – neither of parent, husband, master, civil ruler, or church elder, can remit the obligation to the Christian, at all times, to obey the command of God, even unto death, if need be ...Christ practiced as he taught. He died on the cross, refusing to save his life by a violation of the law of God, at the behest of the civil power ... The apostles, too, one and all, sealed their fidelity to their teachings by dying for refusing to obey the civil power when its requirements came in conflict with the Divine law. A more baseless assumption, one more in direct conflict with God's teaching, was never made by man, than the idea, 'that when the civil authority commands the Christian to do something contrary to the law of God, and he does it, the responsibility rest upon the civil authority, and not on the individual who violates the laws of God at the behest of the civil ruler'. There is not a point of obligation more strongly enforced in the Sacred Scriptures than this – no power of heaven, earth, or hell can come between man and his Maker, to relieve him of his responsibility, under all circumstances, to obey his Maker. The command, then, 'Submit to the powers that be', is clearly limited by the highest duty to submit to God. He who violates the law of God in order to submit to the 'powers that be', surely sins against God. The limit and bound of the Christian's connection with the world-powers, is a quiet and faithful submission to it in all the requirements it makes at his hands, until it demands something contrary to the letter or spirit of God's law, then it his duty to meekly but firmly refuse to obey."

In other words, we are all individually responsible to God for our actions. You do not get a pass because you were just 'following orders'. Full stop.

One year into the Covid debacle, men sit in prison for opening their Churches to their congregations and preaching, no more and no less. James Coates pastors a normal, everyday Church – Grace Life in Edmonton, Alberta, Canada. He has a medium-sized congregation that he preaches the Word to Sunday by Sunday, like any Church. However, since December 2020, they were told to limit attendance and comply with Covid health measures, or face legal consequences. The Church issued a public statement outlining their stance on Covid[300] – essentially one of peaceful civil disobedience as I have advocated – and remained open, unrestricted. In February 2021, Coates was arrested and taken to jail. James Coates is the first of what is likely to be many of such pastors who is facing persecution for obeying the LORD over the authorities – God bless that man and others like him for their bold stance. Other Churches have been given astronomical fines and threats … simply for continuing to function as Church. These are great examples of resisting tyranny to obey Christ. What will it take for other Churches to disobey too?

There are three other key things from Gordan Runyan's book, 'Resistance to Tyrants',[301] that I think it's worth highlighting when it comes to civil disobedience and speaking out against wicked rulers. First, if we have any false notion that 'Christians should stay out of politics and not preach on it', then we need to correct our thinking on that, quickly. Just read the Book of Acts, it is *utterly* political. The disciples were forever getting tangled up in political situations. And no wonder – proclaiming 'Jesus is Lord' is a profoundly political statement, a threat even. The Gospel changes all aspects of life. Second, we may only be at liberty to disobey in the name of righteousness when we are keeping short accounts with the Lord on our own personal sin and not in knowing rebellion to the LORD's commands in any area. Personal godliness is a prerequisite. We should have a pure and holy attitude, with a desire for truth and tempered with good humour, to keep us free from bitterness and resentment in the face of opposition. Third, we need to settle our resolve on the matter ahead of time. Know your convictions and where lines are crossed, know

---

[300] 'Public Statement'. *GraceLife Church of Edmonton*, 16 Feb. 2021,https://gracelife.ca/feb-7-statement/. Accessed 4 May 2021.

[301] Runyan, Gordon. Ibid.

where and how you will act, 'while you're thinking soberly and the sun is shining', says Runyan.

Romans 13:8 – Our Yardstick for Submission

I posit that the parameters for submission, authority and limits to each of the four types of governance that God has ordained can largely be set by Romans 13:8 (NKJV): *"Owe no one anything except to love one another, for he who loves another has fulfilled the law."* We can fully and joyfully submit to the authorities set in place over us when the motivations and mandates are loving, i.e., for our good and in the interests of what is good. When they are evil rather than good, this poses a legitimate submission problem and invokes a different duty from the Christian, who is to remain in good conscience, free from sin in the matter and taking into consideration love for and protection of our neighbours.

We'll conclude Part 1 of this book and round up our thesis evaluation with an allegory on Romans 13 by Pastor Stephen Richardson. It is copied in full, with permission, from his blog 'Come Down Lord!'

A Conversation Between Christian and the Worldly Wiseman – by Stephen Richardson

The following is based in part on actual conversations, but like Pilgrim's Progress its aim is to communicate, by allegory, Biblical truths.

Christian: *"Hi pastor, how are you doing?"*

Worldly Wiseman: *"Great. Never busier. Lots going on in these uncertain times."*

Christian: *"Wonderful to hear. Tell me more."*

Worldly Wiseman: *"The gospel is spreading, many are benefiting from the preaching, much good is being done despite the present challenges. Actually, I am pleased to say the opportunities have never been greater."*

Christian: *"Pastor, this is tremendous news. You must be meeting with a lot of people."*

Worldly Wiseman: *"No. Not all. That would be illegal."*

Christian: *"Oh – but you said the gospel was spreading and many were benefiting. Are you visiting the sick and the poor and the imprisoned?"*

Worldly Wiseman: *"Of course not. That's illegal."*

Christian: *"I see. Is your church gathering?"*

Worldly Wiseman: *"Seriously? I would think by now you wouldn't need to ask. That, too, is not allowed. We are not about to break the law. Please, let's not entertain this conversation any longer. I am not about to discuss illegal activities with you or anyone else."*

Christian: *"Hmm. Ok; but may I ask just a couple more questions for clarification?"*

Worldly Wiseman: *"Fine."*

Christian: *"Will you be gathering again at some point?"*

Worldly Wiseman: *"Depends on whether the government allows us to or not."*

Christian: *"Ok ... but hypothetically speaking, if the government did allow you to gather this Sunday will masks be required?"*

Worldly Wiseman: *"Depends on what the government says."*

Christian: *"How many will you allow to come?"*

Worldly Wiseman: *"However many the government says."*

Christian: *"I see. May we talk realistically for a moment? Setting aside hypotheticals and possibilities let me ask you a simple question. And please understand, I ask this with all respect. But I am hearing from sheep across the country, and they are lonely and anxious and longing to gather with the saints. So can you please tell me, when will you gather again?"*

Worldly Wiseman: *"Easy ... When the government says we can."*

Christian: *"How long will you wait?"*

Worldly Wiseman: *"Until the government says."*

Christian: *"What if its two more years?"*

Worldly Wiseman: *"That's up to the government."*

Christian: *"What if its 10 years?"*

Worldly Wiseman: *"Again – up to the government."*

But now suppose the conversation took a bit of a turn. Naturally, Christian is having a hard time understanding all of this. After all, the church has *never* been defined as anything else but a gathering. And without that gathering there are *no more* baptisms, *no more* Lord's Supper, *no more* congregational singing, *no more* in-person preaching, *no more* Christian fellowship.

No need to debate baptism because it doesn't happen! No need to debate the songs that are being sung because they aren't sung. No need to discuss whether to use grape juice or wine because the table is closed. No need to worry about the 'one another commands' because they don't hardly see one another anymore. No need to worry about whether you are a sheep or a goat, because *no one* visits the sick and poor and the imprisoned any-more.

But all of this is rather puzzling and troubling to Christian because, after all, the history of the church is riddled with examples of believers that did all these things even when doing so meant possible death. So Christian asks Worldly Wiseman for an explanation.

Romans 13 Exegeted

Christian: *"Pastor, I admit I'm having a hard time with all of this. Can you help me understand why you think we must wait for the government's permission before we do things we have always done and things God has told us to do?"*

Worldly Wiseman: *"That's easy. Read Romans 13."*

Christian: *"But I have. Wasn't that written by Paul? I thought he was arrested and executed for disobeying the authorities."*

Worldly Wiseman: *"Careful now. Don't forget that I am the one with the degrees. I have spent my life studying these things. So, how about you listen to the rest of us? You do realize that the defiant rebel churches are in the minority don't you?"*

Christian: *"Yes; but could we just talk about the Bible?"*

Worldly Wiseman: *"Of course. But don't forget that Richard Baxter agrees with me, and I could cite hundreds of pastors who also agree."*

Christian: *"I understand that, but can we get back to the Bible? Tell me why you think Romans 13 means we shouldn't gather for worship?"*

Worldly Wiseman: *"That one is easy. As you know Richard Baxter agrees with us, and hundreds of other pastors ... But, in any case, listen carefully as I quote Scripture to you – 'Let every soul be subject unto the higher powers' ... and 'Whosoever therefore resisteth the power, resisteth the ordinance of God: and they that resist shall receive to themselves damnation.' So you see its right there plain as day. We have to obey them."*

Christian: *"But it says in my Bible that the 'rulers are not a terror to good works but to evil.' If the government forbids us from doing good or commands us to do evil aren't they become a terror to good works rather than evil; and shouldn't they then be disobeyed for God's sake?"*

Worldly Wiseman: *"No, because the government says we shouldn't, and the Bible says 'Let every soul be subject unto the higher powers'. So when you disobey them you are doing bad."*

Christian: *"You mean if the government says we can't and we do it that its therefore bad?"*

Worldly Wiseman: *"Precisely. Again, 'Let every soul be subject unto the higher powers.' And have I mentioned Richard Baxter?"*

Christian: *"Yes, you and a host of other reformed leaders have quoted Baxter. I admit I find that strange considering they rarely quoted him before and have never published his works. Wasn't he a Neonomian? And what about what William Symington and the Covenanters said? Or Thomas Manton and John Owen and John Flavel and Samuel Rutherford and Alexander Henderson? Actually – forget I said that. Never mind them ... what about God? Didn't He say that if you do that which is good you shall have praise of the same and that we must obey God rather than man?"*

Worldly Wiseman: *"When you get your get PhD in church history and the puritans than you can come quoting those men to me. I fear you have misunderstood all of them. And besides Romans 13 is perfectly clear. You are to be subject unto higher powers!"*

Christian: *"Yes, you have said that repeatedly. But Paul himself didn't always obey them. In fact Jesus Himself and all the apostles suffered for their disobedience to the magistrate. And the Bible lists countless examples of disobedience to ungodly laws and instructs us in the way of holiness and tells us what is good. Even Romans 13 makes it plain that their authority is borrowed and that our ultimate authority is God. So how can we disobey God to obey man?"*

Worldly Wiseman: *"I fear for your soul. You are sounding more and more radical as time goes on. I tell you with considerable sadness, the road you are on can only to lead to your own demise and the ruin of your church. The world will hate you, the Church will no longer hear you, and I myself will not entertain this conversation further. But let me offer a parting word before I go. You speak of disobeying God to obey man. That is nonsense. We would never marry a gay couple, we would never condone transgenderism. So have a care. Remember who you are talking to and show me the respect I deserve."*

Christian: *"My apologies. I didn't mean you any disrespect. Before you go, may I ask for a quick clarification? Aren't you disobeying God to obey man when you stop gathering for worship?"*

Worldly Wiseman: *"Alright, I will play along for another moment, and then this is conversation is over. Here's my question to you: where is the command that the Church must gather?"*

Christian: *"What??"*

Worldly Wiseman: *"Show me in your Bible that what we are doing is sinful. We can still pray privately in our homes, worship privately in our homes and do a host of other Christian things in our homes. And when the government says we can we will gather again."*

Christian: *"But the Church has only ever been defined as a gathering. And how can you have baptism and the Lord's supper and congregational singing and congregational prayer meetings without it? Isn't this what the Church has always done? See the practice of the Old Testament and New Testament saints. See how the Old Testament defines the Sabbath. Even the first four commandments have always been understood in relationship to a gathered Church. Who we worship, how we worship, the manner of worship and the when of it all have to do with the corporate worship. And that's just a start."*

World Wiseman: *"But if you are in prison you can't do those things."*

Christian: *"Yes I understand that. But there is a great difference between can't and won't. If a man falls off a cliff it is an accident. If he jumps it is suicide. The one is an innocent mistake. The other is sin. Duty is ours, events are God's. The secret things belong to Him while the revealed things belong to us."*

Worldly Wiseman: *"Enough. You are clearly too proud to listen to anyone but yourself. You are proud, you are stubborn, you are rebellious and you have obviously become distracted from your calling by politics. As for me I am determined to preach Christ and Him crucified. There will be no politics in my pulpit! And I will not participate in illegal activities. Call it church if you like. Call it a prayer meeting. I call it illegal. This discussion ends here."*

Christian: *"Thank you for your time. I won't press the point; but I do hope you will think upon the Scriptures. You have repeatedly cited Baxter but it is to God that we must one day give an account; and it is God's Word that is our only rule of faith and practice. And while I whole heartedly agree that the preacher must make it his life's work to preach Christ and Him crucified, I would urge you to remember that your objection to political preaching was raised by the Gestapo against preachers who preached against Nazism ... and while we must be careful not to get distracted, the preacher must not confine himself to laying again and again the foundation of the doctrine of Christ, but as the prophets of old he must know the times and so preach the whole counsel of God's Word."*

... And so it is that our worldly wise church leaders are reasoning here in Canada and across the world (with the notable exception of countries already persecuted!). You may not know this but many of our church leaders are reasoning with the same logic – even using the same words – as church leaders did before and during the Nazi regime in Germany and Holland. What I have written is fiction. Some of it based on actual conversations, but all of it allegorical. May God help us.

****

In the next chapter, we'll look at misapplications of Romans 13 by past tyrannical governments, who had no desires to act out of love and goodness, with a focus on Nazi Germany. We'll examine the Church's response to see what we may glean for our situation and learn from their mistakes.

Part 2: Authority, Tyranny And The Wider Problems

CHAPTER SEVEN

Misapplication of Romans 13 in Tyrannical Nazi Germany

"If someone can make you believe an absurdity, they can make you commit an atrocity." – Voltaire

"This is the secret of propaganda: Those who are to be persuaded by it should be completely immersed in the ideas of the propaganda, without ever noticing that they are being immersed in it ... Propaganda works best when those who are being manipulated are confident they are acting on their own free will ... Arguments must be crude, clear and forcible, and appeal to emotions and instincts, not the intellect. Truth is unimportant and must entirely subordinate to tactics and psychology."
– Joseph Goebbels

Romans 13:1-7 has been used by many tyrannical authorities in the past to pressurise Christians to settle down and obey the state; most notably during Nazi Germany around World War II, which we will look at. It's been used in the USA on a number of occasions, for instance, by those upholding the Fugitive Slave Law in the 1840s and 1850s and insisting that escaped slaves be returned to their masters. Also, a couple of years ago, former U.S. Attorney General, Jeff Sessions wildly misused Romans 13 to justify the Trump administration's immigration policy which aimed to separate hundreds of asylum-seeking children from their parents at the border. He warned those Christians who objected that they should obey the State and not speak out against it. This line of interpretation takes Paul's letter used in its original context to give coercive advice to those being oppressed by a government, turns it around 180 degrees, and uses it to justify the actions of an unscrupulous government. It ignores the fact that just because something is legal, does not mean it is moral – sometimes law itself is immoral. As people of faith, knowing our history is important, because there is a long, infamous interpretational history used by authoritarian governments to take chapter 13 out of context to bring about evil.

An article in an Israeli newspaper [302] tells us that: *"In July 1933, during Hitler's first summer in power, a young German pastor named Joachim Hossenfelder preached a sermon in the towering Kaiser Wilhelm Memorial Church, Berlin's most important Church. He used the words of Romans 13 to remind worshippers of the importance of obedience to those in authority. The Church was festooned with Nazi banners and Stormtrooper flags, its pews packed with the Nazi Party faithful – including men in the brown shirts of the Sturmabteilung, the Nazis' paramilitary movement. This is one of the most explicit examples in which the German Protestant Church invoked Romans 13. Indeed, following an attempt to assassinate Hitler, a plotter blamed Romans 13 as a reason why there was not more resistance to the Fuhrer within the Third Reich. The idea some Americans have that there was a faction of Christians opposing Nazis – it was not like that, most Christians were Nazis and Nazis were Christians, and that's just the way it was."*

---

[302] Kraft, Dina. 'The Real Story behind the Nazi Establishment's Use of "Romans 13"'. *Haaretz*, 19 June 2018, https://www.haaretz.com/us-news/.premium-the-real-story-behind-the-nazi-establishment-s-use-of-romans-13-1.6194455. Accessed 4 May 2021.

The Romans 13 text was used explicitly by the pro-Nazi German Christian movement as a polemic against the Confessing Church, which was somewhat resistant to the Nazification of the German Church. Through a particular extreme interpretation of Luther's theology, the German Christian movement asserted that the Church's role was to support the State, no matter how cruel or unjust its laws or practices appeared to be.

Catholic Preacher, David Simons[303] writes: *"Here's the thing. Germans of the 1930s were not immoral or stupid. They were highly educated, creative, and diverse by the standards of the time. They went to Church in greater numbers than Americans do today. And yet, they allowed the unthinkable to happen to their neighbours. The sad reality is that the Church largely stood by, at best ignoring, at worst abetting, due to a cherry-picked interpretation of Romans 13 ... If we allow any human government of any party or political persuasion to represent that obedience to its dictates are the will of God, then we will stand under the judgement of history and of God. There will be a real-world reckoning ending in tragedy for all."*

Reverend John E. Warmth, in his paper, 'Our Ultimate Obedience is to God'[304] states that, tragically, Romans 13 became one of the glues that held the Third Reich together. He asserts what the response of the German Churches should have been: *"So, what were Christians in Nazi Germany to do when asked to kill Jews and steal their property? What were Christians in Communist countries to do when told to spy on fellow Christians and turn them in as traitors to the State? What do Christians in dictatorships do when they are told to keep food and basic necessities away from certain ethnic groups in the country? We don't do those bad things! We follow the example of Peter and James in Acts 5:29. When the*

---

[303] Simmons, David. 'Why We as Christians Cannot Ignore the Misuse of Romans 13'. *Medium*, 25 June 2018, https://roodscreen.org/why-we-as-christians-cannot-ignore-the-misuse-of-romans-13-ee7631d5b440.

[304] Reverend John E. Warmuth, 'Out Ultimate Obedience is to God'. http://www.immanuelglobe.org/home/180005487/180005487/docs/Romans%2013.1-10.pdf?sec_id=180005487. Accessed 4 May 2021.

governing authorities forbade them to speak in Jesus' name any more, they answered, "We must obey God rather than men." Peter and James did not go into total, open rebellion against the authorities. They respectfully said they could not obey that particular command. If it meant arrest and jail time for them, so be it. They were not going to stop doing what Jesus had commanded them to do. Listen to what Peter wrote about this in 1 Peter 3:14-17, "But even if you should suffer for what is right, you are blessed ... It is better, if it is God's will, to suffer for doing good than for doing evil. For Christ died for sins once for all, the righteous for the unrighteous, to bring you to God.""

Karl Barth and Dietrich Bonhoeffer are the real notable examples of Protestants in Germany who were earnestly battling with what Romans 13 was actually saying and relating it to a Church response to the Nazi regime. The Church at large in Germany was guilty of ensuring that the foundation was prepared for Hitler. No one spoke out publicly, except Bonhoeffer, Barth and a few others. In his book 'Church and State' (1939),[305] Barth discussed at great lengths how Romans 13 calls upon Christians to obey the rules of the State they live in, but concluding, in effect, that the actions of **Jesus himself contradicted the narrow reading of Romans 13**, favoured by the Nazis: *"Christians would, in point of fact, become enemies of any State if, when the State threatens their freedom, they did not resist, or if they concealed their resistance – although this resistance would be very calm and dignified. Jesus would, in actual fact, have been an enemy of the State if He had not dared, quite calmly, to call King Herod a 'fox' ... If the State has perverted its God-given authority, it cannot be honoured better than by this criticism which is due to it in all circumstances."*

Barth thus ultimately concluded that Romans 13 does not call upon people blindly to obey the State. Quite to the contrary, according to

---

[305] Barth, Karl. *Church and State*. https://ia803001.us.archive.org/16/items/ChurchAndState-KarlBarth/Church%20and%20State%20-%20Karl%20Barth.pdf, (Original work published 1939).

Barth, Paul's epistle to the Romans requires people to rise against the State when the State is the source of injustice.

It was Barth's conclusions on this that made both Bonhoeffer join the resistance to Hitler (a decision that would cause him to be arrested and later sent to a concentration camp where he was martyred), and drove the plotters behind the assassination attempt on Hitler's life in July 20, 1944. Bonhoeffer was explicit that the Confessing Church should not yield on any point to the Nazi State or those elements in the official Church that cooperated with the State. In 1933 Bonhoeffer gave a famous radio speech on leadership, possibly aimed specifically at Hitler. The talk was insightful and timely but was taken off air before he could finish it. In it, he criticised Hitler for being a leader who was a great *misleader* and made an idol of himself.

The Confessing Church & Barmen Declaration

The Confessing Church was set up to oppose the German Church ideology and was led, in part by Pastor Martin Niemoller of Berlin, with Barth and Bonhoeffer as central figures. They formed the Pastors' Emergency League in September 1933, which openly and adamantly rejected the role of the Aryan Paragraph (a regulation to exclude and eventually persecute Jews) in the Church and stood for a Church based on the tenets of the Bible and the Protestant Reformation. While over 2,000 pastors initially joined the League, many Church leaders believed that Niemoller was too alarmist in his warnings about their nationalistic forms of worship.

In May 1934, they met at the first Confessional Synod, which attempted to establish their own doctrine on the foundations of the Christian faith

– The Barmen Declaration.[306] The Declaration laid out the beliefs and doctrinal statements of the group and was largely written by Karl Barth and Bonhoeffer: *"In opposition to attempts to establish the unity of the German Evangelical Church by means of false doctrine, by the use of force and insincere practices, the Confessional Synod insists that the unity of the Evangelical Churches in Germany can come only from the Word of God in faith through the Holy Spirit."*

Thesis 5 of the Barmen Declaration deals with Church-State relations and is as follows: *"(1 Peter 2:17) Scripture tells us that, in the as yet unredeemed world in which the Church also exists, the State has by divine appointment the task of providing for justice and peace. [It fulfils this task] by means of the threat and exercise of force, according to the measure of human judgment and human ability. The Church acknowledges the benefit of this divine appointment in gratitude and reverence before him. It calls to mind the Kingdom of God, God's commandment and righteousness, and thereby the responsibility both of rulers and of the ruled. It trusts and obeys the power of the Word by which God upholds all things. We reject the false doctrine, as though the State, over and beyond its special commission, should and could become the single and totalitarian order of human life, thus fulfilling the Church's vocation as well. We reject the false doctrine, as though the Church, over and beyond its special commission, should and could appropriate the characteristics, the tasks, and the dignity of the State, thus itself becoming an organ of the State."*

Nazi Propaganda & The Failures of the Confessing Church

The Nazi party overtly endorsed the idea of 'positive Christianity' and Hitler's speeches were laden with propaganda to this effect: *"We demand*

---

[306] 'Barmen Declaration'. *United Church of Christ*, https://www.ucc.org/beliefs_barmen-declaration/. Accessed 4 May 2021.

the freedom of all religious confessions in the state, insofar as they do not jeopardise its existence or conflict with the manners and moral sentiments of the Germanic race. The party as such upholds the point of view of a positive Christianity without tying itself confessionally to any one confession." And he insisted: "*There has been no interference with the doctrine of the Confessions or with their religious freedom, nor will there be any such interference ... the State protects religion, though always on the one condition that religion will not be used as a cover for political ends.*"

The long-term goal of the Nazis was to use the power of the Evangelical Church for Hitler's own purposes, which most people just could not see through. *[And I will interject here – this is exactly what is happening to our Churches right now under Covid by similar oppressors.]* Stories about Hitler's supposed piety became widespread and many accepted as fact that these rumours were true. In her thesis 'Protestant Dissent in Nazi Germany: The Confessing Church Struggle with Hitler's Government Struggle with Hitler's Government' (2001)[307], Jenisa Story notes: "*German Church services were distorted in their form and meaning in order to produce emotional responses in the participants that would strengthen the group dynamic. For example, baptism came to symbolize a parent's pledge to raise their baptized child in the community of German believers and with the beliefs of 'positive Christianity'. In essence, parents were giving their children over to the German, or Nazi, Volk.*"

It is well-documented that from his podium, Hitler mesmerised the crowds. In his speech at the 1936 Nuremburg Party Rally,[308] he stated, "*Not every one of you sees me and I do not see every one of you. But I feel you ... and you feel me!*" Then under the 'Cathedral of Light', thousands of Germans swore what they called a 'holy oath': "*Blazing flames*

---

[307] Story, Jenisa. 'Protestant Dissent in Nazi Germany: The Confessing Church Struggle with Hitler\u27s Government'. *Western CEDAR,* 2001, https://core.ac.uk/display/286998821.

[308] 'The Oath Under the Cathedral of Light at the 1936 Nuremberg Party Rally'. *German Propaganda Archive – Calvin University,* https://research.calvin.edu/german-propaganda-archive/pt36dom.htm. Accessed 4 May 2021.

hold us together into eternity. May the times bring what they will, we are a young people ever ready. No one shall take this faith from those who are dedicated to Germany."

Essentially, the Hitler mesmerised the masses with Satanic propaganda. The Nazis kept the Church structure – it was beneficial to do so and enabled the mass deception – but changed it to create an anti-Christian vehicle to further their regime. There is a replay of this situation rolling out right now that we must wake up to and resist. Hitler ultimately failed, but his cause has continued and the next (final?) 'bite at the cherry' is taking place currently, under our noses. We know to expect a false prophet making way for the false messiah, as spoken of in Revelation 13.

Measures brought into and by the German Church under the Nazis included a denial of the canonicity of the Old Testament; they believed that it was just a 'Jewish book' that had no place within the Church, so they removed it altogether, along with denying Jesus' Jewish heritage. In fact, Hitler rewrote the Bible with twelve Nazi commandments, including 'Honour your Fuhrer' and 'Keep the blood pure and your honour holy' and thousands of Churches received copies in 1941. He proceeded to weaken the Confessing Church movement by removing and arresting non-compliant Church leaders and putting Churches under police supervision. Throughout the lifetime of the Third Reich, in tens of thousands of sermons up and down the country, pro-Nazi Protestant pastors quoted from Romans 13: *"The authorities that exist have been established by God. Consequently, whoever rebels against the authority is rebelling against what God has instituted, and those who do so will bring judgment on themselves."* Tragically, as the Nazi regime imprisoned its opponents and wrought havoc across the world, Romans 13 became one of the glues that held the Third Reich together. This scripture had the effect of preventing, or at least delaying, the emergence of more widespread resistance against Nazi policies.

Some members of the Confessing Church, were astute enough to recognize the dangerous propositions being purported by the German Church and recognised that the law contradicted Biblical teachings. However, their failure was in knowing what to do about it, or a having the courage to act in line with these recognitions. There was a significant misinterpretation regarding Lutheran theological positions and the development of a creed based upon the Neo-Orthodox positions of Karl Barth. This left the Confessing Church with a rather weak protest against the Nazi government and a weak stance on the atrocities the Third Reich committed. A small radical faction of the Confessing Church, which included Martin Niemoller, Hans Asmussen and Bishop Otto Dibelius, interpreted Scripture as commanding them to protest against the immoral actions of the government. On June 27 1937, Niemoller spoke out against Confessing Church persecution: *"We have as little thought and as little hope as the Apostles had of escaping from the clutches of the powers-that-be by our own efforts; and we have certainly as little intention as they had of obeying the human command to keep silent regarding what the Lord our God orders us to say; for, as long as the world shall last, one must obey God rather than men!"*

Dietrich Bonhoeffer actively voiced his opposition and concern with Nazi policies. He presented his doctoral thesis, Sanctorum Communio, at the age of 21 and this established a lifelong interest in studying the structure of the Church. Bonhoeffer took a strong stance on anti-Semitism within the Church. He said, *"The Church cannot allow its actions towards its members to be prescribed by the State."* He was able to travel throughout Europe because of his job and connections and he helped Jews escape Germany and he tried to get Allied support for the German resistance. He eventually joined the group of plotters who sought to assassinate Hitler, after much wrestling with Scripture and his conscience, believing this to be the right thing to do and to uphold good and resist evil. He is

239

famously quoted as saying:[309] ***"We are not to simply bandage the wounds of victims beneath the wheels of injustice, we are to drive a spoke into the wheel itself."*** **– Dietrich Bonhoeffer**

Both Niemoller and Bonhoeffer faced imprisonment because of their faith. Martin Niemoller was arrested in 1937 and imprisoned in Sachsenhausen and Dachau concentration camps until his release in 1945. Dietrich Bonhoeffer was held in the Flossenbürg concentration camp until his execution on April 9, 1945. God bless these two brave men who risked everything for their beliefs, standing firmly for Christ and giving all glory to Him.

Taken from 'No Rusty Swords: Letters, Lectures and Notes 1928-1936, From the Collected Works of Dietrich Bonhoeffer',[310] Bonhoeffer muses on the Church and State: *"There are three possible ways in which the Church can act towards the State: in the first place, as has been said, it can ask the State whether its actions are legitimate and in accordance with its character as State, i.e., it can throw the State back on its responsibilities. Secondly, it can aid the victims of State action. The Church has an unconditional obligation to the victims of any ordering society, even if they do not belong to the Christian community. 'Do good to all men.' In both these courses of action, the Church serves the free State in its free way, and at times when laws are changed the Church may in no way withdraw from these two tasks. The third possibility is not just to bandage the victims under the wheel, but to put a spoke in the wheel itself. Such action would be direct political action, and is only possible and desirable when the Church sees the State fail in its function of creating law and order, i.e., when it sees the State unrestrainedly bring about too much or too*

---

[309] 'Notable Quotes'. *The Dietrich Bonhoeffer Institute*, https://tdbi.org/dietrich-bonhoeffer/notable-quotes/. Accessed 5 May 2021.

[310] Marty, Martin E. 'No Rusty Swords: Letters, Lectures and Notes 1928-1936, From the Collected Works of Dietrich Bonhoeffer. Volume I, 384 Pp. New York, Harper and Row, 1965. $4.50'. *Theology Today*, vol. 22, no. 4, Jan. 1966, pp. 562–64. *SAGE Journals*, doi:10.1177/004057366602200421.

little law and order. In both cases it must see the existence of the State, and with it its own existence, threatened."

While a few individuals chose to speak out on these matters and be a 'spoke in the wheel', the Confessing Church as a whole refrained from involving itself in what it deemed unnecessary disputes with the State. Those who did act against the government did so in a way that they hoped would not attract government attention. Many people decided that self-preservation was more important than their beliefs. 6,000 of the 16,000 Evangelical ministers in Germany had declared themselves to be a part of the Confessing Church as of 1934, but only a small number of pastors are considered to have actively opposed the Nazi state.

Professor of History, Donald Wall, in his paper 'The Confessing Church and the Second World War'[311] states: *"The Confessing Church, by its own admission, fell short of fulfilling the mission of the Church. It acknowledged that the Third Reich was an immoral State in which evil was not simply an accident but a principle. Yet the theology of the Church called for implicit obedience to the duly constituted authorities and discouraged political resistance."* Even with all that was going on in Nazi Germany, Confessing Christians continually preached obedience to the State in all earthly matters, limiting obedience only when the State interfered with the practice of religion. Their unwillingness to protest early on had major consequences, which most just could not foresee. Coupled with this, the German Evangelical Church had a longstanding partnership with the German government. Even though they were not officially part of the State government, pastors were strongly identified with governmental authority due to the historically close relationship between Church and State. Many clergy stressed that they wanted to remain politically neutral due to the fear of 'clericalism' that had occurred in the Middle Ages.

---

[311] Wall, Donald D. 'The Confessing Church and the Second World War'. *Journal of Church and State*, vol. 23, no. 1, Jan. 1981, pp. 15–34. *Silverchair*, doi:10.1093/jcs/23.1.15.

Jenisa Story concludes her thesis on protestant dissent in Nazi Germany by saying:[312] *"This lack of strong resistance to the Deutsche Christen racial ideology is a testament to the inability of the Confessing Church to doggedly stand up to its opponents ... Therefore, the struggle of the Confessing Church was a struggle of theologians, backed by a very small group of courageous laymen. While individuals involved in the Confessing Church had to decide for themselves whether or not to publicly proclaim their private objections, men such as Martin Niemoller and Dietrich Bonhoeffer made the decision to risk their lives in order to stand up for what they thought was right ... Even the Barmen Declaration of 1934 was established solely because of the Church's objections to State interference in Church doctrine and not due to the broader actions of the State itself. The fundamental dilemma facing the Christians during the Nazi era was whether they should obey Biblical principles or the State. It is apparent that even the Confessing Christians were not able to discover a clear solution to this problem."*

Nazi Schooling, Hitler Youth and Now

In a speech he made on 6th November, 1933, Adolf Hitler announced what the Nazi's intended to do with the education system:[313] *"When an opponent declares I will not come over to your side. I calmly say, "Your child belongs to us already. What are you? You will pass on. Your descendants, however, now stand in the new camp. In a short time they will know nothing else but this new community.""*

Bernhard Rust, the German Minister of Education in 1934, introduced the Nazi National Curriculum and said *"the whole purpose of education is to create Nazis"*. He changed the curriculum to contain what they saw as the

---

[312] Story, Jenisa. 'Protestant Dissent in Nazi Germany: The Confessing Church Struggle with Hitler\u27s Government'. *Western CEDAR*, 2001, https://core.ac.uk/display/286998821.

[313] 'Bernhard Rust'. *Spartacus Educational*, https://spartacus-educational.com/GERrust.htm. Accessed 4 May 2021.

main needs: 'racial awareness' and a strong sense of national identity, biology and evolutionism to show the superiority of the Aryans and military skills to ready for war. Teachers who were known to be critical of the Nazi Party and its propaganda were dismissed and the rest were sent away to be trained in National Socialist principles. Schools were only allowed to use textbooks that had been Nazi-approved. Tomi Ungerer wrote in 'Tomi: A Childhood Under the Nazis':[314] *"As the teacher entered the class, the students would stand and raise their right arms. The teacher would say, "For the Führer a triple victory", answered by a chorus of "Heil!" three times ... Every class started with a song. The almighty Führer would be staring at us from his picture on the wall. These uplifting songs were brilliantly written and composed, transporting us into a state of enthusiastic glee."*

Out of school, there was the compulsory 'Hitler Youth' movement for 10-18-year- olds, that had enlisted some four million members by 1936. The Nazis had successfully brainwashed a whole generation under their schooling and youth programmes. There are many indications that children in our current societies are also being claimed by the State as theirs, to be indoctrinated in 'good State principles'. There have been many worrying things taught in school for years, especially around sexuality and gender, but even more so in the advent of Covid and around its mandates. John Taylor Gatto was an award-winning American author and school teacher of 30 years, who wrote extensively on how modern schooling is both brainwashing and extremely damaging to children. Here are some of his quotes:

"Schools teach exactly what they are intended to teach and they do it well: how to be a good Egyptian and remain in your place in the pyramid."

---

[314] 'Childhood'. *Tomi Ungerer*, https://www.tomiungerer.com/about-tomi/childhood/. Accessed 4 May 2021.

"What's gotten in the way of education in the United States is a theory of social engineering that says there is ONE RIGHT WAY to proceed with growing up."

"In our secular society, school has become the replacement for Church, and like Church it requires that its teachings must be taken on faith."

– John Taylor Gatto, 'Dumbing Us Down: The Hidden Curriculum of Compulsory Schooling'.[315]

Outside of schools, there have been Freemasonic 'Child ID Programs'[316] in place for quite some time, which takes the vital statistics and unique personal data of local children – including their fingerprints, photos, videos, dental records and even DNA! This is done, so the Freemasons say, in the name of 'keeping your child safe and protected' in case they go missing. They claim that they keep no record of the data harvested, but one might be dubious to trust the claims of an occult organisation.

In February 2021, Los Angeles Unified Schools District rolled out its innovative 'Daily Pass'[317] system for schools re-opening after lockdowns and seeks to normalise and enforce PCR tests, masks, distancing and vaccines within the schooling system from here on in. A press release from LA Unified[318] states: *"Los Angeles Unified today announced the launch of Daily Pass, the first comprehensive system in the nation that coordinates health checks, **COVID tests and vaccinations all in one simple,***

---

[315] Gatto, John Taylor. Dumbing Us Down: The Hidden Curriculum of Compulsory Schooling. New Society Publishers, 1992.

[316] *The Grand Lodge of Florida: Child ID Program for the State of Florida*, https://grand-lodgefl.com/program_childid.html. Accessed 4 May 2021.

[317] 'COVID 19 / Safe Steps to Safe Schools - Daily Pass.' http%3A%2F%2Fachieve.lausd.net%2Fsite%2Fdefault.aspx%3FPageID%3D17313. Accessed 4 May 2021.

[318] 'Los Angeles Unified and Microsoft Announce Groundbreaking Way To Create Safest Possible School Environment (02-22-21)'. https://ca01000043.schoolwires.net/site/default.aspx?PageType=3&DomainID=4&ModuleInstanceID=4466&ViewID=6446EE88-D30C-497E-9316-3F8874B3E108&RenderLoc=0&FlexDataID=103349&PageID=1&Comments=true. Accessed 4 May 2021.

*easy-to-use tool. The Daily Pass is a critical component of Los Angeles Unified's 'Safe Steps to Safe Schools' reopening plan and part of its continuing commitment to create the safest possible school environment ... The Daily Pass sets the highest standard possible for school safety," said Los Angeles Unified Superintendent Austin Beutner. "MERV-13 upgraded air filters in every school, **COVID testing for all students and staff at least every week** and now the Daily Pass – Los Angeles Unified is proud to lead the nation in creating the safest possible school environment." **Developed with support from Microsoft Corp.**, Daily Pass can be accessed from any mobile phone, tablet or a computer ... Los Angeles Unified's **school-based vaccination program** uses Daily Pass to register and schedule appointments, track vaccines in stock, perform check-in and data capture at time of appointment, sort high-risk individuals, offer waitlists to low-risk individuals and dashboards to view data, among other features. All of this information is shared with the appropriate authorities."*

The signs indicate that the State is indeed looking to 'claim a generation' of children for its purposes and it ensure that the Covid narrative and 'Great Reset' is well-established and unchallenged, just like Hitler did in the 1930s.

What We Can Learn From Nazi Germany's Use of Romans 13

When we look back in history at the Nazi and other tyrannical regimes, we often ask, *"where were the people?!"* We've seen that the lack of early and strong resistance was a major factor in allowing the Nazi tyranny to escalate and move ahead, largely unchallenged. There was also the added factor of Statism propaganda and national pride that many people went willingly along with. This led countless 'normal people', 'good citizens' to become 'desk murderers' – who planned and organised the Holocaust without actually taking part in killings personally. They were so brainwashed that white collar workers such as doctors, teachers and administrators went along with the Nazi regime in the name of 'just doing their job' and not having the insight into (or courage to stand against) the real motives and ramifications of the State regimes of the day. Similarly, clergymen were using Romans 13 to justify their apathetic response. Further, those people who were involved in the direct killing of Jews at the Nazi concentration camps, were *normal civilians*. This is the chilling reality; that our minds may become so warped, and evil so rationalised that the average person is totally comfortable with committing atrocities, having believed absurdities. We can see that today with how people defend the genocide of babies under the term 'abortion' and 'women's right to choose'.

Take a look at the following picture of female Nazi concentration camp workers, enjoying some blueberries. As one newspaper notes: *"They underline the sickening hypocrisy of the servants of Nazism – morally bankrupt, illimitably cruel – and yet able to laugh, joke, drink and sunbathe as if they were no different to anyone else."*[319]

---

[319] Hall, Allan. 'Day off from Auschwitz: The Laughing Death-Camp Guards at Play'. *Mail Online*, 19 Sept. 2007. https://www.dailymail.co.uk/news/article-482691/Day-Auschwitz-The-laughing-death-camp-guards-play.html. Accessed 31 May 2021.

Could this be our doctors and nurses of today?

Essentially, people from inside and outside the Church were bystanders to the atrocities. The **'bystander effect'** is a social psychological phenomenon where a bystander is unlikely to help someone in need when there's the presence of other people around. This bystander apathy is inversely proportional to the total number of bystanders. The more the bystanders, the lesser chances of someone helping the person in need, the lesser the bystanders, the more are the chances of someone helping the person in need. In the case of governmental tyranny, the bystander effect creates a 'spiral of silence' – if no one speaks out, it becomes harder and harder for anyone to speak out. Doing nothing becomes tacit approval. In the same manner, under the Covid regulations, a morally corrupt society is being formed; humans in our societies are lacking the fortitude to help and stand up to wrong.

One of the major factors in people not speaking up is Stockholm Syndrome. A condition in which people under rule by coercion or tyranny will often develop an attachment to their oppressors, called 'trauma bonding', where a sense of loyalty or even a perverse love occurs – kind of like an abused wife. Why? Because they see no other option and because, on a subconscious level, the whole surreal world they are now living in makes no sense at all unless their rulers are doing the right thing. Therefore, their leaders must be right, they have to be right. All in all, many people are subconsciously asking this question: *"would I rather wake up and therefore see the mass insanity all around me, or would I prefer to stay asleep and follow orders and pretend that is the best course of action?"* They choose the second option and take part in a big social 'emperor's new clothes' contract to go along with it. That also explains why people can get very angry if you question the official narrative. Sadly, genuine Christians are not exempt from this and we would probably do well to learn from the failures of the Confessing Church in Nazi Germany. Christian author, Stephen Mattson, in his brilliant short article, 'Misusing Romans 13 to Embrace Theocracy',[320] writes: *"Christians have long used Romans 13 as a way to promote their preferred brand of political idolatry. But being "subject to the governing authorities" isn't a free pass to accept and condone anything the government – or the president – says or does. Often weaponized as a way to propagate partisan agendas while simultaneously shut down criticisms, this passage is commonly misunderstood by many Christians... Suggesting that God put the government in place and President Trump should be exempt from any sort of religious criticism is usually a partisan ploy to excuse the words, actions, legislation, and executive orders that are often callous and cruel. Christians who think President Trump is sovereignly chosen by God but shouldn't be judged according to Christ's standards of truth and holiness are succumbing to both moral relativism and cognitive dissonance. If you believe in the constitutional legality of having a separation between the Church and State while also propping up a president as being a divinely appointed servant of God, you are embracing a theocracy. For Trump-supporting Christians, his perceived status as both a president and pseudo high priest who they believe is faithfully carrying out God's plan*

---

[320] Mattson, Stephen. 'Misusing Romans 13 to Embrace Theocracy'. *Sojourners*, 10 Dec. 2019, https://sojo.net/articles/misusing-romans-13-embrace-theocracy.

provides immunity from any type of legal, spiritual, or moral accountability. Are we supposed to respect authorities who are dictators, war criminals, and brutal regimes as being divinely appointed by God? How can we fault citizens living in enemy states who wage war against the U.S.? Aren't they just following a Biblical command and submitting to their rulers and governing authorities, too? Christians should recognize that Jesus and his earliest followers were arrested, persecuted, and killed by the government of their day – often defying Roman orders and being viewed as treasonous."

There are many, many similarities between the Nazi regime and what we are seeing and experiencing under the Covid regime. Right now, a £35 million shared faith centre is being built in Berlin, dubbed a 'churmosquagogue' and to be shared between the city's Christians, Muslims and Jews – there are plans for these to become commonplace, with the tyrannical authorities' desires for a one-world religion rolling out thick and fast (see much more on this in Chapter 10 on Babylon). 'Clergy Response Teams' are being recruited and indoctrinated in the Covid propaganda to disseminate to their congregations around vaccines, PCR testing and ecumenism. They're also being educated in how to 'quell dissidents' within their Churches. We really need to wake up to what's going on. Now.

Let us end this chapter with a quote from Bonhoeffer: *"Silence in the face of evil is itself evil: God will not hold us guiltless. Not to speak is to speak. Not to act is to act."*

CHAPTER EIGHT

Reconciling Romans 13 and Revelation 13

I've heard it said that if you get Romans 13 wrong then you get Revelation 13 wrong too. I hope I have presented enough of a Biblical case, as well as from all the evidence we've seen so far in examining both tyrannical authorities of the past, and what's going on now under Covid, that we are not called to submit to all governmental authorities over us, either blindly or in a blanket fashion. Being prepared to submit to every single thing that governments command, irrespective of what those commands might be, is to make the State our god – the idolatry of Statism. We must not do this. We are to be, at the very least, seriously questioning and thinking and praying deeply about each new rule the government tries to impose on us. Make no mistake – there will be further lockdowns, further erroneous commands and further ineffective, deceptive and dangerous policies.

I have been saying since February 2020 that these rules will disproportionately disadvantage the Church and at this point – when going to Church and worshipping freely has been clearly and repeatedly deemed as a 'non-essential' activity and more dangerous than eating in a restaurant or working out in a gym – we should be very aware that this is designed, strategically, to weaken the body of Christ and to monitor our activities heavily. I believe this has come to a head as a case in point with the arrest and imprisonment of Pastor James Coates in Alberta, Canada in February 2021 and the subsequent barricading of his Church in April 2021, after his release from prison.

The Covid mandates are at least in part, if not in whole, designed with a view to controlling Church activities and the sermons preached in the near future, in the name of being 'inclusive and tolerant' to everyone. The end game here, like we saw under Nazi Germany, is to keep the form of Church as a vehicle to bring in another religion, dictated by the State's agenda: **This is designed to introduce another Gospel, one step at a time; the coming ecumenical, new age, Luciferian one world, Babylonian religion – headed up by Rome.** Depending on when you read this, you may not see this at play now but mark my words, it's coming … we'll look at this more later and we can see it at play in John's prophetic words of Revelation – the whole world wondering after a beastly perversion of true and holy religion, intimately connected to the beastly political system. We know from Romans 13 that we are to have a general posture of joyful submission to the civil authorities. We can observe from Revelation 13, however, that there is a time approaching in history where there will indeed be a Satanic, universal system of government in place, set up against Christ and His Church (or if you take a historicist view, it's already here!). The whole earth will marvel at this beast and we, as Christians must be aware of this and NOT submit to it. We are called instead to endure the persecution that will result from remaining true to Christ, as the saints and martyrs of the past have done. So that's the tension and spectrum we have to deal with, discern, wrestle with and act upon. On the one hand, we choose submission to our political rulers where there is no direct conflict between governmental authority and God's authority. On the other hand, we choose godly disobedience to political rulers when we discern Satanic rules, practices, suggestions, laws, paradigms, ideologies and religion. Let's look at the Revelation 13 text in its entirety, in three sections …

Revelation 13:1-8:

"Then I stood on the sand of the sea. And I saw a beast rising up out of the sea, having seven heads and ten horns, and on his horns ten crowns, and on his heads a blasphemous name. Now the beast which I saw was like a leopard, his feet were like the feet of a bear, and his mouth like the mouth of a lion. The dragon gave him his power, his throne, and great authority. And I saw one of his heads as if it had been mortally wounded, and his deadly wound was healed. And all the world marveled and followed the beast. So they worshiped the dragon who gave authority to the beast; and they worshiped the beast, saying, "Who is like the beast? Who is able to make war with him?" **And he was given a mouth speaking great things and blasphemies,** *and he was given authority to continue for forty-two months. Then he opened his mouth in blasphemy against God, to blaspheme His name, His tabernacle, and those who dwell in heaven.* **It was granted to him to make war with the saints and to overcome them. And authority was given him over every tribe, tongue, and nation. All who dwell on the earth will worship him, whose names have not been written in the Book of Life of the Lamb slain from the foundation of the world.** *"* (NKJV)

We see from this passage that:

- It echoes what is said in Daniel 7.
- The beast has powerful political authority over the earth.
- This authority is for forty-two months (the symbolic time, times and half a time seen in Daniel 7:25, or a literal three and a half years, depending on how you read it.)
- The beast's authority is given by the dragon (Satan).
- The beast blasphemes God.
- The beast wars against Christians and conquers them (persecutes and martyrs them – i.e. the saints experience tribulation).
- Everyone in the world follows after and worships the beast, except saved Christians who follow Jesus.

So we know that a time is coming, or may even be at hand, where the saints will be called to not follow the rest of the world in their Satanic pursuits and marvelling at this beastly system. And we know that in choosing to go against the ways of this system and to not follow it, not submit to it, not worship it, will result in persecution; even unto death in some cases.

Revelation 13:9-10:

"If anyone has an ear, let him hear. He who leads into captivity shall go into captivity; he who kills with the sword must be killed with the sword. ***Here is the patience and the faith of the saints.*** *"* (NKJV)

This makes it evident that Christians can indeed expect persecution in the form of imprisonment and being killed. The counsel our LORD gives us on this is to exercise patience/endurance and faith – fruit that is supernaturally borne of the Holy Spirit. As a slight aside, my strong Biblical conviction on this is that there will be no 'pre-tribulation rapture' as many Christians speak of. It would be reassuring to think that our Lord will sweep us up before a great time of tribulation, but we just do not see this in Scripture. *"And it was given unto him [the beast] to make war with the saints, and to overcome them".* – Revelation 13:7

There has indeed been much time of tribulation in the past and our LORD uses that to refine us. *"Then one of the elders answered, saying to me, "Who are these arrayed in white robes, and where did they come from?" And I said to him, "Sir, you know." So he said to me, "These are the ones who come out of the great tribulation, and washed their robes and made them white in the blood of the Lamb."* – Revelation 7:13-14 (NKJV)

You can read more in this simple and clear article refuting a pre-trib rapture,[321] and this overview of how a pre-trib rapture is not supported

---

[321] Taylor, Justin. '9 Reasons We Can Be Confident Christians Won't Be Raptured Before the Tribulation'. *The Gospel Coalition*, https://www.thegospelcoalition.org/blogs/justin-taylor/9-reasons-we-can-be-confident-christians-wont-be-raptured-before-the-tribulation/. Accessed 4 May 2021.

throughout Church history.[322] I therefore believe it to be a falsehood, with good evidence that it was a concept created by the Jesuits, originating with Jesuit Francisco Ribera in 1585.[323]

We can agree to differ on this if you hold a different view, however, we are called by Jesus to pick up our cross daily. We are repeatedly told that we are to patiently endure suffering, persecution and even martyrdom, just like many saints of the past have done and as we see in Revelation 6. The Bible does not say we will be spared from horrific tribulation; rather it says that as Christians we can expect it, but our LORD will be with us and will sustain us through it and that His grace is sufficient and His yoke is light. And if we read the accounts of people like Richard Wurmbrand in his book 'Tortured for Christ'[324] and the biographies of martyrs and even hear of people in our own lives who have suffered tremendously for their faith or otherwise, we see that our LORD is faithful and indeed close to the broken hearted and sustains us and encamps around those who fear Him. Psalm 34 is wonderful counsel to us in all of this. I can attest to being sustained by the LORD in my own life sufferings thus far and I'm sure you can too. Let's trust in His ability to deliver us from evil, which may not include delivering us from the actual circumstances.

Revelation 13:11-18:

"Then I saw another beast coming up out of the earth, and he had two horns like a lamb and spoke like a dragon. And he exercises all the authority of the first beast in his presence, and causes the earth and those who dwell in it to worship the first beast, whose deadly wound was healed. He performs great signs, so that he even makes fire come down from heaven on the earth in the sight of men. And he deceives those who dwell

---

[322] Pivec, Holly. 'Blessed Hope or False Hope? — What Holly Thinks — Fulfilled Prophecy'. *Fulfilled Prophecy*, 15 Jan. 2008, http://www.fulfilledprophecy.com/commentary/blessed-hope-or-false-hope-what-holly-thinks/. Accessed 4 May 2021.

[323] 'The Origin of the False Pre-Tribulation Rapture Doctrine'. *James Japan*, 12 May 2014, https://www.jamesjpn.net/basic-bible/the-origin-of-the-false-pre-tribulation-rapture-doctrine/.

[324] Wurmbrand, Richard. *Tortured for Christ*. Living Sacrifice Book Co, 1993.

*on the earth by those signs which he was granted to do in the sight of the beast, telling those who dwell on the earth to make an image to the beast who was wounded by the sword and lived. He was granted power to give breath to the image of the beast, that the image of the beast should both speak and **cause as many as would not worship the image of the beast to be killed.** He causes all, both small and great, rich and poor, free and slave, to receive a mark on their right hand or on their foreheads, and that no one may buy or sell except one who has the mark or the name of the beast, or the number of his name. Here is wisdom. Let him who has understanding calculate the number of the beast, for it is the number of a man: His number is 666."* (NKJV)

There is another beast that appears like a lamb – a counterfeit Christ – who will appear and deceive people with all sorts of signs and wonders and cause humanity to worship it. Again, it is reiterated that those Christians who perceive and resolve not to worship it – but rather to stand against it in righteousness – can expect and be prepared to be killed for their faithfulness to Christ. The mark on the right hand and forehead is a direct reference back to Deuteronomy 6: *"You shall love the Lord your God with all your heart, with all your soul, and with all your strength. "And these words which I command you today shall be in your heart. You shall teach them diligently to your children, and shall talk of them when you sit in your house, when you walk by the way, when you lie down, and when you rise up. **You shall bind them as a sign on your hand, and they shall be as frontlets between your eyes.** "* – Deuteronomy 6:5-8 (NKJV)

So, the 'mark of the beast' of Revelation 13:16 is a direct perversion of Deuteronomy 6:8 and is 'man's number' – six, which is a falling short of God's perfect number, seven. An unholy trinity of 'me, myself and I' if you like, or 'missing the mark of perfection' x3. Instead of people loving the LORD God with all their heart, mind, soul and strength and God's commands being the focus of their thoughts (frontlets of eyes) and actions (work of our hands) – it is all in opposition to this – beastly instead. People will be lovers of evil and lovers of themselves. There is much speculation about what this 'mark of the beast is' but we should first remember that receiving a mark on the hand or forehead is figurative, especially given that we know from Revelation 7:3 that God's servants are sealed on their foreheads. Remember too, Romans 8:38-39 tells us that *"neither death, nor life, nor angels, nor principalities, nor powers, nor things present, nor things to come, Nor height, nor depth, nor any other creature, shall be able to separate us from the love of God, which is in Christ Jesus our Lord."* So, we can rest assured that, as truly born-again Christians, even if the authorities force us to take a vaccine and be chipped and marked, we cannot be separated from our God and we can trust that He will keep us until the very end – set apart and sealed for Him and gathered up to be with Him forever at His great coming. However this prophecy is fulfilled, it is clear that it will involve compromising and contradicting God's commands and worshipping a harlot religion. It also seems very likely that a person having proof that they are officially associated in some way with the beast will be necessary for them to be allowed to engage in the commerce – and this is something us Christians should consider carefully and count the cost of and prepare for. We have to decide if we are going to try and resist taking a nanotechnology mRNA vaccine, with a 'Luciferase' mark in it, or a similar somewhat beastly mark, and face heavy restrictions on our buying and selling and travel, work and leisure activities, or if we're going to go along with it. Whatever we decide though, we must not be deceived into thinking that it is for our good – it is not. It is evil.

I think California pastor and theology blogger, Jeremy Marshall, puts it really well in his article on Romans 13 and Revelation 13: *"Even as the Caesar-Beast seems to run amok, however, the Church is invited neither to a) Revolt against Caesar in the name of God or any virtue, nor to b) Excuse Caesar's bad behaviour in God's name and call Caesar's evil good. The Church is called only to endurance and faithfulness, based on a truthful acceptance that, if any are to be taken captive, then into captivity they will go. If any are to be killed by the sword, then by the sword they will be killed. As we observed from Bonhoeffer: The Christian is still free and has nothing to fear, and he can still pay the State its due by suffering innocently. The force capable of animating lives of peaceful, loving goodness in the face of such horribleness is a patience formed by hope. The basis of this hope is resurrection. The Church is shaped by a partic- ular story about God's Son being violently humiliated and crushed by the Beast, but God asserting his sovereignty by defying the death sentence and raising his Son to life again. The Church is capable of patient faith in the face of the Beast because we believe that we who have a share in Christ's death also have a share in his resurrection."*

So what exactly is patient and faithful endurance? What does it look like and what is it not? The obvious things we are unequivocally called to do with patient endurance are as follows:

- Gather corporately and physically in some form or other to wor- ship our Living God.
- Preach the Word – the whole counsel of God with no omissions, in season and out of season.
- Read and meditate on the Word (or recite it, having memorised it as many persecuted Churches do, who no longer have access to Bibles).
- Pray.
- Evangelise the lost.
- Sing hymns of praise.
- Love our neighbour.
- Uphold and partake in the Lord's Supper and Baptism.
- Train up our children in the Gospel and exercise godly discipline.

These are the things that when push comes to shove, we must hold fast to, irrespective of what our secular (or ecclesiastical) authorities say and what the consequences might be – imprisonment or otherwise. Examples of less obvious things we should do with patient endurance could be:

- Upholding the sanctity of heterosexual, one-man one- woman marriage – and performing wedding ceremonies to this end.

- Greeting each other with a holy kiss.
- Not condoning or supporting abortion.
- Not yoking with false religions and ecumenical movements.
- Refuting a social gospel.

There are many other things that we are to discern with wisdom and seeking the Scriptures. So, what is patient endurance not? As Christians, we may or may not choose to partake in any of the following things (they may or may not be wise or good), but they are not the Biblical patient endurance that John is talking about in Revelation or Peter describes in his letters, or that our LORD Jesus speaks of in the Gospels. We should be wary of our participation in such things, as we may be liable to deceive ourselves or others in thinking we are 'standing up for/being obedient to our faith in Christ', when this isn't the case and may actually be anti-Christian.

Patient endurance is not:

- Signing and encouraging others to sign petitions.
- Supporting Black Lives Matter.
- Attending an anti-vaccination/anti-mask/anti-5G, etc. march.
- Writing letters to bishops, councillors, congressman, prime ministers and other State authorities to appeal against Covid (or other) mandates that affect the Church negatively.
- Ceasing to meet, wearing masks and not singing in Church, even though we dislike these things.

These are things to consider, ponder upon and pray about as all of this is not particularly easy to get our heads around and requires real discernment; especially in the face of bombardment from the authorities with their persuasive and hyped agenda, delivered with immediacy via multi-sensory technology. On the other hand, it's fairly simple when we tune out the noise of the world and take what our LORD commands us seriously and with sober and courageous judgement. The themes we see in

Romans 13 and Revelation 13 are that we are to have a submissive posture towards authorities, but also to be wise and discerning of the times, to discern evil and deception and resist it and to patiently endure persecution for righteousness' sake. Caesar and Nero in the time of Romans 13 were evil. The beast in Revelation 13 is evil – all are ultimately instituted and given authority by God. We must submit peaceably until our obedience to God is inhibited. Then we must choose our LORD first.

The beastly system of Revelation 13 is rising all around us and we need to be prepared to stand strong in Christ. We will examine this more in Chapter 10 on Discerning Babylon. The Covid mandates that are in place now and coming down the road are a test of faith for the saints – to refine us, to allow us to exercise our trust in God over man, increase our boldness, courage, wisdom and obedience and experience the joy and privilege to suffer for our LORD Jesus. If, by now (I phrase it this way because you have got this far into the evidence that I've presented in this book to back up my thesis statement), you believe that this 'pandemic' is as genuine, prevalent and destructive as we're being told, 'safety' is not to be our god. We have never been commanded to suspend worship and our obedience to the LORD in favour of 'keeping us all safe'. The safest place to be is in God's will – and be prepared to face whatever consequences that may bring, knowing that Jesus, Yeshua, will sustain us with His grace. Will we embrace that?

CHAPTER NINE

Good Impressions of the Sinful Nature from Galatians 6

The more I dig into the ever-changing and tightening Covid rules and regulations and the Church's response, the more it is very evident that this is not only a Romans 13:1-7 'subjection to authorities' issue, but it is also a Galatians issue. There is a real danger of sincere Christians turning to a 'different Gospel', being 'enslaved to the elementary principles of the world' and 'wanting to impress people by means of the flesh'.

"I marvel that you are turning away so soon from Him who called you in the grace of Christ, to a different gospel". – Galatians 1:6

Similarly, in 2 Corinthians 11:3-4, Paul expresses a 'divine jealousy' for the Church at Corinth and says he is seeking to present them as a 'pure virgin to Christ' – a spotless Bride. But he is concerned that there is danger of being led astray by 'another Jesus, a different spirit and a different gospel'. There is this same threefold danger for us too.

In May 2021, the world's most famous statue depicting Jesus Christ, the Cristo Redentor in Rio de Janeiro, was lit up to promote the Covid pseudo-vaccine. The message projected onto it: *'Vaccine saves, United for vaccines'*. This is a blasphemous depiction of what we'll cover in this chapter.

Paul's sharp letter to the Galatians was a rebuke of the alternative gospel of legalism – adding works to the grace of Christ. This was being brought in by the 'Judaisers' who were Jewish Christians who sought to influence Gentile believers to observe Jewish religious practices. They insisted that the Gentile converts needed to believe in Christ, be circumcised, and observe the festival laws (days and months and seasons and years), in order to be accepted by God (and by each other). In doing this, they had forfeited the freedom they possessed in the truth of salvation by grace alone, through faith alone, in Christ alone. Paul was especially hard on the Galatian Church in this regard since Jewish legalism was and is even more dangerous than outright paganism – being more refined and subtle, on account of its Biblical proximity. William Still explains it very well in his 'Notes on Galatians' (1972): *"That both heathenism and Jewish legalism, very different from one another, are here bundled together in contrast with the liberty of the Gospel is plain from the fact that the observances which are referred to are applied to both. The law observed externally as*

a superstitious system without faith was doubtless a bondage to elemental spirits of this age, as heathenism was. Not only the bad, but often and much more the good, is the enemy of the best!"

Can I tell you about the personal effect that the letter to the Galatians had on me when I read it prior to writing this chapter? I had not read it for about six months, since the beginning of the pandemic, and when I did so many passages stuck out to me as being utterly relevant to our situation under Covid today. Upon reading it, I immediately felt distraught for the Church, could not eat and fasted, prayed and wept most of the day in solitude. This has happened several times throughout 2020, the first time was after reading Ezra, especially chapter 9: *"Now when these things were done, the princes came to me, saying, The people of Israel, and the priests, and the Levites, have not separated themselves from the people of the lands, doing according to their abominations, even of the Canaanites, the Hittites, the Perizzites, the Jebusites, the Ammonites, the Moabites, the Egyptians, and the Amorites. For they have taken of their daughters for themselves, and for their sons: so that the holy seed have mingled themselves with the people of those lands: yea, the hand of the princes and rulers hath been chief in this trespass."* – Ezra 9:1-2

I saw the Church compromised with the nations around us, being influenced and polluted by worldly precepts and 'the foreign woman' and that the higher ecclesiastical leaders, those imposters whose concern is not for the things of our LORD Jesus Christ, were at the forefront of it.

Back to Galatians … As I read it near the end of 2020, I knew that I had to include a chapter in this book to highlight its relevance in our situation and the warnings Paul has for us too. I've selected twelve passages that spoke deeply to me (pretty much the whole letter) and a brief explanation of how I believe it relates to the Church in our Covid scenario.

Galatians 1:6-7:

*"I marvel that you **are turning away** so soon from Him who called you in the grace of Christ, **to a different gospel**, which is not another; but there*

are some who trouble you and want to pervert the gospel of Christ." (NKJV)

As I stated in Chapter 2 on Romans 13, we are in danger of creating a 'peace and safety' gospel, a gospel of utilitarianism and pragmatism. This is no gospel at all and takes away the power, beauty and freedom of the true Gospel of our LORD Jesus Christ.

Galatians 2:4-5:

*"And this occurred because of false brethren secretly brought in (who came in by stealth to **spy out our liberty which we have in Christ Jesus, that they might bring us into bondage**), to whom we did not yield sub-mission even for an hour, that the truth of the gospel might continue with you."* (NKJV)

All these Covid rules that have 'slipped in' have nestled themselves in our Church quite nicely and taken root. 'Don't sit there'. 'Don't get too close to each other'. 'Don't come into Church without covering your face'. 'Don't sing'. This bondage has become quite commonplace in our Church buildings (if they are open at all, that is). Who has introduced them? Governments, yes, but also higher ecclesiastical leaders with dubi-ous motives and commitment to the Gospel at best and being outright wolves at worst (we'll look at this more in Chapter 10 on Babylon). There is many an individual Christian or Churchgoer who is ready to enthusias-tically uphold these rules and boldly call out others who are not towing the line. Unfortunately, we have not been as quick-witted and bold as Paul in discerning and not yielding to this imposed slavery of a new safety gospel. We have embraced it and determined that it trumps the spir-itual freedom we have in Christ – the freedom to be unafraid when it comes to our flesh and not acquiesce to the fear of the rest of the world. We have misguidedly applied Romans 14 to say that we are 'looking out for our weaker brother and not causing them to stumble' by following the Covid rules. In doing this, we are trumping God's commands with trying to please our neighbour – this is a kind of Christian humanism. It is one thing to agree not to eat a certain food in order to love our brother – that

263

is of no consequence. It is quite another to compromise worship in the house of God, especially when it is done to pander to our brother's fear and following worldly, godless propaganda. An analogy that comes to mind is this: Without a resurrection hope (or instead holding some false notion of reincarnation or the like), the heathen world is tempted or resigned to act like the owner of a new Ferrari regarding their bodily condition. It's their prized possession and they're constantly concerned about it not being scratched – cleaning and polishing it and making sure its appearance and performance is in tip top condition, even locking it away under great security measures to prevent it from being stolen or in any other way marred. All of this comes at great time and expense. (That said, it can be observed that very few people take the holiness of a good and temperate diet and healthy habits very seriously, but that's another issue.) This is a clear example of idolatry, delusion and slavery to that perishing item. The thing that was supposed to bring the proud super-car owner joy and happiness, instead brings insecurity, worry and bondage … I have known quite a few Ferrari owners and they all attest to this! The Christian, on the other hand, knows that this life is passing away. We should view our bodies more like owning an old banger of a car: We use it and enjoy it and we look after it, as good stewards of God's gifts, but we do so much more liberally and lightly. We are not concerned if it gets a bump or a scratch here or there. We are relatively happy for the kids to spill drinks in it, or the elderly parent to drop biscuit crumbs in it. We won't lose any sleep over it. When we need to use it as a hard work horse for our job, family and Church purposes, or in any other way expend it in service and love and for practical use and freedoms, we willingly do so. And when the time comes that we must scrap that car, we are not so attached to it or devastated that it shakes our world in any way. We simply shrug it off and hope to get a new one. There is joy and freedom that comes from using it to serve and to enhance our lives and the lives of others in a practical way, rather than us serving it as an idol and in pursuit of status. This may sound flippant, but let's remember – as Christians have the resurrection hope as gloriously described in 1 Corinthians 15 – this body is not our only hope, we wait for our perfected resurrection bodies!

"So also is the resurrection of the dead. It is sown in corruption; it is raised in incorruption: It is sown in dishonour; it is raised in glory: it is sown in weakness; it is raised in power". – 1 Corinthians 15:42-43

This should, therefore, give us huge hope, faith and the ability and freedom to take more risks with this earthly body. We can confidently hold its health and condition lightly, rather than seeking to hide it away and preserve it in some kind of 'Covid pickling jar' by endlessly 'shielding' and 'self-isolating' out of fear – for ourselves and others. (I say this as someone who takes good diet and health practices very seriously.) And let us not forget that 'to live is Christ and to die is gain'. Do we actually believe this and live by it? In many cases, it seems not, despite the firm promise and hope of resurrection, many Christians appear to be holding onto their old banger like a prized Ferrari. The lost world can be somewhat excused in this, since they have no other hope; we cannot. Jesus expended himself fully for us and poured out His precious blood on the cross, so that we may have a hope beyond this earthly life. We all need to be reminded of this, I am ministering to myself in this as much as you – we are all tempted towards self-preservation, safety and love of our own bodies. It's a constant battle for every one of us!

The thing that most concerns me most right now, as I write this, is the prospect of 'no vaccine, no Church' and 'no Covid test, no Church' mandates. Maybe as you read this, they are already in place in Churches? Israel has implemented this. At the very least, this can be seen as the sin of partiality that James talks about and, at worst, it is another gospel that has entered our Churches and like all 'other gospels', it is exceedingly dangerous – not only spiritually in this case but physically and mentally too. I refer back to my original thesis statement at the beginning of the book – this is Statism: idolatry of the State to bring such abominations into our Churches. I have already heard Church leaders discussing dividing their congregations and Church buildings between 'the vaccinated' and 'the unvaccinated'!

"My brethren, do not hold the faith of our Lord Jesus Christ, the Lord of glory, with partiality. For if there should come into your assembly a man with gold rings, in fine apparel, and there should also come in a poor man in filthy clothes, and you pay attention to the one wearing the fine clothes and say to him, "You sit here in a good place," and say to the poor man, "You stand there," or, "Sit here at my footstool," have you not shown partiality among yourselves, and become judges with evil thoughts?" – James 2:1-4 (NKJV)

As we explored back in Chapter 4 on enforced vaccines, I'm very sad to say that shockingly, right now, we have Church wolves in place who are advocating this experimental, novel vaccine as being 'part of Christ's commandment to love each other'.

19th January 2021

FACTS AND FAITH

Justin Welby: Getting Covid vaccine is part of Christ's commandment to love each other

The Archbishop of Canterbury Justin Welby has received his first dose of the Covid-19 vaccine and encouraged others to do the same.

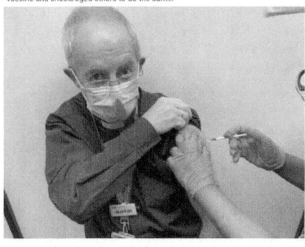

Galatians 2:11-13:

*"Now when Peter had come to Antioch, I withstood him to his face, because he was to be blamed; for before certain men came from James, he would eat with the Gentiles; but when they came, **he withdrew and separated himself, fearing those who were of the circumcision**. And the rest of the Jews also played the hypocrite with him, so that even Barnabas was carried away with their hypocrisy."* (NKJV)

How many people do we see in our Churches, like Peter, drawing away from others who are not following some of the erroneous Covid rules to their liking? Are masks, hand sanitisers, tests and vaccines the new form of circumcision? And people staunchly advocating them (with good intentions or otherwise) the 'coronavirus circumcision party' or the 'Covid Judaisers'? There are certainly parallels.

I have been complained about and avoided because I have not worn a mask in Church or social distanced as 'required' and have witnessed many 'tuts', frowns and haughty, disdainful attitudes. Judgements have been made on my 'falling short' of following Covid mandates to the letter and for expressing concerns with the vaccines. And, if we want to dig deeper into this sinful partiality, in my experience I know for a fact that many of the staunch Covid rules enthusiasts are not sharing the Gospel with unbelievers. Neither are they committed to diligent daily Bible reading (i.e., the renewing of their natural mind and thoughts with God's precepts) and in some cases have been in adulterous relationships. I do not believe that any of my actions that have been met with disdain are sinful, at all. And yet if others, for some reason, do see them as a sin to be confronted, it's certainly not done in a Biblical way. Concerning the woman caught in adultery, Jesus says to the crowd, *"He that is without sin among you, let him first cast a stone at her."* From this passage we learn that we should not accuse others unless we first thoroughly search our own hearts and minds to make certain that we are pure in our motives and that the accusations are accurate (Matthew 7:3). Also, we must always look to

God's glory, assess own selfish motives, and avoid unnecessary division or harm (Matthew 18:15).

Galatians 3:1-4:

"O foolish Galatians! Who has bewitched you that you should not obey the truth, before whose eyes Jesus Christ was clearly portrayed among you as crucified? This only I want to learn from you: Did you receive the Spirit by the works of the law, or by the hearing of faith? Are you so foolish? Having begun in the Spirit, are you now being made perfect by the flesh? Have you suffered so many things in vain – if indeed it was in vain?" (NKJV)

The answer to 'who has bewitched us?' in our situation could be answered with any or all of the following: television screens, news reporters, medical officers, doctors, government officials, ecclesiastical leaders, billionaire computer programmers and more. We have appealed to our fleshly nature in the name of physical safety and to be thought well of amongst men. How much of these worldly influences are spiritually correct or edifying in their nature, assessments and response to Covid?

Galatians 3:11:

"But that no man is justified by the law in the sight of God, it is evident: for, The just shall live by faith."

We must ask, are we trying to please God through our faith and obedience to Christ or please people by obscure, man-made rules?

Galatians 4:3-10:

"Even so we, when we were children, were in bondage under the elements of the world. But when the fullness of the time had come, God sent forth His Son, born of a woman, born under the law, to redeem those who were under the law, that we might receive the adoption as sons. And because you are sons, God has sent forth the Spirit of His Son into your hearts, crying out, "Abba, Father!" Therefore you are no longer a slave but a

268

son, and if a son, then an heir of God through Christ. But then, indeed, when you did not know God, you served those which by nature are not gods. But now after you have known God, or rather are known by God, how is it that you turn again to the weak and beggarly elements, to which you desire again to be in bondage? You observe days and months and seasons and years." (NKJV)

Paul echoes this in Colossians 2:8:

"Beware lest any man spoil you through philosophy and vain deceit, after the tradition of men, after the rudiments of the world, and not after Christ." – Colossians 2:8

It can be so easy to be deceived and enslaved by the philosophies and deceptions of the world. They can often sound good, plausible and inviting; mainly because they match up with our own sinful inclinations, such as fear or the desire to avoid persecution and towards comfort. Our sinful natures can fall for and collude with anything. Therefore, we need to take extra special care that we 'see to it' to check everything out with God's Word to us. It is our responsibility to be constantly going back to Scripture to let our LORD teach us what is right, good and holy for us, remembering that we are children and heirs of the most-high God and to live as such, not as slaves and not as dogs returning to our own vomit.

Galatians 4:16:

"Have I therefore become your enemy because I tell you the truth?" (NKJV)

If we raise any concerns about Covid in our Churches – along the lines of anything discussed in this book – the government propaganda (and thus higher ecclesiastical bodies too, under government direction) has seen to it that we try and condemn any other opinion than the official narrative and even label such people as dangerous and 'mentally unstable'. I have spoken to many Christians who have ventured to challenge the official Covid spin and mandates and have received harsh treatment from within their Churches – attempting to shame and silence them. I have been on the receiving end of this many times and there is a palpable hatred of the message and hostility towards me for telling these truths. And let's not forget courageous Pastors such as James Coates, Jacob Reaume and Stephen Richardson in Canada, who have been reprimanded and even imprisoned by the magistrate for telling the truth of the matter and leading their Churches in Gospel freedom. Yet there are many Christians who have very openly condemned their actions.

Galatians 4:17:

"They zealously court you, but for no good; yes, they want to exclude you, that you may be zealous for them." (NKJV)

Paul is describing manipulation tactics. Sadly, we can see these at play in our Churches right now, albeit subtly in many cases: Covid zealots complaining about people who do not submit to the rules or even just voice an opposing or questioning viewpoint, as just described. In applying this kind of exclusionary peer pressure, which reminds me of my school days, they seek to bring outliers 'in line' with government rules. Again, it surprises me how bold so many people are in touting Covid rules, yet not saying a peep about the Gospel to their friends and in their workplaces – by their own admission. It's hard to determine that such people's affections and allegiance lie firmly and purely with Christ.

Galatians 5:1-8:

"Stand fast therefore in the liberty by which Christ has made us free, and do not be entangled again with a yoke of bondage. Indeed I, Paul, say to you that if you become circumcised, Christ will profit you nothing. And I testify again to every man who becomes circumcised that he is a debtor to keep the whole law. You have become estranged from Christ, you who attempt to be justified by law; you have fallen from grace. For we through the Spirit eagerly wait for the hope of righteousness by faith. For in Christ Jesus neither circumcision nor uncircumcision avails anything, but faith

working through love. You ran well. Who hindered you from obeying the truth? This persuasion does not come from Him who calls you." (NKJV)

The Apostle Paul warned the Church at Philippi that the circumcision party are evildoers, *"Beware of dogs, beware of evil workers, beware of the mutilation!"* (Philippians 3:2), since they have fallen away from grace.

In my estimation and observation, we are deviating dangerously from the grace and freedom that Christ gives us and commands us to live by, we are adding 'good works' to that by adding Covid rules. Of course, we would never admit that. 'We are saved by grace alone in Christ alone, though faith alone' most Christians would protest. But are we acceptable and accepted in our Churches unless we add to it the entourage of Covid rules? If not, we are adding works to grace and enforcing slavery to laws again. The irony being that, just like the Old Testament laws, the Covid rules are impossible and impractical to be kept by anyone anyhow (as well as non-sensical), so we are all failing to meet the perfect standard. I.e., are we always six feet away from other people? Are we not touching the masks we are wearing and do we have them properly fitted at all times? Have we refrained from seeing and socialising with people completely during lockdowns? If by chance and diligence we have, then the problem of legalism and lack of Christian charity, love and disobedience to the Gospel is far more concerning.

Galatians 5:17-21:

"For the flesh lusts against the Spirit, and the Spirit against the flesh; and these are contrary to one another, so that you do not do the things that you wish. But if you are led by the Spirit, you are not under the law. Now the works of the flesh are evident, which are: adultery, fornication, uncleanness, lewdness, idolatry, sorcery, hatred, contentions, jealousies, outbursts of wrath, selfish ambitions, dissensions, heresies, envy, murders, drunkenness, revelries, and the like; of which I tell you beforehand, just as I also told you in time past, that those who practice such things will not inherit the kingdom of God." (NKJV)

271

The desires of the flesh and those of the Spirit are at odds with each other. We cannot seek to please both fleshly man and our spiritual God at the same time. James 1:8 reminds us that a double-minded person is unstable in all his ways. Because of our enforced separation and closure of Churches, it may be hard to see for sure that sexual immorality, impurity and sensuality is flourishing in the Body of Christ as a result of the Covid rules. However, we can see seeds, and in some cases full blown examples of divisions, dissentions, rivalry, strife, jealousy, anger and the like. Paul contrasts these works of the flesh with the fruit of the Spirit.

We can again look to Romans 13 for guidance which corroborates this: *"But put on the Lord Jesus Christ, and make no provision for the flesh, to fulfill its lusts."* – Romans 13:14 (NKJV)

Galatians 6:1:

"Brethren, if a man is overtaken in any trespass, you who are spiritual restore such a one in a spirit of gentleness, considering yourself lest you also be tempted." (NKJV)

Just as Peter was in sin and hypocrisy (Galatians 2:11-13), Paul tells us that Barnabas and others were also led astray by him in this. This is a warning to us. The Covid enthusiasts are leading many others into sin and to follow the false safety gospel and losing sight of the actual Gospel. This goes some way to explaining why whole Churches are just going along with these rules and regulations and, in many cases, not even questioning it and welcoming tighter safety rules, seeing them as virtuous.

Galatians 6:7-8:

"Do not be deceived, God is not mocked; for whatever a man sows, that he will also reap. For he who sows to his flesh will of the flesh reap corruption, but he who sows to the Spirit will of the Spirit reap everlasting life." (NKJV)

Can you see what is happening here? Temptation to follow the safety gospel by many people, out of worldly, fleshly desires is reaping corruption as…. a result within our Churches. There is division, sin and a weakening of our witness to the world, as well as the promotion of a harmful, experimental injection. I've shown the physical, mental and spiritual dangers of this extensively in Chapter 4.

Galatians 6:12:

"As many as desire to make a good showing in the flesh, these would compel you to be circumcised, only that they may not suffer persecution for the cross of Christ." (NKJV)

This really is the pinnacle of the whole letter in my opinion and I suspect in Paul's too. This verse is very, very sobering to me and should be to you as well. He is so compelled to say this twelfth verse of chapter 6 to the Galatian believers that at this point Paul takes over the writing of the ending of the letter from his scribe and writes it in bold, in his own handwriting, to show its importance and urgency. And the ending of the letter does not have the same signature gracious benediction and tone that many of his other letters to the Churches have. It has a reiteration of a sharp warning and gives an explanation as to why. Those Judaisers who were concerned with outward appearance and being well-thought of, enforced these legalistic rules because they are cowardly seeking to avoid Christian persecution.

Christian, let me ask you, how willing are you to be persecuted for the cross of Christ? This is the crux of the issue (pun intended). It is clear that there is a spirit of fear in the Church brought in under Covid. People are afraid of death and disease and have been taught and conditioned to fear other people, fear social contact, fear gathering in Church, fear governments, fear questioning anything we're being told, and more. Fear of persecution is a growing concern too. Fear is understandable, but it is not excusable. It is something we need to identify and rebuke and repent of in our lives. We need to minister to each other in this as a standard part of discipleship.

As believers, we are called into Gospel freedom and that includes freedom from the grips of fear – to be replaced with courage, love and peace of mind and courage. Perfect love casts out fear, as Jesus tells us in 1 John 4:18.

Let's explore this idea of fear of persecution more …

Gregory Barkman from Beacon Baptist Church in North Carolina, USA identifies five key Galatians 6:12 issues (which I am expanding upon) that we should too beware of in terms of seeking to avoid persecution:

1. Image Over Reality

The Judaisers were concerned with making a good show of themselves – being liked and thought well of, over spiritual realities. By forcing circumcision, they were adding tangible works to the Gospel of grace and being kept acceptable to God and others by those works. For us, could it be that to be thought of as a strong or righteous and loving Christian and approved of by others, we must wear a mask, socially distance, not sing in Church, take virus tests and be vaccinated? I'd say that this is the view of many Church folk. Where is Christian freedom? Is faithful adherence to the Covid mandates a measure of spiritual success (and 'loving our neighbour'), as the Judaisers falsely made circumcision to be? We have seen in Chapter 5 the four different types of governance and the limits to each. As clearly outlined back then, these mandates are not within the remit of either government or Church authority, have no place in the Church and should be resisted as a matter of Biblical principle by every Christian. Wearing a mask is an important physical and very visible identifying factor with the new Covid tenets. It's a matter of carnal satisfaction, making a good impression and ticking outward boxes of conformity. It has nothing to do with spiritual health, or physical health for that matter, as we've seen, and most people know this but go along with it all anyway. Instead of working on our Covid image, we need to work upon our hearts, our holiness, our spirituality, love of God, inner man and obedience.

274

Would we be willing to be disapproved of by man in actively not follow-ing all the erroneous Covid rules? Try not wearing a mask for a week and see how much flack you get in Church and society and how much courage and willingness you need to have difficult conversations … That said, I have seen God to be faithful in allowing my complete freedom on this matter. This is training my friend for the harder persecutions to come. Give it a go. The masks are aiding and abetting a lie, why submit to that? The Romans 13 call to submit to government authorities does not call us to sin by submitting to lies that hinder our worship and witness.

2. Psychology and Politics Over Scripture

We should beware of 'fine sounding arguments' and smooth speech which have no grounds in Scripture. I have heard pastors often repeating the line 'we need to slow the spread of the virus' as if it's a new creed. The circumcision party were using mental and psychological coercion and manipulation in Paul's day. We can see the Covid rules enforcers us-ing politics, worldly propaganda and fear psychology now to compel us to keep instituting the ungodly Covid rules within our Church worship. Add to that social pressure, group think and 'collectivism' and we can see the sinful effects. Even Peter would not eat with the non-circumcised and Paul had to rebuke him strongly. There are people in our Churches who are applying such tactics, wittingly or unwittingly. Paul was the only one who stood up and opposed the Judaisers. This takes discernment, humil-ity and guts.

3. Comfort Over the Cross/Truth

Human beings are very adept at self-preservation and seeking comfort. Our souls are made up of the will, the intellect and the emotions. Our will directs the other two and naturally our will has a strong tendency to seek comfort and avoid pain and persecution. We must constantly check our motives and realise that we all filter the world and what we see through our pre-existing beliefs. This is how two people can look at the same ev-idence and one can deny it and believe a lie – sometimes it's because of the will's desire for comforted self-preservation. We can avoid persecution in two main ways: by keeping quiet about our faith and holiness (or certain aspects of it) or compromising on it – we can hide away in communes and keep our faith to ourselves, or have one foot in the world and one in the Church. We want to be liked and respected by our family, friends, co-workers, boss, etc. We want to keep our jobs, our status, our wealth, our homes and our good standing in the community. But Jesus promises us no such things. He tells us that we will be hated and we will suffer if we are faithful to Him. How much of this have you experienced, or have you avoided it?

"Woe unto you, when all men shall speak well of you! for so did their fathers to the false prophets." – Luke 6:26

What about the cost of discipleship? What about the offence of the cross and separation from the world and our call to be salt and light? When personal comfort is preferred over truth and picking up our cross (daily), we partake in false religion. If we are brutally honest with ourselves, we will find that much of what we are entertaining in our Churches under Covid is an elaborate justification of seeking comfort and avoiding persecution, just like the Judaisers. Our motivations are not in seeking to honour and exalt Christ, but sadly in keeping our heads down for ease and conformity and out of cowardice. I would highly recommend reading both Matt Walsh's book 'Church of Cowards'[325] for much more on this and Doug Giles' 'If Masculinity is Toxic, Call Jesus Radioactive'[326] for a good pep talk on the need for courageous men in the Church, like in Biblical times.

---

[325] Walsh, Matt. Church of Cowards: A Wake-Up Call to Complacent Christians. Gateway Editions, 2020.

[326] Giles, Doug. If Masculinity is 'Toxic' Call Jesus Radioactive. White Feather Press, 2020

4. Statistics Over Substance

The Judaisers looked at numbers of circumcisions and kept a tally of names to both condemn the uncircumcised and laud and praise the circumcised. In a different way, we are using erroneous, deceptive, managed and massaged government statistics to inform our Church worship and operations. Corrupt government stats are trumping God's eternal Word of truth. We also need to beware of boasting of ecclesiastical statistics – numbers of people watching live streams, Church giving accounts, new people joining Churches, etc. God measures success by one thing – each person and Church's faithful, loving obedience to His Word, not numbers. Moreover, a 20-second play of a Church YouTube livestream service on a phone whilst watching TV counts as a 'view'.

5. Symbolism Over Obedience

The Judaisers forced the Gentile Christians to submit to the letter of the law, but they themselves didn't and couldn't keep the law, as Galatians 6:13 tells us: *"For neither they themselves who are circumcised keep the law; but desire to have you circumcised, that they may glory in your flesh."* So the law is applied inconsistently and by each person's erroneous standards and ability to keep them. It's lip service, full of hypocrisy, exactly like the Covid rules are today. We can make a show of trying to keep the law by doing a few visible and highly ceremonial practices and observances – hand sanitising before the Lord's Supper, wearing masks at all times on the livestream videos and making pronouncements about social distancing but then loosening the standards at other times. Not at all times, but the point is their inconsistent application. And when our standards are high and we're wanting to virtue signal, we can piously judge others accordingly but then justify ourselves when we might waive them, as I have witnessed time and time again, in otherwise godly Churches. Such people have the weight of government and public health mandates, majority opinion and media propaganda on their side, but that does not necessarily make it true, right and godly.

Forgive me if I'm belabouring these points a little but I think it might be necessary. Where else are we hearing this alternative view and sober examination of all that the Church has instituted and compromised on since the beginning of 2020? Let me reaffirm here, I am not seeking to condemn brothers and sisters in Christ, I am pointing out dangerous error that, if left unchecked, will be even more disastrous for the Church at large. Also, to highlight that, like the Judaisers, not everyone in Church has the LORD as their priority; we need to remember that there are unsaved folk amongst us who will love to adopt religious and secular rules to appear pious.

To round this up, we simply cannot entertain rules that are not Scriptural when they are in direct conflict with what our LORD commands. They are too burdensome and crushing and are fleshly, not of God and weaken the Church and our unity in Christ. They are keeping swathes of people locked up at home in 'self-isolation' for weeks or months at a time. Who authorised each person to select certain parts of the Covid law and which pieces to adhere to and which to waive, even on occasion? I have found various pastors to be giving inconsistent advice and then wondering why congregations are puzzled and making up their own Pharisaic rules. Our fallen nature loves to set up rules and regulations that give us a false ladder to climb and a measure of status to signal how good we are – as well as to avoid the hard assignments of evangelism and true personal holiness. We must be vigilant to regularly check out hearts on this and repent, not encourage it!

"Search me, O God, and know my heart: try me, and know my thoughts: And see if there be any wicked way in me, and lead me in the way everlasting." – Psalm 139:23-24

External observances and outward appearances can foster judgements of others as acceptable Christians or not. We may acknowledge you as a Christian, but we'll judge you as not being a good Christian, nor loving towards your neighbour unless you keep these obscure Covid laws and don't raise questions about them.

The bottom line seems to be this: A proportion of Covid rules enthusiasts have taken a few scriptures (mainly about submitting to authorities and loving your neighbour, from Romans 13 and 14) and have neglected to dig into the true and full meaning of them. They've armed themselves with the most virtue-signalling mandates and determined that we're going to use these as evidence of our holiness and obedience – and possibly to avoid persecution, as per Galatians 6:12 – and we're going to judge you according to these things. We judge you to be lacking in many ways, namely love, righteousness, faith and a submissive spirit. If this is too harsh an estimation, let me offer a more charitable alternative: The Covid rules are serving as a great distraction from the real things of Christ. I have been included in all of the group emails of a local ministry since the first lockdown and all of them, without exception, have been about practical and safety matters under Covid. Not one has said anything about our LORD Jesus and worshipping and honouring Him. These rules have given an excuse to hordes of similar Christian ministries all around the world to look inwards and towards self-preservation, rather than outwards to Christ and to a world that is lost – not all, but many. And of course, maybe it's just bringing to the surface the true nature of people's hearts and allegiances, which has been harder to discern under previous circumstances. Unfortunately, the 'hyper-grace gospel' has also done much to dumb down the Church and sought to bring us into alignment with political correctness. Very few leaders have or are preparing the Bride, Messiah's people, for persecution and learning to let go of self and be privileged to suffer for Christ (Philippians 1:29).

Conclusion – Do Not Be Fearful of Persecution

The Covid rules are becoming dangerously close to, if not already, a Galatians 'different Gospel' and 'appearance of godliness' issue, as well as a Romans 13 'subjection to authorities' issue. They represent superstition and sorcery with their misapplication and inconsistency and bear no root in Scripture. We're veering into obscurity and ridiculousness, as well as the deception of it all. Masking, distancing, incessant sanitising, arbitrary and frequent shutting down and re-opening of Churches, tests and vaccinations are being misapplied. They're applied, not out of common sense, reality or truth but out of cowardice, blind obedience and, in some cases, wilful ignorance (I say that because all the reports on the inefficacy and harm of lockdowns, test, masks and vaccines are now out there for anyone to see, with a little discerning digging), superstition and fear of persecution. Friend, Paul warns us that it is a sin to seek to avoid persecution and to do things for appearance only, making a 'good show of the flesh'. When we turn to the 'elementary principles of this world', sowing in the flesh, we reap and prepare to reap corruption. Let's repent of this path we've taken and get back to the highway of holiness. Is there personal risk involved with this? Yes, absolutely. But Christianity was always supposed to be risky. We risk this current life in abandonment for Christ because we know the next is secure and glorious. What did the two lauded Churches in Revelation, which received no reprimand from Jesus, have in common? Patient endurance in the face of persecution and suffering. Both Smyrna and Philadelphia had the synagogue of Satan against them and stood up to it with patient endurance and were blessed by the LORD in doing so. Jesus' words of encouragement to them should be good counsel for us too:

"Do not fear any of those things which you are about to suffer. Indeed, the devil is about to throw some of you into prison, that you may be tested, and you will have tribulation ten days. Be faithful until death, and I will give you the crown of life." – Revelation 2:10 (NKJV)

"Because you have kept My command to persevere, I also will keep you from the hour of trial which shall come upon the whole world, to test those who dwell on the earth. Behold, I am coming quickly! Hold fast what you have, that no one may take your crown." – Revelation 3:10-11 (NKJV)

We need to hold onto what our Father tells us is precious within our Churches – gathering in close fellowship, breaking bread together, singing heartily in the congregation, observing the Lord's Supper, evangelism and discipleship, as well as the preaching of the Word – rooted in the reality of the world and times we live in. Let's get back to a full-blooded version of all of this, not the anaemic version we've been seeing for over a year now, with no acceptable end in sight – unless we boldly reclaim it. Otherwise, where did the 'power in the blood' go?

CHAPTER TEN

Discerning Babylon in Our Time

"By the rivers of Babylon,
There we sat down, yea, we wept
When we remembered Zion.
We hung our harps
Upon the willows in the midst of it.
For there those who carried us away captive asked of us a song,
And those who plundered us requested mirth,
Saying, "Sing us one of the songs of Zion!"
How shall we sing the Lord's song
In a foreign land?
If I forget you, O Jerusalem,
Let my right hand forget its skill!
If I do not remember you,
Let my tongue cling to the roof of my mouth—
If I do not exalt Jerusalem
Above my chief joy.
Remember, O Lord, against the sons of Edom
The day of Jerusalem,
Who said, "Raze it, raze it,
To its very foundation!"

O daughter of Babylon, who are to be destroyed,
Happy the one who repays you as you have served us!
Happy the one who takes and dashes
Your little ones against the rock!
– Psalm 137 (NKJV)

"And that, knowing the time, that now it is high time to awake out of
sleep: for now is our salvation nearer than when we believed. The night
is far spent, the day is at hand: let us therefore cast off the works of
darkness, and let us put on the armour of light." – Romans 13:11-12

The Relevance and Reality of Babylon in Our Situation

There are around 400,000 Churches in the USA and 50,000 in the UK, but very few teach about Babylon. It's the central subject of end times scriptures. It's the ruling force behind the minds and motivations of the world leaders who set themselves up against Christ (as per Psalm 2, Psalm 110). Babylon as a whole is both an idolatrous religious world system and a political and economic world power. It is mentioned by God more often than any other place except Jerusalem. Yet ministers are not preaching about it and in many cases actively discouraging end times discussions in their congregations; perhaps nervous that it could be divisive, cause fear or be distracting from Jesus. Many people have no idea what you're talking about, nor its relevance, when you mention Babylon.

The Bible is in many ways a tale of two cities or two kingdoms – God's Jerusalem and Satan's Babylon. The key to understanding the end times and last days is by understanding Babylon, in the context of Jesus' supreme authority, as put most explicitly in the Book of Revelation. We'd do well to take heed and discern this and the times we're in, as our LORD tells us to, with our critical thinking heads on.

Key Bible passages about Babylon are found in Isaiah 13, 14, 47, Jeremiah 50, 51, Revelation 17 and 18 – showing the fall of Babylon and warning the saints to flee Babylon and her deceptive power and alluring harlotry. Our Bibles depict all sorts of fantastical evil that takes place – from temple prostitutes to child sacrifices to Molech, to the whole prophets of Baal contest with Elijah at Mount Carmel, to Satan entering into Judas to conspire to have Christ killed. These types of things have not gone away. That kind of spiritual deception and supernatural evil is not ring-fenced for Biblical times only and now we live in a much more rational, scientifically-observable, 'normal' world. No, let's not be naive and unwise – It is all very much active now, as Paul reminds us in Ephesians 6:12: *"For we wrestle not against flesh and blood, but against principalities, against powers, against the rulers of the darkness of this world, against spiritual wickedness in high places."* In verse 5:11 of Ephesians, Paul also says: *"And have no fellowship with the unfruitful works of darkness, but rather expose them."* (NKJV)

What is Babylon?

Babylon is essentially a worldly, spiritually Satanic empire, set up against the Living God and all that He institutes in the name of His Christ.

Ancient Babylon was the capital city of the region of Babylonia, located in modern-day Iraq and it features often in the Old Testament, along with one of its prominent kings, Nebuchadnezzar. It destroyed the temple in Jerusalem and took many Jews into captivity and several of the prophets foretold of this, most notably Jeremiah and Isaiah. Other prophets chronicled the events in Babylonian exile – like Daniel and Ezekiel, who gave us a great example of how to live courageous, godly lives in the midst of an anti-Christian society under pagan authority. Babylon was founded by Nimrod, a descendant of Noah and the first of the demonic hybrid humans – the 'Nephilim', to reappear after the flood. He was the first king of Babylon.

"And Cush begat Nimrod: he began to be a mighty one in the earth. He was a mighty hunter before the Lord: wherefore it is said, Even as Nimrod the mighty hunter before the Lord." – Genesis 10:8-9

Verse 8 states that Nimrod 'began to be a mighty one in the earth'. The term for 'mighty ones', 'gibborim', is the same Hebrew phrase used to describe the demonic Nephilim giants in chapter 6 of Genesis who were 'mighty men'. It is also the same term used to describe the giant Goliath in 1 Samuel 17:51. The Hebrew word for 'began' in the verse is 'halal', which means, 'to profane, desecrate or pollute oneself, to begin – ritually or sexually'.

Matthew Henry, in his Bible commentary, puts it clearly when he says: *"The same spirit that actuated the giants before the flood (who became mighty men, and men of renown, chapter 6:4), now revived in him, so soon was that tremendous judgment which the pride and tyranny of those mighty men brought upon the world forgotten."*

We can see that Babylon's origins are occult in nature, from a revived Nephilim heritage. Nimrod built the Tower of Babel – 'the gateway to the gods', which is a clear representation of humanity, under the influence of Satanic powers, setting itself up against the LORD, to attempt to be as god in a great rebellion. Babel sought to create a one-world system, unified against God and so He scattered the people to prevent this from happening. The Babylonian spirit has been seeking to create a 'reverse Babel' ever since; to again unify humanity, under the reign of Satan, in rebellion against the LORD. So, it should come as no surprise to us when we hear about the establishment of a 'New World Order'[327] – a uniting of all nations in a one-world, global government, a 'reverse Babel' and the desire for complete power by the world's rich elite 'deep state' powers

---

[327] The term New World Order (NWO) has been used a generic term used to refer to a worldwide conspiracy being orchestrated by an extremely powerful and influential group of elites – in order to unite and control the world's resources and people.

(those behind world governments) to establish a totalitarian world regime, with a diabolical head. Further, if we think back to what we looked at in Chapter 4 on enforced Covid vaccinations and in particular the eugenics and transhuman agendas – to both depopulate the world of 'lesser humans' and create a 'super-human' race of people merged with technology (all controlled and under surveillance by the elite powers), this tallies up with their occult desire to 'be as gods'. Further, with the advent of human genome mapping and 3D 'gene printing', as well as the advance in quantum physics, there are plans in action right now to open the 'gateway to the gods' and merge humanity with demonic spirits once again, in a literal Babel Mark II, which we'll look at shortly. Crazy, right? Totally evil. Thanks be to God who has overcome all this. Let's keep going ...

There is much mythology around Nimrod and his supposed wife, Semiramis (or daughter of Baal or the 'Queen of Heaven' as mentioned in the Bible – the same spiritual power behind King Ahab's wife, Jezebel) and son Tammuz. Each false religion's central characters can be traced back to Nimrod, Semiramis and Tammuz as an unholy trinity. They became the gods of Egypt, Greece and Rome and now are worshipped by the Catholic church in the form of the father, son and Mary the mother. The Mary who is venerated by the Roman Catholic church is actually this Queen of Heaven, if you go back through history and Catholic doctrines and look at the overt occult symbolism. Reverend Alexander Hislop's 1853 book, 'The Two Babylons – The Papal Worship Proved to be the Worship of Nimrod and His Wife' gives an excellent treatise of this.

Just so you're aware and can recognise the pervasiveness of this false god worship, here are a few of the alternate names for Nimrod and Semiramis – there are many, presumably owing to the many languages after Babel and each tongue's desire to preserve the legend. Other names for Nimrod include Baal, Bel, Zeus, Jupiter, Apollo, Cupid, Mars, Hermes, Chemosh, Dionysus, Asshur, Vulcan, Nebo, Molech, Atlas, Dagon, Osiris, Gilgamesh, Ninus, Ra, Sun God, Vishnu, Hercules, Horus, Marduk. Other names for Semiramis include Ashtoreth, Ishtar, Inanna, Isis, Jezebel, Aphrodite, Diana, Venus, Moon Goddess, Liberty, Madonna, Queen of

Heaven, Artemis, Minerva, Athena, Astarte, Cybele, Gaia, Columbia, Fortuna. Whatever lies behind these occult characters, it is true that the world's top authorities and organisations worship them (along with Satan himself), seek power from them and offer great sacrifices to them – in both secret rituals and through big, obvious world-stage events. As one example of an in-your-face occult entertainment ritual, you can look at any USA Super Bowl half-time show and it's laden with blatant Satan worship and mind-programming propaganda. Unfortunately, most people have become so normalised to these things through the habit of watching television and Hollywood films (which are both designed to do exactly that – normalise and programme us, to their agenda) that they miss it and even approve of it. You can find short videos online, which give break-down analysis of Super Bowl show occultism.[328]

Here is a brief list of some of the world elite organisations that worship Satan and his false Babylonian god, Nimrod: Freemasonry, Knights Templar, Rosicrucians, Swiss Black Nobility, Jesuits, Sabbatean Frankists, Bavarian Illuminati, Federal Reserve, United Nations (set up as the governing body of the New World Order), International Monetary Fund, Committee of 300, Bilderberg Group, Council on Foreign Relations, Trilateral Commission, Royal Institute for International Affairs (Chatham House), Club of Rome, Vatican (yes, the Vatican), World Council of Churches, The Round Table, CERN, World Bank, Bank of England, League of Nations (UN replaced this), World Economic Forum ... I could go on. Don't take my word for it, these can all be verified as being occult in nature by doing your own homework – much of which can be gleaned directly from their own mission statements, publications and websites, as well as examining the values and background of their leaders and observing their buildings and symbols. Check, for example, the 'Jesuit extreme oath' (which outlines a desire to destroy Protestant Christianity, in no uncertain terms) and the United Nations'

---

[328] Barwick, Steve. 'More Occult and Satanic Symbolism in Superbowl Half-Time Show | Have Ye Not Read?' *Have Ye Not Read,* 3 Feb. 2020, https://haveyenotread.com/more-occult-and-satanic-symbolism-in-superbowl-half-time-show/. Accessed 5 May 2021.

Lucis Trust mission statement: *"The Lucis Trust is dedicated to the establishment of a new and better way of life for everyone in the world based on the fulfilment of **the divine plan for humanity**. Its educational activities promote recognition and practice of the **spiritual principles** and values upon which a stable and interdependent **world society** may be based. The **esoteric philosophy** of its founder, Alice Bailey, informs its activities which are offered freely throughout the world in eight languages."*

You can take your pick from any of Alice Bailey's satanic, channelled books here,[329] although I wouldn't recommend it. If all this is new information to you then it may sound pretty incredulous and may be hard to get your head around, I understand that. It is beyond the remit of this work to go into much detail on this but I would recommend the Christian ministry, The Fuel Project's excellent video series called 'Know Your Enemy'[330] to understand more on this subject.

The Identity and Scope of Mystery Babylon

Revelation 17 refers to 'Mystery Babylon', the harlot Church. She is pictured as having committed adultery with the rulers of all nations and the people throughout the world have become awe-struck by her power. It could be described as the occult, religious spirit behind the establishment of ancient Babylon, but the end-times Mystery Babylon of Revelation is much more far-reaching. It is the harlot Church which paves the way for the eventual religious system from which the Antichrist rules and persecutes Christians before Jesus' return on the Day of the LORD.

---

[329] *Alice Bailey Books - Books & Publications Store (Lucis Trust)*, https://www.lucistrust.org/store/category/alice_bailey_books_p. Accessed 5 May 2021.

[330] 'Know Your Enemy (Part 1 - Introduction)'. *YouTube*, https://www.youtube.com/watch?v=HDDGl79x4Pc&list=PLCED9C361662866BD. Accessed 5 May 2021.

"And upon her forehead was a name written, MYSTERY, BABYLON THE GREAT, THE MOTHER OF HARLOTS AND ABOMINATIONS OF THE EARTH." – Revelation 17:5

This harlot Church's core is Roman Catholicism and its papacy, sitting on the seven hills of Rome, arrayed in purple and scarlet, adorned with gold and pearls, full of sexual immorality (unfaithful idolatry), drunk with the blood of the martyrs of Jesus. This has been the view of Biblical scholars and teachers all down through the centuries, it has only been since the 19th century that differing or less concrete views have appeared. If you are in any doubt about this, please read the excellent classic book 'Romanism and the Reformation' by Henry Gratton Guinness, or 'The Scarlet Woman' by Keith Malcomson. There is a very good video series on Gratton Guinness' book[331] that's worth watching. R. C. H. Lenski expands out to include all heathen religions and spirituality outside of Christ in 'The Interpretation of Saint John's Revelation'[332]: *"Babylon ... the great enemy of Israel, Jerusalem, Zion ... is the entire antichristian empire throughout the whole New Testament Era. Both pagan and also papal Rome would then be included."* But it is important to know that the root of all false religion is Babylon and Nimrod worship, and therefore centred at Rome. You might be surprised to learn that there is much evidence to suggest that even Islam was a creation of Rome. Professor Walter Veith has a detailed lecture on this, showing the clear connections between the Vatican and Islam.[333] Further, ex-Jesuit whistle blower Alberto Rivera, has clearly stated that the Vatican created Islam.[334] It also incorporates all of the esoteric religions – Kabbalistic Judaism, Freemasonry, New Agism and all in between. It is commonly held that the Apostle Peter

---

[331] 'Tom Friess-Romanism and the Reformation-Author-Henry Grattan Guinness'. *YouTube,* https://www.youtube.com/playlist?list=PL-yNUliTpvPlAQbMulAAHFQYmiXEz75Os. Accessed 10 May 2021.

[332] Lenski, R. C.H. The Interpretation of St. John's Revelation. Wartburg Press, 1943.

[333] '216 - The Islamic Connection'. *The Great Controversy,* https://www.thegreatcontroversy.info/216---the-islamic-connectio.html. Accessed 10 May 2021.

[334] Morse, John. 'Former Jesuit Priest Exposes How the Vatican Created Islam'. *The Event Chronicle,* 25 Jan. 2016, https://theeventchronicle.com/vatican-created-islam/.

was referring to Rome when he said, *"She who is in Babylon, elect together with you, greets you; and so does Mark my son."* – 1 Peter 5:13 (NKJV)

'Mystery' Babylon is indeed that – hidden and occult. The guise of Christianity that Papal Rome has succeeded in duping the world with, is a mere cover for the systematic worship of the Babylonian gods of old, just like the Pharisees of Jesus' day – it always has been and always will be until Christ destroys it. Jupiter is the Roman name for the Greek Zeus. A statue of Jupiter was renamed St. Peter and placed in the Vatican. Similarly, a statue of Venus in the Vatican was renamed Mary or Maria. On 18 November 1302, Pope Boniface VIII issued the Papal Bull called 'Unum Sanctum'. On the bull, it says that all of the souls in the world belong to the Roman Catholic church! Did you know that copies of all birth certificates are held within the 66 miles of vaults beneath the Vatican? They deem that your birth certificate is essentially the title of the soul that they own in their registries. The bull ends with the following statement: *"Furthermore, we declare, we proclaim, we define that it is absolutely necessary for salvation that every human creature be subject to the Roman Pontiff."*

Please note: in exploring this, I am not presuming to say that all Roman Catholics are not saved, some are if they trust in Christ's finished work alone (and I've observed that they will then often leave Catholic churches, once they have a saving faith). However, this is not the Catholic doctrine and faith in Christ alone as the means of salvation was pronounced as an anathema (cursed) at the Council of Trent[335] as part of the Jesuit Counter-Reformation in 1545. Of course, Catholics may become Christians, as may any Pope.

---

[335] 'Theology Thursday - Anathema! The Council of Trent on Justification'. *SHARPER IRON*, 2 Mar. 2017, https://sharperiron.org/article/theology-thursday-anathema-council-of-trent-justification. Accessed 11 May 2021.

"Canon 12: If any one saith, that justifying faith is nothing else but confidence in the divine mercy which remits sins for Christ's sake; or, that this confidence alone is that whereby we are justified: let him be anathema."

There is much more we could say about the true nature of Roman Catholicism, such as the blasphemous mass, idol and relic worship, pagan festivals, prayers to the dead, the 'infallibility' of the Pope and his 'ex cathedra' pronouncements, but, again, I invite you to explore for yourself if you are in any doubt. I hope you can see the grave heresy of the harlot Church and why Jesus commands us to *"Come out of her, my people, lest you take part in her sins, lest you share in her plagues"* (Revelation 18:4).

The Mother of all Harlots, Mystery Babylon, the woman who rides the beast, is unequivocally Papal Rome. She is riding a political beast, which is the same beast as identified in Revelation 13.

The Jesuit Order

It's worth noting that behind every Pope is a 'Black Pope' – a Jesuit Pope who pulls many of the strings behind the scenes. There is also a named 'Grey Pope' – an even more shadowy figure with power over the other two and head of the occult bloodlines apparently – but there is much less information about this. The Jesuit Order, otherwise and blasphemously known as 'The Society of Jesus' is the occult military arm of the Vatican and if you have not yet read it, you can see the Jesuit extreme oath to 'exterminate them [Protestants] from the face of the whole earth',[336] in all its lurid detail. The current Pope, Francis, is himself a Jesuit and is openly known to be – this is a first in the Papacy. I cannot state this highly enough – that the Jesuits have been behind nearly, if not all, infiltrations and complete corruption of our modern world. That is no exaggeration. The Jesuits operate with 'fifth column' tactics – they join an enemy organisation

---

[336] 'Jesuit Extreme Oath of Induction'. *Reformation,* http://www.reformation.org/jesuit-oath.html. Accessed 5 May 2021.

and systematically and stealthily dismantle it from within. Their number one target is the Protestant Church and there are Jesuits in high-ranking positions in Churches, ecclesiastical bodies and theological schools. My strong view is that much of the official Church response to Covid can be attributed to Jesuit suggestion; those wolves set in place to deceive. A vital principle of the Jesuits is that 'the end justifies the means', there is no crime or atrocity that is not allowed if this rule is followed. They typically make 50 and 100-year plans, so they are in it for the long game and are patient in bringing about their carefully prepared agendas. Thus, they are very hard to detect and cause untold devastation, that often leave people thinking *"what on earth happened?!"* Keen Bible students can finish theological college with a shipwrecked faith. Children come out of school with humanistic atheism as their predominant worldview. Medical students graduate as doctors believing that drugs and surgery are the only or best solution to any health issue.

The Jesuits are literally and figuratively the Vatican's silent assassins. Of course, all mainstream sources of information on them would refute this, which is simply more lies and cover up, as we can expect from Babylon. But with a bit of intelligent research, like all of what is being presented in this book, we can see the reality of the situation and the nature of its most dangerous deception.

The Society of Jesus is responsible for:

- **Many wars** – including the French Revolution, the First and Second World Wars (Hitler idolised and set up his Nazi regime according to the Jesuit model and ideology). Edmond Paris in his book, 'The Secret History of the Jesuits', states: *"The public is practically unaware of the overwhelming responsibility carried by the Vatican and its Jesuits in the starting of the two world wars – a situation which may be explained in part by the gigantic finances at the disposition of the Vatican and its Jesuits, giving them power in so many spheres, especially since the last conflict."*

- **Corruption of the education system** – over the last 400 years the Jesuits have succeeded in establishing the largest worldwide network of schools and universities, designed to indoctrinate with the Babylonian system. A prominent one being Georgetown University in Washington, DC.

- **Most of USA's congressmen and Supreme Court Justices**, other heads of state, ambassadors, news media moguls, big business owners and presidents – Jesuit trained. Clinton, Trump and Obama are examples. Most political speeches are written by Jesuits.

- **Controlling the powerful secret societies that are shaping the New World Order** – such as the CFR, UN, Federal Reserve, Bilderberg, etc. We'll look at these in more detail.

- **Taking over the office of the Spanish Inquisition** shortly after it was sanctioned and this led to the martyrdom of millions of Christians.

- **Starting Communism** – Marx, Castro, Lenin, Hitler and Stalin were all Jesuit trained. Communism was a brainchild of the Jesuits, beginning with what were known as their Reductions in Paraguay in the 17th and 18th centuries, which were a series of communes in which Jesuit priests exercised authority over the natives there; educating and controlling them to work on their behalf. From the 1933 book, 'The Revolutionary Movement' by J. Findlater[337], we read the following: *"The Jesuits had established twenty strong Mission centres, called Reductions, with many thousands of the Guaranis enrolled as their members ... The Jesuits aimed to set up there a completely communistic system, in the sense that no individual rights were recognized and there was no private property. Everything belonged to the State, and was supposed to be shared in common. But in reality, much the greater part of the proceeds of goods sold was always remitted to the*

---

[337] Findlater, J. The Revolutionary Movement – A Diagnosis of World Disorders. Brodiesword, 1933.

Camarilla (Jesuit superiors) in Europe; and the Guaranis got only the bare necessities of life in return for their toil and sweat." They perfected their system of totalitarian control, all the while telling the world that their oppression over other people was, in fact, 'Utopia'.

- **Corruption of the Protestant Church, Bibles and doctrine** – introducing dangerous heresy, confusion and division. We have not been quick to identify and remove the influence that Martin Luther and his peers fought so hard to do during the Reformation. **We need to understand that the Jesuits created *Dispensational*[338], *Pre-tribulation* Futurist theology[339]**, for example. Also, are you aware that the modern Bible versions (NIV, NASB, ESV, CEB, Living, Message, and even the NKJV and others) are Vatican-controlled, diluted and corrupted? It is worth doing some research into this and surveying the omissions and discrepancies between them and the King James Version. Don't fall for the claims that Christians who exclusively read the King James Bible are outlandish and misguided. Neither be deceived by the pseudo-scholarly trickery of arguments such as *"the modern Bible versions use older manuscripts and are more reliable"* of people like James White. I recommend watching Chris Pinto's comprehensive documentary 'A Lamp in the Dark: The Untold History of the Bible'[340] and its two follow ups (available to stream freely online, as well as to purchase). Authors Gail Riplinger and David W. Daniels have written a number of good books on why the KJV is the best English Bible version (they both have heavy critics). Do reserve judgement until you've delved into this issue.

---

[338] Dispensationalism is an approach to Biblical interpretation which states that God uses different means of working with people (Israel and the Church) during different periods of history.

[339] 'Jesuit End Times Antichrist Deception'. *End Time Deceptions*, 10 Aug. 2013, https://christianitybeliefs.org/end-times-deceptions/jesuit-end-times-antichrist-deception/.

[340] *Chris Pinto DVDs - Noise of Thunder Radio with Chris Pinto.* http://www.noiseofthunderradio.com/dvds/. Accessed 5 May 2021.

The Jesuits were driven out of 83 countries no less between 1555 and 1931 for subversion plots, according to the records of a Jesuit priest of repute Thomas J. Campbell. An example of such is France, with their 1762 Act of Parliament of France, dissolving and banishing the Jesuit Society:[341] *"Their doctrines destroy the law of nature; they break all the bonds of civil society, by authorizing theft, lying, perjury, the utmost licentiousness, murder, criminal passions, and all manner of sins; their doctrines root out all sentiments of humanity, overthrow all governments, excite rebellion, uproot the foundation of religion, and substitute all sorts of superstition, irreligion, blasphemy and idolatry."*

The third General of the Jesuits, Francis Borgia, said *"Like lambs have we crept into power; like wolves have we used it; but like dogs shall we be driven out."* In 'The Secret History of the Jesuits',[342] Edmond Paris concludes his book with following statements: *"Between 1939 and 1945, the storm killed 57 million souls ravaging and ruining Europe. We must be on our guard; another and even worse catastrophe may lie hidden in these same clouds; lightning may strike again, throwing the world into 'abysses human wisdom can foresee', but out of which, if it had the misfortune to let itself be thrown into, no power could rescue it. In spite of what Rome's spokesmen may say, it is not 'anticlericalism' which prompted us to study carefully the Vatican's politics, or those of the Jesuits', and to denounce its motives and means, but the necessity to enlighten the public about the sly activity of fanatics who do not retreat before anything – the past has proved this too often – to reach their aims. We have seen how, during the 18th century, the European monarchies united to demand the suppression of this evil Order. Nowadays, it can concoct its intrigues in peace and the democratic governments do not seem to appear concerned. The danger the world is exposed to because of this Company is far greater today than at the time of the 'family pact',*

---

[341] Hulbert J. Beaufort. *The End Justifies the Means: Proven from Jesuit Authors to Have Been Taught for 350 Years*, Internet Archive, http://archive.org/details/endjustifiesmean00hurl_202010, (Original work published 1890).

[342] Paris, Edmond. *The Secret History of the Jesuits*. Chick Publications, 1975.

and even greater than when the two World Wars broke out. *No one can nurse any illusion as to the deadly consequences another conflict would have."*

Given all of this, it should come as no surprise to learn that major players in the Covid crisis in the US are Jesuit alumni. They include: Anthony Fauci, Governor Andrew Cuomo of New York, Governor Gavin Newsom of California, and former President Donald Trump. Trump studied for two years at the Jesuit Fordham University in New York. Additionally, Robert Redfield, head of the US Centers for Disease Control (CDC), is another Jesuit graduate and a key player in Operation Warp Speed, to roll out the rushed experimental injection.

If we take a look at Revelation chapter 18, it seems to refer to the end times economic and political location of Babylon, from where the Antichrist will rule. This is a futurist view. The historicist position is that, again, this is Papal Rome and the Antichrist is the office of the Papacy. Whichever view you take, it is important to note that *political* Babylon and *religious* Babylon are both activated by Vatican City, which is *actually an independent country.* It could appear that there might be two separate Babylonian entities described in Revelation 17 and Revelation 18 but in actuality, it just shows the true nature and extent of the power of the Roman Beast. The ensuing political and commercial power-base can and does change location. We see much of the epicentre of Babylon in the USA right now, especially in New York City and Washington, DC, as well as the city of London. America is a vassal State of Rome and the engine that is driving the world into the One World Government. But this could quite easily move over to, say, the Middle East, once USA's purpose has been fulfilled and it can be dispensed of. We'll look at this further in this chapter but this image gives an overview.

The Roman Power Pyramid

Make no mistake, Rome may seem insignificant on the political or financial scene on the surface, but it's actually the centre of the world's power and wealth, not just in past times but right now. Avro Manhattan's book of 1983, 'The Vatican Billions' is an interesting read on this: *"The Catholic church is the biggest financial power, wealth accumulator and property owner in existence. She is a greater possessor of material riches than any other single institution, corporation, bank, giant trust, government or State of the whole globe ...The Catholic church, once all her assets have been put together, is the most formidable stockbroker in the world. The Vatican, independently of each successive pope, has been increasingly orientated towards the U.S. The Wall Street Journal said that the Vatican's financial deals in the U.S. alone were so big that very often it sold or bought gold in lots of a million or more dollars at one time."*

So the entirety of end-times Babylon – the harlot Church and the epicentre of commercial and political power before Christ's return – make up an octopus-strangling system that controls the whole world. This seems to be what the apostle John, who wrote Revelation, also might be implying in his first letter – that Babylon is simply 'the world'. *"Love not the world, neither the things that are in the world. If any man love the world, the love of the Father is not in him." –* 1 John 2:15.

In Chapter 8, we looked at how we need to approach Romans 13 in light of Revelation 13. We should thus be aware that as the faithful, holy Bride of Christ, we need to have nothing to do with any kind of Romanism, nor ecumenical movements or groups seeking to conflate Christianity and Roman Catholicism. This was the basis of the Reformation and it still stands today, no matter how many compromisers or people ignorant to this area of Church history are seeking to deny or reverse all that. We should also be exceedingly wary of the world's politics and financial pursuits, which are intimately connected to Rome.

A Nation Paving the Way for End Times Babylon

As I mentioned, the nation that's leading the way in Babylonian indoctrination and activism right now, with its strings being pulled by Rome as a vassal State, is the United States of America. Many Christians are unaware of the USA's origins, true power structure and connections with Rome, Israel and Iraq and the ancient mystery occult. I'll put forth my reasoning to show the USA's Babylonian core and in doing so, show how where we are today with the Covid deception and all that's coming with it, has been carefully planned out over a long period of time.

The USA, as you'll see, was instituted to be a concentrated and all-pervading Babylonian system that captivates all the nations with its occult (hidden) true nature and agenda. In many ways, **it's like a revived Roman Empire.**

All of this to say, I am writing this book at a particular point in history, with much of the plans for a reverse Babel 'New World Order' taking shape in and from the USA, under the directive of Rome. I will therefore focus my attention on what is going on in America to prepare the way for the final Antichrist system to be established. With that in mind, please think of this chapter as a kind of 'end times Babylon case study'.

The USA was formed in 1776, the same year as the Bavarian Illuminati and many of its founding fathers had a plan for America to be a kind of Masonic 'New Atlantis' that Rosicrucian (secret society) head Francis Bacon wrote about in his 1627 book of the same name, to usher in the New World Order. This New Atlantis would represent a utopian Christian society (in name only), ruled by a pagan philosophic priesthood; dedicated to the doctrine and execution of the Luciferian agenda via secret esoteric knowledge and technologies. The entire narrative of the New Atlantis was to use Christian jargon (including much mention of Jesus Christ) mixed with mystery school religion language. This blurring of Christianity with occultism is the essence of the Order of the Rosy Cross (Rosicrucianism) and from it has branched out Freemasonry as well as Christian Gnosticism and Liberalism, Jewish mysticism and Hermeticism. Can you see how this is so deceptive? A blurring of Christianity and its language with that of occultism. A little poison added to the Gospel; Paul has some exceedingly strong words for those who preach 'another gospel' in Galatians, as we have already examined in the previous chapter. These things are not immediately recognisable and very hard to discern. In many ways they seem unbelievable.

If you're in any doubt about the esoteric nature and roots of the USA, grab any one dollar bill and you'll see on it the phrases 'novus ordo seclorum' – 'new world order' and 'e pluribus unum' – 'out of many, one' as well as an image of the 'all-seeing eye of Horus' Freemasonic, Luciferian pyramid. It also says 'in god we trust'. Which god? Plus, if you've listened carefully to any of the presidents of the USA since George Bush Sr, they have all come right out in stating their plans for the New

World Order. The name 'America' is believed by many to mean 'Land of Lucifer', after a Mayan tribe's god Amerrique, 'the serpent spirit of the air'.

Thankfully, at the time that the Rosicrucians, led by Francis Bacon, were busily rolling out their plans for the new nation of America, our LORD (as well as sitting in the heavens and laughing) was also directing another plan ... A group of Christian Puritans, the Pilgrims, boarded the May-flower from Plymouth, England and sailed to this New World in 1620. And so, the duality began in the USA: Rosicrucians, Masons and mystics on the one hand, seeking to carry out their Luciferian plans. While on the other hand, true Christians built godly communities and places of worship and were living according to Biblical standards and seeking to share the Gospel of Jesus Christ to make disciples. Today, 400 years on, the USA represents all that Satan represents – debauchery, deception, pride and even much death, which we will look at. America embodies all aspects of Babylon, to its very core. If you're an American, I may well be offending you right now and it is not my intention to. Of course, there are many God-fearing Christians in America and good Churches, which our LORD has preserved, but we cannot ignore America's Babylonian like-ness.

Let's look at Babylon as described in Revelation 18 and six reasons why USA is like her mother, Rome.

1. **Proud and boastful and lives in luxury** (Revelation 18:7): This is fairly self-explanatory.
2. **Imports and possesses many goods** (Revelation 18:12-13): USA is indeed a vast importer, bringing in huge containers of all types of goods and luxuries every day and is rich in all types of merchandise.
3. **Has sea ports and does much international trade** (Revelation 18:19): The USA has many busy sea ports – even one called Bab-ylon in NYC.

4. **Industrial** (Revelation 18:22): USA is home to an abundance of diverse trades – from the arts to travel to agriculture to finance – all of which are exported and have influence on other nations. Think too about all the fast food franchises the USA exports to the world and that when they operate in other nations, they must conform to the very inch of what is done in America: A domineering message of *"We know what is best for everyone else."*

5. **Babylon revels in entertainment** (Revelation 18:22): Just think of Hollywood, the music industry, Las Vegas, news media, sports, games, pornography … and it exports all of these things to the rest of the world too, which is lured by USA's revelry.

6. **Babylon is occult and deceives the rest of the world with her sorcery or 'pharmakeia'** (Revelation 18:23): As we've seen, the USA has heavy Freemasonic roots with an esoteric, one world agenda. It is home to secular humanism, evolutionism, atheism, new agism and every other kind of false religion. 'Pharmakeia' refers to witchcraft, drugs and medicines – all of which are rife and big business in America. Hollywood and the music industry employ impressionable and money and fame-hungry celebrities, who are willing to literally sell their soul to the evil one and go through rigorous mind programming and sex programming with drugs and shock therapy (named 'MK-Ultra') in order to train them to most effectively administer their occult, bewitching media to the masses in the name of entertainment. This is very sad and most celebrities have no idea what they're signing up to until it's too late. Do you ever wonder why so many celebs seem to go crazy and many commit suicide or die in mysterious circumstances? I pray regularly for celebrities, would you, too?

There is a very good documentary (in two parts) that I recommend watching on the subject of USA and Babylon: 'America the Babylon: Daughter of the Harlot' (Parts 1 and 2) documentary by Pastor Sam Adams.[343]

Before we go further, why not read and examine chapters 17 and 18 of Revelation and examine against the points we've looked at so far? Pray and ask the LORD to give you wisdom in all of this. An advanced warning: What comes next about the USA is going to get pretty weird and pretty alarming, especially if you're new to this. I urge you not to make the mistake of dismissing it as conspiratorial nonsense (see my note on 'conspiracy theories' again in the introduction if needs be). It is certainly conspiratorial, but it is not nonsense. Unfortunately, this is the reality of the world we're living in, before Christ's return.

12 Occult USA Monuments and Symbols

There is an abundance of Babylonian occult symbols and monuments all over the USA. To name but a few:

1. **Statue of Liberty** – it's no secret that the huge statue in the NYC harbour is Freemasonic and is depicting Jezebel, the Queen of Heaven, Ashtoreth ... the whore of Babylon. At the higher levels of Freemasonry, they believe it is Lucifer himself, the 'light bearer'.
2. **Washington Monument obelisk** (and all other obelisks) – symbolises pagan Horus (Nimrod) phallus worship.
3. **US Capitol building** – has a statue to Mars (Nimrod) and occult pentagrams and pagan gods on the ceiling and much more.
4. **Liberty of Congress** – has a statue of Neptune (Nimrod).
5. **Jefferson Memorial** – is modelled after Roman Pantheon to pagan gods.

---

[343] America the Babylon: America in Bible Prophecy - Independence Baptist Church. https://independencebaptist.com/america-the-babylon/.

6. **Lincoln Memorial** – is modelled after Greek Parthenon to pagan goddess Athena (Semiramis).

7. **The street layout of Washington, D.C.** – is designed as an occult pentagram, with the bottom pointing directly at the White House. The whole city is teeming with occult symbolism and statues.

8. **Rockefeller Centre** – has a statue of Prometheus (Nimrod).

9. **Los Angeles Central Library** – has many occult symbols and artwork, such as the Jesuit sun rays and pyramids.

10. **St. John the Divine Cathedral in New York City** – a Jesuit gothic building with hundreds of Masonic and occult representations.

11. **Denver International Airport** – has four disturbing occult new age murals, Masonic stones, a hideous and apocalyptic-looking blue horse statue and a 26-foot tall Egyptian god Anubis statue with a jackal head. I'm not sure it gets any more in-your-face.

12. **Entertainment industry** – the 'all-seeing eye', Masonic chequerboard floors, pyramids and mind programming symbols such as bird cages, monarch butterflies, pentagrams, hexagrams and broken mirrors pepper Hollywood films and music videos. There's so much occult symbolism in Hollywood, as well as overt sexualisation, to possibly list and it goes under most people's radar or it's just seen as 'art'. There is a huge selection of occult symbols and images used in USA, the Vatican and beyond.[344]

---

[344] 'The U.S. Constitution: Symbols of the Illuminati-New World Order'. *The U.S. Constitution*, https://mytreatises.blogspot.com/p/symbols-of-illuminati-new-world-order.html. Accessed 5 May 2021.

The Overt USA Depopulation Agenda

Just listen to what US politicians and rich, powerful American figures in places of great influence say in their own words and we can see that they are looking to get rid of quite a few 'superfluous' people ...

"Depopulation should be the highest priority of foreign policy towards the third world, because the US economy will require large and increasing amounts of minerals from abroad, especially from less developed countries" – Henry Kissinger, Bilderberger Conference, Evian, France, 1991

"Society has no business to permit degenerates to reproduce their kind." – Theodore Roosevelt

"A total world population of 250-300 million people, a 95% decline from present levels, would be ideal." – Ted Turner, CNN founder and billionaire, in an interview with Audubon magazine

"A cancer is an uncontrolled multiplication of cells; the population explosion is an uncontrolled multiplication of people.... We must shift our efforts from the treatment of the symptoms to the cutting out of the cancer. The operation will demand many apparently brutal and heartless decisions". – Paul Ehrlich, Stanford Professor, in 'The Population Bomb'

US independent investigative journalist Jon Rappaport asserts:

"At the highest levels of the medical cartel, vaccines are a top priority because they cause a weakening of the immune system. I know that may be hard to accept, but it's true. The medical cartel, at the highest level, is not out to help people, it is out to harm them, to weaken them. To kill them. At one point in my career, I had a long conversation with a man who occupied a high government position in an African nation. He told me that he was well aware of this. He told me that WHO is a front for these depopulation interests."

"We are on the verge of a global transformation. All we need is the right major crisis and the nations will accept the New World Order." – David Rockefeller, at 1994 UN dinner

… Could Covid 19 be this 'right major crisis' that David was talking about? Let's not forget, his 'Lockstep Scenarios' Report of 2010, which describes in great detail a devastating virus scenario and the control mandates that could be brought in as a result. Congressman Larry P. McDonald was killed in the Korean Airlines 747 that was shot down by the Soviet Union. In 1976 he said this of the Rockefellers:

"The drive of the Rockefellers and their allies is to create a one-world government combining super-capitalism and Communism under the same tent, all under their control … Do I mean conspiracy? Yes I do. I am convinced there is such a plot, international in scope, generations old in planning, and incredibly evil in intent."

Interlude

Let me just interject at this point: You may be thinking all sorts of thoughts and have lots of questions about what you're discovering here. Maybe you've got some strong, uncomfortable feelings too. That's only natural. Maybe you feel angry at me. Maybe you think all this is ridiculous. I'm not meaning to patronise, but I know how difficult this can be if you're coming to this for the first time and the pastoral side to me wants to offer some reassurance here …

I've been investigating the geopolitical landscape and agenda for over 20 years and it's terribly difficult to swallow in many ways; it's one of the things that brought me to my knees in despair and led me to cry out to the LORD to be saved. At this point, I've had those 20+ years to get used to the position we're finding ourselves in now and have prepared myself, to a small extent, for what's to come. As Christians, we all have access to our Bibles, which also shows us and warns us of the evil we face in the world and as the Day of the LORD draws nearer, but I know many people do not necessarily connect the dots between Bible verses and the day-to-day life in our world as we live in it. My aim is to help you to do that, for a number of reasons. Friend, we must have the right and clear diagnosis of the problem in order to administer the right treatment. We can only seek and receive the right and best solution when we understand the extent and true nature of the issue at hand and not be skirting around the real issue in the hope that it will just go away and 'all be back to normal soon'. If you had stage four cancer, would you want your doctor to tell you? My guess is that, painful as the news would be, you'd want to know so that you can take the appropriate measures and grasp the seriousness of the situation, with hope and prayers that you can respond with serious action, proportionate to the problem. To use a Biblical term – to 'gird our loins'.

If we see Covid and its mandates (making way for the 'Great Reset') as a mere flesh wound that will be healed soon enough, rather than the cancer that it is, seeking to pervade the whole body of Christ and destroy it, we will not be serious enough in our prayers, Bible reading, our evangelism, our concern, our love, our fellowship, our defence of the faith, or our perception of the absolute need to gather as the Church and worship our LORD in full and uninhibited reverence.

So, if you'll permit, may I keep on with the diagnosis? We'll be done in this section shortly and then onto the treatment.

The Overt New World Order Agenda

Here are some statements of US government officials on the NWO, in their own words ...

"Today, America would be outraged if U.N. troops entered Los Angeles to restore order. Tomorrow they will be grateful! This is especially true

if they were told that there were an outside threat from beyond, whether real or promulgated, that threatened our very existence. It is then that all peoples of the world will plead to deliver them from this evil. The one thing every man fears is the unknown. When presented with this scenario, individual rights will be willingly relinquished for the guarantee of their well-being granted to them by the World Government." – Henry Kissinger

"Crisis scenarios are the means by which dictators justify control. The most often cited example is Hitler's 'Enabling Act' in the wake of the Reichstag Fire. Another example is the 'Patriot Act' in the aftermath of 9/11. Globalist organizations, behind the usual façade of the most idealistic intentions, such as the Club of Rome, have for decades warned of impending planetary doom unless a world control system is inaugurated ... Hence, one should raise questions when the oligarchs who run the world financial system draw up world improvement schemes." – Dr K.R. Bolton, Foreign Policy Journal

"Fundamental Bible-believing people do not have the right to indoctrinate their children in their religious beliefs because we, the state, are preparing them for the year 2000, when America will be part of a one-world global society and their children will not fit in." – Nebraska State Senator Peter Hoagland, speaking on radio in 1983.

"The Trilateral Commission is intended to be the vehicle for multinational consolidation of the commercial and banking interests by seizing control of the political government of the United States. The Trilateral Commission represents a skillful, coordinated effort to seize control and consolidate the four centers of power – Political, Monetary, Intellectual, and Ecclesiastical." – U.S. Senator Barry Goldwater, from his 1964 book, 'No Apologies'

In volume 2 of his 'Secret Societies and Biblical Prophecy' excellent documentary, Leonard Ulrich claims: *"The bankers and globalists are using Covid-19 and the profits that can be made from it to accomplish a series of goals towards their ultimate aim, which is total control. Covid-19 elim-inated protests against globalization, contributed to depopulation, in-creased dehumanization through social distancing, accelerated the anti-cash movement through perceived contamination, increased dependence on government, and shaped peoples' paradigms through information control. Because a pandemic accomplishes all these goals, you can expect this card to be played again and again until the world complies through familiarity and fatigue."*

10 Primary Source Books Foretelling the Current and Coming Global Tyranny

I stated in the introduction to this book that the mandates that have been instituted under Covid have not been mere quick reactions to a real prob-lem, but rather an extremely well-orchestrated and long-held set of plans and agendas that have been in place and moving forwards towards the end goal of a New World Order for hundreds of years, traversing all aspects of society and life. Here are some books, many of which written many decades ago, that are prophetic in detailing what we are seeing unfold now. They all tie in with each other and attest to this central theme of complete control and depopulation, led by the USA.

1. Carroll Quigley – Tragedy & Hope (1966)[345]

At 1695 pages, this book is an analysis of the real agendas behind the politics and wars of our modern times and is regarded by many as the best history book ever written. It was not written for public reading and it was originally banned as it was deemed to give far too much 'insider in-formation' on what the elites plan and execute. Georgetown University Professor, Carol Quigley states in his book: *"The powers of financial cap-italism had far-reaching aim, nothing less than to create a world system*

---

[345] Quigley, Carroll. Tragedy and Hope: A History of the World in Our Time. GSG & Associates, 1966.

of financial control in private hands able to dominate the political system of each country and the economy of the world as a whole. This system was to be controlled in a feudalist fashion by the central banks of the world acting in concert by secret agreements arrived at in frequent private meetings and conferences ... For the first time in its history, Western Civilization is in danger of being destroyed internally by a corrupt, criminal ruling cabal which is centered around the Rockefeller interests, which include elements from the Morgan, Brown, Rothschild, Du Pont, Harriman, Kuhn-Loeb, and other groupings as well. This junta took control of the political, financial, and cultural life of America in the first two decades of the twentieth century."

2. Edward Bernays – Propaganda (1928)[346] and Crystallising Public Opinion (1924)[347]

It is reported that the earliest attempt to bring about a New World Order was a result of putting into practice the theories of Edward Bernays, the chief theoretician at the Tavistock Institute of Human Relations, the world's premier 'brainwashing' institute. It's probably best that you don't look into the kind of mind programming activities that Tavistock has pioneered and engage in, such as MK-Ultra. Bernays' 100-year-old books talk about using history as a weapon, organising mass false propaganda, organising chaos and the psychology behind public relations and mass manipulation. Here's a quote from 'Propaganda': *"We are governed, our minds are moulded, our tastes formed, our ideas suggested, largely by men we have never heard of. Whatever attitude one chooses to take toward this condition, it remains a fact that in almost every act of our daily lives, whether in the sphere of politics or business, our social conduct or our ethical thinking, we are dominated by the relatively small number of persons (a trifling fraction of our hundred and 20 million, who understand the mental processes and social patterns of the masses. It is they*

---

[346] Bernays, Edward. *Propaganda.* Ig Publishing, 2004 (Original work published 1928).

[347] Bernays, Edward. *Crystalizing Public Opinion.* Ig Publishing, 2011 (Original work published 1924).

who pull the wires which control the public mind, and who harness old social forces and contrive new ways to bind and guide the world."

3. HG Wells – The Open Conspiracy (1928)[348] and New World Order (1940)[349]

Also written almost a century ago, Wells' books have been described as manifestos for the most complete and disturbing form of totalitarianism and tyrannical world government, which includes depopulation and a new age Luciferian religion. (Wells was a member of the Committee of 300, see next.)

4. Dr John Coleman – Conspirators' Hierarchy: The Story of the Committee of 300 (1991)[350]

If you really want to perceive what's going on at the geopolitical level and understand the level of deception, John Coleman's book is one of the best to read. Alternatively, you can listen to a lecture he gave on the Committee of 300 here.[351] It's worth your time listening to it, to improve your spiritual and media discernment. John Coleman is an author and analyst of world affairs and former British Intelligence Officer for MI6 who has written several books and numerous papers analysing the power structure of the world. He argues that a relatively small group of people, whom he identifies as 'The Committee of 300' and names its names, constitute a ruling elite who are pursuing a goal of one-world government. This book took him 20 years to research and write. Here are some key quotes and assertions of the book, which can be corroborated by many of the other books I've listed in this section too. Strap yourself in ...

---

[348] Wells, H.G. The Open Conspiracy: What Are We To Do With Our Lives? Book Tree, 2006 (Original work published 1928).

[349] Wells, H.G. New World Order. Orkos Press, 2014 (Original work published 1940).

[350] Coleman, Dr John. Conspirators' Hierarchy: The Story of the Committee of 300. Bridger House Publishers Inc, 1991.

[351] 'The Club of Rome, Chatham House and The Committee of 300 - a Lecture by Dr John Coleman'. YouTube, https://www.youtube.com/watch?v=HsLqbXbch4g. Accessed 5 May 2021.

"The Committee [of 300] is the ultimate secret society made up of an untouchable ruling class, which includes the Queen of England, the Queen of the Netherlands, the Queen of Denmark and the royal families of Europe. These aristocrats decided at the death of Queen Victoria, the matriarch of the Venetian Black Guelph, that in order to gain world-wide control, it would be necessary for its aristocratic members to 'go into business' with the non-aristocratic, but extremely powerful leaders of corporate business on a global scale.

... Who are the planners and plotters who serve the mighty all-powerful Committee of 300? The better-informed of our citizens are aware that there is a conspiracy and that the conspiracy goes under various names such as the Illuminati, Freemasonry, the Round Table, the Milner Group, and the Royal Institute of International Affairs.

... All of the great historical events are planned in secret by men in high places, with intent to deceive ... No matter what societal structure is examined, there has always been a group of certain individuals, in whom the need to control is paramount. During the last three centuries we have seen a rise in the number of such individuals and societies, generally under the heading of 'secret societies' that have evinced this common characteristic.

... The Club of Rome reported to the Committee of 300, at whose head sits the Queen of England. Her Majesty rules over a vast network of closely-linked corporations who pay no taxes, and are answerable to no one; who fund their research institutions through foundations whose joint activities have almost total control over our daily lives.

... A new plan for the world ... called for an attack upon industrialized nations with advanced mechanized agricultural production in a slow, but sure disintegration of industrial production (and this includes nuclear power generation), the destruction of hundreds of millions of people, referred to by the Committee of 300 as 'surplus population', and the removal of any leader who dares to stand in the way of the Committee's global planning to reach the foregoing objectives.

311

What are the goals of the secret elite group ...?

(1) To establish a One World Government-New World Order with unified Church and monetary system under their direction ...

(2) To bring about the utter destruction of all national identity and national pride ... primary consideration of the concept of a One World Government was to stamp out the individuality of all people ... in order to create 'the masses' ...

(3) To engineer and bring about the destruction of religion, and more especially, the Christian religion, with the one exception, a One World Government concoction of beliefs ...

(4) To establish the ability to control each and every person through means of mind control ... and establish a system of terror ...

5) To bring an end to all industrialization and the production of nuclear generated electric power in what they call 'the post-industrial zero-growth society' ...

(6) To encourage and eventually legalize the use of drugs and make pornography an 'art form', which will be widely accepted and eventually, become quite commonplace ... as part of their strategy to destroy Western culture.

(7) To bring about depopulation of large cities according to the trial run carried out by the Pol Pot regime in Cambodia ...

(8) To suppress all scientific development except for those deemed beneficial by the Committee. Especially targeted is nuclear energy for peaceful purposes. Nations who persisted in building nuclear power stations were to be brought down ...

(9) To cause, by means of limited wars in the advanced countries, a reduction in the number of people called 'surplus to requirements' and by means of starvation and disease pandemics in Third World countries ...

(12) To keep people everywhere from deciding their own destinies through the application of one created crisis after another and then 'managing' such crises. This will confuse and demoralize the population to the extent where faced with too many choices, apathy on a massive scale will result ...

(17) To cause a total collapse of the world's economies and engender total political chaos.

(18) To take control of all foreign and domestic policies of the United States.

(19) To give the fullest support to supranational institutions such as the United Nations, the International Monetary Fund, the Bank of International Settlements, the World Court and as far as possible, cause local institutions to become less effective and gradually phasing them out or bringing them under the mantle of the United Nations.

(20) To penetrate and subvert all governments, and work from within them to destroy the sovereign integrity of the nations represented by them, under the guise of spreading 'democracy' as a bulwark against terrorism.

(21) To organize a world-wide terrorist apparatus and to negotiate with lawful government for their surrender wherever terrorist activities take place, by allowing the U.S. to establish permanent military bases in those nations which will be carried out under the banner of 'bringing democracy'.

(22) To take control of education in America with the intent and purpose of utterly and completely destroying it through graduated change in curricula and teaching methods ...

(23) To establish Socialism in the United States with the purpose of nullifying State Constitutions and the Federal Constitution.

... The Committee of 300 is for the most part under the control of the **British monarch, in this case, Queen Elizabeth II**...*The people of England and indeed the English-speaking world are so brainwashed that they believe the British Royal Family is just a nice, harmless and colorful institution, and so fail to realize just how corrupt, and how all-pervading is this institution called the British Monarchy ... The Knights of the Order of the Garter acts as Queen Elizabeth's most trusted 'privy council' ('private council') which is just that ... There is not one single aspect of life in America that is not watched over, steered in the 'right' direction, manipulated and controlled by the invisible government of the Committee of 300."*

5. Zbigniew K. Brzezinski – Between Two Ages: America's Role in the Technetronic Era (1970)[352]

Brzezinski was president Jimmy Carter's National Security Advisor, a counsellor and trustee at the centre for Strategic and International Studies and a professor of American foreign policy at the School of Advanced International Studies at Johns Hopkins University. He was also a Committee of 300 member and a man pulling a lot of strings on a geopolitical level and masterminding much of the elite's one world strategies and crises for several decades. He was foreign policy adviser to Obama during his time as president. All of his books betray the deceptive and nefarious agenda of the elites, in particular 'Strategic Vision: America and the Crisis of Global Power', 'The Choice: Global Domination or Global Leadership', and 'The Grand Chessboard: American Primacy and Its Geostrategic Imperatives' – the titles say a lot, don't they? His book 'Between Two Ages' outlines the dystopia the elites in society are pursuing through a technocracy. It states: *"The technotronic era involves the gradual appearance of a more controlled society. Such a society would be dominated by an elite, unrestrained by traditional values. Soon it will be possible to assert almost continuous surveillance over every citizen and maintain up-*

---

[352] Brzezinski, Zbigniew K. Between Two Ages: America's Role in the Technetronic Era. Greenwood Press, 1982.

*to-date complete files containing even the most personal information about the citizen. These files will be subject to instantaneous retrieval by the authorities...In the technotronic society the trend would seem to be towards the aggregation of the individual support of millions of uncoordinated citizens, easily within the reach of magnetic and attractive personalities **exploiting the latest communications techniques to manipulate emotions and control reason.**"*

6. David Rockefeller – Memoirs (2002)[353]

David Rockefeller was American billionaire banker, founder of the Trilateral Commission, Director of the Council on Foreign Relations and Committee of 300 member (all Illuminati organisations) from the Rockefeller dynasty, who are members of the Illuminati. He epitomises the Satanic power elite and their mindset and agenda. In his book 'Memoirs' he admits he is part of a secret cabal working to destroy the United States and create a new world order. Here is the direct quote from the book: *"Some even believe we (Rockefeller family) are part of a secret cabal working against the best interests of the United States, characterizing my family and me as 'internationalists' and of conspiring with others around the world to build a more integrated global political and economic structure – One World, if you will. If that's the charge, I stand guilty, and I am proud of it."*

In an address to the Trilateral Commission in 1991, David Rockefeller said: *"We are grateful to The Washington Post, The New York Times, Time Magazine and other great publications whose directors have attended our meetings and respected their promises of discretion for almost forty years. It would have been impossible for us to develop our plan for the world if we had been subject to the bright lights of publicity during those years. But, the work is now much more sophisticated and prepared to march towards a World Government. The supranational sovereignty*

---

[353] Rockefeller, David. David Rockefeller: Memoirs. Random House, 2002.

of an intellectual elite and world bankers is surely preferable to the national auto-determination practiced in past centuries."

7. Annie Jacobsen – The Pentagon's Brain: An Uncensored History of DARPA, America's Top-Secret Military Research (2015)[354]

This book talks about all sorts of nefarious Defence Department schemes that are in earnest action right now with billions of dollars and the smartest brains backing them ... yet you ask most people about this stuff and they dismiss it as fear mongering gibberish. From killer robots and artificial intelligence to total surveillance, Internet of Things, weaponised 5G technology (being rolled out across the world as we were all in lockdown), High-Frequency Active Auroral Research Program (HAARP – 'geoengineering' of weather) cloning and enhanced superhuman soldiers – it's all in there and is scary stuff. It details how DARPA is under orders from the CFR and the other Illuminati think tanks and uses the mind programming techniques of Tavistock Institute.

8. William Guy Carr – Pawns in the Game (1954)[355]

William Guy Carr was one of the earlier whistle-blowers about the Illuminati and their sinister global agenda, emanating from Rome. He goes into great depth about the Luciferian nature of the NWO (World Revolutionary Movement as he calls it). He also considers the wars and revolutions in detail and how they were contrived to fit an agenda – the evidence he supplies is irrefutable. Shocking but educational. It is worth watching his lecture on the book.[356]

---

[354] Jacobsen, Annie. The Pentagon's Brain: An Uncensored History of DARPA, America's Top-Secret Military Research Agency. Back Bay Books, 2015.

[355] Carr, William Guy. Pawns in the Game. St George Press, 1962 (Original work published 1954).

[356] 'Pawns In The Game Lecture by William Guy Carr.' *YouTube*, https://www.youtube.com/watch?v=0hCx1rOmJfk. Accessed 22 May 2021.

9. Marilyn Ferguson – The Aquarian Conspiracy: Personal and Social Transformation in Our Time (1980)[357]

Widely regarded as the 'new age bible', it details much of the mystic religion that's pervading all aspects of society now – and has been instituted into many Churches – falsely promising peace, safety and unity. This is the religion that they're wanting under the New World Order and may well be the precursor to the Antichrist.

10. Aldous Huxley – Brave New World (1932)[358]

Aldous Huxley was a Committee of 300 member. His infamous book depicts a dystopian nightmare, very different to that of Orwell's 1984, but equally totalitarian. It was a good bit of 'predictive programming' since many people speculate that we are moving right into a mix of the two types of one-world dictatorship described in the two books. There's a good video summary of Brave New World here.[359]

I could have picked from over a hundred other primary source books of this nature that outline the desire and plans for total world domination by the globalist elites, but I trust that the ones I've listed and various direct quotes from them have served to show that these deceptive, occult, genocidal, conspiratorial plans centred in the USA are anything but 'theory'. Further, Covid 19's roll-out is a small but integral part of this agenda. If you're still an any doubt about this stuff, why not pick up one of these political books for yourself and take a read?

---

[357] Ferguson, Marilyn. The Aquarian Conspiracy: Personal and Social Transformation in Our Time. Jeremy P. Tarcher, 1982 (Original work published 1980).

[358] Huxley, Aldous. Brave New World. Harper Perennial, 2006 (Original work published 1932).

[359] 'Video SparkNotes: Aldous Huxley's Brave New World Summary'. *YouTube*, https://www.youtube.com/watch?v=raqVySPrDUE. Accessed 5 May 2021.

Other USA and UN Occult Agendas Exported to the World

Here are just a few more covert agendas and ideologies that are being fully promoted, implemented and used to shape policy right now in our governments, media and school systems. The USA 'Common Core' school curriculum is heavily informed by these agendas (and being used as the model in the UK, Canada and beyond), which is very concerning for the future of our children, whom the State is intent on taking from parents and having full 'ownership' of. I refer you again to John Taylor Gatto's book, 'Dumbing Us Down – The Hidden Curriculum of Compulsory Schooling' for a very good overview of this.

Alice Bailey and United Nation's Occult Doctrines

Alice Bailey founded The Lucis Trust (formerly known as Lucifer Publishing Company) in 1922 and under its umbrella she authored 24 books on esoteric occult subjects, influenced by Theosophy and channelled by a demon she called 'the Tibetan'. She is a revered figure in the higher echelons of the United Nations, her work heavily influences UN policy, which in turn directly influences USA policy, and eventually Lucis Trust became the publishing arm of the UN, with consultative status. In her book, 'Discipleship in the New Age' she says: *"Within the United Nations (UN) is the germ and seed of a great international and meditating, reflective group—a group of thinking and informed men and women **in whose hands lies the destiny of humanity**."* – Alice Bailey, 'Discipleship in the New Age' (1955)

"Hundreds in the East and in the West are pressing onwards towards this goal. and in the unity of the one ideal, in their common aspiration and endeavour, they will meet before the one Portal. They will then recognise themselves as brothers, severed by tongue and apparent diversity of belief, but fundamentally holding to the same one truth and serving the same God." – Alice Bailey, 'Initiation, Human & Solar: Unabridged' (1922)

"There is no question, therefore, that the work to be done in familiarising the general public with the nature of the Mysteries is of paramount importance at this time. These Mysteries will be restored to outer expression through the medium of the Church and the Masonic Fraternity ... When the Great One comes with His disciples and initiates we shall have ... the restoration of the Mysteries and their exoteric presentation as a consequence of the first initiation." – Alice Bailey, 'Externalisation of the Hierarchy' (1957)

Above all, Alice Bailey and the UN want to usher in a one world new age religion, headed by Lucifer, who will 'reappear as the Christ' and demand worship as God – utter blasphemy and evil. This ties in with the Biblical prophecy of the Antichrist. Bear in mind that she wrote all her books between 1919-1949, over 70 years ago. When you read her aims to get God and prayer out of schools, to destroy Christianity and the family structure, to make homosexuality, bestiality and incest normal, to debase art, to use media propaganda and to make the one world religion a reality for all, you can see how much headway the UN's made across the world with their agenda. Further, David Spangler, former Director of Planetary Initiative at the United Nations and strong promoter of Alice Bailey's work, writes in his book, 'Reflections on the Christ' (1978): *"No one will enter the New World Order unless he or she will make a pledge to worship Lucifer. No one will enter the New Age unless he will take a Luciferian Initiation."* ... And the whole world is now receiving the Covid vaccine – developed by and pushed from the USA – with talks of including a bioluminescent 'Luciferase' enzyme, whilst simultaneously moving into a financial 'Great Reset' and towards the NWO.

Council on Foreign Relations (CFR)

Based in NYC and Washington, the CFR claims (in its mission statement) to be: *"an independent, nonpartisan membership organization, think tank, and publisher dedicated to being a resource for its members, government officials, business executives, journalists, educators and students, civic and religious leaders, and other interested citizens in order to help them better understand the world and the foreign policy choices facing the United States and other countries."*

However, this is complete propaganda. It is by no means independent; the CFR is a subsidiary of the Committee of 300. It serves to function as much more than a 'resource' to its listed interested parties; it outright controls them and dictates their policies, via its several thousand members and 'experts'. Media and Hollywood mogul, Myron Fagan, gave an in-depth exposé lecture in 1967 on the CFR and UN and their Illuminati origins and occult agenda, called 'The Illuminati and the Council on Foreign Relations.'[360] You can find the audio lecture on YouTube[361] at this point too. The CFR is one of the most powerful private organisations, along with its similarly powerful British sister organization, the Royal Institute of International Affairs (now renamed Chatham House). The group suggested the formation of a League of Nations. All but one of the men of the 'Agenda Group' which drafted the United States proposal for a United Nations were members of the CFR. Carol Quigley called its members the 'international financial coterie' The CFR was instrumental in planning the post-World War II economic and political world order. The first job of the CFR was to gain control of the press. This task was given to John D. Rockefeller who set up a number of national news magazines such as Life, and Time. He financed Samuel Newhouse to buy up and establish a chain of newspapers all across the country, and Eugene Meyer also who would go on to buy up many publications such as the Washington Post, Newsweek, and The Weekly Magazine. David Rockefeller has been chairman of the CFR and has been a major funder. The CFR runs the 'David Rockefeller Studies Program', described by the CFR as its 'first class think tank'. It influences foreign policy by making

---

[360] Fagon, Myron. 'Illuminati and the Counsel on Foreign Relations'. http://www.gwb.com.au/gwb/news/multi/illumin.html. Accessed 5 May 2021.

[361] 'Myron Fagan Exposes the Illuminati/CFR [1967].' *YouTube*, https://www.youtube.com/watch?v=KrUXPn7HCjM. Accessed 22 May 2021.

recommendations to the presidential administration and diplomatic community, testifying before Congress, interacting with the media, and publishing on foreign policy issues.

Historical consultant, PhD, lecturer and author, Laurence Shoup has written a book called 'Wall Street's Think Tank: The Council on Foreign Relations and the Empire of Neoliberal Geopolitics, 1976-2014'[362]. He argues that the CFR now operates in an era of 'Neoliberal Geopolitics', a worldwide paradigm that its members helped to establish and that reflects the interests of the U.S. ruling class. In his book, he boldly dispels the notion that the USA operates in a democracy: *"The U.S. government – led behind the scenes by the CFR – is largely run in an anti-democratic fashion by and for the interests of a financialized capitalist class, their corporations, and the wealthy families that control and benefit from these corporations. No matter who is elected, people from the Council propose, debate, develop consensus, and implement the nation's key strategic policies."*

And Carroll Quigley, in his mammoth book, 'Tragedy and Hope' (1966), states: *"The Council on Foreign Relations is the American branch of a society which originated in England ... [and] ... believes national boundaries should be obliterated and one-world rule established."*

Probably most disturbing for us, we should note that the CFR has its stooges in the Church: Pastor Rick Warren, author of the wildly successful best-selling book, 'The Purpose Driven Life', was appointed as a CFR member to help bring about 'understanding and co-operation among the world's great religions'. Warren has warned against 'extremism in Fundamentalist Christianity, Fundamentalist Islam, and Fundamentalist Judaism'. To achieve its ecumenical new age agenda, the CFR has also elevated to membership another of America's most influential Christian

---

[362] Shoup, Lawrence H. Wall Street's Think Tank: The Council on Foreign Relations and the Empire of Neoliberal Geopolitics. Monthly Review Press, 2014.

evangelical group leaders, Richard Land of the Southern Baptist Convention.

Twelve Objectives of the Frankfurt School of Cultural Marxism – Used by USA Intelligence

Below is a list of the recommendations of the Frankfurt School of Cultural Marxism, an Illuminati organisation that has been responsible for social engineering and political mind programming agendas that inform USA intelligence organisations and government. These objectives have now also become the mantra of the **'Common Purpose' not-so-secret society in the UK**, under the guise of a benevolent British charity to develop 'future leaders':

1. The creation of racism offences.
2. Continual change to create confusion.
3. The teaching of sex and homosexuality to children.
4. The undermining of schools' and teachers' authority.
5. Huge immigration to destroy identity.
6. The promotion of excessive drinking.
7. Emptying of Churches.
8. An unreliable legal system with bias against victims of crime.
9. Dependency on the State or State benefits.
10. Control and dumbing down of media.
11. Encouraging the breakdown of the family.
12. All all-out attack on Christianity and the **emptying of Churches**.

World Economic Forum 'Great Reset'

The World Economic Forum[363] (WEF) wants to 'shape our future'. Its motto is 'Committed to improving the state of the world'. I can't help but wonder if they mean the global, one-world all-pervasive elite state? Its founder and president, Klaus Schwab, is a member of the Bilderberg

---

[363] *World Economic Forum*, https://www.weforum.org/. Accessed 5 May 2021.

Group and the Committee of 300, which tells us a lot about how and why it would like to do that. WEF holds an annual meeting in Davos, Switzerland to discuss its plans and it has relished the opportunity of the 'surprise pandemic' to usher in its 'Great Reset'. Schwab has written a book of the same name. This is a moving forward of its plans for a 'Fourth Industrial Revolution' (a technocracy) that it touted back in 2016 and is made up of over 50 areas of interest that are formed of both 'Global Issues' and 'Industries', which in turn are all part of the WEF's Strategic Intelligence platform. The WEF echoes a lot of what the Club of Rome (another Illuminati think tank) says in its 1970 report 'Limits to Growth',[364] and the UN's Agenda 21/2030 that we looked at in earlier chapters. Like them, it proselytises the fabricated 'global warming' and 'overpopulation' agendas and, yet again, presents depopulation, technocracy and a one world government and currency as the solutions. **There's no area of life that is left out of this Great Reset plan.** The planned reform will affect everything from government, energy and finance to food (think eating genetically-modified lab creations instead of real food), medicine, property, policing and even how we interact with our fellow human beings in general.

Very worryingly, the WEF runs 'Cyber Polygon'[365] – a 'training exercise' in cyber-attacks. This is similar to the Event 201 pandemic wargame, which took place merely weeks before the actual pandemic was announced. The July 2021 event focuses on the following theme and scenario: *"Recent years have seen a surge in the number of attacks targeting supply chains. Given the global trend towards the development of ecosystems across the business community, the vulnerability of supply chains has become a growing concern. With that in mind, the central theme of the training this year will be **ecosystem security and mitigation of supply chain attacks** ... During the online exercise, the teams will practise*

---

[364] Meadows, Donella J., et al. *The Limits to Growth.* https://www.clubofrome.org/publication/the-limits-to-growth/, (Original work published 1972). Accessed 5 May 2021.

[365] *Cyber Polygon,* https://cyberpolygon.com/. Accessed 22 May 2021.

response actions at the moment of a targeted supply chain attack on a corporate ecosystem."

In a short video released in 2020, the WEF has given eight bold and coercive predictions for 2030 (**which includes the surrender of the United States to the United Nations – which at that point could have its HQ in Baghdad if those plans go ahead**):

1. "You'll own nothing." – And "you'll be happy about it." [Oh, ok!]
2. "The U.S. won't be the world's leading superpower." [Iraq instead? A new vassal State of Rome?]
3. "You won't die waiting for an organ donor." – They will be made by 3D printers
4. "You'll eat much less meat." – Meat will be "an occasional treat, not a staple, for the good of the environment and our health".
5. "A billion people will be displaced by climate change." – Soros' Open Borders
6. "Polluters will have to pay to emit carbon dioxide." – "There will be a global price on carbon. This will help make fossil fuels history."
7. "You could be preparing to go to Mars." – Scientists "will have worked out how to keep you healthy in space."
8. "Western values will have been tested to the breaking point." – "Checks and balances that underpin our democracies must not be forgotten."

Joe Biden, elected USA president, as at November 2020, has openly stated his 'Build Back Better' campaign, to prioritise four things: Covid 19, economic recovery, racial equality and climate change (along with transgender rights with the Equality Act). Sounds pretty good right? Except that it's straight from the WEF 'Great Reset' playbook and is following exactly the depopulation agendas that we've examined so far (and in the next section).

Also, as we can clearly see being put in place, 'economic recovery' will involve an authoritarian 'social credit' system rolled out across

the world to assert full control over citizens, as was first introduced in China in 2020. We must be aware of this veiled political speak that sounds plausible, benevolent and rational; it is not.

The WEF scheduled its 'Agenda for the post-Covid world'[366] meeting for January (virtual meeting) and August 2021 (in Singapore), to discuss 'enhancing stewardship of our global commons' and 'harnessing the technologies of the Fourth Industrial Revolution', amongst other things.

Rothschild – Illuminati – Zionist 25-Point Plan for Political Control

In 1773, Mayer Rothschild summoned twelve wealthy men (also Zionist Jews and Illuminati members) to Frankfurt and asked them to pool their resources, then presented the 25-point plan that would enable them to gain control of the wealth, natural resources and manpower of the entire world, directed from the USA. Those 25 points (as identified in William Guy Carr's 'Pawns in the Game' – see above) are:

1. Use violence and terrorism rather than academic discussions.
2. Preach 'Liberalism' to usurp political power.
3. Initiate class warfare.
4. Politicians must be cunning and deceptive; any moral code leaves a politician vulnerable.
5. Dismantle existing forces of order and regulation. Reconstruct all existing institutions.
6. Remain invisible until the very moment when it has gained such strength that no cunning or force can undermine it.
7. Use Mob Psychology to control the masses. 'Without absolute despotism one cannot rule efficiently'.
8. Advocate the use of alcoholic liquors, drugs, moral corruption and all forms of vice, used systematically by 'agenteurs' to corrupt the youth.

---

[366] 'Special Annual Meeting in Singapore to Take Place in August 2021'. *World Economic Forum*, https://www.weforum.org/press/2021/02/special-annual-meeting-in-singapore-to-take-place-in-august-2021/. Accessed 1 May 2021.

9. Seize properties by any means to secure submission and sovereignty.

10. Foment wars and control the peace conferences so that neither of the combatants gains territory placing them further in debt and therefore into our power.

11. Choose candidates for public office who will be 'servile and obedient to our commands, so they may be readily used as pawns in our game'.

12. Use the Press for propaganda to control all outlets of public information, while remaining in the shadows, clear of blame.

13. Make the masses believe they had been the prey of criminals. Then restore order to appear as the saviours.

14. Create financial panics. Use hunger to control and subjugate the masses.

15. Infiltrate Freemasonry to take advantage of the Grand Orient Lodges to cloak the true nature of their work in philanthropy. Spread their atheistic-materialistic ideology amongst the 'Goyim' (human cattle).

16. When the hour strikes for our sovereign lord of the entire World [Lucifer] to be crowned, their influence will banish everything that might stand in his way.

17. Use systematic deception, high-sounding phrases and popular slogans. 'The opposite of what has been promised can always be done afterwards ... That is of no consequence'.

18. A Reign of Terror is the most economical way to bring about speedy subjection.

19. Masquerade as political, financial and economic advisers to carry out our mandates with diplomacy and without fear of exposing the secret power behind national and international affairs.

20. Ultimate world government is the goal. It will be necessary to establish huge monopolies, so even the largest fortunes of the Goyim will depend on us to such an extent that they will go to the bottom together with the credit of their governments on the day after the great political smash.

21. Use economic warfare. Rob the Goyim of their landed properties and industries with a combination of high taxes and unfair competition.
22. Make the Goyim destroy each other so there will only be the proletariat left in the world, with a few millionaires devoted to our cause, and sufficient police and soldiers to protect our interest.
23. Call it The New Order. Appoint a Dictator.
24. Fool, bemuse and corrupt the younger members of society by teaching them theories and principles we know to be false.
25. Twist national and international laws into a contradiction which first masks the law and afterwards hides it altogether. Substitute arbitration for law.

Wow, how many of these do you think have been achieved so far? Bear in mind too that the Federal Reserve – a privately owned bank that runs all of the money in the US – was set up in 1913 and is still owned by the Rothschilds. The Rothschilds also own and run much of the rest of the world's banking systems, including the banks of Iraq, Iran, Israel and Jordan. **In other words, this is the clear, Satanic agenda of the people who own and direct all the money in America and the Middle East.**

Babylon Within the Church

In light of what we've just learned, let's briefly revisit the influence of Mystery Babylon, the harlot Catholic church with her Jesuit army, on the true Church. Here's an example: The Archbishop of Canterbury, Justin Welby, presented a text by the Anglican communion in 1999, affirming a joint declaration by the Roman Catholic church and global Protestant bodies, described as *"a sign of healing after 500 years of division"*. It was adopted by World Methodist Council in 2006 and adopted by the World

Communion of Reformed Churches (representing 80 million congregants) in 2017. So that's it – the Reformation was just a misunderstanding that one archbishop can sign away to effectively reverse?

The former Archbishop of Canterbury was a member of the Committee of 300. Given what we now know about this committee of elites and their agenda, we can draw serious inferences about the Archbishop's role and intentions within the Church of England. As well as the fact that the Queen of England is the head of the C. of E. These are very major problems for our Churches and C. of E. ministers must be very aware of this and the direction that the Church is being steered in – not just around same-sex marriage issues but the grave ecumenical agenda that will seek to undermine and destroy Biblical Christianity.

Pope Francis and the Grand Imam of Al-Azhar, Ahmed el-Tayeb, signed a document on Human Fraternity for World Peace and Living Together,[367] in February 2019. It states: *"Meeting one another in fraternal friendship in this place of prayer is a powerful sign, one that shows the harmony which religions can build together, based on personal relations and on the good will of those responsible."*

Over and over again, the word 'God' is used to simultaneously identify Allah and the God of Christianity and that 'God has willed the diversity of religions': *"We, who believe in God and in the final meeting with Him and His judgment, on the basis of our religious and moral responsibility, and through this Document, call upon ourselves, upon the leaders of the world as well as the architects of international policy and world economy, to work strenuously to spread the culture of tolerance and of living together in peace; to intervene at the earliest opportunity to stop the shedding of innocent blood and bring an end to wars, conflicts, environmental decay and the moral and cultural decline that the world is presently experiencing ... The pluralism and the diversity of religions, colour, sex,*

---

[367] 'Vatican Sends Greetings to Muslims for Ramadan 2020'. *Independent Catholic News – ICN*, 1 May 2020, https://www.indcatholicnews.com/news/39485. Accessed 5 May 2021.

race and language are willed by God in His wisdom, through which He created human beings. "

Pope Francis and Islamic leaders are both heavily promoting the 'Sustainable Development' agenda, AKA Technocracy. In May 2020, the Pope invited many world religious leaders to sign the 'Global Compact on Education', a world educational pact aiming to 'educate young people to the fraternity, learning to overcome divisions and conflicts, promoting hospitality, justice and peace'.

Remember also, as we looked at in Chapter 5 on the four different types of authority, that many churches in the USA are registered as Tax Exempt 501(c)(3) entities, which bans all political activity and effectively makes them legal State Churches.

Zionism, Jewish Mysticism, Kabbalism and the State of Israel

The Bible warns in Revelation 2:9 about a group of people who claim to be Jews but are not genuine Jews and are seeking to deceive people into their false, elitist and legalistic religion and fleece them of their money. These are occult Jews, originating back to the times of Israel's Babylonian captivity and can be seen in Jesus' time as the Pharisees. The Pharisees were a secret order who outwardly appeared to be orthodox Jews but inwardly were of the mysteries of Babylon.[368] That is why Jesus exposed them as hypocrites; that is having two faces and used extremely scathing words with them, calling them 'serpents', 'whitewashed tombs' and 'of their father, the devil'. This Kabbalistic mysticism has perpetuated from generation to generation and exists today in Freemasonry, Mormonism, Judaism, Jehovah's Witnesses, Scientology and other secret societies and false religions. The Bible calls this the 'synagogue of Satan'

---

[368] The Pharisees sought to impose a complex system of oral traditions, the 'traditions of men' as Jesus called it. This taught that man was inherently good and so by daily and burdensome 'good deeds' could redeem himself. These doctrines are very much alive and pervasive today under the umbrella of 'Kabbalah' (Cabala).

(Revelation 2:9). We know that Israel plays a major role in Bible prophecy and world affairs. We must pray for revival in Israel and that the Jews there would see the true Messiah, our LORD Jesus, and repent and be saved. Paul reminds us in Romans 9:4-5: *"who are Israelites, to whom pertain the adoption, the glory, the covenants, the giving of the law, the service of God, and the promises; of whom are the fathers and from whom, according to the flesh, Christ came, who is over all, the eternally blessed God. Amen."* (NKJV)

However, we need to be careful to discern the Kabbalistic deception and avoid Zionist teachings and influence. The Talmud and Zohar are their main texts, which are Satanic (as is their star of David symbol, which was sadly foisted upon the State of Israel by the Rothschilds as it was established in 1948) and are the basis of the Kabbalah, which is the Babylonian foundation of all modern mystery occult religions and belief systems.

Billy Graham – The NWO Ecumenical Prophet

US Preacher and 'evangelist' Billy Graham, like Queen Elizabeth II, is beloved by many and heralded as a great upholder of the faith. He preached most of his life, from the 1940s and was still speaking publicly about Jesus and religion until he died, several years ago. His children, especially Franklin Graham, have continued his ministry and expanded upon it. Beloved by so many saints as he is, many Christians saw big problems with him and his ministry from the outset and claimed him to be a wolf in the Church. These voices were, and still are, heavily suppressed. What I say next might well offend you (if I haven't already!) but I am highlighting this as a matter of discernment and concern for the Body of Christ and I urge you to do your own unbiased research too. There are some clear alarm bells with Billy Graham that you should be aware of, as follows:

- There are many claims that he was a 33rd degree Freemason. His membership is allegedly stated in later editions of 'The History of Freemasonry' – written by the Freemasons as their official history book. He is pictured giving masonic handshakes to various people. His biography cites almost exclusively other Freemasons and he is known to have associated heavily with other Freemasons[369] and endorse many anti-Christian people and doctrines. There is evidence and anecdotal evidence of this. Freemasonry, especially at this high Satanic level, is wholly incompatible with a love for Christ.

- He had many occultist friends. The book 'Billy Graham and His Friends: A Hidden Agenda?' by Dr Cathy Burns gives much evidence of this.

- Staunch anti-Catholic preacher, Ian Paisley wrote a book 'Billy Graham and the Church of Rome: A Startling Exposure' in 1972 that heavily criticises Graham. Paisley preached several sermons on this too.

- He heavily promoted ecumenism and was a great supporter of the Pope and Roman Catholicism throughout his entire ministry, as well as Islam. In 1980 in 'The Saturday Evening Post', Graham stated, *"Since his election, Pope John Paul II has emerged as the greatest religious leader of the modern world, and one of the greatest moral and spiritual leaders of this century ... The Pope came [to America] as a statesman and a pastor, but I believe he also sees himself coming as an evangelist."* His son Franklin has continued promoting his ecumenical and social gospel.

- He supported and openly promoted the false doctrine of universal salvation and that you can be saved in other religions, since people in other religions are also 'seeking God' (that's not what Psalm 14 says). You can hear this in his talk show appearances, especially one of his latter interviews with Larry King[370]

---

[369] 'Freemasons Pay Tribute To Billy Graham as their Great Friend'. *Cutting Edge,* https://www.cuttingedge.org/news/n1742.cfm. Accessed 5 May 2021.

[370] 'Billy Graham with Larry King'. *YouTube,* https://www.youtube.com/watch?v=MhVPOazNWBo. Accessed 5 May 2021.

where he stated that preaching hell and the salvation of only believers in Christ is to 'go off on all kinds of other side trails'. This is anti-Biblical and a very damaging testimony.

- He promoted people making 'decisions for Christ' rather than trusting in the atonement of Jesus's shed blood to pay for our sins. A subtle but diluting and polluting Gospel message.

- Even at the height of Graham's crusades and ministry in the 50s and 60s, he was sending people who made a 'decision for Christ' back to synagogues, Roman Catholic and liberal Churches and not calling them to attend a local truly Biblical Church.

- He is lauded by pagan society, celebrities and institutions, as well as Christians. He has been on the cover of Time magazine, been a guest interviewee on Larry King, even has his own star on the Hollywood Walk of Fame. One has to ask, why? Aren't true Christians hated by the world? Could you imagine Martin Luther or Spurgeon or Lloyd Jones ever being lauded by the secular world and elites in such a way?

- He attended and supported the Jesuit-run World Council of Churches (WCC) meetings from 1961. The WCC is an Illuminati organisation, heavily funded by the Rockefellers and it functions as an organisation intimately aligned with the U.N. and carrying the baton of the Interchurch World Movement of the 1920s to promote ecumenism and towards a one-world religion ideal.

- To look into this more, you can read a free online copy of the book 'Billy Graham's Sad Disobedience' by David W. Cloud.[371]

This blurring the lines between the true Church, the Bride of Christ and the harlot Roman Catholic church is a grave danger that we need to be aware of. Remember, wolves in sheep's clothing appear as sheep.

---

[371] Cloud, David W. *Billy Graham's Sad Disobedience. Way of Life Literature*, March 2018, https://www.wayoflife.org/free_ebooks/billy_grahams_disobedience.php. Accessed 5 May 2021.

Rockefeller Funding of USA Theological Seminaries – to Push Ecumenism and Liberalism

John D. Rockefeller, like his son, was a globalist elite member of the Jesuit-controlled Committee of 300. He was commissioned by the CFR to infiltrate theological seminaries and pervert them – subtly and not so subtly promoting ecumenism and liberalism and allowing the 'little yeast' to take its disastrous effects over time. In 1938, he established the Seatlantic Fund, to give support to institutions and programs which promoted liberal Protestantism. The fund contributed to Protestant theological education and created the Interdenominational Theological Center along with other liberal Protestant seminaries and schools benefited from the fund.

FEMA Clergy Response Teams

I mentioned in the section on the CFR above that Rick Warren is a major stooge to usher in ecumenism and a one world religion, along with Billy Graham. We also have to be aware that the NWO folk could well be coming for your local pastor too. Right now there is widespread recruiting of Church leaders and pastors going on to pave the way for the NWO and we can see that in the heavy promotion of the Covid pseudo-vaccine by pastors, owing in large part to the 'guidance' being issued to them. In May 2006, Cherith Chronicle and in 2007, Prison Planet exposed the existence of a nationwide USA FEMA (Federal Emergency Management Agency) program which is training pastors and other religious representatives to become secret police enforcers who teach their congregations to 'obey the government' (and citing Romans 13, just as in Nazi Germany) in preparation for the implementation of martial law, property and firearm seizures, mass vaccination programs and forced relocation. These were labelled 'Clergy Response Teams' (CRTs) and it is estimated that there are over 100,000 pastors now signed up in the USA! Pastors are specifically told to preach Romans 13 to their congregations, misinterpreting it to command that Christians should obey the government even if they must disobey God and their conscience. They are trained in what to do in the event of a 'worldwide pandemic' – bear in mind this was instituted almost 15 years ago – and have been told they will be backed up by law enforcement and that they will lead SWAT TEAMS and given preferential treatment. Many so-called Church bodies have signed up to the National Voluntary Organisations Active in Disaster (NVOAD)[372] to help 'deal' with crises to help facilitate the NWO agenda – Adventists, Billy Graham Response Team, Co-operative Baptist Fellowship, Brethren Disaster Ministries, Church World Service and more. You can read more about FEMA recruiting of pastors[373] and download an alarming 33 page training document for Clergy Response Teams here,[374] bear in mind it was published in 2006 – fourteen years before Covid. Bottom line, if you're a pastor do not get sucked into this or join and CRT. And if you're a congregation member, keep an eye out for this.

The Growing Desire for a New Age Christ

I mentioned the 'Hegelian Dialectic' principle in earlier chapters (another Jesuit creation, incidentally), whereby deceptive political authorities seek to create a 'third way' out of two seemingly opposing views. They create the problem, and a reaction and then offer a solution; what they wanted all along: Thesis, antithesis, synthesis. This creates the illusion that we, the people, have a say in in what goes on and can 'vote' and have our view counted. For example, they set up Republican vs Democrat and then the synthesis is the 'third way' merging of the two, which was the agenda all along. In relation to religion and Babylon, this is important to keep in mind because of where we are headed. Atheism was introduced in the modern ages and was only meant to be a temporary 'non-religion'

---

[372] *NVOAD*, https://www.nvoad.org/. Accessed 5 May 2021.

[373] Watkins, Jon. 'Clergy Response Teams'. *Exposing Satan,* https://www.exposingsatanism.org/clergy-response-teams/. Accessed 5 May 2021.

[374] 'Pastoral Crisis Intervention: An Overview of Pastoral Crisis Intervention and Debriefing.' *Exposing Satan,* 15 May 2006, https://www.exposingsatanism.org/wp-content/uploads/2017/01/Clergy-Response-teams-PDF.pdf. Accessed 5 May 2021

adopted by the masses – the antithesis to the thesis of Christianity. The synthesis, which is the goal of the elites, is the one world religion, headed by Lucifer (See Alice Bailey's work earlier). We are moving into times where the synthesis is emerging quickly and strongly. Atheism as the popular world view is coming to an end. A merging of religions will occur – also called 'syncretism' and this will then eventually give way to Luciferianism – the worship of an Antichrist. For the most part and especially since events in Covid 19, people are looking for a spiritual solution and comfort. The stark and cold pointlessness of life that atheism espouses is growing wearing for many people and a new syncretic religion of oneness, kindness, tolerance and world peace; a merging of all religions and world views is becoming ever more fashionable and desirable.

Having been delivered from years in the new age movement, I am all-too-familiar with this and how pernicious it is and attractive it can appear. It's all-inclusive, ecumenical, seemingly full of light, encourages a 'higher state of being' and places no burdens on us to turn from sin or change our ways. It touts flowery and alluring terms such as 'universal consciousness', 'the divine within', 'manifesting our desires' and being 'at one with the source'… It is gnostic pantheism and is utterly demonic. It plays to our sense of pride and selfishness and, again, as Satan always does, tries to say that 'we can be as gods' and have divine knowledge – outside of Christ, of course. With the interim merging of religions, there will be a new age Christ. This can take any number of forms but a common one is the ethereal notion of 'Christ consciousness', which is supposed to be the state of being unified with God. It says that Christ is not one man or God but a thing that we step into the realisation of through an awakening of our true nature as an expression of God. It says that we are all Christ, we just haven't realized it yet like Jesus did. This idea draws upon Hinduism, Buddhism and theosophy to give us an esoteric understanding of the ministry of Jesus. Here are some quotes by New Age teachers on the idea that we are all Christ:

"Is he (Jesus) the Christ? O yes, along with you." – A Course in Miracles

"When one has truly awakened to God's Presence within – one is not impressed by anyone claiming to be Jesus. But by having awakened to Christ Consciousness within oneself, one may share the emerging wisdom without any claims to be Jesus or anyone else in the history of religion that people would tend to look up to. Be thankful for such messengers and respect them for the Christ Consciousness Energy that speaks through them - but don't worship them, saving worship for God's Presence within yourself." – Dr Master, 'Theocentric Way of Life'

But to push this concept further, there are many who are looking for and anticipating an actual 'Christ' to 'return' to the earth; a new age Christ. New age occultists such as Benjamin Creme, as well as Alice Bailey and many other spiritual leaders are prophesying a new Christ to come to the earth and they often call him 'Lord Maitreya', an 'ascended master', a demon. In fact, all major religions have some kind of 'enlightened one' who they expect to return to the earth at some point to usher in a new age of enlightenment. However, we know from the Bible that he will actually be the Antichrist – talked about by the Prophets Jeremiah, Isaiah, Daniel, Micah, Paul and John.

From my investigations and reading various other globalist elite documents, I think we can certainly expect some kind of staged 'second coming' of Christ – possibly using holographs and advanced technology, or some kind of demonic resurrection – which we'll look at that shortly! Jesus warns us about this in Matthew 24 and tells us not to believe it. When He returns on Judgement Day, every eye will see and every knee will bow. FYI, we might also expect some kind of staged alien encounter (the elites and now the Pope himself have been seeding this into the mainstream media for years), as well as further financial meltdowns, pandemics, nanobot/RFID chipping (via pandemic vaccination programmes), global warming propaganda, a mega-terror attack of some kind, war in the Middle East and a possible presidential assassination. These will all be masterminded by the elites, ratified by Rome and the Committee of 300, rolled out by governments and media and taken in by the masses.

A charismatic one-world religious Christ-figure will be vehemently welcomed in such circumstances. Christian, as mad as this all sounds, we need to be on guard and with our eyes open. We've seen many such tyrannical regimes in our world before, let us not be deceived and caught without our armour on. I'd highly recommend reading Walter Martin's book 'The New Age Cult' and Tal Brooke's 'One World' to educate and protect yourself from this false religion and coming 'new age Christ' – both of which have crept into many Churches right now.

What About the Antichrist?

There are many differing 'end times' thoughts and perspectives that exist between Christians. What do we make of the Antichrist and also the Great Tribulation that Jesus speaks of in Matthew 24:21? It's important to at least acknowledge the reality that Dr Gratton Guinness points out in his book, 'The Approaching End of the Age': *"It has been calculated that the Popes of Rome have directly or indirectly slain on account of their faith, 50,000,000 martyrs; men and women who refused to be party to the Romish idolatries, who held to the Bible as the Word of God, and loved not their lives unto death, but resisted unto blood, striving against sin"*.

So in terms of tribulation, there is certainly a convincing case that this has happened in the Dark Ages, under Papal Rome. However, I think it's lacking scriptural and historical insight to think that as Christians we can guarantee being spared from awful persecution (via 'the rapture', as plenty believe), since it has been proven in history that so many have not. There are also too many prophecies left as yet unfulfilled. Despite the horror of the Dark Ages, I do think both that things will get progressively worse until Jesus returns (but will cause many to turn to Christ – Jews and Gentiles) and that our LORD will protect and sustain us as He sees fit. We need to make this distinction: that neither persecution, nor tribulation are the same as the wrath of God and we do not need to be taken out of the way in order to be spared God's wrath, as evidenced in the plagues of Exodus. I can sympathise *to a degree* with the Historicist viewpoint, as the Reformers believed. We can see that Revelation begins with the early Church and ends with the second coming of Christ. Thus, the prophecies described *have* to apply to the time in between. I also acknowledge the fair amount of symbolism in Revelation and that it is a book that applies to every Church in all times – not just John's contemporaries (the Preterist view – where the prophecies ended in 70AD with the final destruction of the Jewish temple). Unlike the Reformers however, and after much searching of the scriptures and prayerfully weighing them up, I believe that there will be a *future, single* and final Antichrist – separate from the office of the Papacy of Rome and I will give my reasonings for this with scriptural evidence, as well as some interesting (and very disturbing) facts about the plans and agendas that are going on in high places to try and usher in the Antichrist. Before we look at some points musing on the possible Antichrist figure, I want to preface it with this: I am well aware, as mentioned before, that the prevailing Dispensational Futurist tenets are from the Jesuits, later affirmed by John Darby of the Plymouth Brethren and then made wildly popular by C.I. Scofield. This false doctrine that the Church will be 'raptured' (taken away by Jesus) prior to the Great Tribulation is just not Biblical and is a dangerous heresy that will cause many Christians to be caught off-guard and disillusioned with the very trying times and persecution to come. The books of Daniel and Revelation, as well as Matthew 24 and 2 Thessalonians, contain unfulfilled prophecies and indicate that there will be a *future* tribulation with an apostasy and an Antichrist in power (likely to be seven and three and a half years respectively).

"Let no one deceive you by any means; for that Day will not come unless the falling away comes first, and the man of sin is revealed, the son of perdition, who opposes and exalts himself above all that is called God or that is worshiped, so that he sits as God in the temple of God, showing himself that he is God." – 2 Thessalonians 2:3-4 (NKJV).

Many Christians believe that the prophecies of the 'abomination of desolation' that we see in Daniel and Jesus' Olivet Discourse[375] are referring exclusively to events past. Preterists attribute it to the siege and destruction of the temple in Jerusalem in 70AD by Titus of Rome. The city was surrounded and the Christians fled to the mountains – just as Jesus warns and in Luke 21. The mention of an abomination in Daniel 11 is accepted by some to refer to Seleucid King Antiochus IV Epiphanes' profaning of the temple in around 167BC. However, Jesus warns of an abomination of desolation that is still *future,* when he spoke about it in Matthew 24 (and therefore also the corresponding text in Luke 21). Could it be that these were partial fulfilments and that there will be a third abomination of desolation in a rebuilt temple in the last days before Jesus' return (plans for this are underway in Jerusalem right now)? It's quite possible and there are repeated cycles, patterns and motifs throughout the Bible. All this said, we must not think that we don't need to set our 'eschatological clock' ticking until we see the temple reinstated. Our evangelism must be urgent and we need great wisdom on all of this.

The Son of Perdition – Office or a Man?

You probably don't need me to tell you that many theologians throughout Church history have pronounced the Papacy as the Antichrist. Men such as John Wycliffe, who after translating the Bible into English immediately deemed it as such. Martin Luther, John Calvin, John Ridley, Hugh Latimer, John Knox, John Bunyan, John Wesley, Dwight L. Moody, Charles Spurgeon, Hudson Taylor. There is a very strong and credible case for this position. We can see from Revelation 13 and 17 that the Harlot is ecclesiastical Rome – the Roman Church. The first Beast is a worldwide end-times revived Roman empire – the globalist 'New World Order' political system. The Antichrist is the little horn coming up from amongst others, so it would be natural to think that this horn of power

---

[375] The Olivet Discourse is the name given to the passage containing Jesus' teaching on the Mount of Olives in Matthew 24:1-25:46 (and also Mark 13:1-37; Luke 21:5-36). It includes significant focus on prophecy.

springing from Rome is the Papacy. Chapter 25:6 of the 1646 Westminster Confession of Faith[376] boldly states: *"There is no other head of the Church but the Lord Jesus Christ. Nor can the Pope of Rome, in any sense, be head thereof; but is that Antichrist, that man of sin, and son of perdition, that exalts himself, in the Church, against Christ and all that is called God."*

If you want to read more on this fairly convincing position, there's a helpful and detailed but succinct article called 'The Antichrist' by Shaun Willcock. However, Theologian Tony Garland, in his commentary on Daniel states:[377] *"Three phases of the fourth, Roman, kingdom: (1) iron alone; (2) feet of iron mixed with clay; (3) toes of iron mixed with clay. If iron alone represents unified Rome at the time of the first coming of Christ and the toes of iron mixed with clay correspond to the ten horns (Dan. 7:7,20,24), the final confederation of ten contemporaneous kings (Rev. 17:12-13), then it would seem that we may currently be living in the time of the feet of iron mixed with clay."*

It is evident that there are *not* currently ten kings in place empowering or empowered by Rome. These kings are *contemporaneous* – all reigning at the same time as each other and the Antichrist. So they are to come. Let's look deeper into Revelation 17: *"Here is the mind which has wisdom: The seven heads are seven mountains on which the woman sits. There are also seven kings. Five have fallen, one is, and the other has not yet come. And when he comes, he must continue a short time. The beast that was, and is not, is himself also the eighth, and is of the seven, and is going to perdition. "The ten horns which you saw are ten kings who have received no kingdom as yet, but they receive authority for one hour as kings with the beast. These are of one mind, and they will give their power and authority*

---

[376] 'Free Presbyterian Church of Ulster – WCF-25'. *Free Presbyterian Church of Ulster,* https://www.freepresbyterian.org/wcf-25/. Accessed 14 May 2021.

[377] Garland, Tony. 'Daniel - Sequence of Kingdoms (Daniel 2 and 7)'. *Spirt and Truth,* http://www.spiritandtruth.org/teaching/Book_of_Daniel/11_Sequence_of_Kingdoms/11_Sequence_of_Kingdoms_20130308.htm?x=x. Accessed 13 May 2021.

*to the beast. These will make war with the Lamb, and the Lamb will over-
come them, for He is Lord of lords and King of kings; and those who are
with Him are called, chosen, and faithful." Then he said to me, "The waters which you saw, where the harlot sits, are peoples, multitudes, nations, and tongues. And the ten horns which you saw on the beast, these
will hate the harlot, make her desolate and naked, eat her flesh and burn
her with fire. For God has put it into their hearts to fulfill His purpose, to
be of one mind, and to give their kingdom to the beast, until the words of
God are fulfilled. And the woman whom you saw is that great city which
reigns over the kings of the earth."* – Revelation 17:9-18 (NKJV)

Se we can see that:

1. The woman (Mystery Babylon, Roman Catholic church) is seated
    on seven mountains (city of Rome).
2. There are seven kings – five past kings, one current and one to
    come for a short time. Tallying this up with Revelation 13 and
    Daniel 7, we might muse that that these past kings, from the var-
    ious large empires covering the world might be Nimrod of Baby-
    lon, Pharoah of Egypt (during the time of the Exodus), Sennach-
    erib of Assyria, Cyrus of Medo-Persia, Antiochus Epiphanes of
    Greece. The current one in John's time being Nero of Rome (who
    is deemed as the Antichrist by many Preterists) and then a future
    one (from John's perspective).
3. The eighth king *"that was and is not, it is an eighth but it belongs
    to the seven, and it goes to destruction."* Could this be the king of
    the coming Globalist NWO Roman empire? The king of Babel
    Mark II? The man of sin, the Antichrist, is the eighth and final
    king and will arise from the seventh kingdom. Babel was and is
    coming again. Could Nimrod be also coming again? There are
    certainly many who think so and are trying to usher him back in!
    We'll look at this more.
4. The ten horns are ten kings that receive royal power at the same
    time as the Beast hand over their power to the little horn, the An-
    tichrist.

5. I think Revelation 17:16-17 are the most significant verses that make me doubt that the Papacy is the Antichrist: *"And **the ten horns which you saw on the beast, these will hate the harlot, make her desolate and naked**, eat her flesh and burn her with fire. For God has put it into their hearts to fulfill His purpose, to be of one mind, and to give their kingdom to the beast, until the words of God are fulfilled."* Do you see what it is saying? That the ten kings will hate the harlot – Papal Rome – and will destroy her with fire. She experiences what Jeremiah described long before about the final destruction of Babylon, which has not yet been fulfilled: *"The Lord has raised up the spirit of the kings of the Medes. For His plan is against Babylon to destroy it"*. – Jeremiah 51:11 (NKJV).

Further, the idea of the Antichrist being a dynasty seems to contradict Revelation 13, which depicts a *singular person*, the beast out of the sea. Revelation 19 describes the battle of Armageddon, which ends with both the Antichrist and his False Prophet cast into the lake of fire.

"And the beast was taken, and with him the false prophet that wrought miracles before him, with which he deceived them that had received the mark of the beast, and them that worshipped his image. These both were cast alive into a lake of fire burning with brimstone." – Revelation 19:20

They are individual persons. John also says, *"Little children, it is the last hour; and as you have heard that the Antichrist is coming, even now many antichrists have come, by which we know that it is the last hour."* – 1 John 2:18. Unless this is all figurative of course and it's talking about throwing the 266 or so Popes (and a similar amount of Black Popes ... and Grey Popes?) in the lake of fire?

And what about what Paul says in 2 Thessalonians 2:3 which indicates a single man not a plurality, office or institution? Moreover, 'son of perdition' can be identified as 'Apollyon' or 'Apollo' – a Greek god name for Nimrod. This also ties in with Revelation 9:11 – *"And they had a king over them, which is the angel of the bottomless pit, whose name in the*

Hebrew tongue is Abaddon, but in the Greek tongue hath his name Apollyon."

Could the Antichrist perhaps be another Nimrod? Let's explore this possibility.

The Assyrian

We can clearly see from all our evidence in this book thus far that a united one-world government, like Babel, is well underway and that Covid is a vehicle to accelerate the 'Great Reset', which is another major push towards it.

"We shall have World Government, whether or not we like it. The only question is whether World Government will be achieved by conquest or consent." – James Paul Warburg, while speaking before the United States Senate, February 17, 1950.

Jesus gives us this interesting verse in Matthew 24 concerning the last days: *"But as the days of Noah were, so shall also the coming of the Son of man be."* – Matthew 24:37. There were Nephilim giants on earth in the days of Noah; likely to be the offspring of fallen angels and human women. Nimrod was the first of the Nephilim. All of the false mystery religions have a penchant for Nimrod, as we've seen. At the higher levels of their occult practices, as resurrected Nimrod is part of their writings and doctrines. Consider what Manly P. Hall wrote in 'The Secret Teachings of All Ages'[378] about Osiris (Nimrod): *"The Dying God shall rise again! The secret room in the House of the Hidden Places shall be rediscovered. The Pyramid again shall stand as the ideal emblem of solidarity, inspiration, aspiration, resurrection, and regeneration."*

From the Middle Ages forward, Church leaders have believed that the Antichrist would ultimately represent the return of the Nephilim – the reunion of demons with humans. Augustine wrote of this in 'The City of

---

[378] Hall, Manly P. *The Secret Teachings of All Ages*. A&D Publishing, 1853.

God'. The extra-canonical books of Enoch and Jasher talks about a re-vived Nephilim – but I would be reluctant to trust them, since there is evidence that the ones we have may be fictional counterfeits of those named in the Bible.

I believe that when the Bible talks about 'the Assyrian' (most notably in Isaiah 10 and Micah 5), it is depicting the Antichrist. Hell was made for this individual, Isaiah tells us. 'The Assyrian' was another name for Nim-rod – the King of Assyria, or King of the North. I therefore think that it's very plausible that the final Antichrist will be a resurrected Nimrod, ac-cording to Biblical prophecy. This ties in with all the occult expectations of the Mystery Babylon religions, who have not only worshipped him throughout history but are expecting a 'second coming' of the ancient Babylonian Nephilim king.

*"When **the Assyrian** comes into our land, And when he treads in our pal-aces, Then we will raise against him Seven shepherds and eight princely men. They shall waste with the sword the land of Assyria, And the land of Nimrod at its entrances; Thus He shall deliver us from the Assyrian, When he comes into our land And when he treads within our borders.* – Micah 5:5-6 (NKJV)

*"Therefore it shall come to pass, when the Lord has performed all His work on Mount Zion and on Jerusalem, that He will say, "I will punish the fruit of the arrogant heart of the **king of Assyria**, and the glory of his haughty looks.""* – Isaiah 10:12

*"For through the voice of the Lord shall **the Assyrian** be beaten down, which smote with a rod. And in every place where the grounded staff shall pass, which the Lord shall lay upon him, it shall be with tabrets and harps: and in battles of shaking will he fight with it. For **Tophet [Hell] is ordained of old; yea, for the king it is prepared**; he hath made it deep and large: the pile thereof is fire and much wood; the breath of the Lord, like a stream of brimstone, doth kindle it."* – Isaiah 30:31-33

Daniel 11 describes a 'vile man' in some detail. Whilst it is true that Antiochus fits the description of Daniel 11:29-35, he does not fit verse 36-39, or others. For instance, Antiochus never gained authority or ruled through deceit (v21). He did not distribute the plunder (v24). He did not magnify himself above every god or not had regard for the god of his fathers, nor for any god (v36-37). Finally, the events of the '*time of the end*' (v40-45) do not fit history at all. It would appear as if Antiochus Epiphanes is a type of Antichrist, foreshadowing the final one, which these verses especially describe in detail:

"And the king shall do according to his will; and he shall exalt himself, and magnify himself above every god, and shall speak marvellous things against the God of gods, and shall prosper till the indignation be accomplished: for that that is determined shall be done. Neither shall he regard the God of his fathers, nor the desire of women, nor regard any god: for he shall magnify himself above all. But in his estate shall he honour the God of forces: and a god whom his fathers knew not shall he honour with gold, and silver, and with precious stones, and pleasant things. Thus shall he do in the most strong holds with a strange god, whom he shall acknowledge and increase with glory: and he shall cause them to rule over many, and shall divide the land for gain." – Daniel 11:36-39

There are other theories as to who these verses might be referring to, but I think the text takes a similar direction as that of Ezekiel 28, where the focus shifts from the prince of Tyre (an earthly ruler) to the king of Tyre (Satan). I would recommend reading Peter Goodgame's short series, 'Prophecies of 'The Assyrian': Will the Antichrist Come From Iraq?'[379] for insight on a possible Assyrian Antichrist.

Back to Babylon?

---

[379] Goodgame, Peter. 'Prophecies of 'The Assyrian': Will the Antichrist come from Iraq?'. *Red Moon Rising, 14 Jan. 2008,* http://www.redmoonrising.com/Giza/raiders1.htm. Accessed 5 May 2021.

It follows that in the last days before Christ's return, there will be an actual physical location from which the Babylonian system and demonic beastly rule will take place – and that may not be the Harlot, Rome, or her daughter the USA, if we take Revelation 17:16 at face value. **Biblical prophecy might indicate that the beastly system will locate itself back in the original location of ancient Babylon, in Iraq or Syria.** If we look at Zechariah 5, it tells us that there is a woman (representing religion) sat in an ephah (measuring tool for grain – representing commerce), with a 'wickedness' leaden cover (representing evil political rule), being taken to Shinar (Babylon) to build a house there.

"So I asked, "What is it?" And he said, "It is a basket that is going forth."
He also said, "This is their resemblance throughout the earth: Here is a
lead disc lifted up, and this is a woman sitting inside the basket"; then he
said, "This is Wickedness!" And he thrust her down into the basket, and
threw the lead cover over its mouth. Then I raised my eyes and looked,
and there were two women, coming with the wind in their wings; for they
had wings like the wings of a stork, and they lifted up the basket between
earth and heaven. So I said to the angel who talked with me, "Where are
*they carrying the basket?" And he said to me, "**To build a house for it in***
***the land of Shinar**; when it is ready, the basket will be set there on its*
base." – Zechariah 5:6-11

So, the one world system of religion, economics and politics could end up in Iraq, and from that power base, the Antichrist could arise.

I think it's worth saying that I have come to these end times theological conclusions from much (dogged) study, prayer, listening to sound preaching, refinement of thought and also my perceptions gained from coming out of a long background in the new age occult, where I saw things from a kind of reverse angle – living in 'the world'. If you differ with my eschatology, I'd urge you 'not to throw the baby out with the bath water' so to speak and consider my evidence for the Babylonian uprising that we can see around us now and where it's headed. I hope we can agree that we are all in a process of learning and growth and that we should approach the study of Scripture and especially eschatology, with humility and a desire to learn and grow. I've been led into deeper truths by the Holy Spirit and had to humble myself and change my thinking on many occasions, as I'm sure you have!

If the Antichrist was to arise from Iraq or Syria with a return to the original city of Babylon for 'one last evil fling', one might wonder how this can be, since it is not a national superpower at present and in many ways it's quite barren? Well, what if there were plans to rebuild Iraq and that it was being carefully cultivated by organisations who are intent on ushering in the NWO? It could be that the USA and UN are paving the way for an end times rebuilt Babylon in Iraq. Here are some things to note about present-day Iraq in relation to USA:

- There is much work going on to rebuild Iraq[380] and there is a lot of investment into the country from outside governments and organisations, such as the Bill and Melinda Gates Foundation.
- There has been serious discussion about the UN moving its headquarters from NYC to Baghdad and Iraq already has 21 regional UN headquarters[381] there.
- On September 11th 1991, President George H. W. Bush spoke to Congress about a 'New World Order'[382] (NWO, globalist rule), in relation to the Iraqi-Kuwait Gulf war: *"We gather tonight, witness to events in the Persian Gulf as significant as they are tragic. In the early morning hours of August 2nd, following negotiations and promises by Iraq's dictator Saddam Hussein not to use force, a powerful Iraqi army invaded its trusting and much weaker neighbor, Kuwait ... Once again, Americans have*

---

[380] 'About the Event'. *Rebuilding Iraq,* https://rebuilding-iraq.com/about-the-event/. Accessed 5 May 2021.

[381] 'Link to Agencies', *United Nations Iraq,* http://www.uniraq.com/index.php?option=com_k2&view=item&layout=item&id=1543&Itemid=655&lang=en. Accessed 5 May 2021.

[382] 'Bush Before a Joint Session of Congress (September 11, 1990) - Famous New World Order Speech'. *YouTube,* https://www.youtube.com/watch?v=7iUX3yP9M8g. Accessed 5 May 2021.

stepped forward to share a tearful good-bye with their families before leaving for a strange and distant shore. At this very moment, they serve together with Arabs, Europeans, Asians and Africans in defense of principle and the dream of a new world order."

- Bush spoke to congress again on the NWO, on March 6th 1991 after the end of the Gulf War in Iraq.[383] He made telling statements about his intentions for a united, Babylonian one-world political system: *"Until now, the world we've known has been a world divided – a world of barbed wire and concrete block, conflict and cold war. Now, we can see a new world coming into view.* **A world in which there is the very real prospect of a new world order.** *In the words of Winston Churchill, a 'world order' in which 'the principles of justice and fair play ... protect the weak against the strong ..."* **A world where the United Nations, freed from cold war stalemate, is poised to fulfil the historic vision of its founders.** *A world in which freedom and respect for human rights find a home among all nations."*

- The U.S. has had military interests in Iraq for over 30 years, with significant numbers of troops in Iraq for 18 years. What began as an effort to seek 'weapons of mass destruction', which were never found, and then the events under 9/11, has in effect resulted in almost two decades of U.S. occupation of the country. It is widely speculated that the USA actually covertly funded both sides of the Gulf war.

A Great ConCERN

The Large Hadron Collider (LHC) is the world's largest energy particle collider, a huge 17-mile underground tunnel machine located near Geneva, named 'Appolliacum' (in honour of Apollo) in Roman times. It was

---

[383] 'George Bush's Speech after the Gulf War'. *Jerusalem Media and Communications Centre - JMCC*, 6 Mar. 1991, http://www.jmcc.org/Documentsandmaps.aspx?id=341. Accessed 5 May 2021.

built by the European Organization for Nuclear Research (CERN) between 1998 and 2008 in collaboration with over 10,000 scientists and hundreds of universities and laboratories, as well as more than 100 countries, at a reputed cost of $10 billion. This is clearly a big deal on the science and tech front. What does this have to do with the end times and the Antichrist, you might wonder? The LHC is famous for discovering the Higgs boson particle. The BBC reported back in 2015[384] that *"The next collisions of protons may reveal something about the majority of matter that exists but has yet to be seen – the stuff known as dark matter. They may uncover evidence for the weird notion that there are extra dimensions, or hordes of previously unseen particles that form pairs with the ones we know about."*

The director of CERN from 2009-15, Sergio Bertolucci, said that:[385] *"The Large Hadron Collider could open a doorway to another dimension, and out this door might come something, or we might send something through it".* It's not just that it 'could' open a doorway to another dimension, this is their number one aim in creating and using it. They are trying to create dark 'anti-matter' and they're tampering with 'black holes'! The entire CERN operation is full of occult symbolism – from its Shiva mascot statue (the destroyer god, Hindu representation of Nimrod) outside its HQ, to the occult LHC opening ritual, to its Satanic logo. CERN's logo is three intertwined sixes, to make 666. There is no logical reason for this pattern since the LHC tunnels are not arranged like this. CERN is also the birthplace of the World Wide Web (WWW). Interestingly, the Hebrew equivalent of our 'w' is the letter 'vav' or 'waw', which has the numerical value of six. Anthony Patch[386] is the founder of 'Entangled' magazine, which specialises in quantum computing and mechanics, artificial intelligence, cryptocurrencies and DNA/RNA modifications. He is the leading

---

[384] Shukman, David. 'What Is the Point of the Large Hadron Collider?' *BBC News*, 28 Mar. 2015, https://www.bbc.com/news/science-environment-32087787.

[385] Page, Lewis. *'Something May Come through' Dimensional 'Doors' at LHC.' The Register*, 6 Nov. 2009, https://www.theregister.com/2009/11/06/lhc_dimensional_portals/. Accessed 14 May 2021.

[386] *Anthony Patch*, https://anthonypatch.com/about. Accessed 15 May 2021.

independent researcher on CERN. According to him, CERN is about to 're-animate' or resurrect Nimrod and his demon army by opening the gates of Hell, or as they put it 'a portal to an alternate dimension'. The tomb of Gilgamesh (Nimrod) was announced as found in 2003 in the location as described in the Epic of Gilgamesh – in Iraq. One month later, the American military entered Iraq under the pretext of finding weapons of mass destruction during Operation Desert Storm and supposedly raided the tomb as well as several museums. It took artefacts for 'safe keeping'. It is believed that they are using the DNA they obtained for clandestine purposes. Anthony Patch states: *"Yes indeed, the whole war was staged for the secret retrieval of Nimrod, specifically Nimrod's 'preserved head' which has been preserved in a jar for thousands of years. After the U.S. troops obtained Nimrod's head, it was sent to the Vatican to be stored until the real agenda could take place. The plan is to resurrect Nimrod better known as Osiris, using the Large Hadron Collider 'LHC', a majority of people think the LHC is a particle accelerator used for scientific experiments, but in fact this is a large three-story 3D printer used to print organic material. **They will be able to print a complete organic copy of Nimrod, which is exactly what they will do, and this is how some believe the Antichrist will make his return.**"*

Notice the Vatican link. The Vatican has its own observatory,[387] interested in searching for 'extra-terrestrial life' and takes an active interest in the LHC. George V. Coyne was the Jesuit Director of the Vatican Observatory and headed its research group at the University of Arizona from 1978 to 2006. Why are Vatican Jesuits concerned with astronomy? They of course have a plausible reason why. But if you join the dots, you see a bigger picture. Compare the plans and desires going on at CERN with Revelation 9: *"And the fifth angel sounded, and I saw a star fall from heaven unto the earth: **and to him was given the key of the bottomless pit. And he opened the bottomless pit; and there arose a smoke out of the pit**, as the smoke of a great furnace; and the sun and the air were*

---

[387] *The Vatican Observatory*, https://www.vaticanobservatory.org/. Accessed 15 May 2021.

*darkened by reason of the smoke of the pit. And there **came out of the smoke locusts upon the earth**: and unto them was given power, as the scorpions of the earth have power. And it was commanded them that they should not hurt the grass of the earth, neither any green thing, neither any tree; but only those men which have not the seal of God in their fore-heads...**And they had a king over them, which is the angel of the bottomless pit, whose name in the Hebrew tongue is Abaddon, but in the Greek tongue hath his name Apollyon.***" – Revelation 9:1-4, 11

Under the new schedule, the LHC has restarted in May 2021 and is planned to run until the end of 2024. Who knows what already has been and will be unleashed by way of this sinister machine? Yes, it sounds completely fantastical and like something from science fiction, but not reality. Sadly, this *is the reality* and depravity of where scientism and occultism has taken us. Back to Babel.

Bill Gates also has an active interest in the LHC. Returning for a moment to the issue of the Covid vaccine, would you want to take this experimental injection that has been quickly rolled out, with force, by the various elite associates who are responsible for and interested in all of the following things?:

- CRISPR gene drive technology and 'playing God'.
- Human genome mapping and tampering.
- CERN and 'resurrecting' and cloning demonic entities.
- Opening Satanic portals to other dimensions.

For Your Consideration

I humbly submit my eschatological perspectives and findings to you for your prayerful consideration. My advice would be this – spend less time looking at opinions and commentaries, books and films on Biblical subjects. Spend more, prolonged time in the scriptures and asking the LORD for His wisdom on them in prayer and quiet meditation. I assume that you are reading the *whole* Bible through, often. I have spent up to five hours a day searching and reading through the landscape of the Bible and it's been such a blessed adventure with the LORD! If you want to know the deeper truths of the scriptures, keep yourself unstained by the world and spend much time reading God's Holy Word and prayerfully weighing it up.

Conclusions We Can Draw

There is overwhelming evidence to suggest that we are living in the time where the USA is leading a present-day Babylonian revival to bring in the NWO system, set up against our LORD as a kind of second Tower of Babel and to eventually take its last days position (possibly in the Middle East), before Jesus returns. There are depopulation, transhuman and demonic realm agendas in place and Covid 19 is one large vehicle to aid bringing this about. Churches across the USA and indeed the world are being infiltrated, recruited and polluted into pushing the Babylonian agenda, led by the Jesuit arm of the Roman Catholic harlot Church, and we need to be aware of this and have our wits about us to stand firm against it. Our LORD tells us not to be deceived and not to be ignorant of Satan's designs. We also need not worry – our LORD Jesus has overcome the powers of darkness and our lives are hidden in Him. He is our shield and protector. Thanks be to God! But we need to be ready for what is coming ...

The technocracy we are moving into as a result of Covid 19 affords the leverage for end times prophetic fulfilment like never before.

I hope this chapter has given you a clear whistle-stop tour of what's going on, its demonic and occult nature and the classic covert lies and 'gas lighting' tactics that abusers use to disarm, confuse and wield power over their victims. My aim is to equip you to be discerning and not fall for the news propaganda and to then take wise, decisive, confident, godly action – which we will look at in much more detail in the final chapters of this book.

Come Out of Her, My People

I hope you can see that with everything that's been and will be coming in under Covid, there is a huge spiritual goal here. Yes, it's about control and totalitarianism and depopulation and that's awful enough, but **as Christians we must see the massive spiritual deception and one world religion agenda on the cards simultaneously under Covid rules and the 'Great Reset'**. Right now, as I type this, Churches are again closed in lockdown and are forced to stream services on the technocratic platforms that are in complete agreement and part of the NWO agenda – YouTube and Facebook and the like, which hate Christianity and are fast shutting down free speech. We are being monitored now, censored soon and dictated too in the near future. Just like Hitler infiltrating the German Churches with his ideals, keeping the Church in form but changing it to compromise its Biblical standards and Christ-centredness.

So what is the answer? John tells us in Revelation 18:4-5 (reiterating Jeremiah 51 verses 6-7 and 45-47): *"**Come out of her, my people, that ye be not partakers of her sins**, and that ye receive not of her plagues. For her sins have reached unto heaven, and God hath remembered her iniquities."*

What does that mean? Leave USA? (Or leave Rome or Iraq?) No, not necessarily, although it could do at some point. We are to leave Babylon's ideologies and idolatry. We must leave the harlot Roman Catholic church of Revelation 17 and not take part in the ecumenical movement. Rather, we must share the Gospel with Catholics and pray for their salvation. Are some Roman Catholics truly saved followers of Jesus? Yes, but they are probably a very small minority and they are in a false system of religion that they need to come out of. It also means being very cautious as to where you get your sources of information from and what worldly institutions you engage with – remembering that the Jesuits have infiltrated and corrupted MOST of them. This extends to politics, news media, entertainment (music, movies, games, sport), learning institutions, food system, health system, etc. We should look to minimise and eliminate all forms of worldliness and increase our holiness and purity of heart for Jesus and following Him.

The latter verses of Romans 13 back this position up; that we must be awake and aware of the deception that's going on and shun the darkness of evil and walk in the light of Christ and His righteous commands.

"And that, knowing the time, that now it is high time to awake out of sleep: for now is our salvation nearer than when we believed. The night is far spent, the day is at hand: let us therefore cast off the works of darkness, and let us put on the armour of light." – Romans 13:11-12

At the beginning of this chapter we looked at Psalm 137. The last verse often disturbs and perplexes most people: *"Happy the one who takes and dashes Your little ones against the rock!"* – Psalm 137:9 (NKJV)

I believe this is not referring literally to babies but rather to the offspring of Babylon – the products and fruit of Babylon. Of course, our great King Jesus, the rider on the white horse will finally destroy Babylon. As His followers, we would do well and be blessed if we take the fruit of Babylon in our time and get rid of them from our lives. In the next chapters, we'll look at how we can effectively 'come out of Babylon' and reclaim our Church and personal authority and holiness in Christ and stand firm against the devil's schemes to contend for our faith – even as the elite agendas, to bring in Satan's Antichrist last days reign roll on ahead at a furious pace.

Prayer suggestion – Psalm 35.

Part 3: The Solution

CHAPTER ELEVEN

Reclaiming Rightful Church Authority

In the previous chapter, we have determined that what is going on in the name of a worldwide pandemic, is in fact a major step towards the one world government, one world cashless monetary system and one world religion, spoken about in Revelation. The ultimate goal is a spiritual one – to create a new 'Tower of Babel' so to speak and to destroy the true Church of Jesus Christ. When we see the bigger picture and where we are headed, John's words in Revelation 18:4 – 'Come out of her my people, lest you take part in her sins' takes on a significance and urgency that we could miss otherwise. **We need to get out of Babylon and get Babylon out of our Churches and lives.** We'll look at practical ways to do this in the remaining chapters of this book. There are five main topics we'll explore in this chapter: Five key Church authority errors in the advent of Covid 19, Church family communication, civil disobedience, creating our own 'Church Great Reset' and the underground Church.

Five Key Church Authority Errors in the Advent of Covid 19

Surveying the landscape of what's happened in Churches across the world (although not everywhere, but certainly in Northern America and UK) since the advent of Covid 19, we can observe five key Church errors. This is not meant to condemn, just make a sober appraisal of the situation and then look at what we can do about it moving forwards. Reverend Paul Dowling from Tandragee, Northern Ireland preached an excellent 17 minute sermonette, 'Covid 19 and Churches in UK',[388] on these errors, which I'd highly recommend listening to and I have reiterated and expanded upon his sentiments here.

1. The Sovereign God has been forgotten

Our Lord does not give us get out clauses for what he prescribes – namely gathering for Church worship. He is fully aware and sovereign over the coronavirus and by no means ignorant of it. Do we believe that? Have we trusted that He calls us to worship together at any and all times? Sadly not. In our actions, we have forgotten to consider Him. Let us remind ourselves that our Heavenly Father, our Lord Jesus and Holy Spirit have feelings - they are jealous for us, they are grieved by our idolatry and sidelining of them and will not sanction the neglect of their Holy Word. We cannot visibly see our triune God right now and we do not always feel the immediate force of their commands, like we may do with our governments. But do we believe and understand that they are every bit as real and to be taken into our considerations as the secular governments? Of course, this is a huge understatement – the two are not to be equated, but it would appear that many Christians do not even view our God as equal in consideration, much less supreme and high above all. Our God exercises great patience and grace with us, which we can take for granted

---

[388] Dowling, Paul. 'Covid19 and Churches in UK'. *SermonAudio*, 27 May 2020, https://www.sermonaudio.com/sermoninfo.asp?m=t&s=527201322131101. Accessed 5 May 2021.

in our folly. You may be tempted to refute this and give all sorts of rational, expedient and well-motived reasons for why we stopped gathering, but it does not change this stark reality and we should remember that we are easily motivated by comfort, ease, the world, our flesh, the devil and our hearts are liable to deceive us. So, we must look to God's Word to renew our thinking, where we see no provisions to change the command to worship as the LORD invites us to. Which brings us on to point two ...

2. Where is our regulative/normative principle now?

The regulative principle of worship states that the corporate worship of God is to be founded upon specific directions of Scripture – and not added to, mostly upheld by reformed and other conservative Protestant and Baptist denominations. The normative principle teaches that worship in the Church can also include elements that are not prohibited by Scripture – such as using instruments, announcing Church notices, tithes and offerings, and is mostly practiced by modern evangelical Churches. Neither approach has anything to do with levels of formality nor do they commit the Church to a 'cookie-cutter' style or liturgical sameness; there is more than ample room for variation. Rather, they are both concerned with **upholding unadulterated Scriptural directions as the basis of Church worship**: In the public worship of God, specific requirements are made, and we are not free to ignore them or change them to suit ourselves. The Second London Baptist Confession of 1689 states: *"The acceptable way of worshiping the true God, is instituted by himself, and so limited by his own revealed will, that he may not be worshiped according to the imagination and devices of men, nor the suggestions of Satan, under any visible representations, or any other way not prescribed in the Holy Scriptures (22.1)."*

Could it be that the safety rules under Covid are the 'suggestions of Satan'? We can see how seriously our LORD takes this in the incidents of the golden calf, Nadab and Abihu and the offering of 'strange fire' (Leviticus 10), His rejection of Saul's non-prescribed worship. The LORD said, *"to obey is better than sacrifice"* (1 Samuel 15:22) and Jesus' rejection of Pharisaic worship according to the 'tradition of the elders' (Matthew 15:1-14). These all clearly show a rejection of worship offered according to values and directions other than those specified in Scripture. We examined this in Chapters 3 and 5, but have to ask ourselves, again: Is the new 'Covid 19 prescribed worship', dictated by our secular governments, in line with Scripture and is it acceptable to our LORD? When we examine the specific Biblical directions around gathering as Church and fellowshipping with each other, preaching the Bible, singing as a congregation, baptism and the Lord's Supper, I think we have no choice but to answer, once again – 'No.' Which leads us to point three ...

3. Now We Obey Men Before God

Acts chapter 5 clearly tells us that when the commandments of men and the commandments of God are at odds, we are to always obey God. Under Covid, we have set a precedent of obeying man rather than God. This needs to be truly repented of. Even if at the beginning of Covid we obeyed the rules out of genuine trust and to maintain the Christian default posture of submission to the ruling authorities, belief that the rules were for our own good. Perhaps out of good-willed charity in the spirit of Matthew 5:41, we are now at a stage where all of those reasons are in question. (*"And if anyone forces you to go one mile, go with him two miles."*) At this stage, we can clearly see that the Church is being disproportionally disadvantaged compared to other sectors of society. After lockdowns, the re-openings of Churches have been largely limited to 'private prayer only', whilst supermarkets, gyms and restaurants have been in full flow.

4. We Have Treated Healthy People as Unclean Plague Bearers

Instead of quarantining the sick only, as the Bible teaches, we have treated everyone as if they are contaminated with a deadly disease, must be feared and kept away from us, which is not only a fallacy and gross misinterpretation of the situation but is anti-Biblical and anti-Christian in spirit. Isolation, distancing, masks, vaccines have been employed and promoted by our Churches, which have greatly harmed the body of Christ

– hindering worship, spiritual vigour, intimate fellowship, evangelism, administering the Lord's Supper, baptisms, weddings and loving our neighbour … And ironically 'loving our neighbour' has been cited as the very reason we have submitted to the authorities' mandates. Brother or sister, let us see this folly and deception for what it is. I have witnessed several situations where someone in need has entered a Church, looking for spiritual, emotional and practical help and has been ignored by Church folk. I have seen a spirit of fear and contempt come across people in situations like this and no doubt rationalisation that they are 'following the safety rules' and so should other people be. It has been very saddening to see. There is a refusal of many to fully acknowledge the harm done by these rules but if you were to sit for ten minutes and put yourself in the shoes of various different people in your Church family and ponder on the ramifications of all these rules, then we can quickly appreciate the awfulness of this situation, leading to point five …

5. We Have Short-Sightedly Neglected the Spiritual, Mental, Financial and Even Physical Health of People in Favour of Following Erroneous Covid 'Safety' Rules

Rev Dr Richard Turnbull, in his very good talk at the Christian Institute in November 2020, 'Failure of Spiritual Leadership: The Contemporary Church Response to Covid-19',[389] states that *"Policies which prioritise bare existence at the expense of those things that give quality, meaning and purpose to life are deeply, deeply troubling, These matters include the freedom to worship, to work and to maintain family relationships. None of this means we don't care for our neighbour … **The obsession with safety has increased the level of fear, anxiety and concern among congregations.**"*

---

[389] Turnball, Rev. Dr Richard. 'A Failure of Spiritual Leadership – the Contemporary Church Response to Covid-19'. *The Christian Institute,* 13 Nov. 2020, https://www.christian.org.uk/resource/a-failure-of-spiritual-leadership/. Accessed 5 May 2021.

We are only beginning to see the huge negative ramifications of the Covid rules, such as elevated suicide rates, businesses and livelihoods destroyed and people becoming severely ill from isolation and staying indoors too much. Here are some very real examples that I've either seen or heard of from ministers and friends …

Take 83-year old Anna, a widow who did not see anyone in person in her home or in Church for months during the first lockdown. She has no access to the live streaming technology, nor the capabilities or desire to engage with a computer screen. She wants to meet with her Church but cannot as the people who used to take her are 'shielding'. She did manage to go to Church once during a period of re-opening but not being able to get close to people or sing or see people smile because of faces being covered – it was just horrible. She feels alone, sad, neglected, confused, spiritually flat, fearful and her physical health has declined.

Or 22-year-old James, a student who's away from his family at university. In-person lectures have ceased and relationships with his house mates have grown very fractious. He suffers with asthma and wearing a mask makes him feel claustrophobic and panicky at times but he doesn't have the emotional strength to refuse to wear one. Church fellowship and Sunday services were a real anchor and high-point in his week and spiritual life and he now feels adrift – online services leave him cold. On top of that, he was forced to 'self-isolate' for two weeks and is struggling with porn addiction, over-eating and dark thoughts of depression and even suicide at times.

Or 71-year-old Duncan, whose wife Gill died of breast cancer during lockdown. The death certificate says 'Covid' which angers him as this is untrue. He could not see her in hospital and is heartbroken that Gill was left to die without Church family around her. He was not able to give his wife a proper funeral and emotional support has been very limited and stifled in the weeks since her passing. He feels not only heartbroken but totally let down and cannot believe the situation in the Church has become like this.

Or 85-year-old Barbara, who's in a residential home and is forced to stay in her room and not see anyone. Her Minister who usually visits to share the Lord's Supper is not able to since the home's restrictions and security is so tight; no visitors have been allowed for over nine months. She has been heard by the staff crying 'help me' several times but her cries are largely ignored.

Or 35-year-old Adam, who would say he's 'spiritual but not religious'. Since the first few months of Covid, he's been questioning his spirituality and 'the meaning of life' and would like to attend Church and speak to a Minister. Unfortunately, all the Churches are closed. This doesn't seem right to him. He doesn't know much about Church life, but aren't they supposed to be there to help people?

6. A Non-Gathered, Non-Functioning Church is Not Church

A reminder of what Scripture prescribes for Church worship ... We are commanded to:

- Gather in His name and do not neglect meeting together (therefore making no provision for universal isolation and lockdowns).
- Greet one another with a holy kiss and have good fellowship with each other (therefore not entertaining social distancing and masks).
- Partake in the Lord's Supper (therefore rejecting a 'bread only' version).
- Baptise.
- To sing to the LORD (therefore rejecting mandates to stop congregational singing and to play a music video only, or be sung to by a small music group).

If we have not heeded these Scriptural commands and rejected the secular Covid ones, we are teetering on the edge of ceasing to be Church, if not already. We may be doing all sorts of things to 'keep Church afloat' – conducting high tech online services, Zoom prayer meetings and Bible studies, calling Church family members to see if they're ok. We could be dropping off food parcels and leaving them outside homes, writing Church newsletters, recording music videos. These are all seemingly good things and can be helpful to people and can ease our consciences about the shutting of Churches. The alarming reality is that they are all elaborate ways of avoiding, obeying and skirting around the LORD's clear commands. I admit, I have been to some of the best group intercessory prayer sessions I've ever experienced via the Zoom platform, which I would not have been able to attend in person due to locational distance; but I do not see this as 'Church'. In essence, this is self-justification, not too dissimilar to that of a couple who are not married but living together: *"We've both been married before and not sure we are ready to commit fully to marriage again yet, we feel God brought us together, we feel spiritually alive together, our children get on really well, we can't afford to get married just yet, God is gracious and loving ... "* All sounds very plausible but is in stark disobedience to what our LORD commands around relationships. Of course, we may not always be able to do 'structured Church' and indeed in many countries where Christians are heavily persecuted, there are no structured Churches or Church buildings at all. In these cases, and where we're likely headed as well, the body of Christ gathers in small house fellowships, prayer groups and in doing community together, like in the book of Acts. This is gathered Church and is where the body flourishes – not in non-gathered online meetings. That's the distinction. Some Churches have started doing this since Covid.

The Remedy for Our Errors

We are not to simply think about obeying, or be trying to obey, or considering deeply when we might obey, or planning to obey soon, or praying about obeying, or obeying as far as we can given the government rules, or adapting how we obey given the situation. No, we are to simply OBEY. **Just because we are putting in a lot of time, effort and prayer into our activities, we should not mistake disobedience for true obe-**

dience. Similarly, we are told to 'put on the LORD Jesus Christ' (Romans 13:14), not simply look at him in wonder; we are to be *followers* of Jesus – doing what He tells us, having counted the cost upfront; not mere admirers. I am belabouring this point because we are all sinners and we are all, at times, bent on justifying our own disobedient and sinful actions and this can lead to a seared conscience. Let's repent, recalibrate our holiness and walk in obedience – enjoying the complete freedom and peace of mind that comes with it. Do not worry about the possible consequences, that's the LORD's business. We'll look more at that later.

Church Family Communication

One of the big things I've observed since Covid 19 was first announced is a major muting of the Church. Yes, we have discussed hand sanitisers, locking down the Church, live streaming and the like – the mandates that secular authorities have instituted (and as we've seen by now, are not in fact there for our good, but are there for harm). We've prayed for the streaming technology, we've prayed for things like 'good fellowship', 'strong faith' but these are all compliant and vague enough to not cause any kind of offence, not sticking our necks out and avoiding the elephant in the room: Mass vaccination and implications for the Church, possible civil disobedience, the fact that we're not baptising, singing, observing the Lord's Supper in its entirety, not laying hands, not greeting with a holy kiss, etc. I would estimate that it would be a minority of Churches who have had honest, robust, challenging and multi-viewpoint conversations either within the congregation, or the leadership team, to assess whether or not we should be implementing what the authorities tell us and side-lining what our LORD tells us. Neither are we reassessing this at regular junctures. For example, most Churches deemed that we should lockdown back in March 2020, with very little discussion and a fairly straightforward acceptance of it since it was 'only for a few weeks' and the 'governments were doing it for good'. But now, when lockdowns have happened repeatedly and for long periods, and we have the data and hindsight to know that there is confusion, bungling, heavy handedness, uncertainty, ineffectiveness, disproportionate negative bias towards Churches, danger to the spiritual vigour of the Church and nanny-statism in their institution, many still don't seem to question whether we should defy the mandates or not. Masks were brought in to 'keep everyone safe', but they've been proven to be a nonsense, and now Christians are still sat in Churches muzzled, with compromised fellowship, steamy glasses, itchy faces and breathing difficulties, not singing … for what exactly?

The first step in effectively reclaiming our Church authority and the freedom we have in Christ to worship Him in song, evangelise, fellowship, partake in the Lord's Supper, etc. is to pray for boldness and to SPEAK to each other, inviting viewpoints advocating civil disobedience, as well as compliance. We need to have honest discussions about the details of what's going on and our response – as a whole Church, or at the very least the leadership team – in love, truth and humility. I have spoken to several Church leaders who are doing this and their Churches are spiritually flourishing in this time.

At the moment, we are like a married couple that have been together for years and have major underlying problems with intimacy and meaningful communication. There are so many things that are unspoken and neither one wants to bring any of it up for fear of upsetting the applecart and opening a can of worms that would mean vulnerability, courage, and difficult action needing to take place in order to heal the years of hurt, resentment and deadness that has set in, which can often happen in relationships. It's just easier and more comfortable to say nothing, even though the relationship has been reduced to an unfulfilling transactional one without the satisfaction and aliveness of real intimacy and devoid of the power of Christ. Yes, there is always the risk that opening up such discussions could result in permanent breakdown of the relationship (and in the Church context could mean congregation members leaving the Church – we'll look at this more in the next chapter), but the relationship has become one only in name anyhow, so we have to ask how much would actually be lost? We might be in a Church that was spiritually and emotionally alive before Covid but by now, whether you realise the full extent of it or not, there are huge spiritual dangers of where we've got to, potential for division and most people are either blind to what's really going on in our world situation, refusing to see it, or afraid to talk about it. None of it is good and all of it needs to be spoken about. Yes, it's a risk, but saying nothing is a much bigger risk. The world situation and where it's going is a real one and we cannot afford to ignore it, bury our heads in the sand and piously say, 'just give me Jesus'. Our Jesus loves truth and integrity and hates evil. He calls us to root our faith and obedient actions in the here and now – 'in the field', including world politics, not just in theory and theological study. If we fail to have honest conversations about what's going on (which will include naming names of people and situations to watch out for, as we see many times in Paul's letters and as I have done in this book), the current state of play could quite easily lead to Jesus being stood outside our Church walls saying, *"Behold, I stand at the door, and knock: if any man hear my voice, and open the door, I will come in to him, and will sup with him, and he with me."* – Revelation 3:20

We are not Gnostics and we're not antinomians, gliding through a disobedient and superficial Church life on Jesus' grace and thinking that as long as we're talking about how much we love Him, we're all good and can detach ourselves from getting involved in the physical reality and gritty mire of applying His Word in difficult circumstances, such and the one we find ourselves in presently. I can hear the rebuttals now: *"We just want to preach Christ in our Church. Discussions or, God forbid, preaching about Covid and politics will only seek to detract from the Gospel and divide the body of Christ."* This sounds reasonable and rational. But friend, the Church is already divided. You may not be seeing the full fruit of that division yet but that's largely due to the enforced separation of our congregations. If you've seen a falling away of some members in recent months,[390] that in itself is an indication of division. Further, there is a sin in keeping silent on matters of evil when we are called to expose and resist it. I have witnessed and heard stories of lots of subtle and not-so-subtle divisions, in the course of my research. Story upon story of irritations, fractured relationships, arguments and hurts over various Covid-related things. This time requires strong leadership to unite in honesty and equip for what's ahead.

"While the errors of perfectionism have been and always will be a threat to true Christian religion, the opposite error of practical antinomianism, whereby preachers fail to exhort their people to obey God with a pure heart, is equally pernicious because such a view undermines the grace of God in saving sinners from the power of sin." – Mark Jones, 'Antinomianism: Reformed Theology's Unwelcome Guest?'[391]

We need frequent, open, courageous and humble conversations where we resolve not to take offence and keep loving each other and take a stance as a Church on the matters at hand. We must also understand that we will inevitably lose Church members by doing this, and to a degree this will be a necessary 'trimming of the wick' and calling out of a faithful remnant. We'll explore this more.

The Church's Reasonable Response – Time is Up

Under Covid, the Church has lost a number of its key freedoms. The government has taken them from us without following due process. They have not been written into law, they have not been worked out in the courts or through parliament and congress. Instead, we have given our authorities (often medical officers) almost unilateral authority to take whatever they deem necessary. That said, there have been some key

---

[390] 'One in Three Practicing Christians Has Stopped Attending Church During COVID-19'. *Barna Group*, 8 July 2020, https://www.barna.com/research/new-sunday-morning-part-2/. Accessed 5 May 2021.

[391] Jones, Mark. Antinomianism: Reformed Theology's Unwelcome Guest? 1st ed. P&R Pub, 2013.

Christian contests of these things that have shown that the governments are not willing to stop further encroaches on Church life. At this stage, various Christian leaders have done what is reasonably practicable to petition governments not to lockdown Churches again, explaining their reasoning for the necessity of our buildings to remain open and functioning.

In September 2020, in an open letter written by five pastors from across the UK and signed by over 600, Church leaders called on the UK governments to 'refrain from socially damaging restrictions' and 'not to close Churches again'.[392] The Church leaders stated that:

"The public worship of the Christian Church is particularly essential for our nation's wellbeing. As we live in the shadow of a virus we are unable to control, people urgently need the opportunity to hear and experience the good news and hope of Jesus Christ, who holds our lives in his hands ... We have been and will remain, very careful to apply rigorous hygiene, social distancing and appropriate risk assessment in our Churches. As a result, Church worship presents a hugely lesser risk of transmission than pubs, restaurants, gyms, offices and schools; and it is more important than them all. We therefore wish to state categorically that we must not be asked to suspend Christian worship again. For us to do so would cause serious damage to our congregations, our service of the nation, and our duty as Christian ministers."

Leaders of Churches in England and Wales joined together in challenging the governments over the forced Church closures in the last months of 2020. The October 2020 Letter from Welsh Church Leaders to the Welsh Assembly,[393] cites various protections in law (namely Article 9 of the ECHR and s.13 of the Human Rights Act 1998) for Church worship and

---

[392] 'Over 600 UK Church Leaders Urge the Government Not to Close Churches Again'. *Christian Concern*, 24 Sept. 2020, https://christianconcern.com/comment/over-600-uk-Church-leaders-urge-the-government-not-to-close-Churches-again/.

[393] 'Letter from Welsh Church Leaders to the Welsh Assembly'. *Christian Concern, 26 Oct. 2020.* https://christianconcern.com/wp-content/uploads/2018/10/CC-Resource-Misc-Judicial-Review-Wales-Firebreak-Church-Pre-Action-Letter-201026-1.pdf. Accessed 5 May 2021.

makes some very good and poignant points on our need and right to self-govern, in accordance with God:

"20. While the short-term practical difference between State regulation and Church self-regulation may be limited in present circumstances, the principle of Church autonomy is extremely important in the broader constitutional context and must be protected for the benefit of present and future generations.

Rationale behind the principle

21. The principle identified above is important for the simple reason that a believer's worldview is radically different from a non-believer's worldview. It may seem natural for a temporal authority, well-meaning and intending no disrespect to religion, to see a Church service as simply an example of a 'public event' which attracts a peculiar kind of people interested in it – roughly similar to entertainment. In that worldview, Church services are important for welfare of those who need them, but obviously less important than things like steady food supplies and protection of health.

22. By contrast, in a believer's worldview, Church services are part of our means for achieving eternal salvation of the soul, which is infinitely more important than even a survival of the body. The Bible and centuries of tradition oblige Christians to gather weekly for worship and witness around the Word of God and sacraments; we need one another to flourish in our service to Christ (Ex. 20: 9-11; 1 Cor. 16: 1-2; Heb. 10:24-25; Acts 2:42, 20:7). Neither confessional Christian faith nor the Church as an institution can faithfully exist without a Lord's Day gathering. The Church has adhered to that obligation through long periods of persecution, where fulfilling it meant a risk of death at the hands of temporal authorities. The Church does not exist by permission of the State, for its establishment and rule is found in Jesus Christ himself.

23. The restrictions imposed on the Church activity principally affect the believers. Hence it is important that the decisions about them are taken by believers – not by people who, in their minds and/or as a matter of professional duty, live in a wholly different world. If Churches are to be closed, that must not be done by people who may well have never been to a Church in their lives, or at least, have little understanding of the role, functioning, and ministries of the Church."

Various statements were also given by individual pastors, saying such things as: *"I can confirm that as a Church the main effect of the pandemic we are seeing, is on families that are struggling with the Church not open-ing, due to the lack of consistent input into whole family. As a Church we are looking after 200+ families weekly. Sadly, we are seeing marriage break ups, parenting issues, loneliness and suicides of fathers. Worship and gathering together is their lifeline."* – Pastor, Welsh Church

However, these petitions largely fell on deaf governmental ears and from November 5th, a month-long national lockdown was enforced across England and, once again, most Churches closed and then again in January 2021 for further months. There have been many similar situations across the world where Church leaders have written to and petitioned govern-ments and local councils around the Covid mandates, but have been dis-regarded. We have seen such examples in California,[394] Canada[395] and across the USA with the 'Peaceably Gather'[396] petition. In January 2021, English and Welsh Church leaders withdrew their pursuit of a judicial re-view, after restrictions on public worship were lifted in England and Wales following sustained political, legal and media pressure. However, this was done only after national outrage to a legal online Church service

---

[394] 'PETITION: Support Pastors Fighting against Oppressive State Mandates'. *LifeSite Petitions*, https://lifepetitions.com/petition/petition-support-pastors-fighting-against-oppressive-state-mandates. Accessed 5 May 2021.

[395] Wakerell-Cruz, Roberto. 'Canadian Petition to Declare Church an Essential Service Gains Traction as Lockdowns Continue'. *The Post Millennial*, 8 June 2020, https://thepostmillennial.com/Church-is-essential-petition-started.

[396] *Peaceably Gather*, https://peaceablygather.com. Accessed 5 May 2021.

wrongly being shut down by police[397] and the pastor of the Church being prosecuted on his doorstep. Mourners at a funeral service were also prevented from saying the Lord's Prayer together.[398] Again, we have done what is reasonably practicable to explain to our secular authorities the reason why Churches should be able to both stay open and self-govern, why we are an 'essential service' (to use their worldly terms) and why we are a totally different entity to all other necessitous and leisure organisations within society. But we have not been heeded in this and this should come as no surprise. **A secular authority that disadvantages Churches because it does not see or concede the need for the things of God, will unlikely rescind their decisions because of the things of God.** Which leads us to only one Biblical course of action: Civil Disobedience.

Necessary Civil Disobedience

When the commands of civil authorities are at odds with the commands of God, Scripture is clear – we must obey God and that means we disobey the civil authorities. It's as simple and as difficult as that. **We need to contend for the faith!** It has been said that if you give up freedom for security, you get neither and we'd do well to remember that the freedoms we enjoy as Church today were not gained through passivity. No, many a predecessor of ours fought (again, non-sinfully) and died to uphold Biblical principles and freedoms in the face of despotic rulers. The new culture of fear, and not a holy fear of God, within our Churches, needs to be stopped in its tracks before it gets a stranglehold on us. There are 365 'fear not' verses in the Bible; one for each day. It is a sin to be in fear.

---

[397] 'Police Storm Church Broadcast in Milton Keynes over "Loud Music"'. *BBC News*, 29 Nov. 2020, https://www.bbc.com/news/uk-england-beds-bucks-herts-55122859.

[398] Nikolic, Isabella. 'Council BANS Mourners' Lord's Prayer as "chanting" Breaks Covid Rules'. *Mail Online*, 13 Oct. 2020, https://www.dailymail.co.uk/news/article-8833157/Mourners-BANNED-reciting-Lords-Prayer-workers-South-Wales-crematorium.html.

We are not to indulge it, we are to rebuke it, repent of it and ask the LORD for trust, faith, courage, wisdom, strength and discipline to overcome it.

Freedom to worship is not an automatic right, *it's a skill that's activated by prayerful courage and practice.* We are called to freedom, not a spirit of fear and not a yoke of slavery – as Galatians 5:1 tells us. What's more, freedom to worship and be faithful is possible whether granted by our governments or not. The accounts of the martyrs show this – they exercised their God-given right and command to worship and faithfully obey the LORD, irrespective of worldly opposition. They paid the worldly consequences of torture and death, but gained the heavenly rewards of an eternal crown of glory from our LORD. Hallelujah! The moment we see that the civil authorities' commands are at odds with God's, we have to take an immediate stand, whatever way we do it. Later is too late – we are not to tarry in our obedience or there will be too much compromised, too many consciences seared, too many casualties within the Church, too many truths lost and too much ground taken by the enemy. Hebrews 3:15 warns us *"As it is said, "Today, if you hear his voice, do not harden your hearts as in the rebellion.""* In terms of the Church needing to stand in truth and against evil, we are commanded to worship 'in spirit and truth'. Truth is vitally important. I would go so far as to say that where truth has gone from the midst of our fellowship, there is no fellowship.

In the Encyclopaedia of Biblical and Christian Ethics, civil disobedience is defined as, *"... a conscious demonstration of disloyalty toward some enactment, statute, or ordinance promulgated by a body that has power to make legally binding regulations ... it describes defiance of promulgations enacted by the state. Through disobedience of particular ordinances it poses a direct challenge to the authority of the promulgating body."* When we civilly disobey, there should be some likelihood of achieving a successful end – i.e., normative Church worship and freedom to resume, and we should be willing to accept any penalty for law-breaking. Also, while it may be necessary to disobey individual commands of a government, we are not thereby free to rebel against that government – our general attitude should still be one of submission. This attitude demonstrates respect for the principle of the rule of law and distinguishes the action from insurrection or anarchy.

So How Do We Do Civil Disobedience Well?

Civil disobedience as exercised by the Church is peaceful and non-violent (usually, but not always, as we can observe in Scripture), dignified, respectful and non-sinful. We would never seek to overcome sin with sin; we are generally not looking to start a revolution or a violent protest. Keep in mind though that what the world deems unlawful does not necessarily mean it's sinful and vice versa. The example of Shadrach, Meshach, and Abednego in the book of Daniel is to be our model here. When hauled up in front of King Nebuchadnezzar and asked why they would not worship his golden statue that he set up on the plain of Dura, they answered: *""O Nebuchadnezzar, we have no need to answer you in this matter. If that is the case, our God whom we serve is able to deliver us from the burning fiery furnace, and He will deliver us from your hand, O king. But if not, let it be known to you, O king, that we do not serve your gods, nor will we worship the gold image which you have set up.""* – Daniel 3:16-18 (NKJV)

Notice a few things about their response: Their freedom from seeking/ having to explain their reasoning to him – since they have already cleared it with the LORD and resolved upfront. Their faith in God's deliverance. Their respectful attitude – 'O king'. Their faith and obedience were not based on outcome, it was there whether the LORD delivered them or not – 'But if not...'. Their clarity and courage in stating what they would not compromise on – 'we do not serve your gods, nor will we worship the gold image which you have set up'. We can learn so much from this great example.

There are two main options for en-masse Church civil disobedience: Let's call them 'The MacArthur Way' and the 'The Quiet Way' ...

The MacArthur Way

As you probably know, John MacArthur, the well-known and long-standing octogenarian pastor of Grace Community Church (GCC) in Los Angeles, California, has been very bold and outspoken in his stance that 'we must obey God rather than man' and has preached on this[399] since the get-go of the pandemic. He has outright rejected all of the Covid mandates, stating that they're at odds with what God commands and have been proven to be both blatant lies and ineffectual. He's even asserted that 'there is no pandemic'. This man has his critical thinking head screwed on and the courage to back up his convictions! He kept his Church open throughout lockdowns and rejected social distancing, masks and non-singing. Since Covid, at times his attending congregation has reportedly swelled by several thousand up to 8,000 people; a fair few more than the 100 people allowed under California law at the time. MacArthur has stated: *"We know there are reasons for this [lockdown] that have nothing to do with the virus. There's another virus loose in the world and it's the virus of deception. And the one who is behind the virus of deception is the arch-deceiver Satan himself. And it's not a surprise to me that in the midst of all this deception the great effort that is going on is to shut down Churches that preach the gospel ... It does not surprise me that they want to shut down those who preach the Gospel because the architects of this level of deception are not a part of the Kingdom of Heaven; they're a part of the kingdom of darkness."*

Grace Community Church's[400] elders wrote in a statement first posted on the Church's website on July 24, stating: *"Although we in America may be unaccustomed to government intrusion into the Church of our Lord Jesus Christ, this is by no means the first time in Church history that Christians have had to deal with government overreach or hostile rulers, persecution of the Church by government authorities has been the norm,*

---

[399] 'We Must Obey God Rather Than Men'. *YouTube*, https://www.youtube.com/watch?v=t2ixUp5KKn8. Accessed 5 May 2021.

[400] *Grace Church*, https://www.graceChurch.org/news/posts/2039. Accessed 5 May 2021.

not the exception, throughout Church history ... We must recognize that the Lord may be using these pressures as means of purging to reveal the true Church. Succumbing to governmental overreach may cause Churches to remain closed indefinitely. How can the true Church of Jesus Christ distinguish herself in such a hostile climate? There is only one way: bold allegiance to the Lord Jesus Christ."

Grace Community Church opened its doors for unrestricted worship in July 2020 (after a brief period of shutting, when it deemed there might be a genuine pandemic threat) and L.A. county sent MacArthur a 'cease-and-desist' letter, noting that violating its health orders is a crime punishable by a fine of up to $1,000 and imprisonment of up to 90 days, for each day the laws are violated. The county and Grace Church went back and forth for months on this in contention with each other and it was eventually ruled in GCC's favour. At time of writing, the Church is open, unrestricted and three services and a full mid-week program are in operation, with MacArthur preaching and speaking into this situation as it relates to the Bible at regular intervals. There will no doubt be continued struggles with the authorities at GCC and maybe intense persecution to come, who knows. But what is evident is that John MacArthur has stated that he does not fear going to prison for exercising his faith and that it would be an honour. Much of his Church, and people in agreement on his stance who have joined the Church in the past year, have followed his lead – weighing the consequences upfront.

Other bold examples of 'The MacArthur Way', include the Liberty Coalition Canada,[401] which issued a Declaration called 'The Church Must Gather'. It states: *"Over the course of the pandemic, there has been much confusion in the Church about gathering together for worship. Some Churches continue to gather in-person. Other Churches have been 're-imagining themselves'. Many pastors have slipped into using the word 'together' in reference to pre-recorded videos or virtual meetings. Still*

---

[401] 'The Church Must Gather'. *Liberty Coalition*, https://www.libertycoalitioncanada.com/the-church-must-gather. Accessed 5 May 2021.

others are advocating that gathering in-person is not 'essential'. As the government begins to use our confused behavior against us, the time for clarity is now. Simply put, public worship is a non-negotiable principle. Beyond science, and every natural reason we can give, we ultimately bow the knee and pledge our lives to King Jesus who is the Head of the Church and our only Sovereign. We the undersigned, believe that Churches or believers must continue to gather in person for public worship with or without the permission of the civil authorities. " The Declaration has thousands of signatories at this point, as does The Niagara Declaration on the liberty of Church from the state,[402] and various Churches in Canada have taken the staunch stance to remain open – and have faced the consequences squarely. Most notably at this point, Pastor James Coates of Grace Life Church in Alberta, Canada has been imprisoned for keeping his Church open at unrestricted capacity (the Covid mandates stated a 15% cap) and Pastor Stephen Richardson of Faith Presbyterian Church in Ontario, Canada who has been issued with over 100,000 CAD in fines for remaining open during lockdowns. Possibly most shockingly, Trinity Bible Chapel in Waterloo, Ontario under Pastor Jacob Reaume has been issued with *40 million dollars of fines*, simply for remaining open.

The MacArthur way takes a strong man in leadership who is able to rally his congregation to also make a bold stand, or at least be prepared to take the consequences singlehandedly, head on and probably very publicly. That said, Paul reminds us well that: *"And He [the LORD] said to me, "My grace is sufficient for you, for My strength is made perfect in weakness." Therefore most gladly I will rather boast in my infirmities, that the power of Christ may rest upon me."* – 2 Corinthians 12:9

So actually, this stand actually just takes great faith, which comes from the LORD. Why not ask Him for this kind of faith?

---

[402] 'The Niagara 2020 Declaration'. *Niagara Declaration*, https://www.niagaradeclaration.ca. Accessed 5 May 2021.

The Quiet Way

The second option for Church civil disobedience can be called the 'The Quiet Way'. This is much more discreet and subtle. Rather than openly and, in some cases, loudly proclaiming and making it known that your Church is open as usual and you have shunned the civil regulations in respect to Covid, it is a peaceful, internal dissent that employs underground Church tactics.

Again, this is where internal Church conversations are so important because it could well mean meeting in secret, meeting in homes, splitting the Church into 'cell groups', meeting at unusual and differing times, locking the doors once services are in operation, etc. I know of several pastor friends who have employed this approach and have continued to meet as a Church all through the lockdown; sharing the Lord's Supper each week, singing and shunning social distancing. This requires shrewdness, wisdom, trust between people and to be 'wise as serpents and gentle as doves'. It also requires faith and courage. We'll explore more on the underground Church at the end of this chapter.

One friend wrote to me: *"We need to continue to be the Body of Christ gathering together to worship Him, break bread and minister to each other in psalms hymns & spiritual songs. We disobey God at our peril. Look at what happens when we honour God – Paul and Silas singing in prison, and the disciples refusing to obey the authorities when told not to preach any more in the name of Jesus, and Jesus making Himself known at Emmaus in the breaking of bread. Hallelujah!"*

It should be noted that whether we choose to take 'The MacArthur Way' or 'The Quiet Way' in our civil disobedience, we may be called to do both. For example, if we go with The Quiet Way and the authorities discover what we're doing and it causes public attention and retribution, we will then be required to take an open public stand – The MacArthur Way.

'Church Great Reset'

Whilst the World Economic Forum has been hatching its plans at Davos for an economic 'Great Reset', Christians are in need of our own 'Church Great Reset'. Our Church life as we know it has changed drastically since Covid and we will not be going back to how it was. There are Christians out there who are still harbouring notions of it all getting back to normal soon enough but it's becoming quite embarrassing and unsettling to see such naivety within the body of Christ.

In my estimation, our Church Great Reset needs to consist of seven key actions. We need to:

#1 Increase prayer – we need to hold more prayer meetings than we are maybe used to doing. We also need to increase our repentance and fasting. My friend in Canada holds daily prayer meetings each morning and the LORD has blessed his Church with favour and boldness in this time.

#2 Increase Church family communication – as mentioned above, this time necessitates that we communicate often, honestly, clearly and humbly – about these issues at hand and decisions to be made and letting the relevant people know how, what, when and why you are doing things to function as a civilly disobedient Church. This will require strong and bold leadership. This is none of the authorities' business; it's family business only.

#3 Purge the profane and plead the Blood of Jesus – there is much that has crept into our Churches that should not be there under Covid. Specifically; social distancing rules and signs, test and trace protocols, ban on singing, ticketing of services, mandatory masks, mandatory vaccines (not in place at the time of writing this but well may be at the time you're reading this). Now is the time to reset these things – get rid of those 'suggestions of Satan' that should not be in operation in the house of God and reinstate those holy things that have been lost – greeting each other with a holy kiss, fellowship meals, laying on of hands, baptisms, etc. Also, as we've looked at in previous chapters, where Churches are registered are Tax Exempt 501(c)(3) Corporations (or their equivalence in other countries), they should look to dissolve this State-Church bondage. Lamentations 1:10 (NKJV) seems pertinent here: *"The adversary has spread his hand Over all her pleasant things; For she has seen the nations enter her sanctuary, Those whom You commanded Not to enter Your assembly."*

We should seek to revert to Church normality – i.e., either the Scriptural normative or regulative principle – as much as possible, exercising compassion and common sense. If people want to wear masks and sanitise, that's fine but it should be optional and not particularly encouraged. Sick people should quarantine if necessary. Also, as well as purging the profane, we must plead the Blood of Jesus in every aspect of our Church life and physical worship. Saint, do not neglect this, it is the means of overcoming our accuser – there is much power in the blood, as the old hymn states.

"Then I heard a loud voice saying in heaven, "Now salvation, and strength, and the kingdom of our God, and the power of His Christ have come, for the accuser of our brethren, who accused them before our God day and night, has been cast down. And they overcame him by the blood of the Lamb and by the word of their testimony, and they did not love their lives to the death. Therefore rejoice, O heavens, and you who dwell in them! Woe to the inhabitants of the earth and the sea! For the devil has come down to you, having great wrath, because he knows that he has a short time."" – Revelation 12:10-12

#4 Seek out your watchmen – great discernment is needed in the Church at this time. There are people within our congregations who are able to distinguish the spirits (1 Corinthians 12:10) and have been appointed as 'Kingdom watchmen'.

"Again the word of the Lord came to me, saying, "Son of man, speak to the children of your people, and say to them: 'When I bring the sword upon a land, and the people of the land take a man from their territory and make him their watchman, when he sees the sword coming upon the land, if he blows the trumpet and warns the people, then whoever hears the sound of the trumpet and does not take warning, if the sword comes and takes him away, his blood shall be on his own head. He heard the sound of the trumpet, but did not take warning; his blood shall be upon himself. But he who takes warning will save his life. But if the watchman sees the sword coming and does not blow the trumpet, and the people are not warned, and the sword comes and takes any person from among them, he is taken away in his iniquity; but his blood I will require at the watchman's hand.' "So you, son of man: I have made you a watchman for the house of Israel; therefore you shall hear a word from My mouth and warn them for Me. When I say to the wicked, 'O wicked man, you shall surely die!' and you do not speak to warn the wicked from his way, that wicked man shall die in his iniquity; but his blood I will require at your hand. Nevertheless if you warn the wicked to turn from his way, and he does not turn from his way, he shall die in his iniquity; but you have delivered your soul." – Ezekiel 33:1-9 (NKJV)

We'd do well to seek out such people and humbly enquire as to what they discern, for the edification, wisdom and safety of the Church. Charles Spurgeon wisely said: *"Discernment is not a matter of simply telling the difference between right and wrong; rather it is telling the difference between right and almost right."* On a natural level, Carroll Quigley, author of one of the most insightful books on world history ever written, 'Tragedy and Hope', stated, *"To know is not too demanding: it merely requires memory and time. But to understand is quite a different matter: it requires intellectual ability and training, a self-conscious awareness of what one is doing, experience in techniques of analysis and synthesis, and above all, perspective."*

#5 Educate – we need to educate ourselves as Church congregations. Why not arrange weekly/bi-weekly get togethers to watch relevant films, documentaries and to share insights. I would highly recommend reading, maybe as a Church, 'Live Not By Lies: A Manual for Christian Dissidents' by Rod Dreher (2020) and 'Church of Cowards' by Matt Walsh (2020) and watching three of Leonard Ulrich's comprehensive documentaries that I've mentioned before (all currently available on YouTube), to give a whistle stop lowdown on the deception going on in the world, which over-arches the Covid landscape:
NWO: Secret Societies and Biblical Prophecy Vol. 1[403]
NWO Volume Two: The Illusion of Money[404]
Christians and Conspiracies[405]

Also, why not prayerfully share this book and invite group discussions. Dr Josef Tson, evangelist and former president of the Romanian Missionary Society, has some great videos on overcoming fear and how to prepare your family for persecution.[406] The book and film 'The Insanity of God' will really open your eyes to what Christian persecution means and how our LORD is faithful to His Church under great trial. Finally, Doug Wilson's frequent podcasts, books and blogs at Canon Press and his Blog and Mablog YouTube channel[407] speak incisively into the current situation, with wit and wisdom.

#6 Preach to the times – if you're a Church leader, or house group leader, prayerfully ask the LORD what He is wanting you to preach on in

---

[403] 'NWO: Secret Societies and Biblical Prophecy Vol. 1'. *YouTube*, https://www.youtube.com/watch?v=jYZksdzVxic. Accessed 5 May 2021.

[404] 'NWO Volume Two: The Illusion of Money'. *YouTube*, https://www.youtube.com/watch?v=HH1qQ9YXMYg. Accessed 5 May 2021.

[405] 'Christians and Conspiracies'. *YouTube*, https://www.youtube.com/watch?v=7Vbv3A2HK-4. Accessed 5 May 2021.

[406] 'Dr Josef Tson'. *Embassy Media*, https://embassymedia.com/speaker/dr-josef-tson. Accessed 5 May 2021.

[407] 'Blog & Mablog'. *YouTube*, https://www.youtube.com/channel/UCEeDTCe9GnbRPbUf-NwoqEYQ/featured. Accessed 5 May 2021.

these times and resolve not to avoid or skirt around hard issues and the details of what's going in in the world. Whilst we are not to turn our pulpits into political platforms by any means, neither are we to avoid all discussion of the kind of issues raised in this book … and nor can we be let off the hook by regurgitating conventional political lines or merely lamenting the current Covid situation and frustrations.

Jesus preached right into current affairs of His day, the real issues; the issues that much of the crowds did not see or were not wanting to see and what's more, he provoked the religious leaders who were preaching non-sense (have you read Luke 6 recently?). He did this to bring truth and insight into situations and to warn and equip the Church. He did it out of love. If we fail to preach the whole counsel of God and in particular these pertinent issues, we could be in danger of the sin of omission – the sin of keeping silent on an issue that the Church needs exhortation on. Do not be afraid to lovingly warn, train and rebuke, as necessary. As an example, are we preaching on Romans 13 at this time? Babylon? Prophecy? The book of Revelation portrays the committed opposition of the Church to State authority (Revelation 11:19-14:20) – are we digging into these meatier topics? Hebrews 5:14 (NKJV) reminds us that the mature Christian needs solid food: *"But solid food belongs to those who are of full age, that is, those who by reason of use have their senses exercised to discern both good and evil."* Thus far, I have had to seek sermons online from pastors overseas to hear preaching on subjection to authorities, end times signs, the implications of Covid on the Church, Babylon, etc. Psalm 94:16 poses and emphasises a question to us, which may be useful for preachers in considering the content for sermons: *"Who will rise up for me against the evildoers? or who will stand up for me against the workers of iniquity?"*

#7 Equip – we need to prepare and equip ourselves for what's ahead as a local Church. It would be helpful to be reading books on persecution, the underground Church and even martyrdom. We should think about and discuss resolving to reject the experimental injection (or at least rejecting any 'no vaccine, no Church' mandates). We should resolve to know that

God goes ahead of us and fights our battles and He is faithful and true and can deliver His people from every trial and enemy. Pray fervently for protection and guidance and for our Church leaders, who have such a lot on their shoulders. Encourage your leaders and work with them.

Underground Church

In many ways, we are in exciting times. This is an opportunity to re-evaluate what it means to be 'Church', to do a kind of existential inventory and assessment. There are probably quite a few things that we can identify in all our Churches that might be 'nice to do' but are actually extraneous to what true Church is and may be inhibiting the essential activities. For example, it might be nice to have a well-rehearsed Christmas programme of events (if its pagan origins are not too much of a stumbling block), but is this taking time and focus away from evangelism? We are called to 'patient endurance' (Revelation 13:10), as we explored in some detail in Chapter 8.

Church, in essence, operates to do four key things, with endurance:

1. Worship – in submission to and love towards Jesus Christ.
2. Community – as the body of Christ, fellowshipping and ministering in love.
3. Missions – evangelising the lost world.
4. Equipping to serve – training, shepherding and discipling.

All of these four things are guided by the authority of Scripture. We might want to think about stripping our Church life back to refocus and re-emphasise these areas. That could well might mean operating as an underground or 'secret' local Church as we anticipate the squeeze on Christianity continuing and heightening through Covid and beyond – moving into a more communist regime and into the one world order. Again, I'd highly recommend reading Rod Dreher's 'Live Not By Lies', or 'The United States of Socialism' by Dinesh D'Souza (2020) to understand the kind of 'soft totalitarianism' that we are heading into.

At its basic level, underground Church can be as simple as house Church with several other Christians – meeting together in homes to read and discuss Scripture, pray, worship the LORD in song, partake in the Lord's Supper and have fellowship meals. Many Christians have done this quietly during Covid lockdowns. It is beyond the remit of this book to go into a lot of detail about possible preparations for more sophisticated underground Church where great secrecy and caution is needed because of danger levels – the very real possibility of imprisonment, torture and death. Also, there will be a need to think about how to implement Church order and discipline, etc. I would highly recommend reading this short piece 'Preparing for the Underground Church' by Richard Wurmbrand,[408] who was tortured in a Romanian communist prison for 14 years and wrote the acclaimed book 'Tortured for Christ'. You can also listen to his very interesting four-part series 'How To Organize An Underground Church'[409] on Sermon Audio.

He talks about how we need to:

- Prepare for suffering for God's glory.
- Be careful with the truth and who we share information with.
- Be diligent in our spiritual exercises and disciplining ourselves for resilience.
- Seek to resolve Biblical doctrinal doubts before the real trials come.
- Understand the test of torture, how it can be used spiritually and only focus on the moment at hand.
- Learn to be silent and not speak carelessly.
- Decide upon and employ our underground Church stratagems and codes.

---

[408] 'Preparing for the Underground Church'. *Richard Wurmbrand Bio,* http://richardwurmbrand-bio.info/prepare.html. Accessed 5 May 2021.

[409] Wurmbrand, Richard. 'How To Organize An Underground Church - Part 1'. *SermonAudio*, 5, Feb. 2020, https://www.sermonaudio.com/sermoninfo.asp?m=t&s=2520149594943. Accessed 5 May 2021.

- Prepare to resist brainwashing, including that from our TVs and media!
- Prepare for solitary confinement – memorise Scripture.
- Seek the joy of the LORD.

Here are some good books on this topic that you might like to check out now:

- 'Preparing for the Underground Church' – Richard Wurmbrand (2000)
- 'Underground Church: A Living Example of the Church in Its Most Potent Form' – Brian Sanders (2018)
- 'MicroChurches: A Smaller Way' – Brian Sanders (2019)
- 'The Underground Church: Reclaiming the Subversive Way of Jesus' – Robin Meyers (2020)

The underground Church has represented the majority of normal Christian Church life throughout history and has generally been the most fruitful in making new disciples of Christ. The underground Chinese Church is a great example of this – with an estimated collective congregation of 100 million Christians. When asked, Chinese Christians often attribute their fervent faith and fruitfulness to five things:

1. A high commitment to reading and preaching the whole counsel of God.
2. A high commitment to their corporate and individual prayer life.
3. Commitment of all Church members to engage in evangelism.
4. Expectancy of miracles.
5. The expectancy and embracing of suffering.

Could you imagine how fruitful our Churches would be if every member was committed to these five principles? There would be no passengers or lukewarmness and no devolving all the tasks of evangelism, training and discipling to 'one man at the top'. We should seriously consider and pray about reforming our Churches towards the fruitful, fervent underground model. And we should do it now, before the real persecution comes, we're caught unprepared and we've given too much ground to the lies of Satan … and there are too many vaccine casualties.

A Testimony from Trinity Bible Chapel

Let me conclude this chapter with an encouraging account of the bold stance that Pastor Jacob Reaume at Trinity Bible Chapel (TBC) in Ontario, Canada has taken – a glowing example of civil disobedience done well and a testament to the favour and strong presence of the LORD in the midst of their fellowship. On 22nd January 2021, the Ontario Superior Court of Justice ordered that Trinity Bible Chapel and her elders not hold gatherings of more than ten people. The same day, Jacob Reaume issued this invite to the Sunday services at TBC:[410]

"Dear Neighbours and fellow Ontarians:

I hereby cordially invite you to learn of the good news of Jesus Christ and experience the joy of Christian worship. We are opening the doors of Trinity Bible Chapel this Sunday when we will hold in-person Lord's Day services at both 9:00am and 11:15am. Ten months have passed since our provincial government called us to shut down our regular lives for four-teen days to flatten the curve. Since that time, officials and media have provided regular updates on case and death counts. As of today, 98.03% of Canadians have not tested positive for Covid-19 and more than 99.9499% of Canadians have not died of Covid-19. While I see every death as tragic, I believe that life is much greater than avoiding a vi-rus. We will never get this time back, and we are not guaranteed tomor-row. The focus on mitigating the risk of spreading this contagion has now superseded nearly every aspect of our lives. Commerce has slowed almost

---

[410] Reaume, Jacob. 'Trinity Bible Chapel Is Open Sunday (DV): You're Invited!' *Trinity Bible Chapel*, 22 Jan. 2021, https://trinitybiblechapel.ca/trinity-bible-chapel-is-open-sunday-dv-youre-invited/.

to a halt. Childhood education has been compromised. Families are for-bidden from visiting each other. Weddings and funerals are im-peded. Most importantly, as I pointed out in an earlier blog,[411] the Chris-tian Church is forbidden to exist in its most basic essence which is as a gathering. People are lonely, afraid, despairing of life itself, and facing financial ruin, among many other deprivations and tribulations. This is all during the darkest and coldest season of the year. If ever our fellow Ontarians needed hope, it is now. Out of neighbourly love, I am person-ally openly inviting anyone and everyone to experience the hope of the Gospel and the warmth of Christian worship at Trinity Bible Chapel this Sunday during our two Lord's Day services."

The services went ahead. The police showed up and issued steep fines. Trinity Bible Chapel are facing 40 million dollars in potential fines right now, *yes – forty million*, for gathering the Church for Sunday wor-ship. Here's Jacob's testimony so far:[412]

"Personally, I have never experienced a more palpable manifest presence of God's Holy Spirit during public worship than I did on that Sunday. Many others – I have lost track of how many – shared similar experiences ... On Sunday, February 27, we baptized 13 individuals, some of whom traced their conversion to those weeks in January, especially January 24 ... This week the Ontario Superior Court of Justice handed down our sen-tence for having Church on January 24. The service cost us $83,000. That is our fine, and here is how it breaks down. Pastor Will and I each owe $5,000. Pastor Randy owes $4,000. Each of the other elders owe $3,000. The Church itself owes $15,000. And we have been ordered to pay $45,000 to cover the legal fees of the Ministry of the Attorney Gen-eral. The Ministry of the Attorney General [MAG] claims their lawyers

---

[411] Reaume, Jacob. 'Here We Stand: The Church Must Meet'. *Trinity Bible Chapel*, 3 Dec. 2020, https://trinitybiblechapel.ca/here-we-stand-the-Church-must-meet/.

[412] 'Huge Fines for Single Church Service: "We Worshipped Christ Extravagantly at the Price of $83,000"'. *Protestia*, 26 Feb. 2021, https://protestia.com/2021/02/26/huge-fines-for-single-Church-ser-vice-we-worshipped-christ-extravagantly-at-the-price-of-83000/.

spent 104 hours to prosecute us for holding services on January 24 – charges for which we pled guilty. Evidently, the MAG was very motivated, and the prosecutors worked tirelessly against our Church. So that is a grand total of $83,000. These fines will not and cannot be appealed. They are final. We will pay $83,000 for having Church on January 24. I could say it was the most extravagantly priced service I've ever held, but that would not be factual. Every service I've held has cost Christ His very own blood, which is worth infinitely more than any dollar amount. I was heartened by something Pastor Steve Richardson recently pointed out. In reference to Matthew 26:6-13, he explained the anointing of Christ by Mary with the alabaster jar. The alabaster jar of ointment would have been worth the equivalent of a retirement savings. It was expensive, and that dear woman paid a lot of money for one quick act of worship. She thought Christ was worth it. The disciples, however, were indignant, saying, "Why this waste? For this could have been sold for a large sum and given to the poor?" Jesus defended her saying, "She has done a beautiful thing for me." Chief among the woman's accusers was Judas (John 12:4-5). The woman thought Christ was worth the money, but Judas thought He wasn't. She went down in history for doing good, but Judas was a traitor who would have been better off not being born. On January 24, we worshipped Christ extravagantly at the price of $83,000. He is worth that and so much more. Our fine is nothing near what Mary spent on Jesus for her one quick extravagant act of worship. And we cannot compare it to the price of blood He paid so that we would worship Him. As we've sung many times:

Were the whole realm of nature mine,
That were a present far too small;
Love so amazing, so divine,
Demands my soul, my life, my all."

Let's pray for the LORD's grace to give us all similar boldness, courage, faith and love of Jesus in the face of orders to compromise.

CHAPTER TWELVE

Reflection and Preparation for Church Leaders

Our Church leaders have such a difficult job on their hands at this time. This is unchartered territory. Not that government tyranny, or plagues, or set-backs or Christian lukewarmness is anything new, but what is new is this: Mass deception and affirmation of evil – on a world-wide scale, even within the Church.

What has happened in the advent of the Covid Trojan Horse has caused much of the world, including our Church congregations, to perceive the creeping authoritarian control that's been introduced and embraced as good and beneficial for the safety and health of everyone. There are many layers to this deceitfulness as we have explored in some depth and there are many subtleties in it that are missed by even the most discerning minds: For example, the pushing of collectivism over individualism 'for the greater good' (this is more selfless, right?), the tacit agreement with lies and submission to the 'god of safety' by the wearing of masks in our Churches and an affirmation of a spirit of fear ... *"Jonathan and Liz are not coming to Church at the moment because they're vulnerable and shielding. They're being sensible."*

Isaiah 5:20 warns us: *"Woe unto them that call evil good, and good evil; that put darkness for light, and light for darkness; that put bitter for sweet, and sweet for bitter!"*

If we put liberal Churches aside, most Bible-believing, Jesus-centred Churches and leaders would ardently claim that they want stand for the truth and on matters such as sexuality and marriage, gender and the sanctity of life in the womb. However, when it comes to Covid 19 and the theological minefield that it's brought with it, we are at sea. We are unsure in knowing where or how to draw godly lines and take a stand against evil. Fear, cowardice, idolatry and lack of spiritual disciplines – to name but a few sins that are rampant in our Churches right now – are flourishing, largely uncontested.

If you're a Church leader in any capacity, this chapter is written specifically for you, to help and give some considered things to think, pray, reflect and act upon – as you deem appropriate for your particular setting, in how to lead your ministry in our current time. Since most Church leaders are men, I am addressing this section to men and using male pronouns. But, in less conventional circumstances where women are leading Churches, this applies equally to them too. My hope is that you will read it with humility and an attitude of investigation, curiosity and open-mindedness, rather than seeing it as a threat, condemnation or personal attack on your work and labour of love within your Church. I do not doubt that you are toiling hard in your ministry and with great concern and care for your flock. You have such a weighty job on your hands right now and my heart is for you and with you, as are my prayers. And if you're not a Church leader, it is helpful for you to consider the kinds of issues your pastor is facing, so you can pray for him. I'd encourage you to share this book or at least these latter chapters with him. It's always healthy to have an attitude of 'semper reformanda', 'always reforming', within our Reformed Churches; appraising and, where needs be, bringing our doctrines, practices and worship back to Biblical standards. Whilst not all the advice and topics in this chapter are direct Biblical principles, they are rooted in them and draw on best practices and wisdom from Church leaders of the past. There's also knowledge and pointers about the current Covid issues and some helpful advice from the world of personal productivity, disciplined work and effectiveness. Use this chapter as a guidepost and a springboard to give you ideas, food for thought and to help you discern the barrage of information and communication that's being thrown your way on a daily basis, no doubt. This article from iBelieve[413] gives a good indication of how many pastors are feeling, the pressure they're under and things they must wrestle with presently. I wonder if you can relate?

"Everyday pastors are forced to answer questions about their Covid-19 response. From Church members quoting scriptures with a sense of condemnation about the Church 'choosing fear', to social media threads of pastors and congregations becoming infected, it seems everyone has an opinion. Debates over masks, temperature checks, if online services are really spreading the Gospel, are constant and causing great division among the body. Everyone has an opinion on what the local Church should be doing. However, ultimately, it falls on the pastor and the leadership to make the final call. Although it would seem they should be the strongest in the room, your local pastor has to reconcile the voices of their congregation, their Church leadership, their overseers, social media critiques, government officials, the enemy, and the Lord."

Dear pastor or leader, these are difficult but exciting times! The LORD has called you for such a time as this. May He strengthen you with joy.

Perfect Love Casts Out Fear

Remember, from the last chapter, that there is a new culture of fear (not a holy fear of God) within our Churches, which needs to be stopped in its tracks before it gets a stranglehold on us. There are 365 'fear not' verses in the Bible; one for each day. It is a sin to be in fear. We are not to indulge it, we are to rebuke it, repent of it, renew our minds by God's Word and

---

[413] Riollano, Victoria. '7 Things Pastors Wish You Knew about the Church's Response to COVID-19'. *IBelieve.com*, https://www.ibelieve.com/faith/things-pastors-wish-you-knew-about-Church-response-to-covid.html. Accessed 5 May 2021.

ask the LORD for courage, wisdom, strength and discipline to overcome it. How do we do that, when there is seemingly so much to be afraid of and congregations have so many mixed views on exactly what the perceived threats are? How do we minister effectively to people who are afraid? What if you yourself are afraid? Remember, the antidote to fear is love, which by nature is rooted in truth: *"There is no fear in love; but perfect love casts out fear, because fear involves torment. But he who fears has not been made perfect in love."* – 1 John 4:18 (NKJV)

John reminds us that if we are in fear, it is because we are afraid of punishment. That could be a fear of punishment from God, but in our current situation that perceived punishment is more likely to be in the form of any of the following:

- The punishment of rejection – angry and dissatisfied congregation members, colleagues or superiors who are disapproving of your choices and decisions.
- Legal punishment – if you put your 'head above the parapet' or in any way defy the authorities' Covid rules, or outright civilly disobey.
- The punishment of loss – of status and credibility, friendships and relationships, earnings, job, property, etc.

The reality is that whatever decisions you make, you'll experience the first thing listed above; you're never going to please all your flock all of the time, as you well know! If you do make decisions against the official government guidelines and laws, there is a very real possibility that you could also face the 'punishment' of the second two things listed above. You have to give headspace to that. Let's extrapolate a bit more …

So, if you were to decide to go against the Covid mandates in civil disobedience, believing that this is what God is calling His Churches to do – let's say you announce to your congregation that as of the next service, no one is required to wear a mask, socially distance or refrain from sing-ing, what then? You'll probably have a minority who rejoice, you'll have some who are indifferent and some who are very angry at your decision, calling you irresponsible and endangering everyone's health. You could well face being reported to the authorities, which is encouraged of course, with the added blow that it was by one of your own Church members. The next week, the police turn up, see that you've defied the rules and issue a friendly warning. The following week, there is a drop in attendance of 30%. Persisting in your stance, the following week the police turn up again and issue a fine. On top of that, your ecclesiastical body has heard what you're doing and called you to a meeting. They sharply warn you to reinstate the Covid legal rules, or disciplinary action will be taken. You continue in your stance, in good conscience before the LORD and not wavering due to the opinion of man, but at the same time pained by the rejection and condemnation of people you love and feeling the accusatory attacks of the enemy on your mind. What next? More fines, forcible shut-ting of your Church by authorities? Imprisonment? These things could well happen and are happening right now, like in Canada, where, in Jan-uary 2021 six pastors were charged 10.8 million dollars and threatened with imprisonment for gathering,[414] and let's not forget Canadian Pastor James Coates' imprisonment as a direct result of his Covid civil disobe-dience. Even if you take 'The Quiet Way' of civil disobedience that we discussed in the last chapter, where you organise your faithful congrega-tion into underground house Church cells, or meet in your Church build-ing in secret, you could be found out. You could still face punishment and you'll still face the condemnation of those that disapprove.

So why do this? **Faithfulness**. The LORD calls us to be faithful. Not pop-ular, not successful in the eyes of men, not growing in numbers, not con-forming to the worldly ways, but faithful. Faithful in feeding the sheep and applying the Holy Word in all areas of life. Pastor, there is a lot you

---

[414] 'Six Elders and Church Charged for Meeting: Max Total Penalty Is $10.8 Million plus Jail Time'. *Trinity Bible Chapel*, 8 Jan. 2021, https://trinitybiblechapel.ca/press-release-jan-8/.

could and may well lose, including your liberty, but there are some things that will remain intact – your peace and trust in the LORD and commitment to Biblical commands and the truth (and your Church being rooted in truth). Further, two things will grow – your faith and joy right now and your eternal rewards in the new creation (yes, we can think about these things – Jesus encourages us to). This will be your gift from the LORD for your faithfulness and bold stance.

"You keep him in perfect peace whose mind is stayed on you, because he trusts in you." – Isaiah 26:3

Our LORD has something to say about those who are not committed to the truth, that includes the truth of the situation and deception of Covid. Do we believe that? Do we believe that Jesus has authority over all areas of life and calls us to live in the light rather than darkness, or not, or only in some compartmentalised circumstances?

*"Now as Jannes and **Jambres withstood Moses, so do these also resist the truth**: men of corrupt minds, reprobate concerning the faith."* – 2 Timothy 3:8

*"So you shall say to them, 'This is a nation that does not obey the voice of the Lord their God nor receive correction. **Truth has perished and has been cut off from their mouth.**"* – Jeremiah 7:28 (NKJV)

*"This witness is true. Wherefore rebuke them sharply, that they may be sound in the faith; Not giving heed to Jewish fables, and commandments of men, **that turn from the truth.**"* – Titus 1:13-14

Here is the truth of our situation, which we've looked at chapter and verse in this book: **We have been deceived, are being deceived and will be deceived and this will be to our great harm unless we recognise and address the issue now, before the next round of play, and it starts with Church leaders.** You might ask, but is standing up to the Covid tyranny really that crucial? I know pastors who can clearly see the deception, tyranny and totalitarianism that's coming in, but think that it's not their job to discuss it or make a stand against it in their Church. They'd rather say 'just give me Jesus' and encourage their flock to focus on His gentle and lowly nature, rather than get too riled up about truth and righteousness and turning more than a blind eye to Jesus's commitment to it. Well yes, calling out and standing up against deception, evil and despotic leaders is that important ...

The 15,000 Tonne Freight Train

When there's a 15,000-tonne freight train loaded with 75 wagons on it coming towards your Church at a rapid pace, and the whistle is sounding loud and there are diesel fumes coming into your Church doors and the noise of the wheels is getting louder and louder, is it good and right to say, *"Were just gonna keep preaching Jesus"*? Or would it be better to warn everyone and take action in response to the situation at hand? And when I say 'action', what I am not suggesting is protests, political manoeuvres and the like, although there is some Biblical precedent for this – Moses petitioning Pharoah, Elijah confronting Ahab as but two examples. I am simply putting forward that we keep meeting (closely), keep singing (corporately), keep evangelising (closely), keep taking the LORD's Supper, etc. The harmful and spiritually disarming Covid rules being imposed on the Church and the associated and coming 'Great Reset', ecumenism, one world religion, persecution and the rest of what we've looked at are that freight train and we need to call a spade a spade and act accordingly. You might say, as I've heard lots, *"I'll cross that bridge when we get to it"*. Too late, in my view. Far too late. Your Church may be deceived, fearful, isolated, in secret sins (including idolatry of governments and the medical authorities) … right now. Do you think that all this will suddenly be resolved when the noose is tightened or slackened? That we'll all suddenly gain the necessary courage and desire for obedience?

Do you suppose it's good and right to say, along with the world, that *"the vaccine is our pathway out of this"*? Heaven forbid, no! Just like the child at her swimming lesson who's scared of getting in the water, the longer this fear and evil is negotiated with by watching parents and teacher, the more it will gain a paralysing grip on the child. The antidote to fear is faith and love – put into action. Not timidity. We need to 'jump right in' so to speak with doing the right thing. Yes, we may fear and tremble but Paul exhorts us to work out our faith anyhow. I know that I had to keep going out all through various lockdowns to evangelise, in person, or else I'd lose my nerve and get comfortable with not doing it. It would have been easy to rationalise the neglecting of Jesus' Great Commission in the name of coronavirus.

Why 'Just Give Me Jesus' is Not Enough

It is so tempting for us all to say *just give me Jesus'*. It seems so pious and so right; what could possibly be amiss with 'just looking to Jesus'? Well, only that our Jesus spoke directly into the issues of the day and has a fierce commitment to truth, knowledge, reading the signs of the times, calling out evil, living holy lives, walking in the Spirit and worshipping in spirit and truth. It is a sin to stand passively by to evil and to not refute, rebuke and turn from the schemes of the enemy to deceive and defile our minds.

Unless we root the Gospel and our 'just give me Jesus' attitude to our practical lives and circumstances, we risk falling into mysticism. Instead of Jesus being the very real and present friend, ally, Saviour, counsellor and LORD of our life, He takes a kind of Buddha like place – where we're happy to quote Him and look at Him and claim our allegiance and love, but then carry on with 'real life' without Him.

Further, Peter Hammond from Frontline Fellowship in Cape Town, South Africa states why it's not OK for pastors to say, *"I'm just gonna preach the Gospel"*. He says it's a convenient excuse for disobedience, laziness and cowardice and asks which preacher in the Bible just preached the

Gospel? John the Baptist, Elijah, Jesus? He asserts that we are called to do far, far more than preaching the Gospel. To constrain our faith and Church life by 'just preaching the Gospel', seeks to put limits on God's sovereignty on earth, fuelled by cowardice and censoring much of the Bible. All throughout the Scriptures we see that God looks for people to oppose injustice. Ezekiel 22:25-27, 30 (NKJV) is one such example:

"The conspiracy of her prophets in her midst is like a roaring lion tearing the prey; they have devoured people; they have taken treasure and precious things; they have made many widows in her midst. Her priests have violated My law and profaned My holy things; they have not distinguished between the holy and unholy, nor have they made known the difference between the unclean and the clean; and they have hidden their eyes from My Sabbaths, so that I am profaned among them. Her princes in her midst are like wolves tearing the prey, to shed blood, to destroy people, and to get dishonest gain ... So I sought for a man among them who would make a wall, and stand in the gap before Me on behalf of the land, that I should not destroy it; but I found no one."

Timothy and Chuck Baldwin in 'Romans 13: The True Meaning of Submission'[415] state: *"As government actions become more and more evil, the cause of resistance towards government becomes more and more righteous."* C.S. Lewis asserts: *"Christianity is a fighting religion. I don't want retreat I want attack ... let us go down fighting for the right side."* Francis Schaeffer reminds us in his book 'A Christian Manifesto' that: *"If there is no final place for civil disobedience, then the government has been made autonomous, and as such, it has been put in the place of the living God...since tyranny is Satanic, not to resist it is to resist God, to resist tyranny is to honour God."*

---

[415] Baldwin, Timothy and Chuck Baldwin. *Romans 13: The True Meaning of Submission.* Xlibris, 2011.

We Need Courageous, Direct Leadership

It is a leader's duty to seek Christ's will diligently, to keep themselves unstained by the world, as James exhorts (which will otherwise inevitably influence thinking and decision making), to not negotiate with tyranny (i.e. to stand firm against the devil) and then boldly follow the course of truth and justice and freedom in Christ. This is very different from many Church situations right now where the pastor has one eye in Scripture and one eye on the news media and Covid hype and then weighs up all opinions and bents of congregation members and settles for a kind of spurious middle ground approach. Not really staking their flag anywhere in particular, sending unclear messages and pussyfooting around the Covid rules; hoping it will all go away soon … and then, sadly, in many cases I have heard of, having a nervous breakdown under the pressure and confusion.

"The fear of man brings a snare, But whoever trusts in the Lord shall be safe." – Proverbs 29:25

"You who love the LORD, hate evil! He preserves the souls of His saints; He delivers them out of the hand of the wicked." – Psalm 97:10 (NKJV)

Again, pastors have an exceedingly hard job on their hands and there are nuances of their specific individual settings to consider, but that does not negate the necessary, unpopular and uncomfortable action to be taken. A bold stand against this particular evil, because it has deceived so many, will be met with resistance from within your own flock, as well as without – as I have seen when interviewing several pastors from around the world who have resisted Covid directives from the get-go. It is hard enough to stand against tyranny with your Church, like in classic persecution scenarios, let alone without the Church. That's heart breaking in many ways and a tough blow to take. But it is the right course to take and to affirm again, you'll have the joy and peace of obedience to your LORD, Saviour and King Jesus and you'll have the support of and deeper fellowship with your Christian stalwarts, who are also willing to engage in the battle we are called to. We simply cannot afford to acquiesce to the wishes of the fainthearted and those refusing to see the truth of what's going on. If we see our pastor taking a bold stance against evil, facing it squarely in the face and following Scripture over governments, we (the flock) have a duty then to heed, obey and support this bold leadership, with courage and faith.

"Obey them that have the rule over you, and submit yourselves: for they watch for your souls, as they that must give account, that they may do it with joy, and not with grief: for that is unprofitable for you." – Hebrews 13:17

Church planter, author and missionary, Jeff Christopherson gives an interesting and encouraging insight that some Churches are experiencing in his article '10 Leadership Qualities of the Post-Covid-19 Church':[416]

---

[416] Christopherson, Jeff. '10 Leadership Qualities of the Post-COVID-19 Church'. *Christianity Today*, 21 Aug. 2020, https://www.christianitytoday.com/edstetzer/2020/august/10-leadership-qualities-of-post-covid-19-Church.html. Accessed 5 May 2021.

"The purging effect of this pandemic is allowing leaders to more accurately discern those truly invested in Jesus' mission and work. This analysis focuses equipping to be directed toward those desiring to be a disciple of Jesus. With the 'prime customer' squarely in their vision, leaders have shifted from tickling the sensibilities of the lowest common denominator to a much deeper spiritual investment of equipping into an already deployed mission force. But the Covid-19 scattering has caused missionary leaders to rise to the surface. They are the ones who intuitively are finding ways to advance the mission of the Church when the structural programs are no longer possible. Those who actually missionally engage, not simply those who wear a leadership title, are those best positioned to lead the Church into its next iteration. Many have been asking for a long time as to where our next teams of Church planters come from – the answer will be found within the Church. Early on in this pandemic, I sensed God saying to me, "Speak courage to leaders." For years I have heard the heart cries of pastors who know a better way, but feel trapped by the inevitability of the ecclesial system. If they lead change, they fear they will be leading alone. But in a few short weeks, God has allowed His Church to stop, reflect, and perhaps dream again. And so now, many leaders are courageously choosing 'mission' over 'model' – and preparing for a future Church that becomes pandemic-proof."

Leading courageous change in this time via civil disobedience of one kind or another, overtly or quietly, requires great strength of character from our Church leaders and to be well-established on the matters at hand in their hearts and minds. It's a very good idea for pastors to do an inventory of holiness and faith and look at the issues for self-examination, which we'll do next ...

Self-Examination Areas for Church Leaders

I'm sure you're well-schooled and take mindful precaution already in the things that I'm describing next with these areas of self-examination for pastors, so please use them as reminders and pointers, which we all need from time to time.

3 'P's That Keep Us from Following Jesus Wholeheartedly and Discerning His Will

The apostle John tells us in 1 John 2:16 that *"For all that is in the world, the lust of the flesh, and the lust of the eyes, and the pride of life, is not of the Father, but is of the world."* These three things make us and keep us worldly if we are not vigilant to purge them from our day-to-day lives.

#1 Pride of life – honour and status among men: This can include arrogance and thinking we're above others. But it can also be much more subtle and 'rational' but equally stubborn and sinful – wanting to keep a good standing amongst people, Christians and non-Christians alike, and anything that exalts us above our station and offers the illusion of God-like qualities. It could be that all your pastor friends think that it's good and right to submit to the Covid rules. Are you worried about losing favour with them and their support? Are you concerned about going against your ecclesiastical body or Church elders or your local council? Afraid of ridicule and slander and fractured relationships and people avoiding you? (I've experienced all these things in writing this book, before it had even been published!) This is the pride of life and we are reminded in Proverbs that the fear of man is a trap. Paul tells us not to conform to the pattern of the world but to be transformed by the renewing of our minds by the Word (Romans 12:2). These two things – worldly precepts and godly ones – are at enmity and we must shun the former and embrace the latter. We are not to look like the rest of the world in our response to Covid and pander to the newspeak. Ask yourself, how much mainstream news and television are you watching and relying upon (even unconsciously)? Would you get rid of your television? If not, why not? Do you feel like you'd not be able to 'keep up with what's going on'? If so, why do you feel that? Do you really need to let worldly, mostly hyperbolic and deceptive tenets enter your mind to be an effective pastor? I'd argue not and that it hinders you much more than you realise ... Do re-read 'The Modern Metal Image' allegory at the beginning of this book. I have interviewed pastors who agree; and they're the ones taking a bold civil disobedience stance. And what about doctors and medical professionals? Are you listening to those voices in your congregation and the 'scientific community' and weighing your decisions on 'hospital numbers', 'positive Covid tests on the rise' and the like? If so, this is not what you are required to do, it is at odds with our LORD's commands. James reminds us ...

"If any of you lacks wisdom, let him ask of God, who gives to all liberally and without reproach, and it will be given to him. But let him ask in faith, with no doubting, for he who doubts is like a wave of the sea driven and tossed by the wind. For let not that man suppose that he will receive anything from the Lord; **he is a double-minded man**, *unstable in all his ways."* – James 1:5-8 (NKJV)

We have a situation where pastors are earnestly asking the LORD for His wisdom and then, upon surveying the latest Covid advice and 'statistics' have gone against clear commands in Scripture – the obvious ones being the closure of Churches and ban on signing. It's akin to the Christian man who is praying about leaving his wife for another woman, trying to work out if that's the LORD's will. It clearly is not, but he continues to pray anyhow, especially since the new woman seems so much godlier than his wife, who is critical of him (i.e., self-justification, with no basis in Scripture). Paul goes on to tell us in Romans 12:2 (NKJV), *"do not be conformed to this world, but be transformed by the renewing of your mind, that you may prove what is that good and acceptable and perfect will of God."* So, if you're wanting to seek God's will for your Church – shun worldliness and the subtle but deadly pride that comes from thinking you need to keep yourself 'well-informed' on the Covid advice and increase your Bible reading, study, meditation, fasting and prayers instead.

#2 Pleasure – lusts of the flesh and eyes: This concerns the unhealthy (even idolatrous) desire for that which satisfies any of the physical needs and is contrary to the will of God. It can include the obvious things such as sexual immorality and greed but can also include the more 'respectable sins' such as envy, covetousness, materialism, excessive desire for safety and health, excessive and wrongful enjoyment of entertainment, sports, music, news, food, clothes, family, etc. In Matthew 6:22-23 (NKJV), Jesus asserts that the eye is the lamp of the body *and "If therefore your eye is good, your whole body will be full of light. But if your eye is bad, your whole body will be full of darkness. If therefore the light that is in you is darkness, how great is that darkness!"* Your eyes are closely related to your heart. Proverbs 17:24 (NKJV) says that *"Wisdom is in the sight of him who has understanding, But the eyes of a fool are on the ends of the earth."* We need to be vigilant to guard our eyes and heart and very careful about we let into each. Jesus commends the 'pure in heart' who seek wholeheartedly after the LORD. Are you doing this?

#3 Prosperity – wealth and comfort: It's ok to have money and comfort but if you are elevating these above God's will and unwilling to let go of them for the fear of poverty and persecution, if that's the path ahead that the LORD is or may be calling you to, then this is a sinful snare. **As Christians, we should have counted the cost of our discipleship up-front**, but it is good to do so again now, with the growing squeeze on Christianity and with the prospect of civil disobedience and what that might incur. If you are caught up in any ongoing secret or not-so-secret sins, now is the time to get really serious about turning from them. As long as you are indulging in sin, you are compromising your walk with the LORD, sensitivity to the Holy Spirit's promptings and discerning of the LORD's will in your Scripture reading.

4 'P's That Can Keep Pastors from Taking A Stand Against Lies and Tyranny

#1 Propaganda: The News media is full of it. Do not swap comforting, conforming lies for the unpopular, hard truth – Jesus calls us to truth. We've highlighted this point enough. This sermon on media deception and dangers by Peter Hammond[417] is very good on why we need to avoid it, proactively.

#2 Purpose – work: Examine yourself to make sure that your views and decisions are in no way attached to your desire to keep your job and income, i.e., we must be careful not to compromise obedience to the LORD, integrity and our conscience for the sake of keeping our job position.

#3 Property – vicarage, etc.: If your role as a pastor of a Church comes with a vicarage or manse then you also need to be diligent not to base your decisions on your attachment to your home or your Church building. Hold them lightly and trust that the LORD will provide a home and place of gathering for you, should you need to vacate your Church properties. As we explored in the section on the underground Church in the last chapter, it looks very likely that we may be conducting Church in our homes as standard practice in the not-too-distant future, if not now.

#4 People – family, friends, colleagues, etc.: If you are afraid of the views of people around you or have a deep fear for what might happen to your family if you are attacked in your stance or even imprisoned, then this fear needs to be repented of. It's not our job to sort out the consequences of our obedience, the LORD does that. We can trust that He will care for us and our family one way or another. This is hard to get our heads around and to have faith in, but we must! I think it's worth stating that a pastor's wife holds a pivotal and powerful role in the life of the Church. If she is firmly against any kind of civil disobedience stance or is totally for the mainstream narrative and rules, then it will be very difficult for you to make a contrary decision for your Church. Brother, it's your job to keep the worldliness out of your home and to lead your wife and family well; lovingly, reassuringly and strongly in the ways of following the LORD, truth and righteousness and counting that

---

[417] Hammond, Peter. 'Dealing with Deception in the Media'. *SermonAudio*, 7 Feb. 2013. https://www.sermonaudio.com/sermoninfo.asp?m=t&s=5131365140. Accessed 5 May 2021.

cost of that. It may be that you need to counsel her first on possible persecution and the costliness of decisions you are thinking of making. If this is not something you have spent much time doing, do not delay any longer. You are head of your family before you are the leader of your Church and your wife needs time, headspace and reassurance to come to terms with what's ahead. Fear of man leads to cowardice, let's explore that a little as a problem that's becoming quite evident within our Churches right now.

Cowardice

Cowardice is defined by Wikipedia as: *"a trait wherein excessive fear prevents an individual from taking a risk or facing danger. It is the opposite of courage. As a label, 'cowardice' indicates a failure of character in the face of a challenge."* It's a lack of bravery and courage, timidity, spinelessness, faint-heartedness, fearfulness and feebleness. Not a popular term, in fact quite taboo, within our Churches today, cowardice is a huge issue that we need to address, repent of and work through with the LORD and in our Church settings. There is clear lack of men standing up to do the unpopular right thing and being willing to face the condemnation and persecution that might go with it. This is a sin and is the first listed sin that Jesus mentions in Revelation 21 on who will face the second death of the lake of fire: *"But the cowardly, unbelieving, abominable, murderers, sexually immoral, sorcerers, idolaters, and all liars shall have their part in the lake which burns with fire and brimstone, which is the second death."* – Revelation 21:8 (NKJV)

We know that by the blood of the Lamb and our faith in Him, we will not face the second death, but we also don't want to partake in the sin Jesus takes so seriously, listing it along with murder, witchcraft and sexual immorality. Now, I will say at this point that it is very tempting for me, owing to the so-called 'snowflake generation' we're living in where people are overly sensitive and so easily take offence and umbrage at the slight hint of rebuke, for me to say that I am not pointing the finger at you, dear reader. I'm tempted to talk quite generally about a problem 'out there', but I'll refrain from doing that and deliver my point with a more Puritan-like admonishment. I credit you with more awareness of your sinful heart, which is bent towards comfort, and to be made of 'sterner stuff' and the humility to at least consider that you, me, all of us could be acting with more than a little cowardice in this whole coronavirus nightmare. I would estimate that the tyrants have got as far as they have with this because of cowardice to a large degree.

I often wonder why cowardice is a sin not talked about or addressed in our Churches, much like gluttony or laziness. It has been a neglected area of discussion, discipleship and prayer for a long time, and it has now caught us off-guard. We are reaping what we've sown ... or failed to sow. The sin of cowardice is one we've been either quite blind to or comfortably entertaining. This does not make it right. Now is the time to recalibrate our holiness and start taking it seriously. Better late than never. Christian writer, Allan Stevo in his article 'Face Masks Refusal Says so Much, Because Courage is the Prerequisite to All Virtuous Behaviour'[418] states quite strongly that: *"**Courage is the prerequisite to virtue.** If a person doesn't have guts, they can't be trusted. The rest of their qualities are worthless because the foundation of their character is weak and promises to give way under pressure. I will always choose a courageous man I agree with 25% over a coward I agree with 95%. One, I know where he stands. The other, I know where he stands until he pulls his head out of the book and walks out into the real world, at which point the cowardly man is a syncope."*

In my experience and opinion, I tend to agree with Allan's viewpoint. There have been numerous occasions in my life, in various settings, where

---

[418] Stevo, Allan. 'Face Masks Refusal Says So Much, Because Courage Is the Prerequisite to All Virtuous Behavior'. *LewRockwell.com*, 20 Dec. 2020, https://www.lewrockwell.com/2020/12/allan-stevo/face-masks-refusal-says-so-much-because-courage-is-the-prerequisite-to-all-virtuous-behavior/. Accessed 5 May 2021.

people with whom I was in agreement with on an issue in theory and principle were nowhere to be seen or heard when it came down to standing up for that thing in a difficult situation. We need guts and courage to ensure that we are free to act upon our convictions. Cowardice paralyses us; it stops us from doing the virtuous and right things that we know we should. And virtue is the foundation for other godly attributes, as Peter reminds us: *"But also for this very reason, giving all diligence, add to your faith virtue, to virtue knowledge, to knowledge self-control, to self-control perseverance, to perseverance godliness, to godliness brotherly kindness, and to brotherly kindness love. For if these things are yours and abound, you will be neither barren nor unfruitful in the knowledge of our Lord Jesus Christ."* – 2 Peter 1:5-8 (NKJV)

Author and podcaster Matt Walsh's challenging book, 'Church of Cowards' is challenging and eye-opening reading on this topic (though, as he's a Catholic I do not agree with some of his doctrinal stances). He says that one solution to Christian cowardice is for Churches to *"call their flocks to deeper and more authentic faith. The message needs to be sent that faith is something that we live, something we do, not just a passive feeling."* On virtue and sacrifice for Christ's sake, he says: *"It is easy to be virtuous in our world because we have adopted easy virtues. We applaud ourselves for our goodness, but it costs nothing to be 'good' in modern times. A man can be good just by sitting in his living room. The couch potato is the new paragon of virtue, exceeded in goodness only by the man in a coma. Virtue has been pulled down from its lofty perch and made accessible to the inert. By this standard, the most virtuous thing on the planet is a turnip or a blade of grass. It just sits there and says nothing and does nothing and does not get in the way. The Church, once the stalwart defender of real virtues, now promotes cheap and shallow ones. Christians are not often exhorted to courage, chastity, fidelity, temperance, and modesty anymore. Those virtues require action and sacrifice and intention and thought and sometimes pain. They ask you to do something for their sake, become something, be something. These are the formidable, inconvenient virtues. You must rise to them because they will not come down to you. Luckily for us, we are no longer asked to strive for those high virtues. Instead we are encouraged to be welcoming, accepting, and tolerant. The turnip virtues. Compassionate, too. Always compassionate. And I agree, of course, that a Christian ought to be welcoming, accepting, and tolerant. Certainly, he must be compassionate. But these virtues have superseded and ultimately consumed all the others ... God does not want my bare minimum. God does not want me to go just one step further than other people. He does not say, "Be good enough." He does not say, "Be better than most." He says, "Be perfect." Of course, it's hard to shoot for perfection. It is all the harder when you are surrounded by people who are not even trying. The world tells us that there is no such thing as good or bad. All is permissible. Sin is no big deal. Some sins are even laudatory. There is no perfection. But Christ calls us out of that relativistic fog – all the way out. Not to mere acceptability or decency, but to holiness, to sainthood. He will settle for nothing less, so neither can we ... How many of us are willing to give up anything – let alone everything? Most of us will lash out bitterly if we are asked to make any sacrifice at all, any adjustment to our lives, any change to our lifestyles. We will shriek in horror if anyone suggests, say, that we give up watching certain television shows or listening to certain music. We will explode in fury if anyone questions whether a Christian ought to watch pornography, or dress provocatively, or use profanity. We will laugh and mock and practically spit at any critic who dares to look at something we do, something we enjoy, something that gives us pleasure, and question whether it is proper. Most of us, if we are being perfectly honest, cannot think of one thing – one measly thing – that we greatly enjoy and have the means to do yet have stopped doing because we know it is inconsistent with our faith. I do not believe that I exaggerate when I say that the average American Christian has never given up one single thing for Christ."* – Matt Walsh, 'Church of Cowards: A Wake-Up Call to Complacent Christians'.

Food for thought.

Not All Opinions Are Equal – Choosing Wisely Who You Listen To

It's fair to say that most pastors are receiving a deluge of correspondence at this time from congregation members, as well as all the Covid guidance being issued from various authorities. I'm sure that on a day-to-day basis you receive many emails, texts and calls from your flock – sincere and earnest, some encouraging, some critical and ranging from *"we must shut our Churches, what an earth are you doing opening at this time? We need to keep everyone safe!"* to the kind of things mentioned in this book – which most pastors dismiss and pigeonhole as 'conspiracy theories' or paranoid hype. I've obviously dealt chapter and verse here to coax you out of that pigeonhole in your thinking if that's where you were tempted to go!

I spoke earlier in this chapter about your need to discern the LORD's will and then ignore the voice of the crowd. That said, and as we looked at in the previous chapter, there are people within our congregations who are very adept at distinguishing the spirits and have been appointed as 'Kingdom watchmen'. There are those who are thinking and acting in fear and those who are doing so from courage. That needs to be a big consideration in who you choose to listen to and seek advice and counsel from. You are called to consider and care for the weaker in faith members of your congregation, for sure, but you are not called to take heed of advice on leading your Church which is rooted in fear, cowardice and neglect of discerning the truth. **Work pastorally with everyone, heed the advice of few.** There is a Biblical precedent for this in Deuteronomy: *"And the officers shall speak further unto the people, and they shall say, What man is there that is fearful and fainthearted? let him go and return unto his house, lest his brethren's heart faint as well as his heart. And it shall be, when the officers have made an end of speaking unto the people that they shall make captains of the armies to lead the people."* – Deuteronomy 20:8-9

You cannot possibly know and do everything. Determine wisely your counsellors at this time, let them help you and where possible in the framework of your Church leadership system, place them in positions of leadership. For example, if you choose the path of civil disobedience, there may well be people in your congregation who are very experienced in facing persecution and maybe you are not. Seek their advice. Ask how they employ courage and hear their stories of how the LORD brought them through tough times and what godly disciplines helped strengthen them in their times of great need. This kind of counsel is obviously found in Scripture and we need no more than that, but it can really help with encouragement and resolve to hear first-hand practical examples and anecdotes, as well as building richer relationships. Again, check your pride in this – you may be reluctant, as the Church leader, to go to that little old lady, or man thirty years younger than you and openly admit that you have little experience where they have much and ask for help. The key here is obviously humility. Ask questions, lots of them and then listen. Seek first to understand and it will serve you well.

Good Health Disciplines and Personal Habits

An area easily neglected by pastors and all at this time is personal health disciplines. The world is caught up with the Covid health and safety non-sense, which makes zero health sense, and we must be different, else we'll severely compromise our physical and mental health. Staying indoors too much, not meeting with people, stifling your breathing and oxygen flow with masks and hand sanitisation are all exceedingly unhealthy, as we looked at in Chapter 3. We need to be taking an alternative path, of truly healthy habits and practices. It is critical to have clarity of thought, stable energy and mood and enough sleep and rest – under normal circumstances but especially now – and this takes good health disciplines and personal practices. You simply cannot expect to deal with all you have to deal with in your pastoral role if you're eating junk food, neglecting exercise in the fresh outdoor air and not getting enough sleep.

We'll look more at good health in the next chapter but think for now about making improvements in your diet – eating natural foods that are free from chemicals and toxins, lowering your carbohydrates and increasing healthy fats, meats and vegetables, for example. You also want to consider certain supplements, your exercise regime, hydration with fresh, filtered water, your sleep hygiene and screen-time limitation.

Wesley's Questions for Self-Examination and Spiritual Appraisal

The following questions were used by John Wesley for self-examination[419] and are sure to be a bit convicting and motivating even for us today. Have a look through and note areas where you are falling short and plan to prayerfully work on them:

1. Am I consciously or unconsciously creating the impression that I am better than I really am? In other words, am I a hypocrite?
2. Am I honest in all my acts and words, or do I exaggerate?
3. Do I confidentially pass on to another what was told to me in confidence?
4. Can I be trusted?
5. Am I a slave to dress, friends, work, or habits?
6. Am I self-conscious, self-pitying, or self-justifying?
7. Did the Bible live in me today?
8. Do I give it time to speak to me every day?
9. Am I enjoying prayer?
10. When did I last speak to someone else about my faith?
11. Do I pray about the money I spend?
12. Do I get to bed on time and get up on time?
13. Do I disobey God in anything?
14. Do I insist upon doing something about which my conscience is uneasy?
15. Am I defeated in any part of my life?

---

[419] 'John Wesley's 22 Questions of Self Examination'. *The United Methodist Church*, 28 May 2020, https://www.umc.org/en/content/john-wesleys-22-questions-of-self-examination. Accessed 5 May 2021.

16. Am I jealous, impure, critical, irritable, touchy, or distrustful?
17. How do I spend my spare time?
18. Am I proud?
19. Do I thank God that I am not as other people, especially as the Pharisees who despised the publican?
20. Is there anyone whom I fear, dislike, disown, criticise, hold a resentment toward or disregard? If so, what am I doing about it?
21. Do I grumble or complain constantly?
22. Is Christ real to me?

Being Highly Effective and Prioritising the Important Over the Urgent

The best-selling business and self-development book, 'The 7 Habits of Highly Effective People' by Stephen Covey[420] was a game changer for me when I read it decades ago. It borrows a lot from Biblical principles, and it did what it says on the tin and helped me to greatly increase my effectiveness in life and work. The habits are as follows:

1. Be Proactive
2. Begin with the End in Mind
3. Put First Things First
4. Think Win-Win
5. Seek First to Understand, Then to Be Understood
6. Synergise
7. Sharpen the Saw

If you haven't read it, I'd recommend it, or at least listening to one of the detailed presentations or summaries freely available on YouTube and podcasts. One of the most helpful things I found in the book was the Time Management Matrix, which puts activities into Four Quadrants. It's a

---

[420] Covey, Stephen R. *The 7 Habits of Highly Effective People*. Simon & Schuster USA, 1990.

good idea to assess where your time is spent and how you can be maximising it to ensure that the important things are given enough of your time and attention – many of which are new or require increased prioritisation, such as fasting about Church leadership and planning for civil disobedience.

- **Quadrant One: Urgent and Important** – this is the meat and bones of your work as a Church leader and includes things such as preparing and delivering sermons, pastoring your congregation, Covid crises and new rules being issued, taking weddings, funerals, baptisms.
- **Quadrant Two: Not Urgent, but Important** – this is harder to give time to since there is no immediate (or at least obvious) urgency. It is crucial that you're diligent in making time for Quadrant Two activities, since they will not clamour for your attention like the other quadrants, but Covey argues that this is where effective people focus their time and energy. They will greatly benefit your Church life in the long term if you invest the time in them. These things can include quiet, alone time thinking and praying about civil disobedience. It could also include strategically building new relationships and collaborations, thoughtful creative work, giving presentations and holding meetings to equip and lead your family and congregation, clarifying your values, fasting and reading this book!
- **Quadrant Three: Urgent but Not Important** – these activities include your everyday Church admin stuff that you should be largely delegating. If you're not careful or in pursuit of a bit of escapism, you can find yourself wasting time in this quadrant that you could be spending on the non-urgent important things. Activities here can include interruptions and some meetings, phone calls and emails.
- **Quadrant Four: Neither Urgent nor Important** – these are things you may do for enjoyment (but are not helpful and restful), procrastination or out of confusion about what's truly important.

Activities can include web surfing, idle talk, self-indulgence, excessive dog-walking, over-thinking on the wrong things and pointless 'busy work'. Be vigilant in eliminating these activities when you catch yourself wasting time in this quadrant.

In summary, be mindful and proactive in spending as little time as possible in Quadrants Three and Four and more time in Quadrants One and Two – being especially diligent in making time for Quadrant Two. It may be a good time, as a Quadrant Two activity, to spend some time focusing on your weaknesses as well as strengths. Are you feeling fearful or cowardly? Do you need to repent of a sin that you can identify with from the list of self-examination areas above? Take more time than usual to focus on this work and prayer. Chess champion, Garry Kasparov, says in his book, 'Deep Thinking: Where Machine Intelligence Ends and Human Creativity Begins':[421] *"Focusing on your strengths is required for peak performance, but improving your weaknesses has the potential for the greatest gains. This is true for athletes, executives, and entire companies. Leaving your comfort zone involves risk, however, and when you are already doing well the temptation to stick with the status quo can be overwhelming, leading to stagnation."*

Losing Congregation Members

Let's briefly revisit this painful topic. It's not just likely, it's inevitable that in taking a bold stance for Christ in leading your Church out of the deception and bondage of the Covid rules and into godly civil disobedience, reclaiming Church's rightful authority, you will lose people along the way. You have already lost quite a few people since March 2020 I'm sure, be prepared to lose more … and that's OK.

---

[421] Kasparov, Garry. Deep Thinking: Where Machine Intelligence Ends and Human Creativity. John Murray, 2017.

Civil disobedience is not for the faint-hearted. It's not for the nominal or lukewarm Christian. It's for the radical, all-in, 'let's step up my allegiance to Christ' Christian and there are fewer of them than we tend to realise. It is for the true and faithful remnant Church – the virgin Bride of Christ being prepared for her Bridegroom. Many people have never given up or suffered anything for their faith in Christ, let alone risking fines, liberty and more and they will just not be prepared to now (others will). Others won't want to bother with the inconvenience of moving into underground house Churches and meeting in more difficult circumstances. It will hurt you to see close friends and long-time congregation members choose not to stick with your Church. It will be very painful to hear accusations that you're being irresponsible and endangering people. It will alarm you to see Church giving figures decrease and people in key positions abdicate. No matter – your commitment to doing the uncomfortable, Christ-honouring thing is paramount. In doing so, God will honour and bless you in it in way that you can't yet imagine. The alternative is for your Church to slide into a situation akin to the German Church back in Hitler's time – the ecclesiastical arm of the Nazi government. Compromised, bound, full of sin, detached from Biblical doctrine and 'Church' only in name. So be prepared for this pruning of your Church, maybe a severe one. But be expectant for God to do some remarkable things too. Where pastors are taking a bold stance now, they are drawing lots of similarly fervent Christians into the fold and are making new disciples because of their strong and evident love of Christ and each other and unity of mind. This is the soil that produces revival. Again, we can look to Deuteronomy for counsel on this: *"When you go out to battle against your enemies, and see horses and chariots and people more numerous than you, do not be afraid of them; for the Lord your God is with you, who brought you up from the land of Egypt. So it shall be, when you are on the verge of battle, that the priest shall approach and speak to the people. And he shall say to them, 'Hear, O Israel: Today you are on the verge of battle with your enemies. Do not let your heart faint, do not be afraid, and do not tremble or be terrified because of them; for the Lord your God is He who goes with you, to fight for you against your enemies, to save you.' Then the officers shall speak to the people, saying: 'What man is there who has built a new house and has not dedicated it? Let him go and return to his house, lest he die in the battle and another man dedicate it. Also what man is there who has planted a vineyard and has not eaten of it? Let him go and return to his house, lest he die in the battle and another man eat of it. And what man is there who is betrothed to a woman and has not married her? Let him go and return to his house, lest he die in the battle and another man marry her.'"* – Deuteronomy 20:1-7

Five Covid Issues to Be Alert to and Avoid

Lastly to cover in this chapter, there are five things that I have observed and identify as being dangers to watch out for and avoid in your ministry at this time:

#1 Pressure to work with community bodies: More and more, Churches are being encouraged to engage and partner with established bodies and networks that deal with care in the community and crisis management – councils, food banks, domestic abuse services, hospitals and the like. Whilst there may be a limited place for such partnerships, they should not become too intertwined nor take time away from the Church's main role – to proclaim the salvation of Christ and make disciples. We are not a social service, and we are not proclaiming a social Gospel. We are at odds with much of what the rest of society and the secular world is doing, and it needs to stay that way. We are a holy and royal priesthood, and the secular world is not. We can of course engage in our own community 'good deeds'.

#2 'Clergy Response Teams': Related to the last point, be very aware that FEMA and other governmental bodies are coming for you, pastor, to join allegiance with them in administering and upholding Covid regulations. As detailed in Chapter 10, there are 'Clergy Response Teams' which are trained (indoctrinated) in the Covid propaganda. Churches are being enlisted as vaccination centres, what an awful situation! Be aware and do not compromise under any circumstances.

#3 Increasing and focusing on the tech: It is tempting and there is much pressure to focus on upgrading your tech and live streaming services. Do not succumb to this – remember that a big part of what is going on is the move into a technocratic society where everything is under surveillance and censored. I would strongly encourage you not to stream your services on YouTube nor rely heavily on Facebook pages and groups. **What you post online now may be held against you in the future.** YouTube is already shutting down many channels that they deem to be 'fake news', 'hate speech' and the like. We are a stone's throw away from free speech disappearing altogether and a banning of preaching the Bible on mainstream platforms. So, you don't want to be investing time, resources and energy into a precarious platform, nor encouraging your congregation to rely on them. You will have to find alternatives sooner than you may realise. Keep things simple – keep your Church gathered as much as possible and do not place your whole service recordings in the public domain for non-participants. It's not public business, it's Church family only and anyone who wants to join, in person. I'd advise sticking to ring-fenced and closed circuit Zoom meetings at the most. Yes, send emails and you could even look at some kind of membership site software platform or private messenger channel for communication, where you retain ownership and privacy, but avoid mainstream social media. And just to be clear, I'm talking about your services, prayer meetings and internal communication, not outward facing evangelistic materials. However, be prepared that any kind of online evangelistic materials could very well be shut down, so again, I'd keep it simple and easily reproducible at low cost. Making sermon recordings available online is a separate matter for pastors to make a judgement call on.

#4 Speaking too much with other pastors and not your own Church family: Whilst it may be wise to seek the advice of and talk through some issues with other pastors and your clergy friends, do not do this at the expense of open, honest conversion and communicating your thoughts and actions with your own Church family. I see many pastors making this mistake and it's kind of like a man who seeks marital advice from his male friends but never actually speaks about the issues at hand with his own wife. This can lead very quickly to breakdown in relationships, confusion as to where you are leading the Church and resentments. Your commitment lies with your own Church, does it not? Your duty is to them to work things through together. You don't need to have things all sewn up and sorted before you start talking to your congregation about what you're going to do. Involve them in your thinking and decision making – but again be wise in who you seek actual advice from. For example, before you've worked out the nuts and bolts of civil disobedience, it's a good idea to relay to your congregation the huge problems with the Covid mandates and their anti-Biblical nature and that we must take a different path. This allows your flock time and headspace to come onboard with where you are steering the ship and prepares them for your stance – increasing the likelihood that faith-filled Christians will stand in agreement with you.

#5 Burn out: This is related to keeping healthy disciplines and personal habits (or lack thereof) that we looked at earlier. What started as what many people thought to be a sprint under Covid has turned into a marathon. Pastors and Church leaders who are continuing at an unsustainable pace are needing to reassess for long term sustainability, both for their Churches and themselves. This means that conversations and practices around self-care – physical, mental and spiritual – are vital and perhaps more vital than ever.

Desire Versus Duty

Men – Church leaders and heads of households – I am addressing this section specifically to you. I fully appreciate that in some circumstances, the LORD will raise up women to lead Churches but generally, men are called to lead and women to follow, as outlined in the Bible and as per the model of headship ...

Have you ever read the excellent book by John Eldredge called 'Wild at Heart: Discovering the Secret of a Man's Soul'? If not, I'd highly recommend it and it will help you greatly in your Church leadership at this time. (The counterpart book for women, written by John and his wife Stasi, is called 'Captivating: Unveiling the Mystery of a Woman's Soul'). 'Wild at Heart' really delves into the core of men's deepest desires and validation. It describes how God has put certain desires in our hearts and that we are meant to have those desire fulfilled – and not just in the New Creation, but also in a smaller way right here and now. These desires are essential in order to live life as the man God has designed you to be; they provide the power for your life. If you neglect or misdirect these desires, they do not go away, instead they go underground and resurface later in anger, addiction and compulsion and you pay the high price for the consequences of these sins. John states that men have three core desires: For a battle to fight, an adventure to live and a beauty to rescue. If you have a wife, then you have rescued the beauty – and you will need to keep doing so, going after her heart, in order for your marriage to flourish. Let's look in more detail at the other two desires that are especially relevant to your role in the Covid Church situation …

Your Desire a Battle to Fight and an Adventure to Live

Every boy knows he is made for battle, and he longs to be the mighty hero. Give him a cape and a sword and he comes alive in a world of superheroes and combat. This is good and natural because men are made in the image of a Warrior God: *"The LORD is a man of war, the LORD is his name"* (Exodus 15:3). Our LORD Himself is a warrior and men are uniquely created (unlike women) to be like Him in this specific way. Thus, every man needs a battle to fight. A man also craves a wild adventure to live. Think about it – the greatest moments of your life and where you've felt truly alive have been when you've been on a risky adventure of some sort. That sailing trip on the open sea, or trekking across mountains with your buddies, or preaching a sermon from the pulpit that you've put your heart and soul into is risky in some way. That's also why every time God gets hold of a man in the Biblical record, he takes him into high-stakes adventure ... Abraham, Moses, Elijah, David, Peter, Paul, John – all swept up into great adventures designed by God. John Eldredge states that *"Christianity is not an invitation to be a really nice guy; it is an invitation into a Larger Story in which you play a decisive role."*[422] The trouble is this: Your heart as a man slowly dies when you are stuck doing humdrum, bureaucratic, red tape tasks that are not your highest calling, where your hands are tied and where you have no sense of adventure in them. The Covid rules and mandates that have come about since the beginning of 2020 are in danger of, if they have not already, quashing that warrior spirit in you and your sense of adventure – in your role as a pastor, preacher and leader. Your masculine, warrior, adventurous nature is desperately needed, by the women in your life and by the Church. But in order for a man to fight for his life, his marriage, his children, his dreams, his integrity, his Church and live a wild adventure in Christ, he must first get his heart back as a warrior. John Eldredge says this in his blog post on becoming a warrior:[423] *"God gave you a warrior heart because you were born into a world at war. Surely you are aware of this – your life is opposed. Your love is opposed. Your hopes, your dreams, your friendships, your joy [your Church] – all fiercely opposed. How much hardship a man will endure, how long and tenaciously he will persevere, is determined by the warrior within him ...The heart of the warrior says, "I will put myself on the line for you. I will not let evil have its way. There are some things that cannot be endured. I've got to do something. There is freedom to be had." It's time to quit asking, "Why is life so hard?" and take the hardness as the call to fight, to rise up, face it down, set your 'face as flint', as Jesus had to do to fulfil his life's greatest mission (Isaiah 50:7). You are a warrior, and your destiny is to join the Great Warrior in his battle against evil. And, by the way, **Jesus was not the poster child for pacifism; he wasn't the World's Nicest Guy. Christianity does not ask men to become altar boys; it calls them up as warriors."***

---

[422] Eldredge, John. Wild at Heart: Discovering the Secret of a Man's Soul. Thomas Nelson Publishing, 2001.

[423] 'Becoming a Warrior'. *Wild at Heart*, https://wildatheart.org/story/real-men/becoming-warrior. Accessed 5 May 2021.

Man of Christ – what we are facing within the worldwide Church now is the biggest call to adventure of your life. This is your chance to shine in your God-ordained role as a warrior; to lead your Church in truth and with courage and boldness, like never before. Do not miss this opportunity. If you do not answer this call, you will be stuck in deception and bound by duty (the wrong sort) and it is likely that your heart and identity as a man will slowly wither, as I have seen and heard of in many instances in the past months. Many Church leaders are deeply discouraged at this time and facing mental health struggles, which I am convinced is rooted in this. Yes, it may mean severe persecution for you, but wouldn't you rather be alive in your faith, alive as a man and with a stunning sense adventure and noble battle to be fighting (as men who are standing up at this time are attesting to), or would you rather be 'safely' cowering in your leadership and following the deceitful lies that have been imposed on us, with no sense of real agency and recovery from this situation? I hope and pray you will choose the former path and that you will ask the LORD for His grace and strength to answer the call and lead your Church in truth and righteousness – to boldly contend for the faith, as the Christians and martyrs of old have done. Remember, we are not called to 'safety' as the Covid authoritarians would have us believe. We are called to peace with God through obedience, as Bonhoeffer astutely wrote in 'A Testament to Freedom': *"There is no way to peace along the way of safety. For peace must be dared. It is itself the great venture and can never be safe. Peace is the opposite of security. To demand guarantees is to want to protect oneself. Peace means giving oneself completely to God's commandment. Wanting no security, but in faith and obedience laying the destiny of the nations in the hand of almighty God. Not trying to direct it for selfish purposes. Battles are won not with weapons, but with God. They are won when the way leads to the cross."*

Encouraging Scriptures for Pastors

Let's end with some verse from Scripture to help and encourage you in your role in these difficult circumstances:

"And the Lord, He is the One who goes before you. He will be with you, He will not leave you nor forsake you; do not fear nor be dismayed." – Deuteronomy 31:8 (NKJV)

"When a man's ways please the Lord, he makes even his enemies to be at peace with him." – Proverbs 16:7

"Fear not, for I am with you; Be not dismayed, for I am your God. I will strengthen you, Yes, I will help you, I will uphold you with My righteous right hand." – Isaiah 41:10 (NKJV)

"So that we may boldly say, The LORD is my helper, and I will not fear what man shall do unto me." – Hebrews 13:6

"Have I not commanded you? Be strong and of good courage; do not be afraid, nor be dismayed, for the Lord your God is with you wherever you go." – Joshua 1:9 (NKJV)

"For you did not receive the spirit of bondage again to fear, but you received the Spirit of adoption by whom we cry out, "Abba, Father."" – Romans 8:15 (NKJV)

"What shall we then say to these things? If God be for us, who can be against us?" – Romans 8:31

CHAPTER THIRTEEN

Twelve Step Recovery Plan for All Christians

We have looked at reflections and guidance for Church leaders and pastors, let's now look at how all Christians can reclaim and live in godly personal authority throughout these troubling times – a 'twelve step recovery plan' if you will. These twelve points are helpful at all times, not just in the wake of Covid, but are particularly important now. They include some physical health tips and mindset advice as well as solid and standard Biblical precepts. This is your plan for living with patient endurance and shining bright for Christ in this dark world as we move further into this tyranny.

1. Come Out of Denial

It is so very tempting to doubt the tyranny that is going on; we are constantly confronted with Covid. We hear of people who have the virus and a friend of a friend who has been ill for months with it, government statistics rising, 'new variants' and hospitals supposedly over-run. Then there's the shutdown of the economy, everyone wearing masks and the whole world pushing the experimental vaccine. It is easy to doubt our position, easy to start questioning whether we might have got this whole thing wrong, or even wondering if we should just acquiesce and go along with the world's (and sadly, most of the Church's) viewpoint: Maybe, *"if you can't beat 'em, join 'em"?* Even in writing this book, I've had several moments where I've thought, *"well, there's nothing you can do to stop this, so why not just submit to it all and chill out?"*

I've been accused many times of wasting much time and energy in writing this book and that I should 'just focus on Jesus'. I've wondered at times if this is indeed a valuable endeavour or not (and the LORD has swiftly confirmed that it is, in many remarkable ways, praise Him). Maybe you have been accused of similar if you've tried to blow the whistle on any of the Covid deceptions and dangers? Well, the fact is, this is the reality we are living in. We are living in times of *great deception,* like the world has never known. Jesus tells us that this will happen. Just because the whole world has believed a vast set of lies, it does not excuse us doing so. We know the truth, and we will be blessed and retain sound minds if we 'live not by lies' as Aleksandr Solzhenitsyn famously stated, and Rod Dreher sets forth in his book of the same name. Again, I'd highly recommend reading that book to help you resolve to come out of denial and live in truth, no matter how hostile it gets. Aleksandr Solzhenitsyn reminds us, *"You can resolve to live your life with integrity. Let your credo be this: Let the lie come into the world, let it even triumph. But not through me."* Our love, speech and contending for our faith must be rooted in truth: *"Love suffers long and is kind; love does not envy; love does not parade itself, is not puffed up; does not behave rudely, does not seek its own, is not provoked, thinks no evil; does not rejoice in iniquity, but rejoices in the truth."* – 1 Corinthians 13:4-6 (NKJV)

"Stand therefore, having your loins girt about with truth, and having on the breastplate of righteousness". – Ephesians 6:14

"Lying lips are abomination to the Lord: but they that deal truly are his delight." – Proverbs 12:22

One thing I have noticed in more and more Christians as this goes on, is a departing from seeing what's going on in the world and the truth of

Scripture. Many people are increasingly unable to reconcile the two, wondering 'where's God in all of this'? It is my suspicion, and I could be wrong in this, but I do wonder if, as people are refusing to come to a realisation of what's going on and watch and pray and understand the times we are in, the Bible becomes increasingly mythologised, instead of utterly relevant and speaking to us directly in our situation. I have found that as the lies and oppression increase, the truths of Scripture have become vividly real to me. When David speaks of 'enemies surrounding me' in Psalms, I can relate to it completely and my fervency in praying his pleas to the LORD has increased. I have heard other Christians say naively that *"we can't relate to that in our situation here, we just have a virus going on, we don't really have enemies in this country."* Oh dear.

Will it be hard to swim against the tide of lies? Yes, it will. Will there be a freedom of conscience and soundness of mind in it that the world and even other Christians will forfeit from not doing so? Yes! And for you, dear reader, you know too much. You have read this book; you cannot unlearn what you've read and seen here (and possibly known or suspected long before doing so). You've seen 'behind the curtain', you've had the magic trick explained to you, so you have to act in that knowledge and it is good and righteous to do so. To try and ignore this will cause you great cognitive dissonance and could cause mental health issues and depression. I see Christians who have a little knowledge of this stuff but are refusing to live in truth and call out the lies and they are losing their strength of character; sadly, their faith is waning, and many are suffering with depression. Keep in good conscience, keep calm and resolve to live in the truth, if only in your little area of life and thought and sphere of influence. There is power and godliness in that and much blessing from the LORD, who wants us to live in truth.

2. Resolve to Have No King But Jesus

Keep your eyes, mind and heart fixed on Jesus. Remember that He goes before us and fights for us, so keep in close behind Him and resolve to follow Him in any and all circumstances and at any cost. Set your face like flint and be prepared to exercise patient endurance under trial and without compromise. Remember, you are a child of the Most-High King and a citizen of His Kingdom, not of this world, so set that as your standard and do not defile yourself with idols of any kind, nor follow any human precepts in favour of His.

3. Get Serious About Fasting, Prayer and Praise

We are amidst an astronomical world crisis and many people are not seeing the true picture, but you have a glimpse at least into the real nature of it all ... Now is the time to get serious about your prayer life and fasting, especially if fasting has not been part of your godly disciplines prior to now. There are huge spiritual strongholds and demonic forces at play in the world and in various situations in your life and relationships, with deception in high places and many of your loved ones being deceived and unsaved. Jesus tells us that in these instances, the only way to breakthrough in the spiritual realm is through prayer and fasting (Matthew 17:21). If you are new to fasting, you may not want to start with a three-day water fast. It's probably a good idea to start off gently – skip one meal, then two, then try a complete day. Most people find fasting difficult, and I think it's supposed to be (although not always). It's an opportunity for us to depend on the LORD instead of our usual sustenance. We get a chance to focus on Him, undistracted by and denying our physical comforts for a time, to draw close to Him in extended prayer. I find the LORD speaks to me in a much deeper and richer way when I fast and pray – I love it! It's been used by Christians all through the ages for their maturity and intimacy with God and to bring powerful warfare in the spiritual realm. Keep it in your arsenal and use it often. Also, it's not just food you could fast from – you can fast from TV, music, certain foods, luxuries and indulgences, etc. Remember too that our LORD loves to hear your worship with hymns, songs and Psalms of praise to Him. It doesn't matter if you have a good singing voice or not. A heart rendered in praise and adoration to our LORD is sweet music to His ears, gladdens our hearts and is powerful spiritual warfare against the enemy.

4. Guard Your Senses and Increase Your Holiness

TURN OF YOUR TV. TURN OFF YOUR TV. TURN OFF YOUR TV! In fact, why not get rid of it altogether? The people whose eyes are open to what's going on know that the television is exceedingly danger-ous and is bewitching people, non-Christians and Christians alike, into their destruction by Satanic forces. Your TV is pushing the world into both Satanism and Statism. This is not an understatement, nor am I using hyperbole here. Anton LaVey, founder of the Church of Satan and author of 'The Satanic Bible' (1969) says this of the television: *"The TV set is the Satanic family altar. Many of you already read my writings in-dicating that TV is the new god. There is a little thing I neglected to men-tion up until now, television is the major mainstream infiltration for the new satanic religion ... There are television sets in every home, every res-taurant, every hotel room, every shopping mall-now they're even small enough to carry in your pocket like electronic rosaries. It is an unques-tioned part of everyday life. Kneeling before the cathode ray god, with our TV Guide concordance in hand, we maintain the illusion of choice by flipping channels (chapters and verses). It doesn't matter what is flashing on the screen-all that's important is that the TV stays on ... In previous centuries, the Church was the great controller, dictating morality, stifling free expression and posing as conservator of all great art and music. In-stead, we have TV, doing just as good a job at dictating fashions, thoughts, attitudes, objectives as did the Church, using many of the same techniques but doing it so palatably that no one notices. Instead of 'sins' to keep people in line, we have fears of being judged unacceptable by our peers (by not wearing the right shoes, not drinking the right kind of beer, or wearing the wrong kind of deodorant). Coupled with that fear is im-posed insecurity concerning our own identities. All answers and solutions to these fears come through the television, and only through television. Only through exposure to TV can the new sins of alienation and ostracism be absolved."*

In light of this, I don't think my allegory in this book – 'The Modern Metal Image' – is an exaggeration in assessing the TV as a modern idol set up in every home. According to Cicero, Roman statesman and philosopher around before Jesus' incarnation, the goal of education was to free the student from the 'tyranny of the present', to give them a greater historical context. But TV aims to keep us in the perpetual present and a fantasy one at that. Adding visual context to meaningless, soundbite information gives it the illusion or relevancy, but the image does nothing to make it valuable. All subjects are presented as entertainment, since the average TV shot is less than three seconds and aims to keep you captivated by novelty. Professor Neil Postman prophesied in his book 'Amusing Ourselves to Death' (1985)[424] that we are becoming a trivial culture by our entertainment and that the truth is drowned in lies. Postman argues that our enemy is not Big Government and that ultimately the tyranny is not coming from them, but that it is self-inflicted through entertainment and TV, taking over the culture, history and true religion (Christianity) of a society and form a trivial culture, unable to distinguish between truth and lies and indifferent to the two anyhow. We are captive to our own distractions and we have become people who see all of life through the lens of entertainment and news media. Also, you've seen from Chapter 10 who owns and controls the mainstream media and what their agendas are. The fact is that every idea communicated (and we are subject to many thousands each day) has consequences for shaping our reality and affects our levels of understanding and being able to discern and value truth. Postman asserts that: *"Form will determine the nature of content ... What is happening here is that television is altering the meaning of 'being informed' by creating a species of information that might properly be called disinformation. Disinformation does not mean false information. It means misleading information – misplaced, irrelevant, fragmented or superficial information – information that creates the illusion of knowing something but which in fact leads one away from knowing ... When news is packaged as entertainment, that is the inevitable result. And in saying that the television news show entertains but does not inform, I am saying something far more serious than that we are being deprived of authentic*

---

[424] Postman, Neil. *Amusing Ourselves to Death.* Methuen Publishing, 1987.

information. I am saying we are losing our sense of what it means to be well informed ... What shall we do if we take ignorance to be knowledge? Spiritual devastation is more likely to come from an enemy with a smiling face."

If we think about it, the ideas being communicated to us via our TVs are not being argued, debated or backed up unbiasedly – especially around Covid and vaccines in our situation (I refer you back to the dark web of influence that Bill Gates, for example, has on shaping the information we receive – medical 'science', university research, vaccine information, news media, government policy, food, and technology information, etc. – see Chapter 4). And with the fiercely hostile censorship and labelling of any opposing view to the mainstream narrative as 'fake news', there is zero room for critical analysis via the mass populace's conventional means of receiving information – TV, news and social media, science and government websites. C.S. Lewis said that *"The most dangerous ideas in a society are the ones not being argued, but the ones that are assumed."* That is exactly what is going in now and the squeeze is getting rapidly tighter. Free speech is disappearing at a furious pace – we need to take measures to protect it, if only in our own lives and homes. Our TVs and devices go on and our brains go off. Further, being 'informed' about something is not the same as acting upon it. Disliking something on social media does not constitute standing against it. The worse-case scenario is that we stop caring about truth and righteousness, throw our hands up in downtrodden surrender and indifferently say, *"who can know?!"* Or with the appearance of piety, *"well, God is in control!"*

As Christians, we do not have the option of succumbing to lies, Jesus forbids it and we cannot afford to choose style over substance, nor looking good and rational over being good and rational. We are told in Scripture to test everything. We must ask of the information we take in: *"How is this defining terms? Who is putting out this information? Why? What is it saying about reality, morality, justice? Is it true?"*

Popular is different from good, right and excellent. If we wish to seek entertainment, that's fine. But don't confuse TV entertainment with serious information, it is not. TV is the 'soma' (the all-purpose drug) of the Brave New World that Aldous Huxley talks about. It is wise to seek entertainment that takes you deeper into life and its meaning, not detract from it – via excellent quality books such as Bunyan's 'Pilgrim's Progress' and Christian biographies and music from the likes of Bach and Handel, for example. C.S. Lewis proposed that we are far too easily pleased with nonsense and junk entertainment. So, let's look for excellence in both our entertainment and information. Our information should be tested and true and received via well-written books, lectures, sermons and other reliable sources, not news media soundbites, nor biased 'science' reports and statistics coming from the Gates/Fauci camp.

We are reminded in Revelation 18 to come out of Babylon. Do not revel in satanic entertainment such as Disney, Marvel films, Harry Potter, news media, Hollywood films, mainstream music, etc. Far too many Christians are blissfully unaware of the spiritual strongholds and dangers of these things; Christians of the past were not. Get smart, read godly books, limit your screen time and be vigilant on what kind of media you consume. Be very careful what enters your body through your eye gate, ear gate, mouth and what you do with your hands and feet – what you put your efforts to and where you go. Remember, again, Matthew 6:22-23 (NKJV): *"The lamp of the body is the eye. If therefore your eye is good, your whole body will be full of light. But if your eye is bad, your whole body will be full of darkness. If therefore the light that is in you is darkness, how great is that darkness!"* Just think how the world would be in a very different place if no one had a TV. Without the bombardment of psychological warfare being thrown at us via the black box altar in the corner of the living room, we'd probably be carrying on as what used to be normal, with little, if any, consequence. Dr Joel Beeke, president and professor of systematic theology and homiletics at Puritan Reformed Theological Seminary and pastor of the Heritage Reformed Congregation in Grand Rapids, Michigan since 1986 affirms my position on the TV:[425] *"TV is a flood of sin. It numbs its watchers against all ten commandments ... Do yourself a favor: for the Word of God's sake, the Church's sake, your own soul's sake, your family's sake, your conscience's sake, dispose of your television today. Do it permanently before you become its lifelong slave."*

Christian, let's heed Paul's exhortation in Philippians and filter all our information input through this test: *"Finally, brethren, whatsoever things are true, whatsoever things are honest, whatsoever things are just, whatsoever things are pure, whatsoever things are lovely, whatsoever things are of good report; if there be any virtue, and if there be any praise, think on these things."* – Philippians 4:8

5. Repent

The world and the Church are in a dire state and it didn't happen overnight. It's a result of decades of sin and unrighteousness and, for Christians, not taking our holy living and commitment to following Jesus seriously enough. We need to repent of that. We must repent of our own personal sins – such as watching too much Satanic television, as we've just looked at, but also those other 'acceptable' sins, such as gluttony, pride, anger, jealousy, envy, cowardice, fear, etc. I'd highly recommend reading Jerry Bridges' book 'Respectable Sins' on this. As well as repenting personally, do you repent on behalf of your nation, Church, world and other people? I do this often and you can see a clear precedent for this kind of intercessory confession and repentance prayer in Scripture. Nehemiah is a good example of this: *"And I said: "I pray, Lord God of heaven, O great and awesome God, You who keep Your covenant and mercy with those who love You and observe Your commandments, please let Your ear be attentive and Your eyes open, that You may hear the prayer of Your servant which I pray before You now, day and night, for*

---

[425] Beeke, Dr Joel R. 'Is TV Really So Bad (Joel Beeke)'. *Simplemann*, 11 Jan. 2010, https://simplemann.wordpress.com/2010/01/11/is-tv-really-so-bad-joel-beeke/.

the children of Israel Your servants, and confess the sins of the children of Israel which we have sinned against You. Both my father's house and I have sinned. We have acted very corruptly against You, and have not kept the commandments, the statutes, nor the ordinances which You commanded Your servant Moses." – Nehemiah 1:5-7 (NKJV)

Here's a few of our national and world sins we can be repenting of:

- Abortion mass murder
- Sodomy
- Lies of evolutionism
- Pornography
- Child trafficking and sacrifice
- Freemasonry
- Love of money and comfort
- State idolatry
- Humanism
- Utilitarianism
- Eugenics
- Scientism
- Health service idolatry
- Television 'modern metal image' idolatry.
- Medical 'pharmakeia' sorcery ... to name but a few.

We can repent on behalf of our Churches for things such as fear of man, cowardice, fear of disease, allowing the profane to enter our holy worship, not following the LORD's commands as prescribed concerning our worship (neglecting to gather, sing, partake in the Lord's Supper etc.) and dissension and rivalry within the body of Christ, as well as some of the sins listed above. If we do not confess and repent of our sins within the Church and of our yoking with the world, especially in the advent of Covid, it will not go well for us. Let us also not forget that revival starts with repentance.

"Do not be unequally yoked together with unbelievers. For what fellow-ship has righteousness with lawlessness? And what communion has light with darkness? And what accord has Christ with Belial? Or what part has a believer with an unbeliever? And what agreement has the temple of God with idols? For you are the temple of the living God. As God has said: "I will dwell in them And walk among them. I will be their God, And they shall be My people." Therefore "Come out from among them And be separate, says the Lord. Do not touch what is unclean, And I will receive you."" – 2 Corinthians 6:14-17

6. Memorise Scripture

Who knows where we are headed and how much longer we may have free access to Bibles and Biblical teaching? The reasons for memorising Scripture are manifold - as Psalm 119:11 tells us: *"Thy word have I hid in mine heart, that I might not sin against thee."* Once the Bible is in us, it cannot be taken from us and the Holy Spirit can bring Scripture passages to our minds and lips for preaching and to counsel, guide, discipline and comfort us as needed. You may have heard it said that *"either the Word keeps you from sin or sin keeps you from the Word"*. There's wisdom in heeding this. If you're not used to memorising the Bible, or have let it lapse, why not start by learning a few Psalms? Psalms 1 and 2 to get started. Then try a chapter of one of Paul's letters, then why not the whole letter? My friend Peter has committed a lot of the Gospels to memory so far and he delights in reciting to us when we go for walks. He has suggested that his Church commit to learning the whole New Testament between them – each person taking a book and committing it to memory, so that between them, if their Bibles are taken away, they have access to it. Of course, saints of old have always memorised great swathes of Scripture – many, many people knowing the whole Bible by heart, which is just mind-blowing in our generation to think about isn't it! So, let's make our attempt – we are reminded not to despise the day of small beginnings (Zechariah 4:10), as in time we will rejoice to see the great work Christ has done.

433

7. Evangelise

Share the Gospel. Quite simply, time is short – go follow Christ's command to make/teach disciples. It keeps your faith active and sharp, and it keeps you depending on Jesus and experiencing a deeper joy in Him, not to mention showing a pure and deep love to lost people and storing up treasures in heaven for yourself.

"And Jesus came and spake unto them, saying, All power is given unto me in heaven and in earth. Go ye therefore, and teach all nations, baptizing them in the name of the Father, and of the Son, and of the Holy Ghost: Teaching them to observe all things whatsoever I have commanded you: and, lo, I am with you always, even unto the end of the world. Amen." – Matthew 28:18-20

8. Keep Good (Underground) Church Fellowship

We need to keep gathering and meeting in worship and fellowship, *"not forsaking the assembling of ourselves together, as is the manner of some, but exhorting one another, and so much the more as you see the Day approaching."* – Hebrews 10:25 (NKJV). Friend, the Day is drawing near and the times are getting more and more evil and we desperately need each other. It is my strong belief that the days of big, open Churches are over – at least for the true and faithful Church. As we have looked at in Chapter 7 on Nazi Germany and how the German Church kept its form and name but lost its Biblical adherence, compromising heavily with the State, we can see many parallels now and would be wise to heed where all this is going – into a soft or hard totalitarian regime. We need to make our provisions for Church accordingly, which will inevitably mean starting underground Church fellowships: Meeting in homes and other discreet locations with like-minded Christians who have a level of understanding of what's really going on in the guise of a 'pandemic' and beyond. I refer you back to Chapter 11 on Reclaiming Rightful Church Authority for more information and recommended books on how to organise your underground Church fellowship. As this situation progresses and as we can see now, there are many believers who, for whatever reason, refuse or are unable to see what's really going on and the bigger picture. They are still convincing themselves that this is a legitimate virus, that the government is here to help 'keep us safe' and that soon enough things will return to normal. Sad as this is, it makes it increasingly harder to fellowship and pray with these Christians. You're praying about protection from government tyranny, opportunities to evangelise in person and about how best to meet in secret and the like and they're praying that we have access to more vaccines, for people who are 'shielding', 'self-isolating' and 'tested positive' (yet showing no symptoms) and about implementing more restrictions to Church worship. How can there be true unity in these two very differing opinions? This is an awful situation and is causing schisms between brothers and sisters in Christ and the enemy is relishing this. But if you have warned people and they will not listen, you need to find other likeminded believers who you can walk in step with, through this situation, ready for what is to come. Also, this is a time to be seeking and offering good and honest discipleship, counselling and healing within your fellowship circles. We can often have emotional or spiritual wounds that may be keeping us in bondage, fear and negative or sinful patterns. We may need to talk and work things through. Seek the counsel and healing ministry of a close few, wise friends. There are a couple of great resources and teaching aids that spring to mind: The book 'Instruments in the Redeemer's Hands'[426] by Paul David Tripp and the 'Wild at Heart' ministry resources[427] of John and Stasi Eldredge.

9. Make Wise Decisions

Make very careful, well-considered decisions on what the authorities are telling us to do and what is best for us, weighed up against Scriptural commands. We are to use our God-given mind and apply critical thinking to our reasoning. Test the spirits and act with wisdom and shrewdness. If

---

[426] Tripp, Paul David. Instruments in the Redeemer's Hands: People in Need of Change Helping People in Need of Change. R&R Publishing, 2002.

[427] *Wild at Heart*. https://wildatheart.org/. Accessed 5 May 2021.

you have children, you may want to strongly consider removing them from public schools, owing to their sinful teaching on sexuality, heavy New World Order and Covid brainwashing and regulations around testing and vaccinations.

10. Improve Your Diet and Health Disciplines

We are under attack from all angles. We have unjust, autocratic governments seeking to seize our minds and free-thinking, shame us for our Christian beliefs, inject us with poison, zap us with massive doses of 5G radiation, feed us junk foods that sabotage our good diet and health, take our property (via the 'Great Reset) and isolate us ... we need to take steps to combat these, even if small ones in comparison. We need energy and good physical mental and spiritual health to live fully in Christ. So, let's improve our diet and health disciplines. This is a huge topic, but here are a few simple and powerful actions you can take to defend against the warfare being wrought against us:

- Get a high-quality water filter – one which removes fluoride, chlorine and smaller toxin particles such as medical waste and volatile organic compounds (VOCs).
- Take immune-boosting foods and supplements, such as vitamins D, C and Zinc.
- Eat plenty of prebiotics and probiotics to improve your gut microbiome health.
- Eat fresh, natural foods – including plenty of organic meats and vegetables. Lower your refined carbs, sugar, refined vegetable oils and margarines and GMOs (especially wheat). Cook from scratch rather than getting packaged goods with added chemicals.
- Get daily exercise and fresh air – a simple brisk outdoor walk each day for 30 minutes should be your minimum.
- Minimise your screen time and EMF (electromagnetic frequency) exposure. Turn off your Wi-Fi at night, wear blue-blocking

glasses to protect your eyes and where possible, connect to the internet via ethernet cable instead of Wi-Fi.

- Consider getting an infrared sauna and/or and oxygen concentrator machine to boost your immunity and oxygenate your body.
- Avoid medications as far as possible (check with your doctor), they are toxins and compromise your gut and immune health, which can, surprisingly, negatively impact your mental health.

11. Do Not Fear the World – Fear God

The Bible tells us 366 times not to fear. When it says this, it means do not fear your enemies, do not fear lack of provision, do not fear men and their opinions, do not fear death, do not fear suffering, etc. In other words, our LORD tells us not to fear worldly and temporal things. But we are told that the fear of the LORD is the beginning of wisdom (Proverbs 1:7, Proverbs 9:10); we are to fear Him, the One who reigns eternal. There is a wrongful teaching in the Church which says that 'fearing God' does not actually mean fearing Him, but it only means respect and reverence. I would disagree. We can absolutely love our LORD and fear Him at the same time and it is totally Biblical to do so – look at Isaiah's reaction to facing the reality of Jesus' awesomeness in the temple in Isaiah 6. Our God is stunning in power and might and He exercises judgement on wickedness. Personally, I do not want to be on the receiving end of His judgement and discipline. I fear for myself when I am wilfully going against His will. An improper fear of the LORD tells us that God is gracious and loving and forgives us, full stop. Yes, He does, but He is also full of righteousness and we are not to take advantage of His grace, patience and mercy and we can expect bad consequences when we do. Why would we ever want to presume upon His kindness? Jesus Christ gave up His life for us. Thus, the antidote to fearing the world is a greater fear of the LORD. Fear Him more and your fear of man and suffering will diminish. Put another way, when you preoccupy yourself with pleasing God alone, opinions and consequences from doing so matter much less and do not stop you from taking the right actions with bold courage. We should be prepared to stand alone in righteousness if necessary, and it's not only OK but a privilege to do so.

12. Prepare for Persecution

"And all that will live godly in Christ Jesus shall suffer persecution. But evil men and seducers shall wax worse and worse, deceiving, and being deceived." – 2 Timothy 3:12-13

Here are some great prayers to prepare us for persecution, even if we pray them with trepidation. Ask the LORD to tear down your idols and give you the grace to give up your comforts and security other than Him. Ask Him to give you the strength and courage to endure to the end, even if it means persecution and martyrdom. Ask Him to remove your fear of man and fear of suffering and give you His perspective on suffering for His sake (as per Acts 5:41 and Philippians 3:10-11). Ask the LORD to give you a love of the truth. Read Christian biographies of people throughout history who have suffered for Christ's sake. Buy and read books such as 'Foxe's Book of Martyrs', 'The Autobiography of George Muller', 'The Insanity of God' by Nik Ripken, 'Through Gates of Splendour' by Elisabeth Elliot, 'The Heavenly Man' by Brother Yun, 'Tortured for Christ' by Richard Wurmbrand and other persecution and martyrdom books. Great preparatory reading and very faith expanding!

'Live Not By Lies' (by Rod Dreher) recommends doing six things to prepare for the persecution to come in the West:

1. Value nothing more than the truth.
2. Cultivate cultural memory.
3. Prioritise family as resistance cells.
4. Understand that religion is the bedrock of resistance.
5. Stand in solidarity.
6. Accept suffering as a gift.

Subscribe to Voice of the Martyrs[428] to educate yourself about persecution around the world and intercede for your brothers and sisters in Christ who are suffering. Remember that your true home is not here but it is coming soon. We are but foreigners and sojourners here on the earth right now. This physical life is only temporary, a mere breath. We will be at home eternally with Christ in the New Creation soon enough!

Bonus: Prepare Practically

You might want to prepare yourself for a disaster situation and protect your home, buy land, source alternate energy and food sources (plant vegetables and keep animals and the like) and gather other supplies. Just remember to temper this with faith and point 11 (do not fear).

Conclusions

As you can see from this 'twelve step recovery plan', the key to thriving as a Christian in these times is not so much about asking, *"what do I need to do?"*, but rather, *"who do I need to be?"* We cannot afford to be lukewarm. We need to be people of fervent prayer and tenacious Bible scholars; readers and learners. We need to be disciplined, repentant, worshipful, watchful and obedient to God and then wise actions and the fruit of the Spirit will flow from these things.

---

[428] *The Voice of the Martyrs*, https://www.persecution.com/. Accessed 5 May 2021.

CHAPTER FOURTEEN

Your One and Only True Solution to Overcome This Mess

If you are a believer in Christ, then you will already know the one and only ultimate solution out of this dark mess is your salvation in Jesus and the firm and blessed hope we have in Him. We know that He is returning to the earth soon in righteous judgement to get rid of all sin, evil and death once and for all. He will renew the heavens and the earth and will raise us to eternal life in our glorious resurrection bodies. Hallelujah!

"And the Spirit and the bride say, "Come!" And let him who hears say, "Come!" And let him who thirsts come. Whoever desires, let him take the water of life freely." – Revelation 22:17 (NKJV)

Hell is No Joke

If you have not yet put your faith and hope in Christ, then you need to as soon as possible – today! The Bible tells us that *now* is the favourable time, today is the day of salvation (2 Corinthians 6:2). Do not delay any longer because no one knows the day or time of their death and if you die in your sins, then you will be condemned to Hell forever. This is not popular, not politically correct, not nice to hear, but it is the truth and I tell you this out of love, so that you take what I'm saying seriously.

You were put on this earth, by Him, for Him, the one who loves you and knows you better than anyone else. He desires to see you accomplish the purpose and plans He designed you uniquely for. It's the reason for life, He is the reason. You were made to glorify God by shining His image, in Christ.

"For God so loved the world that He gave His only begotten Son, that whoever believes in Him should not perish but have everlasting life. For God did not send His Son into the world to condemn the world, but that the world through Him might be saved. He who believes in Him is not condemned; but he who does not believe is condemned already, because he has not believed in the name of the only begotten Son of God." – John 3:16-18 (NKJV)

You might think, *"but I'm a pretty good person"*. Don't you believe it. We have all sinned and fallen short of the glory of God (Romans 3:23). Pastor and author, John MacArthur once remarked, *"people do not have to do something to go to hell; they just have to do nothing to go to hell."* This is true, since we are sinful in our very nature and we act continually from that sin nature, whether we choose to realise it or not.

Hell is a real, physical place, eternal, horrific, exceedingly painful, terrifying and isolated and Jesus warned of it often. He really doesn't want anyone to go there and you certainly don't want to either. It's not meant for people who are created to be loved by Him, but for the devil and his angels.

""Then He will also say to those on the left hand, 'Depart from Me, you cursed, into the everlasting fire prepared for the devil and his angels: And these will go away into everlasting punishment, but the righteous into eternal life."" – Matthew 25:41 and 46 (NKJV)

"And to you who are troubled rest with us, when the Lord Jesus shall be revealed from heaven with his mighty angels, In flaming fire taking vengeance on them that know not God, and that obey not the gospel of our Lord Jesus Christ: Who shall be punished with everlasting destruction from the presence of the Lord, and from the glory of his power". – 2 Thessalonians 1:7-9

Leonard Ravenhill remarked that Hell has no exits. There are no second chances. You need to repent and turn from your sins and receive forgiveness from God to secure your place in the new heavens and new earth.

In the advent of Covid and the dark deception and evil that it's brought with it, you might think that things are pretty bad. But if you do not put your faith and hope in Jesus then this is the very *best* it's going to be for you, compared to your eternity. This will feel like utter heaven compared to the literal Hell that is coming. Conversely, when you put your faith in Christ, even as this situation descends into deeper darkness and tribulation, this is the very *worst* it will ever be for you. Soon enough, you'll be in blissful eternity with the Living God forever. Can you see why this is so vitally important? It really is the biggest and most crucial thing to consider in your whole life.

The Gospel Remedy

The word Gospel simply means 'good news', which is the message of forgiveness for sin through the sacrifice Jesus Christ made on the cross as He was crucified, buried and then resurrected from the grave after three days. It is essentially God's rescue plan of redemption for those who will trust in His divine Son in order to be reconciled to a just and holy God and receive eternal life. This love story of God saving His people is laid out for us very clearly, rationally, historically, relationally and evidentially in the Bible.

"For I delivered to you first of all that which I also received: that Christ died for our sins according to the Scriptures, and that He was buried, and

that He rose again the third day according to the Scriptures, and that He was seen by Cephas, then by the twelve. After that He was seen by over five hundred brethren at once, of whom the greater part remain to the present, but some have fallen asleep. After that He was seen by James, then by all the apostles. Then last of all He was seen by me also". – 1 Corinthians 15:3-8 (NKJV)

"For Christ also suffered once for sins, the just for the unjust, that He might bring us to God, being put to death in the flesh but made alive by the Spirit". – 1 Peter 3:18

The Gospel message can be summed up by the following verse from the New Testament letter to the Romans, written by the apostle Paul:

"For the wages of sin is death; but the gift of God is eternal life through Jesus Christ our Lord." – **Romans 6:23**

Let's break down each part of this verse to clearly reveal what it is saying to us.

The wages – wages are earned or deserved. They are just payment for actions or services rendered.

Sin – anything that falls short of God's perfect standard of holiness. This standard of holiness and perfection is laid out in the Ten Commandments in Exodus 20:1-17, but in fact there are hundreds more laws listed in the Old Testament. If we break even one of these laws, we have committed a sin and it is regarded as breaking the whole of the law.

We are familiar with the commandments not to murder or not to commit adultery. But Jesus ups the ante on this. In His sermon on the mount in Matthew chapter 5, he says that if we even *think* an angry thought against someone, we have committed murder in our heart and will be subject to judgement and that if we lust after someone, we have committed adultery in our heart. If we examine ourselves for even a moment, we will see that we commit a great number of sins on a regular basis. Let me ask you, have you ever lied? Stolen? Been cowardly? Gossiped? Lusted after someone? Blasphemed? Envied? I know I have, countless times.

Further, sin is often an attitude as well as actions and omissions. A hostile or apathetic response to God is a sin. At any point in your life has God seemed non-existent? If so, this is a sin. Unless we are giving God proper acknowledgement, thanks, reverence and worship for who He is and what He has done, we are sinning profoundly – because we have made other things gods.

I hope you can see that by God's standard, we are all sinners.

Death – no more life! In the Biblical sense it has a physical and spiritual aspect. In death, we are cut off from the living God. This verse is saying that as sinners, all of us therefore deserve death and separation from the God who created and sustains us.

But – this is the most important word! It means that there is a 'however', or a hope of avoiding our just wages of death. This is the beginning of the good news of the Gospel.

Gift – Freely given, something not earned or deserved but given independently, usually out of kindness and paid for by the giver rather than the receiver.

God – The Holy Trinity who is Father, Son and Holy Spirit are the three persons of the Godhead. They are perfect and sinless. Jesus is the all-powerful Creator and sustainer of the universe. He is abounding in love and mercy but also in perfect righteousness and justice and will punish all sin.

Eternal life – Life that does not end. Eternal life refers to a relationship with God in blissful harmony forever. It starts in this life and extends into eternity. Sin cannot end it once you repent and are forgiven, but it does depend on our sins being forgiven to receive it.

Christ Jesus – The Messiah, Yeshua, Emmanuel – God taking on flesh and dwelling amongst us in human form. He is the means by which we obtain the gift of eternal life. He is the only one who can offer us the gift because he purchased it. He paid for it with His life, by dying as an atonement for our sins on the cross and shedding His precious blood. We must accept the gift Jesus wants to give us. He will not force it upon us. We can refuse a gift from the giver if we want, but you will, for sure, want to receive this most amazing gift …

Lord – Master, someone who we submit to, who has authority over us. He is none other than the eternal 'I Am' – LORD, Yahweh, Jehovah. The gift of eternal life is available to everyone who makes Jesus Christ, eternal Son of God the Father, Lord over their life. For Jesus to be Lord, we have to give him control and submit to His wisdom and authority – acknowledging in this that he knows what's better for us than we ourselves do. This can seem scary or strange but wouldn't the God who created you and the whole universe and who also died for you, in the most horrific way, know what is best for you and have your best interests at heart? Yes!

So, the essence of the Gospel is acknowledging Jesus as the God who became man and died for the sins of humanity and putting our faith in Him as our Saviour, Lord and King of our life (our eternal life with Him). It is not about trying to be better or a moral person, or going to Church and engaging in religious activities; although once you trust in Jesus, he regenerates us to become better people and we are commanded to be and delight in Church fellowship, with other believers in the 'body of Christ'. It's about a living, personal, intimate relationship with our Creator God.

Receiving the Holy Spirit

At the point when you become a true Christian by faith in Jesus, you are given the Holy Spirit – God's Spirit who comes to dwell in your heart and changes you to be more and more like Jesus over time and to testify with your own spirit in truth and wisdom.

"Then Peter said to them, "Repent, and let every one of you be baptized in the name of Jesus Christ for the remission of sins; and you shall receive the gift of the Holy Spirit." – Acts 2:38 (NKJV)

You can only know spiritual truth once you are born again and receive God's Holy Spirit. Receiving the Holy Spirit is a life-changing experience. The Holy Spirit regenerates your heart and gives you eternal life – starting now and lasting past physical death and into a physical resurrection to be forever with God in the new heavens and new earth when Jesus one day returns for His people.

You may have heard some Christians say that they have been 'born again' – that is exactly true. Once you receive the Spirit through faith in Jesus, your old sinful life has passed away and you have a new life in Christ. Your sins are completely forgiven and you are reconciled to God the Father, who you can now call your heavenly Father. Astonishingly, you are also declared completely righteous!

The Glorious and Risen Christ

Believing in Jesus is neither 'blind faith' nor merely some mental assent to Him as God. Rather, our knowledge and love of Him gives us immeasurable power, assurance, beauty and practical application in our lives – we are never the same again once we 'see' Jesus! He is utterly astounding, wonderful and is the fulness of both God and how humans are designed to be, if we were able to be free of sin. He is our best friend, our advocate, our wise guide, our strong protector, our rich provider of all things and He makes sense of all our deepest desires and questions about life and death.

"That the God of our Lord Jesus Christ, the Father of glory, may give to you the spirit of wisdom and revelation in the knowledge of Him, the eyes of your understanding being enlightened; that you may know what is the hope of His calling, what are the riches of the glory of His inheritance in the saints, and what is the exceeding greatness of His power toward us who believe, according to the working of His mighty power which He

worked in Christ when He raised Him from the dead and seated Him at His right hand in the heavenly places, far above all principality and power and might and dominion, and every name that is named, not only in this age but also in that which is to come." – Ephesians 1:17-21 (NKJV)

Get Right with God Today

You may have some insight into what's been taking place under Covid and maybe you can see the deception that others are not seeing, but this will not matter one jot on the day of judgement, unless you repent and be saved. You need to get right with God, today.

The Bible tells us how to be saved.

"That if you confess with your mouth the Lord Jesus and believe in your heart that God has raised Him from the dead, you will be saved. For with the heart one believes unto righteousness, and with the mouth confession is made unto salvation." – Romans 10:9-10 (NKJV)

So, take this seriously. Receive salvation that is available only through Jesus; place your faith in Him. Fully trust that His death is the sufficient sacrifice for your sins and rely on Him alone as your Saviour. If you have received Jesus as your Saviour, by all means, say a prayer to God. Tell God how thankful you are for Jesus and praise Him for His love and sacrifice. Thank Jesus for dying for your sins and providing salvation for you. If you do repent and believe upon Jesus, then you can pray a prayer like the one following, but be aware that merely reciting a formulaic prayer will not save you; it has to be a heart change and a turning from your sins.

Prayer – Acknowledgement of Sins and Thankfulness for Salvation

Dear Lord,

I admit that I am a sinner. I have done many things that don't please you. I have lived my life for myself only and have neglected You. I am sorry and I repent. I ask you to forgive me, cleanse me, Father, and make me Your child. Jesus, I believe that You died on the cross for me, to save me. You did what I could not do for myself. I come to you now and ask you to take control of my life; I give it to you. Please fill me with your Holy Spirit. From this day forward, help me to live every day for you and in a way that pleases you. Help me to grow in my love and obedience to you. I love you, Lord, and I thank you that I will spend all eternity with you.

Amen.

What Next?

It's important that you tell someone of your faith in Christ, to make it public, secure, and firm. Find another believer in Christ and let them know what has happened.

Now that you have a relationship with the Living God, talk to Him every day. You don't have to use formal words and stuffy language. Just come to God as a friend and in thankfulness and awe for what He has done for you. Tell Him your struggles, ask for help. He is a truly faithful and wonderful Friend and Counsellor. Draw near to Him and He will draw near to you as well.

Thank the Lord daily for your salvation. Pray for others in need. Seek his direction. Pray for the Lord to fill you daily with his Holy Spirit. There's really no limit to prayer. You can pray with your eyes closed or open, in your head or in written prayers, while sitting or standing, kneeling or lying on your bed, anywhere, anytime. Pray for yourself, the Church and other people, the mess of the world! You have access to the throne room of Heaven because of Jesus and you can come to your Heavenly Father at any time and He will listen to you and answer your prayers, in the ways He sees as best.

Also, find a Church or fellowship group and serve and be connected with other believers in Christ. You are an integral part of the Body of Christ and you need other people and they need you to flourish in faith and as His Bride. Jesus commands us to be baptised too – so if you have not yet been, ask a mature Christian or pastor about how and when you can be baptised. There is also the baptism of the Holy Spirit where His gifts are given to us and we are filled anew.

Make sure you read your Bible daily, this is the Word of God – God's love letter to you. It reveals Jesus to us and helps us to know, love and become like Him more and more. It will equip and train you for all the testing circumstances that life throws at you. It will comfort you, encourage you and show you how to grow in love, grace, spiritual maturity and effectiveness.

Life as a Christian may not be easy but it is full of joy, peace, rich fulfilment and security. To be a child of the Most-High God is a wonderful blessing and only found by the believer in Christ.

"Jesus said to him, "I am the way, the truth, and the life. No one comes to the Father except through Me." – John 14:6 (NKJV)

CONCLUSION

From Ephesians

I n concluding this book, rather than giving my best estimate on a summary of how to deal effectively with what the Church has, is and will be going through under the name of the 'Covid pandemic' and its associated mandates, I'll defer to the Bible's empirical wisdom instead. Looking at Ephesians chapters 4-6, we have some practical and inspired advice from Paul on how to deal with the situation we find ourselves in under Covid, which is merely a microcosm of the wider battle against darkness that we are always in, until Christ's return. Let's explore.

Disunity and the 'H' Word

Paul commands us to bear with one another in love and maintain unity in the Spirit (Ephesians 4:1-3). This will be harder to do as these corrupt and odious Covid mandates remain and increase within our Churches, as well as what's unfolding in the next stages of this game plan. If there is division in understanding and viewpoint on what should be accepted and adopted within our Churches, then there will be disunity and factions. Churches have split over differing views on baptism, the nature of Mary and the charismatic gifts, to name a few doctrinal issues. I have shown clearly that what has been instituted under Covid is a Gospel issue imposed upon us – an issue that interferes severely with Church being Church as Jesus commands us in Matthew 28. If you think I'm going too far on this, we need to refresh our memory on our lack of baptisms, gathered and fulsome worship, breaking bread together and evangelising the lost – a compromise on our practical belief that all authority in heaven and earth has been given to Jesus. Not to mention the deference of Churches to 'return to normal only once we have the vaccine'.

Covid mandates were originally brought into our Churches to be both temporary and in good faith, that they are for everyone's good. We are now well beyond a year into this thing and it's not going away. Not only is it no longer temporary (this stuff is here to stay), but there really is no excuse for anyone not to see that the Covid rules have been erroneous, contradictory and ineffective at best. But actually, as we have seen, it's much more sinister than that – they are designed to harm and disarm. Therefore, if we continue and do not purge our Churches of these rules and regulations and apply good and godly civil disobedience, we are in *heresy* – at great odds with established Biblical teaching and authority.

I have not mentioned the 'H' word up until now and I would have liked to have been able to refrain from using it. But given all we have seen and how most Churches are just accepting more and more compromise as a 'normal' part of Church life, I have no choice but to call it what it is. Heresies divide Churches, for good reason. So, expect more and more disunity within the wider Church as a whole and within individual Churches if we do not walk in the truth and purge the Covid profanity from our holy places of worship and Christian life. Church unity is maintained in upholding Gospel and doctrinal truths and righteousness, expressed lovingly. Let's up the ante here and counter the secular and Babylon-inspired 'Great Reset' with our own 'Church Great Reset', as outlined in Chapter 11.

Embrace Our Gifts for A Well-Functioning, Mature and Steadfast Church

Paul tells us in Ephesians 4:11-12 that Jesus has given His Church many gifts that we are to use for our benefit, edification and power – to make more disciples of Christ on earth. We therefore need to recognise and use all the gifts to be a discerning and effective Church and witness to the dying world. Now is a good time to embrace, increase and hone the work of our preachers, teachers, watchmen and evangelists in particular, in order to counter the deception, to avoid being tossed around by 'every wind of doctrine' that is blowing our way and to grow in our Christian maturity.

"That we henceforth be no more children, tossed to and fro, and carried about with every wind of doctrine, by the sleight of men, and cunning craftiness, whereby they lie in wait to deceive; But speaking the truth in love, may grow up into him in all things, which is the head, even Christ".
– Ephesians 4:14-15

Proverbs 17:15 reminds us of the importance of discerning truth: *"He who justifies the wicked, and he who condemns the just, Both of them alike are an abomination to the Lord."* (NKJV)

We need those with well-developed skills and gifts of spiritual discernment and good judgement to speak up and be listened to. Also, we each need to seek to increase in these things ourselves, since there are many right now trying to *"deceive us with empty words"* and Paul tells us to not become partners with them (Ephesians 5:6-7). Steadfastness is the order of the day and that comes with wise judgement, shrewdness, courage and strength to withstand strong winds of deception, compromise and oppression.

Time is Short – Let's Use it Wisely and Worshipfully

In Ephesians 5:15-17, Paul exhorts us to examine ourselves; to *"See then that you walk circumspectly, not as fools but as wise, redeeming the time, because the days are evil. Therefore do not be unwise, but understand what the will of the Lord is."* (NKJV)

Each day that passes brings us closer to the day of our LORD Jesus' return and we should bear that in mind. We simply cannot afford to entertain endless 'lockdowns' and singing bans, etc. Neither can we afford to bide our time on when we go out and evangelise, which in effect has become illegal in many places – since gatherings, approaching people closely and speech freedoms are being outlawed and as 'conversion therapy prohibition' bills are being passed in governments. The will of the LORD is to gather as the Body of Christ, preach the Gospel and to worship Him in spirit and truth, fellowshipping intimately with each other as we do so – let's return to this in its fulness, for our benefit and safety. We must remember that to be out of the LORD's will and timing is more dangerous and tragic than to be out of our governments' will.

We have explored many Biblical passages previously to show the necessity of gathered and united congregational singing and Paul really brings this issue into land in what he says in Ephesians 5:19-21: *"Speaking to yourselves in psalms and hymns and spiritual songs, singing and making melody in your heart to the Lord; Giving thanks always for all things unto God and the Father in the name of our Lord Jesus Christ; Submitting yourselves one to another in the fear of God."* We cannot get around the fact that we must sing as God's gathered people. It is not acceptable to merely sing at home on Zoom, or to only *watch and listen* to a music video from the front of the Church. No, we are to make melody and sing, *ourselves*, as a gathered ekklesia. It is part of our battle plan against the enemy and a huge part of our own edification and joy in Christ and our fragrant offering to Him. We may well have to evacuate our actual Church

453

buildings and commune in house Churches, but either way, we must sing together in that gathering.

We're at War – We Need our Armour

"Blessed be the LORD my Rock, Who trains my hands to war, And my fingers for battle." – Psalm 144:1

We are at war. We're living on a battlefield not a playground; we need to equip ourselves and act accordingly. Our Lord has given us the battle plan. He's given us the armour we need. He's given us the rules of engagement and the means of grace and power to execute. He's counselled us in the opposition we'll face and the reassurance that when we act by His rules, we need not fear as He goes before us into battle and fights for us. Covid has sought to disarm us and render the army of Christ impotent in many ways and trying to do Christianity and Church in our own strength and 'worldly wisdom'. Harsh, but true. As a non-Christian, I used to like the film 'The Big Lebowski' (ungodly as it is) and sometimes now as a Christian, I can find myself empathising with Walter Sobchak's fervent sentiments of wanting to uphold the rules of his beloved bowling game *"Smokey, this is not 'Nam, this is bowling, there are rules."* In other words, hungering and thirsting for righteousness and grieving its compromise. Ephesians 6 gives us the righteous rules for battle that we need to heed for success ...

"Finally, my brethren, be strong in the Lord and in the power of His might. Put on the whole armor of God, that you may be able to stand against the wiles of the devil. For we do not wrestle against flesh and blood, but against principalities, against powers, against the rulers of the darkness of this age, against spiritual hosts of wickedness in the heavenly places. Therefore take up the whole armor of God, that you may be able to withstand in the evil day, and having done all, to stand. Stand therefore, having girded your waist with truth, having put on the breastplate of righteousness, and having shod your feet with the preparation of the

gospel of peace; above all, taking the shield of faith with which you will be able to quench all the fiery darts of the wicked one. And take the helmet of salvation, and the sword of the Spirit, which is the word of God; praying always with all prayer and supplication in the Spirit, being watchful to this end with all perseverance and supplication for all the saints – and for me, that utterance may be given to me, that I may open my mouth boldly to make known the mystery of the gospel, for which I am an ambassador in chains; that in it I may speak boldly, as I ought to speak." – Ephesians 6:10-20 (NKJV)

Covid authorities say: The battle is a virus.
Our Bible says: The battle is in the spiritual realms of darkness.

Covid authorities say: Sit at home, stay safe, don't risk it.
Our Bible says: Get out onto the battlefield where there's danger, pick up your weaponry and stand and fight.

Covid authorities say: Believe lies, hype and propaganda, designed to deceive and cause fear and compliance.
Our Bible says: Gird ourselves with truth.

Covid authorities say: Compromise with doing what seems expedient and pragmatic over what is right and good.
Our Bible says: Put on righteousness and do not compromise on the truth.

Covid authorities say: Stay home and shelter from the world and 'unclean' people.
Our Bible says: Be ready to go out and share the Gospel with the world, heal the sick, cast out demons in the name of Jesus. These are the only means to make spiritually unclean people clean.

Covid authorities say: Walk in fear, which is from the enemy.
Our Bible says: Walk in faith, which is from Jesus.

Covid authorities say: Fill your mind with news of danger, death and rules issued about Covid, which leads to compliance and cowardice. **Our Bible says: Be mindful of your eternal life that is purchased and safe, which should give courage and power over fear.**

Covid authorities say: Fight an erroneous danger with hand sanitisers, tests, masks, vaccines, distancing from other people and staying isolated. **Our Bible says: Fight the real danger with the Word of God and renewing our mind, body, heart and soul with its immutable truths.**

Covid authorities say: Defer to us, we know best. **Our Bible says: Pray to our LORD, listen to Him, heed His Word, He knows best.**

Covid authorities say: Go to sleep, we'll tell you what to think and do. **Our Bible says: Stay alert. Watch and pray.**

Covid authorities say: Give up – your rights, your sense of agency over your life, your income, your freedom, your beliefs. **Our Bible says: Persevere, stand firm.**

Covid authorities say: Christian, be timid, shut up and comply; you talk hate speech and intolerance and we will not tolerate it. **Our Bible says: Christian, be bold, speak up; share the Gospel of life, love and truth.**

A Pure and Fervent Love of Jesus is Key

In the final verse of Ephesians 6:24, Paul signs off with these last words: *"Grace be with all them that love our Lord Jesus Christ in sincerity. Amen."*

Having a sincere, whole-hearted and zealous love of the LORD sums up the key to it all really, His First Commandment to us: *"Thou shalt have no other gods before me."* – Exodus 20:3

"And thou shalt love the LORD thy God with all thine heart, and with all thy soul, and with all thy might." – Deuteronomy 6:5

If our love for Jesus is able to be corrupted and negotiated with; with an attitude of – *"I'll love Jesus this far but no more"* or *"I'll follow Jesus until it means I am risking X, Y or Z"*, then we are not only in spiritual danger ourselves but compromising the power and effectiveness of the whole Church army. This is the attitude of apostasy, which the Bible warns of in the last days. Christian, we must not be found in this corruptible company. Rather, when our love for Yeshua is pure and incorruptible, we will stand up for what is right, and we will have the courage and power to take necessary action, in the power of the Holy Spirit and with the protection that comes from being obediently in the centre of God's will. Before giving us the First Commandment, our LORD reminds us of how He delivers His people when we love and obey Him wholeheartedly: *"I am the Lord your God, who brought you out of the land of Egypt, out of the house of bondage."* – Exodus 20:2

Moving Forwards

We have no idea how we will be delivered from this Covid satanic tyranny when we courageously stand against it and act in righteousness. We know we will be persecuted and will suffer for being an uncompromising Christian, that is a Bible promise. We only have to read through a few pages of books like 'Foxe's Book of Martyrs' to see the hideous suffering of the saints throughout history. But the LORD will deliver us one way or another and will give us the grace to endure and withstand when we follow Him, even unto death if necessary.

Whatever you decide to do in light of reading this book, my prayer is this: That you make your decisions in the full light of knowing that the coronavirus rules and regulations that are being imposed on us are *not in any way for our good but are evil and part of a much bigger control and depopulation plan*. Be under no illusions about this. If you decide to continue to submit to them, that is your choice, but you cannot say that they are righteous because it has been shown, without any shadow of a doubt, that the agenda behind this virus is a 'great reset', eugenics, a one world order and to usher in a new level of Satanic governance and control for all people on earth and to get rid of the true Jesus from all aspects of society. Therefore, I would strongly urge you to use Part Three of this book on the solution to this problem as your blueprint for action moving forwards.

"If my people, which are called by my name, shall humble themselves, and pray, and seek my face, and turn from their wicked ways; then will I hear from heaven, and will forgive their sin, and will heal their land." – 2 Chronicles 7:14

Immediate Practical Actions

Follow the reference links in this book

It's probable that you've skipped over many of the references to external resources and supplementary materials listed and peppered throughout this book. I'd strongly suggest going back, following the links and taking a little time to investigate these things for yourself – don't just take my word for it, but also be mindful not to dismiss anything as nonsense until you have double checked corroborating materials. Many of the links are to primary sources; the first-hand and raw materials data such as laws passed, books written by policy makers and official statistics, as opposed to secondary sources – accounts or interpretations of events created by someone without first-hand experience. I'd suggest prioritising those sections and chapters which pose the most scepticism in your mind. We can see that God, in His grace and mercy, has given us Bibles and also the internet at present, in order to open our eyes to truth – we would be wise to use both, before they are taken away from us! We have a window of opportunity right now to discern the truth of what's going on in order that we are not deceived, as Jesus commands us in Matthew 24.

Re-read and use as a reference

Your first reading might have caused some distress and raised a lot of questions and some doubts, or it may have confirmed everything you suspected! When you pray into those things and read the book again, it will probably allow you to do it more dispassionately and with greater discernment and critical thinking. Part Three is designed to be a reference and practical action guide, so keep it to hand to refer to regularly as we move through this world situation and you pray into your response and actions as a disciple wanting to follow Jesus wholeheartedly.

Share this book and leave a positive review

If you've found it enlightening, helpful, challenging, affirming, disturbing, engaging, poignant, questionable, etc. – why not share with other people and discuss with them? Would you also please consider giving a positive review on the platform where you bought it? This helps other people to find it. If you're a Church leader, prayerfully share with your congregation as many already have. As I write this, various draft versions have been shared with whole Churches and overseas workers. There are very few books written on this subject in real time, yet it is highly relevant to each and every believer in Jesus and should be a topic for discussion. If you're worried about causing divisions, do not be – I refer you back to Chapter 11 on Reclaiming Rightful Church Authority. If you would like to order the book in bulk for your Church or community, please email me.

Keep in contact and consult with me on this

I invite your prayerful and considered feedback and contact on the topics and material covered. Feel free to email me and I will endeavour to respond when I am able. Alternatively, you can write for an appointment, I have been a consultant and speaker in the business and health worlds for over 20 years and have much experience in coaching people. I help people improve their mindset, overcome struggles and succeed in an area they're spinning their wheels in. Increasingly, I'm speaking and consulting on the specifics and practicalities of this book's subject material. If you wish to donate to this ministry, you may do so via the donation page on my website or via email and bank transfer. That would be greatly appreciated and will help further this work to help lead the Church in truth and courage in the face of great worldly deception and fear.

I thank you for taking the time to read this book and pray that it will continue to bless you in your walk with our LORD Jesus.

An Epilogue on Time – from Romans 13

We started this book by looking at the opening verses in Romans 13 regarding subjection to authorities and we have examined its application and limits in our Covid situation. Let us end with the latter verses of Romans 13 and some final thoughts on using our time wisely.

"And that, knowing the time, that now it is high time to awake out of sleep: for now is our salvation nearer than when we believed. The night is far spent, the day is at hand: let us therefore cast off the works of darkness, and let us put on the armour of light. Let us walk honestly, as in the day; not in rioting and drunkenness, not in chambering and wantonness, not in strife and envying. But put ye on the Lord Jesus Christ, and make not provision for the flesh, to fulfil the lusts thereof." – Romans 13:11-14

Here's a paraphrased summary:

- **Wake up, Christian!**
- Time is ticking, Jesus is returning soon – use your time wisely.
- Cast off evil, falsehood and the restraints of sin. Mobilise ourselves in God's army to walk in truth and light.
- Increase holiness, get rid of worldliness and works of the flesh and unite with Christians in truth and love.
- Put on Jesus (incorruptible love for Him, which will increase faith, boldness, truth, love, courage). Kill our natural, selfish sin tendencies – fear of man, fear of death, comfort, ease, status, wealth, pride, lusts of flesh and eyes.

Let's focus in on Romans 13:11, concerning the issue of our time and the times, to end: *"And that, knowing the time, that now it is high time to awake out of sleep: for now is our salvation nearer than when we believed."* I was very challenged recently by listening to a sermon on the parable of the ten virgins in Matthew 25, which focused on the five wise virgins who had oil in their lamp; that is, saved Christians who had the Holy Spirit but who were also found *sleeping along with the unsaved*, foolish virgins when the Bridegroom returned. We are exhorted by Jesus in this chapter to *"Watch therefore, for you know neither the day nor the hour"*. – Matthew 25:13. The preacher posed this question in the sermon: ***"What would you do if you knew that Jesus was returning in three weeks?"*** In other words, time is short, so how will you use your time, Christian? Three weeks is not tomorrow, so there is still a small window of time to go and do what we feel is utterly urgent. It also spans at least two Sabbath days, so it gets us to ask how we would conduct our Church worship, fellowship with one another and daily activities.

Let's break this question down into further, more specific and practical questions related to our time:

- Would we be concerned with Covid rules and regulations?
- Would we socially distance or wear a mask?
- Would we fear a virus?
- Would we fear getting closer than six feet from other people?
- Would we be avidly watching the news media, or even at all?
- Would we be binge-watching Netflix?
- Would we be renovating our house, redecorating the spare room, or planning an extension?
- Would we be seeking unnecessary job promotions?
- Would we be putting our feet up?
- Would we be concerned about holding onto our income and saving for retirement or a 'rainy day', instead of giving to Kingdom work and the poor and needy with abandonment?
- Would we be worried about the crashing economy?
- Would we fear the governments?

462

- Would we be looking to emigrate abroad to somewhere we deem to be more favourable?
- Would we fear standing up against or disobeying unjust laws?
- Would we be encouraging Zoom prayer meetings and YouTube streaming over gathered Church services?
- Would we refrain from singing in our Churches?
- Would we be focusing on delivering and upgrading our Church tech?
- Would we encourage people to stay home and keep everyone safe?
- Would we care about a vaccine?
- Would we think evangelism could wait until we are told we can meet with people again?
- Would we continue to neglect meeting for fellowship and meals together?
- Would we put off baptisms, weddings, the laying on of hands and the Lord's Supper until such a time as when governments tell us it's 'safe' to do them again?
- Would we fear persecution?
- Would we be doing all we could to avoid persecution and rationalising our avoidance?
- Would we try to avoid prison or death at all costs?
- Would we be biding our time and waiting for government announcements 'allowing' us to go about our Church business?

My guess is that your answer to the vast majority of these questions, if not all, would be a bold and resounding 'NO'. In which case, what makes us think that we have the time or permission and blessing of God now to answer 'yes' to some or even all of them? Paul tells us that we are to *"Owe no one anything except to love one another, for he who loves another has fulfilled the law."* – Romans 13:8 (NKJV). That love for each other is to be both towards the Christian and the non-Christian and is to be a concern for the whole person – body, soul and spirit, but primarily a concern for spiritual matters and the state of a person's soul before the

LORD, over physical wellbeing. Therefore, we cannot afford to put off caring for our unsaved neighbour by evangelising and meeting to talk and serve and share the Bible with them. Nor can we put off caring for our saved neighbour by meeting for discipleship, confessing sins, having table fellowship, singing hymns of praise together, studying and reading God's word in the public assembly, praying intimately with each other and serving in practical ways.

We Must Obey God Rather Than Man

We have a situation under Covid whereby our governments are making laws and mandates that conflict with God's Law … and this is increasing at a rapid rate. Therefore, the only choice we have is to say along with Peter and the apostles in Acts 5:29 that *"We ought to obey God rather than man."* In doing so, we need not be afraid of the consequences and persecution. Why? Because we have sanctified the Lord God in our hearts, and He is our fear. God is with us and He will make a way, even in seemingly impossible circumstances. He delights in doing this to show off His glory and help us to trust Him rather than ourselves. It is our divine duty to preach the Gospel – to arise and let our light shine and when we do that, God will hold the winds if they need to be held. The Gospel will never be brought to the world by people who keep quiet about it and are fearful, but by those who have their trust in God, and are not afraid to speak the words that He has given them. We can too trust that our LORD will open the eyes and ears of those destined to 'hear'. In doing this we will not be taking our lives into our own hands; our lives will be hidden with Christ in God and He will care for us. To have the spiritual vigour to obey God over man in times when Christians do not have the favour of the authorities and a free pass to preach the Gospel without reproach, we must be spiritually awake.

Christian, Wake Up!

The Bible has many other verses aside from those in Matthew 25 and Romans 13 about waking up out of spiritual slumber.

"How long will you slumber, O sluggard? When will you rise from your sleep?" – Proverbs 6:9 (NKJV)

Jesus addresses the Church in Sardis on this issue: *"I know your works, that you have a name that you are alive, but you are dead.* ***Be watchful, and strengthen the things which remain, that are ready to die, for I have not found your works perfect before God.*** *Remember therefore how you have received and heard; hold fast and repent. Therefore if you will not watch, I will come upon you as a thief, and you will not know what hour I will come upon you. You have a few names even in Sardis who have not defiled their garments; and they shall walk with Me in white, for they are worthy."* – Revelation 3:1-4 (NKJV)

Do you want to be the Christian that is found with soiled garments in a spiritual stupor when the LORD returns? Or would you rather be in that fewer number that have kept their garments clean and are wide awake, spiritually alive and productive and watching for the LORD when He returns? I know which group I'd rather be found in. And when Jesus tells us to wake up, He means that we should wake up and act. It's not enough to give intellectual assent to Jesus' teachings and our faith. We are to bear true spiritual fruit. When Jesus raised Lazarus from the dead, notice that He said *"Lazarus, come out"* rather than *"Lazarus, wake up"*. The waking up was inferred in the command to get up and come out – to show clear evidence of his being revived from the dead. If we are a sleeping Christian, we may very well be saved and in fellowship but quite indistinguishable in many or all ways from the lost world. When the Bible talks about those who sleep (but are still physically alive), the connotation is that the person's righteousness, received through their faith in Jesus, is not visibly evident, and therefore the person appears to be no different than someone who is unrighteous. This is the worldly, lukewarm Christian, who looks dead from a spiritual perspective, but since they are in fact alive to God, they are called 'sleeping' Christians. Spiritual slumber appears as fear, insecurity, cowardice, playing it small, comfortable, safe and predictable in our faith, keeping quiet about the Gospel and other matters of truth and so on. Just as with Lazarus, Jesus is wanting to 'take away the stone' of the tomb of the slumbering Christian and order him to 'come out' and become fully alive.

Paul exhorts one of the most spiritually alive Churches of the New Testament to *"Awake, O sleeper, and arise from the dead, and Christ will shine on you."* – Ephesians 5:14. As A.W. Tower puts it, there were some at Ephesus that were *"morally good but unenlightened. They were religious but unanointed. It is perfectly possible for a good, faithful, loyal Church member to be spiritually asleep – being in a spiritual state that parallels natural sleep."*

Christian, we are not called to a life of spiritual deadness, we are called to be vigilant, valiant, and victorious in Christ! Let us be found in this state – of great use to God's Kingdom and a great threat to the enemy.

Fellowship of the Unashamed – by a Rwandan Martyr

I am part of the 'Fellowship of the Unashamed'.
The die has been cast. I have stepped over the line.
The decision has been made.
I am a disciple of Jesus Christ.
I won't look back, let up, slow down, back away, or be still.
My past is redeemed, my present makes sense, and my future is secure.
I am finished and done with low living, sight walking, small planning, smooth knees, colorless dreams, chintzy giving, and dwarfed goals.
I no longer need pre-eminence, prosperity, position, promotions, plaudits, or popularity.
I now live by presence, lean by faith, love by patience, lift by prayer, and labor by power.

My pace is set, my gait is fast, my goal is Heaven, my road is narrow, my way is rough, my companions few, my Guide reliable, my mission clear.

I cannot be bought, compromised, deterred, lured away, turned back, diluted, or delayed.

I will not flinch in the face of sacrifice, hesitate in the presence of adversity, negotiate at the table of the enemy, ponder at the pool of popularity, or meander in the maze of mediocrity.

I am a disciple of Jesus Christ. I must go until Heaven returns, give until I drop, preach until all know, and work until He comes.

And when He comes to get His own, He will have no problem recognizing me.

My colors will be clear.

Further Resources

Here are 20 very useful resources to further your knowledge and understanding of our times and how we should best respond and take wise action.

1. 'Come Down, Lord!' Canada Revival Blog – the articles of Pastor Stephen Richardson from Faith Presbyterian Church in Ontario, Canada – www.canadarevival.blogspot.com. I especially commend 'The Worldly Wiseman Exegetes Romans 13' from January 2021. His sermons on Sermon Audio are excellent too.

2. 'Blog and Mablog' – Vlog and podcast from Pastor Doug Wilson on the current tyranny and our Christian response – www.dougwils.com/audio/blog-mablog.

3. 'Resistance to Tyrants – Romans 13 and the Christian Duty to Oppose Wicked Rulers' – excellent short book by Gordan Runyan.

4. 'Civil Government. Its Origin, Mission, and Destiny, And The Christian's Relation To It' – very good book by David Lipscomb.

5. 'Defy Tyrants' – Romans 13 teachings and resources from Pastor Matthew Trewhella – www.DefyTyrants.com.

6. 'America The Babylon: Daughter of the Harlot' – documentary and excellent, timely sermons from Pastor Sam Adams of Independence Baptist Church, Florida – www.independencebaptist.com/america-the-babylon/.

7. 'Live Not by Lies: A Manual for Christian Dissidents' – book by Rod Dreher, warning of coming communist dangers in the West. (One caveat – it lauds the work of a Jesuit.)

8. The Great Reset sermon series – excellent preaching by Keith Malcomson speaking directly into this hour to alert the Church

and counsel us on how we can prepare – https://keithmalcom-son.weebly.com/the-great-reset-exposed.html.

9. Romans 13 sermon by imprisoned Canadian Pastor, James Coates – www.gracelife.ca/sermons/directing-government.

10. 'We Must Obey God Rather Than Man' sermon – by Pastor John MacArthur of Grace Community Church in California – https://www.youtube.com/watch?v=t2ixUp5KKn8.

11. Clash Daily Radio – podcast and books by Doug Giles, on how to be bold and courageous in Christ in our current times – www.douggiles.org.

12. Lew Rockwell – daily news articles from a non-mainstream, well-informed source – www.lewrockwell.com.

13. Now the End Begins – 'the front lines of the end times' Christian news site – https://www.nowtheendbegins.com.

14. Health Impact News – helpful health resources and alternative news articles – https://healthimpactnews.com.

15. Life Facts and Lifesite News – alternative news source for Covid info and updates – https://lifefacts.lifesitenews.com.

16. Richard Wurmbrand on the Underground Church – author of 'Tortured for Christ' on how to prepare for persecution – http://richardwurmbrandbio.info/prepare.html.

17. Eric Metaxas Radio Show – interesting interviews on where the political landscape is going – https://metaxastalk.com.

18. Technocracy News – excellent website and podcast on the NWO, rise of technocracy and the 'Great Reset' with Patrick Wood – www.technocracy.news.

19. NWO Truth documentaries – two excellent, well researched documentaries from a Christian perspective by Leonard Ulrich – https://nwotruth.org.

20. Romans 13 Revival – author website with more resources associated with this book – www.Romans13Revival.com.

"Having seen all this, you can choose to look the other way, but you can never say again, "I did not know."" – William Wilberforce

Romans 13 and Covid 19
– Knowledge, Warnings and Encouragement for the Church and World

by J.L. Fuller

This unique, timely book gives a comprehensive analysis and exposure of the deceptive dangers and errors entering the Church under Coronavirus mandates ... and a clear, Biblical roadmap out of it.

'Romans 13 and Covid 19' is for Pastors, Church leaders, disciples of Jesus Christ and anyone who is concerned by what's being imposed on the Body of Christ and world at large by our Governments, as a result of the Covid crisis.

The book examines Biblical principles on the scope and limits of civil authority, looking at examples from both the current situation and the past (namely the misuse of Romans 13 in 1930s Germany to quell resistance to Hitler). It surveys the key aspects and implications of the Covid directives – from the medical mandates, lockdowns and gene therapy rollout, to systematic State propaganda and the 'Great Reset'. You'll find much-needed knowledge and wisdom about not only what's going on now but also the wider, one-world technocratic agenda at play and where it's headed: Equipping you with all you need to know to accurately understand the times and obey Jesus' command in Matthew 24:4 to *"Take heed that no one deceives you"*, as well as to watch and pray, wake up from sleep, cast off the works of darkness and to put on the armour of light.

Unlike the news media and official guidance, this book is free of hype, spin and Covid fear-mongering. Whilst it's eye-opening and shocking, it will give you encouragement and practical guidance for living fully and fearlessly and in the joy of a closer walk with God – especially as the squeeze on the Western Church gets tighter, world deception increases and Jesus' return draws nearer.

Reviews

"In more than 25 years of Christian leadership, I have not read a book which sets out the truths behind the headlines in such a fearless and relevant way for the times we now live in. This is essential reading for every Christian. The facts will shake you to the core; they did me, but they are vital for us to know, so that we can effectively pray God's Kingdom into a world where hope is fast disappearing."
– Ian Dodgson, Pastor, UK

"Romans 13 and Covid-19 courageously and meticulously presents much-needed light to a very darkened world. I heartily recommend this book as a thoroughly documented 'must-read' for all Christians."
– Sam Adams, Pastor, US

"Reading this is akin to reserving for yourself and your loved ones the best seats in the lifeboat just before the Titanic hits the iceberg."
– Jonathan Stuart-Brown, LLB, Author

"In an age of spin, fake news, lies, propaganda and manipulation by media and governments alike, it is refreshing to find an author who clearly questions the current given narrative of Covid, along with the concomitant reaction of the Church in general. This is a must-read for all Berean Christians, who would claim to be men and women of Issachar, able to read the signs of the times."
– Ruth Campbell, Retired Teacher

"'Romans 13 and Covid 19' will enlighten and shock you in equal measure. It is one of the most timely and relevant books published in the advent of Covid, speaking directly into the situation we all find ourselves in. Make no mistake, this book will open your eyes but also equip you to be the Church of tomorrow in an ever-changing world that may never go back to 'normal' again. The only question I ask is 'are you ready for it?'"
– Val Thorpe, BA (hons)

About the Author

J.L. Fuller is an entrepreneur, author of several books and Law graduate with a decade of professional experience in legal policymaking, medical law and ethics and business consultancy, as well as almost two decades in natural health research and consultancy. J.L. was saved out of the occult new age and humanistic self-development worlds and is a dedicated follower of Jesus and His great commission, with a keen interest in Biblical doctrine. J.L. has been studying the official documents and factual criminal agendas of the Luciferian New World Order globalist elites for more than 20 years and delights in seeing people set free from this pervasive deception and bondage, through faith in Christ.

www.Romans13Revival.com

Email: book@Romans13Revival.com

Thank you for reading my book!

I appreciate and welcome your constructive feedback.

Please would you leave a positive review on the platform where you bought it, to let me know what you thought and found useful. This will help the book to be found by other people and help me to continue to improve my work.

Thank you so much, God bless you,

– J.L. Fuller

Printed in Great Britain
by Amazon

79557572R00271